Kayaking
the Maine Coast

Bass Harbor Light

Kayaking the Maine Coast

A Paddler's Guide
to Day Trips from
Kittery to Cobscook

Dorcas S. Miller

Second Edition

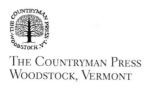

THE COUNTRYMAN PRESS
WOODSTOCK, VERMONT

Over time, directions and access points as described in this book may change. We welcome your feedback and corrections so that we may incorporate new information into future editions. Please address all correspondence to:

Editor
The Countryman Press
P.O. Box 748
Woodstock, Vermont 05091

Copyright © 2000, 2006 by Dorcas S. Miller

Second Edition

Library of Congress Cataloging-in-Publication Data
Data has been applied for.

ISBN-13 978-0-88150-705-8
ISBN-10 0-88150-705-9

Cover and interior design by Faith Hague
Front cover photograph by Jim Dugan
All interior photographs by Dorcas S. Miller unless otherwise noted.
Maps by Ruth Ann Hill, © 2006 The Countryman Press
Illustrations on pages 33, 35, 321, 322, 324, 346, 349 by Ruth Ann Hill
Illustrations on pages 325, 326, 328, 329, 330, 331, 332, 334, 341, 344 © Phyllis Evenden

Published by The Countryman Press
P.O. Box 748
Woodstock, VT 05091

Distributed by W.W. Norton & Company, Inc.
500 Fifth Avenue
New York, NY 10110

Printed in the United States of America
10 9 8 7 6 5 4 3 2 1

In memory of

Audrey Ingersoll

Mellen Shea

Contents

Preface

THIS EDITION OF *KAYAKING THE MAINE COAST* celebrates the vital work of Maine's conservation organizations, land trusts, and state agencies.

No one is making land anymore—indeed, sea level rise is quietly taking it away—and the only way to increase access is to purchase it. In various ways, Maine's people have stepped forward to shoulder the task.

In 1987, 1999, and 2005 Maine voters approved bond issues to fund the Land for Maine's Future (LMF) program. Local land trusts, towns, and other organizations have used matching grants from LMF, sometimes in addition to federal money, to buy or gain easements with the goal of protecting key lands across the state. Many of these lands lie along the coast. In addition, LMF has set aside money to be used specifically for obtaining water access so that the people of Maine can enjoy the rivers, lakes, and shores with which the state is blessed.

Statewide organizations have been active as well. In 2001, Maine Coast Heritage Trust kicked off its Campaign for the Coast, an initiative to raise $100 million over three years to fund coastal acquisitions. The organization has been very active in purchasing land, obtaining easements, and helping local groups as well as the state broker land deals. A spinoff organization, the Maine Land Trust Network, provides education and other assistance and promotes collaboration among local organizations.

More than forty local land trusts from Kittery to Quoddy now serve as guardians of some of Maine's finest islands, peninsulas, marshes, and uplands. Some are nationally outstanding; others have statewide significance; and still others are of great local importance.

Although The Nature Conservancy has recently shifted its work to focus on protecting whole ecosystems in the North Woods, in the past it had acquired significant coastal parcels, some of which it has since passed on to local groups to manage. Maine Audubon Society, although not a major player in shoreline conservation, does manage eight coastal nature preserves.

It is clear, however, that continued efforts are needed in the face of a spurt of growth in residential and commercial development. If you appreciate the efforts of a land trust, even though you don't live in the area, send along a thank-you note and a check. If you are already a member, give to the annual fund or special campaigns. Enroll in a statewide group to support overarching goals. And when the next referendum for the Land for Maine's Future program comes up, please vote yes.

Dorcas S. Miller, 2006

Preface to the First Edition

"WE'RE STARTING A SEA KAYAKING PROGRAM in Stonington and we'd like you to work with it," my boss said to me in the early 1980s. I was a whitewater guide at the time, leading raft trips on the Kennebec and Penobscot Rivers. I'd also worked as an instructor for Outward Bound and other outdoorsy organizations. Assisting with saltwater trips sounded like fun. I'd lived near the coast most of my life but never learned how to sail, so I had spent little time on blue water. Here was my opportunity.

My paddling skills transferred well, but I faced a steep learning curve with respect to the ocean as an environment. I knew the tide went in and out but didn't know anything about tidal currents, spring tides, marine weather systems, wave dynamics, and other intricacies related to sea kayaking. I did know that saltwater paddling was in a different safety category: On a river or lake, if the wind blew up I could capsize or become windbound; on the ocean, I could get blown out to sea.

As the summer progressed, I taught basic paddling skills, pointed out birds and flowers, and generally assisted with the weekend programs. The following year I got a boat of my own—a demonstration boat that had made its debut at a sea kayaking symposium and then made the rounds of local paddlers. I did several point-to-point trips—Lamoine to Jonesport, South Portland to Georgetown, and Bremen to South Thomaston—as well as lots of day trips.

I took my husband out paddling (he in my sea kayak and me in my river kayak) in conditions that might have stressed the marriage but didn't. We eventually got him his own boat. Together, we focused on day trips, exploring all of the rivers, bays, and islands that I'd paddled out and around on my earlier journeys.

One summer we did twenty-four day trips, never going anyplace twice. In the process, we checked out launch sites, researched the location of public islands, and learned about nonprofit preserves that are open to visitors. After one venture I said, "Gee, the way we're going, we could write a sea kayaker's guide to Maine." His response was of the "What do you mean, we?" variety.

I knew the task would be a big one and I was right. I have almost sixty pages of notes about launch sites alone and a file drawer bulging with area-specific information. Along the way, of course, I've picked up a lot myself. That's one of the things I like about being a writer: I get to learn while I'm working.

The coast of Maine is an intricate and beautiful place. It offers protected bays for people just learning to paddle and the open coast for people who are more skilled. The coast can accommodate almost every interest, whether you like to watch birds or botanize, putter along the shore or sprint from one place to another. But the coast is not idyllic. A fast-moving front can speed in and almost instantly change a sparkling afternoon paddle into an ominous struggle against waves and wind. Judgment and skill are both necessary for safe paddling. Maine offers limitless possibilities for developing—and using—both.

Acknowledgments

THANKS TO THE MANY INDIVIDUALS, organizations, agencies, and towns that manage launch sites, parks, preserves, and other natural areas along the coast, and provide critically important public access to these areas. Thanks also to the dozens of people from state agencies, town offices, kayaking businesses, and conservation organizations who have generously shared information about the Maine coast.

Particular thanks goes to Ken Fink, of Poseidon Kayak Imports, who reviewed the manuscript carefully and educated me about tidal delay, the relationship of period to tidal rise, and other topics concerning tides and currents. His comments have strengthened the book considerably. Thanks also to Steve Spencer, recreation specialist at Maine's Bureau of Parks and Recreation; Karen Stimpson, executive director of the Maine Island Trail Association; Brad Allen, seabird biologist at Maine's Department of Inland Fisheries and Wildlife; Steve Kress, director of the Seabird Restoration Program at the National Audubon Society; Nancy Sferra, director of science and stewardship at the Maine chapter of The Nature Conservancy; Linda Welch, biologist at the Petit Manan National Wildlife Refuge; Dawn Kidd, executive director of the Boothbay Region Land Trust; Jane Arbuckle for Maine Coast Heritage Trust; and many other individuals, for reviewing all or parts of the manuscript. Any mistakes, of course, are my own.

Thanks to Jean Hoekwater, Steve Kress, Hank Tyler, and the Maine State Planning Office for allowing me to include their excellent photographs in this book.

I've listed my well-thumbed reference books in the bibliography, but special mention is due to *A Birder's Guide to Maine* by Liz and Jan Pierson and Peter Vickery. I consulted this book regularly throughout the paddling season as well as when I was writing. Jan and Liz also answered my questions. Although I have included information from my own observations, I also relied on their expertise when reporting species likely to be seen. In the same way, I relied on Charles McLane's exhaustive series about the islands of Maine for information about island history, and Fanny Hardy Eckstorm's classic book for the meaning of Native American place names.

I want especially to acknowledge the staff at the Maine State Library, who have been generous with time and goodwill, procuring every arcane report, government document, and book on my wish list. These resources were tremendously valuable as I worked on the manuscript.

Helen Whybrow, Ann Kraybill, and Jennifer Goneau at The Countryman Press have been exceptionally patient with me. Kristin Camp and Pamela Benner hammered out the rough edges of the manuscript and brought the various sections into harmony.

A long overdue thanks goes to Brian Henry, president and chief designer of Current Designs. Brian was a fledgling sea kayak builder when he sold me a demonstration version of his Equinox at a price I could afford. (He still says I got a good deal—and I did.) I enjoyed the Equinox for many years and have only recently traded it in for a spiffy new Solstice.

I remember with gratitude all my paddling cohorts over the years.

And of course a special thanks goes to my main paddling partner and husband, Ben Townsend, whose humor, good spirit, and general love and support have gotten me through difficult moments of paddling as well as difficult days of writing. During every major writing project, I reach a point where I max out and have no more energy. When I went looking for sympathy, Ben cheered me on with the same words that I'd once used to cheer him: Pull up your socks and keep on plugging. So I did and now the book is done.

Dorcas S. Miller
1999

PART I
Read This First

Introduction

SEA KAYAKING PROVIDES ACCESS to another world, one that lies just beyond the shore. It's a world where ospreys nest on channel markers, and harbor porpoises surface with barely a splash to acknowledge their presence. The pulse of the sea rises with each swell and wave. In good conditions, sea kayaking can be fun in the sun. In adverse conditions, sea kayaking can be fraught with danger and require every bit of concentration, skill, energy, and steadfastness that can be summoned.

This book is designed to meet the needs and interests of a wide variety of paddlers. Everyone, though, should read "Low-Impact Paddling" on pages 24–31 because coastal resources are being squeezed and it is important to travel lightly. Information about tides and weather begins on page 32. Defensive paddling and planning a trip are covered beginning at page 38.

Part II of this book covers paddling opportunities from Kittery to Cobscook. Because of space limitations, some areas (North Haven, Vinalhaven, the coast along Passamaquoddy Bay, and some offshore islands) have not been included. Although information in this book can be used to plan multiday sea kayaking trips, the emphasis is on day trips. Why day trips? There are lots of reasons, including flexibility, comfort, safety, and stewardship.

Part III presents information on the geology, flora, and fauna of the coast—what you'll see when you're out there. The appendixes contain answers to questions such as: How cold is the water in June? (In Bar Harbor, it averages 54 degrees.) If I want to take a sea kayaking lesson, where can I call? (Lots of options.) If a flag is rippling in the wind, what is the wind speed? (Between 19 and 24 miles per hour.) The bibliography includes publications that I used when researching this book as well as a small selection of instruction books and magazines.

> **Warning**
> This is a guidebook for an activity that is potentially dangerous. Sea kayakers risk injury and death from hypothermia, drowning, being swept against rocks, and many other hazards.
> This is not a sea kayaking instruction book. This book does not replace proper instruction by a qualified instructor, nor does it replace the skill, proper equipment, experience, and judgment that every sea kayaker needs.

How to Use This Book

Each chapter in part II presents information on seven topics: trip ideas, charts, tides, safety considerations, access, points of interest, and land ownership.

Why Go on a Day Trip?

1. You can luxuriate in a hot shower at the end of the day.
2. You can dry out your gear at night.
3. You have more opportunity to explore coves and bays without the pressure of having to cover distance to get to the next campsite.
4. You need plan only for one day's weather.
5. It is easier to choose trips that are commensurate with your skill level.
6. You have more flexibility: You can factor in the tide and predicted conditions as you choose a trip, and you are not committed to staying in one area more than a day at a time.
7. You need less gear and have to do less planning.
8. You can kayak one day and hike or bike the next.
9. It's easier to get away for one day than several.
10. Because people on day trips have less impact on islands than those who camp, you help protect the very resources you enjoy.

Trip Ideas

This entry lists some of the trips you can take from launch sites within the area. You will notice that this book does not give an exact itinerary for each trip, nor does it say how long the trip will take or whether it is for beginner, intermediate, or advanced paddlers.

When hiking, the trail goes from point A to point B. If the wind starts blowing, you'll still follow the trail. But when you are sea kayaking, if the wind starts blowing you may decide to alter your route to take advantage of shelter offered by an island or shore. Because tide, weather, and wind conditions are major factors in determining the exact route a sea kayaker takes, I have not provided a specific itinerary with a dotted line on the map. Trip suggestions give the approximate mileage and note possible destinations or dangers but leave the actual route up to you. Trip distances are estimates, not exact measurements.

I have not included an estimate of the time needed to complete each trip because wind and water conditions—plus your approach to sea kayaking—will determine trip times. An excursion against the tide and wind can take more than twice as long as a trip with these elements in your favor. Paddling style and interests also influence the rate of travel. Some paddlers like to explore every shore and bay, while others prefer to speed toward a destination.

Once you figure out your average paddling speed in average conditions (conditions that are neither very adverse nor very favorable), you can factor in actual conditions and estimate how long it might take to complete a given trip. My own average is about 3 miles per hour. I'm neither a speed demon nor a gunkholer but paddle steadily with regular breaks.

Charts

Charts are for use on water; maps are for use on land. This entry gives the number and name of the National Ocean Service (NOS) chart for the area covered. I have generally suggested charts with a scale of 1:40,000 because that is the scale most useful to sea kayakers. I have not listed harbor charts that have more detail. Charts are crammed with useful information; get them and use them.

The second listing gives the page number of the chart as found in *Chart Kit: Cape Elizabeth to Eastport Maine*. This large-format spiral-bound book contains reproductions, slightly reduced, from NOS charts. *Chart Kit* is 12 inches by 17 inches, a bit large for carrying on the deck of a kayak but useful because it covers the coast from Casco Bay to Cobscook Bay. If you plan to do a trip on the Damariscotta River but decide to head for Muscongus Bay instead, you'll still have the chart you need. Also, *Chart Kit* costs less than buying all of the individual charts that it contains. Charts and the *Chart Kit* are available at marinas, marine supply stores, and outdoor stores that sell sea kayaks.

The third listing gives the map number in *The Maine Atlas and Gazetteer*, commonly known by the publisher's name, DeLorme. *The Maine Atlas and Gazetteer* is extremely useful for navigating Maine's highways, roads, and back roads. As the atlas says on its front page, it is not intended for water navigation.

Tides

This section gives information about the timing and height of the tide. The entry for Bath, for example, reads: "1 hour after Portland; 6.5 feet average rise." This means that high tide in Bath is 1 hour later than high tide in Portland. If high tide in Portland is at 2 PM, high tide in Bath is at 3 PM. Usually, the delay for low tide is within 15 minutes of the delay for high tide, but on some tidal rivers the delay may be longer or shorter. In Augusta, high tide is 4 hours and 3 minutes after high tide in Portland, while low tide is 5 hours and 30 minutes after low tide in Portland. If the difference is more than 20 minutes or so, I have noted the timing of both tides.

I have chosen Portland as the baseline because it is one of the two sites—the other is Bar Harbor—for which National Oceanic and Atmospheric Administration (NOAA) Weather Radio gives daily tide information. (The tide at Bar Harbor occurs 22 minutes before the tide in Portland, so if you are using Bar Harbor as your base, adjust accordingly.) Daily tide information is also available from annual tide tables and from local newspapers.

The average rise is the average distance between low water and high water. The actual rise for a given day may be more or less than the average rise. (See pages 32–37 for more about tides.)

Safety Considerations, Strong Currents, and Caution Areas

Trips suggested in this book are not designated as beginner, intermediate, or advanced, nor are they assigned numerical ratings of difficulty. Why? Because the route and the conditions—not the route alone—determine the degree of skill required. True, some areas are generally more difficult than others because of their orientation and position along the coast. Paddling on the open ocean is always harder than paddling well up in an estuary. Headlands are more challenging than embayments. The mouths of tidal inlets and estuaries can be treacherous. Fast currents require the specialized skills used in river kayaking.

But in some cases, the difficulty of paddling can be entirely related to weather. An easy (beginner) 2-mile trip one day may be an extremely challenging (advanced) trip the next. Ratings offer false security by making a decision that you should make for yourself. You must be able to evaluate your own skills, the safety considerations described for each paddling area, predicted conditions, potential conditions, and actual conditions when deciding whether to set out in a given area.

With sea kayaking, judgment is as important as paddling skills. Although judgment is largely developed through experience, facts can help considerably. This section gives facts about fast tidal currents, reversing falls, areas with heavy boat traffic, and other potential dangers. If I err by stating the obvious ("This site is open to the south, so wind and waves from that direction can make launching difficult") it is because sometimes paddlers do not recognize the obvious until they are faced with launching into the surf.

For information about dangerous areas, I frequently cite the *United States Coast Pilot (1) Atlantic Coast: Eastport to Cape Cod*. The *Coast Pilot* is the National Ocean Service's compendium of marine information, and it describes every halftide ledge, island, bay, and tidal river along the coast. It also provides information on currents, tidal falls, and other hazards. The *Coast Pilot* is generally written for vessels larger than sea kayaks, but it does direct some comments to operators of small boats.

The Maine Island Trail Association (MITA) notes some danger areas in its *Maine Island Trail Guide*. (See appendix D for more about the association.) Because MITA's members consist of people with small boats—sea kayaks, sailboats, rowing boats, and powerboats—the recommendations and cautions are directly applicable to sea kayakers.

Anyone who ventures into the woods or onto inland waters should be keenly aware that fall is hunting season in Maine. Deer hunting season begins in late October or early November and lasts through the Saturday after Thanksgiving; hunting is not allowed on Sunday. If you are paddling on tidal rivers during deer season, it's a good idea to wear hunter orange or other bright colors.

Duck hunting generally starts in early October. The length of the season varies from year to year and from species to species; some species can be hunted well into January. Duck hunters generally prefer to hunt in the early morning hours but may hunt later in the day. Avoid popular areas like Scarborough Marsh and Merrymeeting Bay and proceed carefully through coastal areas during sea duck season. Hunter orange or other bright colors make you more visible. For more detailed information about either deer or duck season, contact the Maine Department of Inland Fisheries and Wildlife (IF&W, see appendix A).

Access

This entry tells you where you can launch your boat. The sites listed include ramps supported or assisted by Maine's Department of Conservation, ramps owned and managed entirely by towns, and ramps that are part of a marina or other business. Access listings are current as of the writing of this book; things do change over time.

Access is a valuable commodity along the coast. The increase in the number of sea kayakers and boaters with small craft of every kind has promoted two trends. In the first, some launch sites have become so crowded that towns have begun to limit users. At the launch ramps in Falmouth Foreside and Georgetown, for instance, ramp users must have town stickers to launch and park. In Sullivan, only people from the town may use the ramp.

The other trend is for marinas, campgrounds, and other businesses to offer access, charging a fee for launching or parking. Although it may grate to have to pay to use a public resource (the ocean), commercial sites offer an important service. At Bethel Point in Cundy's Harbor, for example, recreational boaters were crowding out people who depend on the ramp for their livelihood. One option would have been to close the ramp to nonresidents. Instead, a local individual opened a parking lot within easy walking distance of the ramp. Use of the launch ramp, parking lot, and toilet facilities is included in the fee.

Some of the launch sites listed in this book have parking lots so small that I hesitated to list them, even after town officials said it was okay to do so. If the lot is small, please make an effort to accommodate local users by carpooling so as not to monopolize parking. These sites are obviously inappropriate for a trip with a large group, so look elsewhere when you go with your paddling club. When using a ramp in any area, please defer to people who make their living on the water (see "Low-Impact Paddling" on pages 24–31).

If you own *The Maine Atlas and Gazetteer,* you may have noticed that launch sites are shown with a boat icon. Not all of the sites shown on the atlas are places that you can launch your boat. Take it from me—I have turned around in a lot of driveways. Some of the sites are privately owned and are posted with conspicuous NO TRESPASSING signs. Others are not located in the indicated position. Still others are town-owned access sites, but with so little parking that if they start getting heavy use there may be conflicts with local users.

Points of Interest

Anything I thought might be of interest to paddlers—places you may want to visit, birds you are likely to see, the derivation of island names that might arouse curiosity—is included under this heading. I have described public islands on the Maine Island Trail as well as sanctuaries and preserves that are owned by conservation organizations and are open to the public. In most cases, I have provided a telephone number to call for more information. All numbers in Maine are in the 207 area code.

With regard to wildlife, I have given priority to birds that can be seen easily from a sea kayak, such as birds of the open coast and wading birds of

Launch areas are almost always limited in size. Be prepared to get your boat into and out of the water as efficiently as possible; do not block access.

Camping

The list of public islands available for camping can change each year, and management policies—such as capacity limits—are constantly evolving. Therefore, camping information is not included in the "use" column of the *At a Glance* section. An island that is described as being available for "careful day use" may in fact be a camping island.

If you are interested in camping, contact Maine's Bureau of Parks and Lands for a list of public islands that are available for overnight use, or join the Maine Island Trail Association to gain the privilege of camping on certain private islands. MITA provides a guidebook with information on all islands on the trail, whether public or private, as well as extensive information about low-impact camping. Information from the bureau and the association is updated annually.

Many saltwater campgrounds are available to sea kayakers (see appendix E). For more information on shoreside accommodations, refer to *Hot Showers! Maine Coast Lodgings for Kayakers and Sailors* (see bibliography).

Most of the launch sites listed in this book are not suitable for overnight parking. *Hot Showers!* describes where you can safely leave your vehicle overnight.

the mudflat and salt marsh. Although shorebirds are included in the salt-marsh chapter in part III, I have not included them in *Points of Interest*. Birders can refer to *A Birder's Guide to Maine* for more information on shorebirds, land birds, and other species.

At a Glance: Land in Conservation or Public Ownership

This section summarizes information on areas that are open to visitors. It is imperative that paddlers respect the dates of closure for both state and private islands. Otherwise, wildlife populations can suffer—and islands could be closed altogether.

If you see someone else misusing a resource—for example, you watch as a boatload of people stop at a seabird island during the nesting season, or you notice that an unleashed dog is romping through a brushy area that is likely eider nesting habitat—report this information to the regional IF&W biologist (see appendix A).

Onshore Threats: Poison Ivy, Insects, and Lightning

Poison ivy thrives on shores exposed to prevailing winds because it holds up well against steady salt desiccation when other plants do not. Despite its name, poison ivy on coastal shores and islands may appear as a low-lying

Choosing a Kayak

A touring sea kayak (14 to 18 feet long, less than 25 inches wide, usually with hatches and bulkheads) is the boat of choice for kayaking along the Maine coast. Touring boats are more efficient, so they stand up well in wind and adverse currents, as well as on longer trips. They are the safest and most versatile style of sea kayaks.

The popular short, wide sea kayaks (less than 13 feet long, more than 25 inches wide, generally without hatches or bulkheads) are suited to trips in calm, protected waters without objective dangers.

Sit-on-top kayaks, which are long and thin with an open cockpit and no bulkheads, are less popular in Maine because the water is so cold. In any case they, too, are less efficient than touring kayaks.

Touring kayaks like the ones shown here are long, narrow, and efficient.

Recreational boats are short, wide, and stable.

plant, a vine, a shrub, or a shrubby tree. Each leaf has three shiny leaflets. The edges of the leaflets are smooth, sometimes with a few large, wavy teeth.

Dog ticks are common in late spring and early summer. Some areas, like Perkins Island in the Kennebec River, are known for their infestations. Dog ticks are about ⅜ inch long.

Lyme disease, which is carried by the much smaller deer tick, is quickly spreading across the state. In its nymphal stage (mid-May through July), the deer tick looks like a fleck of dirt; in the adult stage, it is about ⅛ inch long. The first symptom of Lyme disease is often, but not always, a red bull's-eye around the bite; long-term, the disease can be debilitating. Dog ticks and deer ticks are most likely to be found in brushy areas. If you walk on trails through bushes, it is a good idea to inspect yourself for ticks at the end of the day.

Maine's coast also provides habitat for mosquitoes, no-see-ums, deer-flies, and greenheads. Paddlers are more likely to encounter mosquitoes in and around salt marshes, especially when there is no wind. No-see-ums generally come out at night. Unlike mosquitoes, which leave an itchy reminder, deerflies and greenheads (which are even larger than deerflies) have a painful bite. Although biting insects are not a big problem for day paddlers, it makes sense to carry some repellent in case you find yourself in need.

For information about the browntail moth, see the sidebar on page 91.

In case of lightning, follow the usual guidelines: Do not take shelter under the only tall object, such as a tree in a field. Instead, sit on your PFD and any other insulation you may have with you, keeping your feet close together. Never take shelter in concrete bunkers, such as the ones at Fort Foster in Kittery and elsewhere along the coast, because these damp areas are capable of conducting an electrical charge.

Low-Impact Paddling

Maine's coast is a place of soaring eagles, beautiful isles, and inviting coves. It is also a place of private property, vulnerable seabird nests, and sensitive ecological areas. You can help protect important resources along the coast—so that you and others may continue to enjoy them—by following 10 guidelines.

1. Respect private property, including intertidal land.

This guide lists islands and shoreside properties—both public and private nonprofit—that are open to visitation. For the most part, the rest of the coast is privately owned and not open to the public. Like good guests anywhere, sea kayakers need to respect private property.

In some states, the strip of intertidal land is public property. In Maine, it is not. May sea kayakers use this convenient strip? The answer, which is rooted deep in Maine's history, is complicated. In the 1640s, the Puritans passed an ordinance that declared that the intertidal zone was privately owned, but that the public had the right to fish, fowl, and navigate there. The ability to catch fish, to shoot waterfowl, and to launch a boat were deemed so important to survival in the early days of the colony that they were specifically protected. When Maine split off from Massachusetts and became a state in 1820, the new state carried with it the laws of Massachusetts, including this colonial ordinance.

But over the years, as Maine became a vacation mecca, the public began using the intertidal zone in ways not envisioned by the Puritan lawmakers. Sunbathers crowded onto beaches. People played boom boxes and left trash. Eventually landowners in Moody Beach, a community in southern Maine, challenged the public's use of the intertidal zone, specifically the land between their upland property and the Atlantic Ocean.

In *Bell v. Town of Wells*, which is often called the Moody Beach case, Maine's Supreme Judicial Court declared that the 1640s ordinance is still in effect. The land between high water and low water is privately owned. Furthermore, the court took a narrow view of public rights, stating that because only fishing, fowling, and navigating had been named by the Puritans, these are the only activities available to the public. Any use of the intertidal zone must be tied to one of these activities. The court gave several examples of navigation, saying that it includes the right to moor vessels on intertidal land and to go ashore and walk on intertidal land. (A minority of the court said

Ten Low-Impact Guidelines

1. Respect private property, including intertidal land.
2. Respect the needs of people who live and work along the coast, both at launch sites and on the water.
3. Always be aware of how your presence affects wildlife.
4. Respect closure dates for islands with nesting birds.
5. Give seals a wide berth, especially during the pupping season, which is mid-April through mid-June.
6. When visiting the shore, follow established paths or stick to rocky shores or beaches that can withstand use. Picnic at established sites.
7. Build no fires.
8. Travel in a smaller rather than a larger group.
9. Do not dig in or walk on shell middens.
10. Carry out trash and (yes) human waste.

that the public trust doctrine had evolved over the years far beyond the horizons set by the Puritans and that sunbathing, picnicking, and swimming should be allowed.)

Although people engaged in navigation—including sea kayakers—have a right to use the intertidal zone in a limited way, many landowners believe that because the intertidal area is private property, they have exclusive use of the entire zone. A few individuals have even used force to protect their property.

For practical purposes, it is easier to avoid conflict than to invite it. If you need to use the intertidal zone for navigation, be considerate. Instead of stepping out of your boat right in front of a private home, choose a more isolated place to consult your chart. Public use of private property is a sensitive issue on the coast; please don't abuse this colonial right.

2. Respect the needs of people who live and work along the coast.

Remember that while you are taking a day off to paddle, other people are busy earning a living. Clammers, wormers, and many fishermen depend on local launch sites to get to their work. So if the parking is limited, don't in-

vite a crowd of friends and take up all the spaces. If a launch area is described as one that clammers use, expect that they will be launching on the lower half of the ebb tide and landing on the lower half of the flood tide, and arrive at another time. Develop a system so that you can carry and launch promptly to avoid clogging ramps. One option is to pack boats in the parking lot and then carry them or wheel them (using a two-wheeled dolly) to the water.

Lobstermen complain that sea kayakers paddle too close to their boats, limiting their mobility and getting in the way. Do not paddle right up to a lobster boat. Either go around or be patient and wait until the boat has moved on. (And remember: It's just as hard for fishermen to anticipate the course of some sea kayakers.) Sometimes you can avoid lobster boats by paddling outside the concentration of lobster buoys.

3. Always be aware of how your presence affects wildlife.

Follow these tips for watching wildlife: Stay at a safe distance. Avoid nests. Become familiar with stress signals and back off when animals begin ex-

Suggestions from a Harbor Master

Harbor masters know everything that happens on their turf, and they can spot patterns that lead to problems. When asked about launch ramps in his area, John Bridges, harbor master of the Town of York, gave some advice to paddlers as well.

"Get lessons first from a qualified instructor," he says. "We have problems with untrained kayakers. They take little kids with them and get upriver. When the tide changes, they can't get back because the little kids can't paddle." Bridges has rescued stranded boaters four or five times.

Many beginners expect calm water. "We have tidal areas with a lot of water rushing in" as well as strong currents with eddies, he says. Paddlers aren't prepared and so get into trouble.

Because York harbor is small and crowded, he warns, "Don't get too close to boats. My fishermen all complain that they can't see the kayakers. It's like a trailer truck backing up; any boat over 40 feet has blind spots."

His last suggestion? "Everyone should wear a life jacket"—all the time.

hibiting them. Move slowly and carefully. Carry binoculars for close-up views. Most of all, watch the behavior of the animals around you. When your presence makes that behavior change, alter course or back off. In the long run, you will see more if you watch from a distance. If you approach, you will inevitably flush wildlife, and then the birds or marine mammals are gone.

When eagles are disturbed, for instance, they will begin to vocalize and fly with laborious wing beats in low circles. This showy flight pattern is designed to drive off intruders, but it is also energy intensive. If an eagle is flushed off its roost or nest repeatedly, it has less energy to hunt for food and raise young. While a powerboat goes by quickly, paddling can produce lingering, sustained disturbance.

Leave your dog at home. A dog's short romp on a seabird nesting island can do tremendous damage in a very short time. Barking can disturb wildlife whether you are on land or water.

4. Respect closure dates for islands with nesting birds.

State and federally owned islands that are closed to visitors during the spring and part of the summer because of nesting birds are listed under *At a Glance* at the end of the material for each geographic area. Some additional islands held by private, nonprofit organizations are listed as well. A few state-owned islands are closed to visitors year-round.

It is imperative that sea kayakers abide by closures and other regulations that protect wildlife. Nesting and raising young are perilous processes, and poorly timed disturbance from a single sea kayaker can influence the success or failure of this effort. Birds disturbed during the nesting season can be flushed out of the nest, leaving eggs or chicks exposed to heat, cold, and predation.

Female common eiders and their young raft up in brood flocks early in the summer; chicks that are separated from adults are more vulnerable to predation. Later, during molting, eiders gather in mixed groups. Go around rather than cutting through these flocks.

Migratory birds are protected by the Migratory Bird Treaty Act, state laws, and federal laws, all of which forbid disturbing migratory birds and their nests. The roseate tern is further protected because it is federally listed as an endangered species.

For more information about the lives and habits of island birds, see part III, under "Birds and Marine Mammals of the Open Coast."

5. Give seals a wide berth, especially during the pupping season, which is mid-April through mid-June.

Specifically:

- ▰ Avoid known seal ledges.
- ▰ Back off if you turn a corner and discover seals hauled out nearby.
- ▰ Watch seals only from a safe distance (which means that seals are not raising their heads, looking at you, or acting agitated).
- ▰ Leave stranded or apparently stranded seal pups where they are.

SEABIRD NESTING ISLAND

Area closed to public use April 1 - July 31 to protect sensitive nesting birds. Please help us conserve this island and the future of Maine's seabirds.

All agencies and organizations that manage seabird nesting islands in Maine are now using the same sign.

If seals raise their heads and turn toward you, they are showing the initial signs of alarm; if they point their heads toward the water, they are preparing for escape. Even if seals are acting spooked, they sometimes remain in place if you back off carefully and paddle as far from them as is reasonably possible. If seals flush, leave the area; they may return to the ledge. Unfortunately, seals often see you before you see them, so you must act promptly.

Seals are particularly vulnerable during the pupping season. Mothers usually nurse their young on ledges rather than in the water. If you scare mother seals off a ledge, especially first-time mothers, they may become separated from their pups and not find them again. The abandoned pups may starve. Rarely does another mother adopt an abandoned pup.

Seal pups that appear to be abandoned may simply be waiting for their mothers. Even if the pup is actually abandoned, trained per-

In 2004, more than eighty pairs of arctic terns nested on Eastern Egg Rock in Muscongus Bay. Stephen W. Kress

sonnel are needed to evaluate the pup and decide the proper course of action. If you see what you believe to be an abandoned pup or a stranded seal, leave it in place. Contact one of the organizations listed in appendix A. This conservative action is better for the seal and better for you, as seals can be dangerous—they have teeth and they will use them.

6. When visiting the shore, follow established paths and stick to rocky shores or beaches that can withstand use. Picnic at established sites.

Many coastal islands and peninsulas have shallow soil that erodes easily. When you arrive on an island, walk the shoreline until you find an estab-

lished path leading to the interior rather than scrambling up a bank or cutting through brush or trees. Likewise, use established picnic sites rather than freelancing. If you start a new trail or brush out a new lunch site, others will follow, and soon there will be more paths, more picnic places, more erosion, and less vegetation. If there are no paths, walk along the rocky shore or on the beach—but not in the fragile area above the beach where beach grass and other plants are established.

7. Build no fires.

Once a fire starts, it is virtually impossible to save an island from being devoured. If you want a hot drink while on a day trip, carry a vacuum bottle or heat water on a small camping stove set up below the high-tide line.

Survival is the only acceptable reason to light an open fire on an island. The fire should be made in the intertidal zone on the side of the island away from the wind. All traces of the fire should be removed when the fire is no longer needed.

8. Travel in a smaller rather than a larger group.

Larger groups have a greater impact on vegetation and other coastal resources than do smaller groups. A group of, say, 12 causes more damage than two groups of 6, even if everyone is careful. Why? In a large group, more people need space at any one time. That means more trampling of vegetation and greater disturbance of wildlife. A larger group also has a disproportionate impact on whether other island users enjoy their experience. Large groups tend to be louder and to take over an area. If you are sitting on a rocky outcrop, would you rather have a large group or a small group come ashore and share your space for lunch? You'll likely answer a small group, or even several small groups, rather than a large group.

How large is too large? In its guidebook, the Maine Island Trail Association states, "The best experience can be had by small parties of four persons or fewer." Some of the larger islands can accommodate 6 to 10, but for smaller islands only smaller groups are appropriate.

9. Do not dig in or walk on shell middens.

For thousands of years, Native Americans harvested clams and oysters along the coast of Maine. As they ate, they tossed the shells and other refuse such as food, animal bones, broken pottery, and tools into piles. Today these piles, or middens, appear as a dense layer of shells in the subsoil. Sometimes these layers are quite thick and sometimes they are only a few inches deep. Because middens can reveal information about the history and culture of the people who created them, they are archaeological sites and should be treated with care.

The greatest damage occurs to middens when people dig into them or walk on them, causing erosion. If you see anyone digging into a

Shell middens (in eroded area above the beach) are archaeological sites and should not be disturbed.

midden, quietly write down the boat registration number and alert Arthur Spiess at the Maine Historic Preservation Commission (287-2132 or arthur .spiess@maine.gov).

10. Carry out trash and (yes) human waste.

Successfully practicing low-impact paddling on day trips means that when you leave a stopover site it looks just as it did when you pulled up to it— except maybe you're taking away trash that you found there. As a rule of thumb, if something did not come from the land or sea, it should not be left on the land or in the water.

- Carry out all your trash—plastic bags, apple cores, uneaten food— everything.
- Leave the flora undisturbed and in place. Take photos rather than specimens.
- Leave the wildlife undisturbed. Even though they are begging, those gulls don't need your crusts of bread.
- When you gotta go, you gotta go, but don't leave it there.

This book notes the location of toilets at launch sites and public islands. But sometimes "the facilities" are not at hand when you need them. Because many of Maine's islands have only a thin layer of soil and because so many people are now visiting the islands, it is not appropriate to bury human feces. For suggestions on how to appropriately handle human waste, see appendix G.

Tides and Weather

Tides are created by the gravitational pull of the moon and the sun on the earth. The moon, being closer, exerts a little more than twice the pull of the sun. This gravitational force creates a slight bulge of water under the moon. Because the earth and moon are rotating as a pair as they revolve around the sun, they create a centrifugal force that produces a matching bulge on the other side of the earth. As water is drawn toward the two bulges, two areas that are relatively depressed develop in between.

When the shoreline rotates toward either of the bulges, the water level along the shore rises and tidal currents flow up into bays and estuaries. These bulges create high water (*high tide*). When the shoreline rotates toward either of the relatively depressed areas, the water level drops, creating low water (*low tide*).

The tide is high in any given place (1) when the moon is directly overhead or (2) when the moon is directly overhead on the opposite side of the earth. One cycle from high to low and back to high takes about 12 hours and 25 minutes. Two cycles take about 24 hours and 50 minutes, which is the time it takes for the earth to make one rotation on its axis (24 hours) plus the time for that given place to "catch up" to the moon (which has been revolving around the earth) and move directly beneath the moon once more. If high water occurs at 11:00 AM, it will occur at about 11:25 that night and again at 11:50 the next morning.

If you pay attention to the position and phase of the moon, you can predict the tidal cycle:

New moon. We can't see the moon when it is new because it is located between the earth and the sun, so its unlit side is toward us. New moons rise in the morning, so they are overhead at the middle of the day. Therefore, high tide occurs in the middle of the day and the reciprocal high tide occurs in the middle of the night.

First quarter. Approximately one week later, by the first quarter, the moon has moved 90 degrees relative to the sun and we can see part of the moon. The moon in the first quarter rises around noon, which means that it is overhead in the evening. High tide is in the evening and, reciprocally, in the morning.

Full moon. Approximately one week later, the moon is full. It has moved 180 degrees relative to the sun so we can see reflected sunshine on half of its surface. The full moon rises roughly at the time that the sun sets, which means that it is overhead in the middle of the night. The tide, therefore, is high in the middle of the night and, reciprocally, in the middle of the day.

Last quarter. Approximately one week later, the moon has moved 270 degrees relative to the sun and once again, we see only a part of its surface.

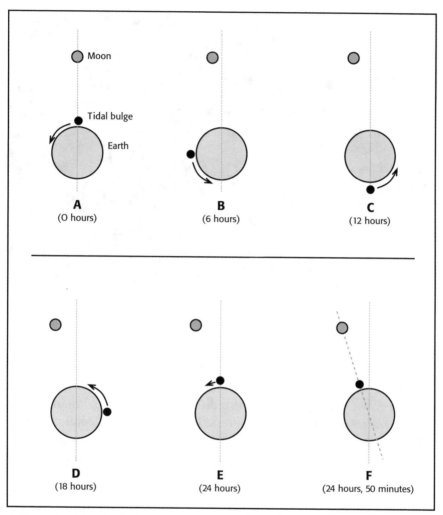

*As the earth rotates (**A–D**), the moon moves around the earth. After 24 hours, the earth is in its original position (**E**), but the moon has moved relative to the earth. It takes the earth another 50 minutes (**F**) to catch up to the moon. Because the tidal bulge tracks the moon's movement, if high tide occurs at 7 PM one day, it will occur at 7:50 PM the next day. (The reciprocal bulge will have produced a high tide in between, at 7:25 AM.)*

This phase of the moon rises in the middle of the night, so it is overhead in the morning. The tide is high in the morning and, reciprocally, in the evening.

Spring and Neap Tides

When the moon and sun are aligned, as they are during the new and full moons, the pull is strongest and the bulges are greatest. These tides are called

The tidal range in the Great Wass archipelago is 11.5 feet.

spring tides, but the word *spring* has nothing to do with the season that follows winter. Spring high tides occur during midday and relatively near midnight. Spring tides are strongest on the two solstices, June 21 and December 21.

When the moon and sun are not aligned, which occurs during the first and last quarters, the pull is from two directions. The moon dominates, but the two bulges are smaller and depressed areas are not as depressed. These tides are called *neap tides*. Neap high tides occur early in the morning and in the evening. Neap tides are most pronounced at the two equinoxes, March 21 and September 23.

Spring and neap tides can be important to paddlers. For example, you may plan to launch at a ramp that just barely has water at the average low tide. During the spring low tide, you'll be slurping through mud. Or, you may plan to land on a favorite area that is exposed during the average high tide. With a spring high tide, the area may no longer be available.

Range (Rise) and Slack Water

A tide approaching high is *flooding* and a tide approaching low is *ebbing*. The difference between high water and the next low water is the *tidal range*; tide charts usually refer to this number as the *rise*.

To understand why the range is not the same in every coastal town, let's first look at waves in a bathtub. If you sit at one end of a bathtub you can make a wave that will travel to the far end of the tub, bounce back to your end of the tub, and then dissipate as it reaches you from behind. But if you slosh

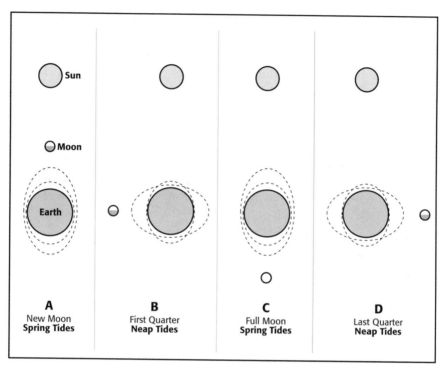

	A	B	C	D

A
New Moon
Spring Tides

B
First Quarter
Neap Tides

C
Full Moon
Spring Tides

D
Last Quarter
Neap Tides

A and C: The gravitational pull of the moon and sun combined create a relatively large bulge in the earth's seas, and a reciprocal bulge forms on the opposite side of the earth; these two bulges are manifested as the highest tides. The bulges create two areas of relative depression in between; these areas are manifested as the lowest tides. These extra high and extra low tides are called spring tides. **B and D:** *When the moon and sun are no longer aligned, the gravitational pull of the moon creates a bulge (manifested as a not-very-high high tide) and the pull of the sun creates a smaller bulge (manifested as a not-very-low low tide). These diminished highs and lows are called neap tides.*

again at just the right moment, you cannot only keep the wave going, you can make it larger. If you keep timing subsequent sloshes properly, you can create a sizable wave that will reach up, first to one edge of the tub and then to the other. These waves have a period, the time needed to travel from one end of the tub to the other end and back. If you do not time your subsequent sloshes with that period, your waves will plow into each other and peter out.

The Gulf of Maine is essentially a large tub, except that it is mostly open at the Cape Cod end in Massachusetts and entirely closed at the Bay of Fundy end in Canada. The period of the Gulf of Maine—the time it takes water to slosh back and forth—is very close to 12 hours and 25 minutes, which happens to be the length of time between one tidal bulge and the next tidal bulge. From its position above the earth, the moon exerts the correctly timed force needed to amplify the tidal bulge so it sloshes high at both ends of the Gulf of Maine. The bulge grows to more than 40 feet in the Bay of Fundy but cannot get as large at the other, open end; in Barnstable Harbor on Cape Cod, the range is 9.5 feet. The range is smaller at coastal areas located partway between the two ends, including Kittery Point (8.7 feet), Portland Harbor (9.1 feet), and Owls Head (9.4 feet).

There is no rule for tidal range on rivers. On the Kennebec, the range decreases as you move upriver to Augusta. On the Penobscot, the range increases as you move upriver to Bangor.

Along the ocean, where the tide moves freely, there are two times during the tidal cycle—at high water and at low water—when there is no movement or almost no movement of water. These times are called slack water. The duration of slack water depends on the speed of the current preceding and following it.

Tidal Delay

In tidal rivers or long, narrow channels, slack water can be delayed or even absent at low water because the freshwater flow can continue on the surface even as salt water pours in below. (As paddlers, we are on the surface, so we have to contend with the downriver freshwater flow.)

To reverse the flow, the incoming tide must overcome the hydrostatic head—that is, the force of the outflowing water caused by the sloping surface of the water and its momentum in downhill flow. Depending on the strength of this force, it can take between 1¼ and 2 ½ hours to overcome the head, which means that the time of low-water ebb flow is lengthened, and the time during which the water floods is shortened. (During the ebb flow, the elevation of the water may actually be rising.) Because the water must rise relatively quickly, the flood current is between 50 and 100 percent stronger than the ebb current.

Wind and Tides

Wind can influence the height of tides. Onshore wind out of the northeast, east, southeast, south, and southwest can cause both high tides and low tides to be higher than usual. Offshore wind, principally out of the northwest, can cause both high and low tides to be lower than usual. Storms, seasonal floods, and the state of the atmosphere can also alter tidal heights. Usually, a low barometric reading predicts higher tides overall, while a high barometric reading predicts lower tides.

Wind can even influence the direction of tidal current. In Deer Isle Thorofare, south of Stonington, the tide usually floods east and ebbs west. With a strong west wind, the current floods east and ebbs east; with a strong east wind, the current floods west and ebbs west.

See appendix C for information about the Beaufort Scale, which is used to rate wind conditions.

Estimating the Strength of the Tide

Depending on the lay of the land, the tide in Maine generally floods to the north or east and ebbs in the opposite direction. Tidal currents generally run between 0.5 knot and 2.0 knots. (A *knot* is a unit of speed defined as 1 nautical mile per hour. A nautical mile is equal to 1.15 statute miles.) Most currents with a greater speed have been noted in the text. Tidal currents are strongest during the third and fourth hours of the cycle; during these 2 hours, the tide gains (or loses) half of its total rise (or fall).

In most circumstances, it is easiest and makes most sense to paddle with the tide. One exception might be when encountering a tidal falls, where it is safer to paddle at slack water rather than at the current's greatest velocity. But if your trip must include some paddling against strong tidal currents, aim for the time shortly before or shortly after slack water and avoid the middle 2 hours. The greater the speed of the tidal current, the more important it is to calculate your position relative to it.

The faster the tidal current, the smaller the window of relatively easy paddling. At the Reversing Falls in Cobscook Bay, for example, the maximum velocity of the current is estimated at 9 to 12 knots. Slack water lasts only a few minutes. If you go there at an hour past slack, you will find a swift, strong current with more to come.

Weather

Air temperature, water temperature, wind direction and strength, and fog are all important factors to consider when paddling along the coast of Maine. Air temperatures are highest in June, July, and August. In Bar Harbor, which is representative of other points along the coast, the average high during these months runs between 72 and 76 degrees Fahrenheit, while the average low temperature runs between 51 and 57 degrees. (See appendix B for more detail.)

For paddlers used to warmer parts of the country, Maine waters are positively frigid. Even at its warmest, in August, sea temperature hovers between 63 degrees (Bar Harbor) and 51 degrees (Eastport). Temperatures in tidal rivers and inlets, of course, can be much warmer.

Danger occurs when paddlers dress for maximum air temperatures (say, 72 degrees in July) instead of sea temperatures (54 degrees). A short-sleeved shirt may be adequate for someone on land in the sun, but it is not adequate for a paddler in the water. There is no single rule about when to wear wetsuits and drysuits, except to dress for immersion.

Because it is easier to heat air than water, air temperatures shoot up more quickly in the spring and drop off more quickly in the fall. Water temperatures warm more gradually in the spring and they take longer to drop off in the fall. The average air temperature is roughly equal to the average sea temperature in April and September. In October, the average air temperature is actually lower than the average sea temperature.

Prevailing winds in Maine blow from the northwest in winter (November through March), move into the west or southwest in April, and blow from the southwest through October. Using a yearlong average, the strongest winds come from the northwest through the northeast and the southeast through the south. The biggest danger when paddling is the northwest wind. It is always strong, it occurs with fair weather, it builds during the day, and it blows offshore.

Fog is more prevalent during the summer than during the winter, and the *degree of obstruction* (times at which visibility is less than half a mile) is greater during the summer than during the winter. There is, however, much variation with the fog. The upper reaches of tidal rivers and inlets can be fog-free when open water is shrouded. (For tips about paddling in the fog, see "Defensive Paddling and Planning a Trip," below.)

For daily weather information and forecasts, consult a weather radio or online information from the National Weather Service. This agency has two offices in Maine, one in Gray (reporting weather conditions and predictions for southern and central Maine) and the other in Caribou (reporting for northern Maine). The Web site for the Gray office is: www.nws.noaa.gov/er/gyx/. This site has a link to the Caribou office, so information on the entire coast is available.

Defensive Paddling and Planning a Trip

It is imperative that sea kayakers engage in defensive paddling. Quite simply, you must take responsibility for yourself—always. Assume that lobster boats, large sailboats, and other large vessels cannot see you, and plan accordingly.

Defensive Paddling

As a defensive boater, stick to waters where other boats cannot or are unlikely to go, such as along the shore and near ledges and exposed rocks. Avoid paddling in congested areas and main channels where there is likely to be other boat traffic. Take special care near shipping lanes and anchorage areas for large vessels, boat ramps where there is frequent congestion, and ferry terminals. Ferries often leave their motors on so that they can push up to the dock;

Tide and Weather Guidelines

- If high water occurs at 10 AM, the next high water will occur at about 10:25 PM and the next at about 10:50 AM. From one day to the next, add about 50 minutes.
- The four phases of the moon are a little more than a week apart, so if there is a spring tide one week there will be a neap tide the next.
- During spring tides, high water occurs at midday.
- During neap tides, low water occurs at midday.
- The range (or rise) is the difference between low water and high water; the range increases as you move north and east along Maine's coast.
- At the mouth of rivers and tidal inlets, surface water can continue downriver even as salt water begins wedging underneath.
- At the mouth of rivers and tidal inlets, the incoming tide can be delayed for up to 2½ hours by the force of the downriver flow.
- Wind can influence the direction and height of the tide.
- Tidal currents are strongest during the third and fourth hour after low, and the third and fourth hour after high. Avoid paddling against strong tidal currents at these times.
- Weather Tip: The biggest danger is northwest winds, which are strong, build during the day, and blow offshore.

there may be strong wash currents. Be especially careful around motorboats, as some operators have no idea of the effect that their wake has on small craft.

If you need to cross the channel, do so by crossing at the narrowest point, crossing perpendicular to traffic, and crossing quickly. Wait until you reach the other side to consult the chart, raft up with other paddlers, or adjust your paddle jacket. In theory, the guiding principle when determining who has the right-of-way is that whichever craft can maneuver more easily gives way. Motor gives way to sail, and both give way to ferries, tugs, tows, larger fishing vessels, and deep-draft ships that are confined to a channel. Size is not the determining factor. But with muscle-powered sea kayaks, the guiding rule is more practical than technical. Use common sense and never assume that you have the right-of-way.

Although it is difficult to know for certain which way a lobster boat will turn, sometimes it is possible to make an educated guess. By law lobstermen must display their uniquely colored buoy on the bow or cabin of their boat. By matching the buoy on the boat with the buoys on the water, you can tentatively predict the course of the boat.

Fog

Fog is a great challenge for paddlers because it is difficult to predict. Sometimes it burns off by noon. Sometimes it hangs around all day. Sometimes it

---

Paddling Tips

- Paddle where others cannot go—near shores and islands—but not in the main channel.
- Avoid areas that are congested.
- Cross main thoroughfares quickly and at a right angle to the boat traffic so you are in the traffic lane the least amount of time possible.
- In fog, listen for the motors or flapping sails of approaching boats, and once you have located the boat, position yourself so you won't be run over.
- Never assume that other boats will give you the right-of-way.

---

lifts and then settles again, shifting in ghostly movements. With dense fog it is difficult to locate the other, much larger, boats whose path you do not want to cross. These days, vessels with electronic navigation systems are likely setting their course from LORAN signals or Global Positioning System (GPS) data rather than peering closely into the fog for landmarks or other boats (yours included). Moreover, kayaks don't register on radar.

It is imperative to paddle defensively in the fog. Be familiar with traffic patterns. Avoid heavily used areas like ferry crossings and main channels into coastal villages. Use previously developed navigation skills. Listen for approaching boats—the whine of a motor, the flapping of sails, the splash of a bow wave. Give a blast with a handheld foghorn to alert the approaching boat to your presence. Once you have ascertained the boat's direction, paddle forward or back to avoid the vessel.

Planning a Trip

The coast of Maine is a big place with widely varying conditions. When I plan a trip I look at the chart and then consider five sets of questions (see the sidebar "Questions to Consider When Planning a Trip," page 42), matching the answers to the first three sets with the answers to the last two sets. If I don't have a good match, then I look at other possibilities. The beauty of day trips is that you are not committed to a particular destination and can plan around the actual conditions of the day. Here are a couple of examples.

Trip #1

My partner for the day is an enthusiast of Arctic travel lore and wants to visit Eagle Island, where Admiral Peary once lived. From the launch site on Basin Point in Harpswell, it's about 2 miles out and 2 miles back. The state of the tide is not critical because the current is not especially strong and the distance is relatively short. The forecast is for a sunny, windless day, and the morning of the paddle the forecast holds. The fog has burned off just as we arrive. The trip is well within our capabilities, and we can cope if conditions begin to deteriorate; we've both done a lot of paddling. We hop in and head for Eagle Island, keeping in mind that there will likely be many recreational powerboaters and sailors in Casco Bay.

Trip #2

I've been wanting to paddle around Little Deer Isle. The route is about 9 miles, within my ability and just what I had in mind for length. My paddling partner and I are well matched in terms of abilities and goals for the day.

The tide is low at 10:40 AM and high at 4:57 PM (Portland). The tide at Little Deer Isle is 6 minutes ahead of Portland, not enough to factor into planning. The tide in Eggemoggin Reach floods northwest and ebbs southeast. If we launch at 11 AM near the ME 15 bridge, at the eastern end of the island, we can catch the incoming tide up the reach. If we paddle about 3 miles an hour, we'll circle the island and reach Carney Island by the causeway in about 2½ hours. The chart shows a border of mud along the Little Deer Isle/Deer Isle causeway at low tide, but when we arrive around 1:30 PM, there will be plenty of water. The tide will still be coming in as we paddle back out into Eggemoggin Reach and on to the launch site, returning at around 2 PM.

Eggemoggin Reach tends to funnel wind from the northwest or southeast, but the forecast calls for steady conditions with an onshore breeze (from the southwest) of 5 to 10 miles per hour. My partner and I are both comfortable paddling in wind of that speed. If the wind blows harder, we can paddle in the lee of Little Deer Isle when we're in the reach, and in the lee of several islands when we are south of Little Deer Isle.

The route looks feasible and we're ready to paddle. We'll check the forecast once more in the morning to make sure conditions haven't changed since yesterday's prediction. If they haven't, it's a go.

Trip #3

Two friends have been wanting to circumnavigate Verona Island. The launch site is at the northern end of the island, and the trip is about 11 miles. The tide for the upcoming Saturday is low at 11:57 AM and high at 6:12 PM (Portland); Bucksport is 2 minutes earlier than Portland—again, not enough to worry about. My paddling partners are comfortable in winds up to about 10 miles per hour (mph).

Ideally, my partners and I would want to go out with the tide in the Main (western) Channel and come in with the tide in the Eastern Channel. The ebb tide current in the Main Channel will be strong because it includes both river current and tidal current. The swiftness of the ebbing current in the main channel will give us a boost, so we're likely to travel faster than our normal speed (normally, the circumnavigation would take us about 4 hours, traveling at 3 mph for 11 miles).

Questions to Consider When Planning a Trip

My goals for the day
What length trip am I interested in paddling?
Do I want to have an easy day or am I willing to work hard? How hard?

My capabilities
How far can I paddle in a day?
What is my average paddling speed per hour, including breaks?
What is the maximum wind speed, wave height, wave steepness, and current speed at which I feel comfortable paddling?
How good are my navigational skills?
Can I handle a surf landing?
Am I prepared for a rough- and cold-water self-rescue?
Am I ready for an emergency bivouac?

Capabilities of my traveling companions
What answers do my paddling partners give for these questions?

Weather
What is the weather prediction concerning wind direction and speed, sea state, swell, fog, and precipitation?
How will the state of the tide influence these elements?
Are conditions predicted to improve, stay the same, or deteriorate?

Proposed route
Are there known dangers along the way—reversing falls, heavy boat traffic, or anything else—that need to be considered?
Will the tide be ebbing or flooding? How can I use the tide to my best advantage?
Will I encounter currents and countercurrents that I can use to my advantage?
Can I avoid currents and countercurrents that will be to my disadvantage?
How does the wind affect my plans? Will I be paddling into the wind? Will it be behind me? Will it come at me from the side?
Are there places that I can seek shelter from the wind or bail out, or is my proposed route fully exposed?
If I plan a trip with the weather prediction in mind and the prediction is not accurate (for example, the wind remains from the north instead of swinging around to the south), can I still complete the trip?

If we leave at 10:30 AM, we'll ride the last third of the outgoing tide, arrive at the southern end of Verona around noon, and then turn north. If we were simply going to retrace our route, we would expect a long delay before the tide would give us a boost on the return trip. The Penobscot is a large river and it will take some time—perhaps 2½ hours—for the incoming water to overcome the hydrostatic head of the outflowing water.

Because we are circumnavigating the island, and the Eastern Channel carries much less water than the Main Channel, there will be much less of a delay there. The chart shows that although mudflats line both sides of the Eastern Channel at low water, the depth of the channel is adequate for our return.

The long-term forecast calls for a storm to arrive from the south on Sunday.

On Saturday morning, the wind is blowing from the south at 10 mph and is predicted to increase during the day. Wind against current means chop, so there will likely be chop in the Main Channel and south of Verona. My partners are at the edge of their comfort zone; I'd rather have a fun day than an epic.

We look at other trips in the area. The South Branch of the Marsh River is just around the corner. That trip is shorter, maybe 6 or 7 miles, and although it's best done on the top half of the tide, the channel is open at low tide. We'll be largely protected from the wind. Sounds like a good choice, given what we have for weather.

Maps

Each chapter in Part II has a map (not a chart) for use in locating launch sites, points of interest, and geographic features. The maps in this book are not adequate for water navigation.

Key

[53] Launch site

[R] Launch site with restricted access, usually to town residents

[124][A] Campground; anyone may launch

[A 1] Campground; patrons only may launch

* Point of interest

Scale

Mileage is in statute miles (not nautical miles)

Abbreviations

Contact information for each agency or organization is listed in appendix D.

BPL: Maine's Bureau of Parks and Lands

IF&W: Maine's Department of Inland Fisheries and Wildlife

DMR: Maine's Department of Marine Resources

MCHT: Maine Coast Heritage Trust

MIT: Maine Island Trail

MITA: Maine Island Trail Association

TNC: The Nature Conservancy

USFWS: United States Fish and Wildlife Service

PART II

From Kittery
to Cobscook

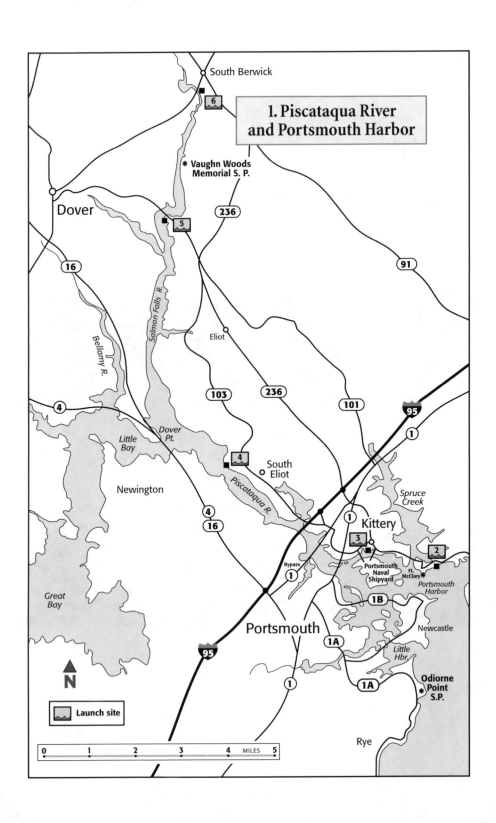

1. Piscataqua River and Portsmouth Harbor

South Berwick

6

* Vaughn Woods
Memorial S. P.

236

Dover

5

91

16

Salmon Falls R.

Eliot

103

236

101

95

1

Bellamy R.

Little
Bay

Dover
Pt.

4

Piscataqua R.

South
Eliot

4

16

Newington

Spruce
Creek

1

3

Kittery

2

Bypass

1

Portsmouth
Naval
Shipyard

Ft.
McClary *

Portsmouth
Harbor

Great
Bay

1B

Portsmouth

Newcastle

95

1A

Little
Hbr.

N

Odiorne
Point
S.P.
*

Launch site

1

1A

0   1   2   3   4 MILES 5

Rye

1.

The Southern Coast

Piscataqua River and Portsmouth Harbor

The Piscataqua River is the fastest-flowing tidal river on the East Coast of the United States, which explains why the *Coast Pilot* features an extensive description of danger areas along the river and in Portsmouth Harbor. Sea kayakers who choose to paddle here will do well to heed the warnings. The river and harbor are also heavily industrialized. Deep-draft vessels steam through the harbor to a long line of wharves on the New Hampshire shore, while the Portsmouth Naval Shipyard occupies center stage on Seavey Island.

Still, the lower Piscataqua can provide enjoyable, if urban, paddling. There are several interesting historical sites, including Fort Constitution, which supplied munitions to the patriots at Bunker Hill, and Wood Island, the eastern anchor for an antisubmarine net that was set up at the entrance to the harbor during World War II.

The Salmon Falls River, which flows into the Piscataqua from the north, and Chauncey Creek, which flows into the harbor from the east, offer paddling along shores that are surprisingly undeveloped given the proximity of an urban center.

Trip Ideas (weather and experience permitting)

From Pepperrell Cove (Launch 2) or Fort Foster, follow Chauncey Creek north into Brave Boat Harbor (7 miles round-trip from Pepperrell Cove, 8 miles from Fort Foster). Cross under the bridge to Gerrish Island, then turn left under a second bridge and proceed through salt marsh; if you go straight instead of turning left, you will dead-end in the marsh behind Seapoint Beach. There's a nice picnic area just inside the southern arm of the inlet at the mouth of Brave Boat Harbor. At its most interior point, the channel in the creek is about 4 feet deep at high water, so you don't have to be there at dead high tide, but it makes sense to go in with the flood tide sometime near high. The paddling between the mouth of Chauncey Creek and Brave Boat Harbor is very protected, and this route is popular with boaters. Look for herons and egrets along the way.

To circumnavigate Gerrish and Cutts islands, launch from Fort Foster (8.5 miles) or Pepperrell Cove (8 miles). There is no protection on the ocean

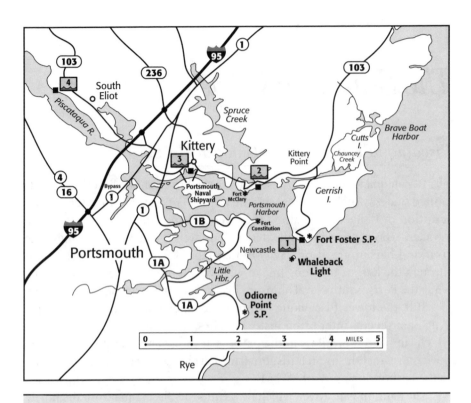

Charts

Charts: 13283, Cape Neddick Harbor to Isles of Shoals (1:20,000)
     13285, Portsmouth to Dover and Exeter (1:20,000)
Chart Kit: Not available in the Cape Elizabeth to Eastport pack
Maine Atlas locator map: 1

Tides (hours:minutes relative to Portland; average rise)
Gerrish Island Wharf: 0:02 before; 8.7 feet
Kittery Point: 0:07 after; 8.7 feet
Seavey Island: 0:23 after; 8.1 feet
Dover Point: 1:33 after; 6.5 feet
Salmon Falls River entrance: High1:35 after, low 1:52 after; 7 feet

side of the trip, and Brave Boat Harbor can be extremely difficult to enter or leave.

From Pepperrell Cove, circumnavigate New Castle Island (about 5 miles) or New Castle and Seavey islands (about 7 miles). A calm day is suggested, as the outer harbor is exposed to the wind. Also, the entrance to Little Harbor can be nasty in a southeast wind.

From Pepperrell Cove or Back Channel (Launch 3), explore Spruce Creek (5 or 6 miles). At low tide, this creek has extensive mudflats; catching the creek on the top of the tide allows more paddling freedom.

From Back Channel, explore the harbor; your mileage will depend on your route.

For a trip on the Salmon Falls River that is as rural as the Piscataqua is urban, put in at the ME 101 bridge, paddle north to the dam in South Berwick, and return (5 miles). Or, from the new launch in South Berwick, catch the tide downriver. The Salmon Falls River is beautiful—largely undeveloped, with either woods or pastures along the shore. The best timing for this trip is a rising tide to the dam and a falling tide back to the launch site, but the current in the river is not so strong

The view up Chauncey Creek

as to preclude paddling against the tide—it's just more work. If you are interested in historic buildings, pull over and visit Hamilton House, which is located on the eastern shore of the river.

Safety Considerations, Strong Currents, and Caution Areas

Piscataqua River and Portsmouth Harbor. From the approaches to Portsmouth Harbor to above Dover Point, the Piscataqua is subject to strong tidal currents. The swiftness of the currents varies from place to place because of variations in the depth and width of the channel.

Opposing tidal and river currents can create dangerous chop and rips in the outer harbor.

Particularly strong eddies form near Fort Point (check your chart) as the Piscataqua turns the corner in Portsmouth Harbor. There is a fierce eddy at Cod Rock, northwest of the point, just before low-water slack. Another eddy reportedly forms in the cove west of the point after slack water.

The average maximum ebb current at Seavey and Badgers islands is almost 4 knots. The average maximum flood current is 3.0 to 3.3 knots.

The current at Nobles Island, located in the narrows where three bridges span the river upriver from the harbor, exceeds 4 knots at maximum ebb.

The current at Dover Point, about 4 miles upstream of the bridges, averages about 3 knots at maximum velocity (flood and ebb) and can exceed 4 knots. Some buoys are reported to tow under here. Wood pilings located along the shores can be hazardous to small boats because they can act as strainers in tidal currents. The swift current at Dover Point is a product of the configuration of tributaries to the Piscataqua. The Oyster, Lamprey, Squamscott, and other rivers draining New Hampshire flow into Great Bay and Little Bay. The riverine waters, combined with the tidal waters stored in the two bays, provide for a huge outflow during the ebb tide. The combined flow of the Cocheco and Salmon Falls rivers from the north further adds to the speed of the current in the Piscataqua.

The direction of the current in the Piscataqua does not always follow the direction of the channel, and perilous crosscurrents may form. Because of the dangerous currents and crossccurrents, deep-draft ships may navigate the river only during the 3-hour periods centered on high slack and low slack water.

In addition to the previous considerations, sections of the harbor and its approaches are vulnerable to wind, particularly from the south and east.

Paddlers who venture into the harbor and onto the Piscataqua River should have experience in evaluating tide, river current, and wind conditions and the skills to deal with these conditions. Also, because Portsmouth Harbor and the Piscataqua River north to Dover Point see heavy boat traffic, from tankers to tour boats to pleasure craft, paddlers must be aware of their position relative to these other vessels and know how to paddle safely and defensively.

Special note regarding Seavey Island. Seavey Island in Portsmouth Harbor is home to the Portsmouth Naval Shipyard. This island is a restricted area and is closed to boaters. Do not land on Seavey Island or paddle into the cove formed by Seavey, Clarks, and Jamaica islands. Even if you're just taking a snapshot, you may find yourself being checked by a patrol. Although the Cold War is over, those charged with protecting the shipyard's secrets take their jobs seriously.

Brave Boat Harbor. Brave Boat Harbor lies to the north of Portsmouth Harbor. The *Coast Pilot* says that surf breaks across the entrance "with the least sign of weather," so the derivation of the harbor's name isn't exactly a mystery. When sea kayaking, bravery is not a substitute for good judgment.

Gerrish Island. The eastern, southern, and western shores of Gerrish

Portsmouth Naval Shipyard on Seavey Island

Island, as well as the eastern shore of Cutts Island, are exposed to the wind and may see considerable surf. (Cutts Island is actually connected to Gerrish Island.)

Access

1: Fort Foster. The windsurfing beach at Fort Foster Park is the designated launch site for sea kayakers. From the bridge between Kittery and Kittery Point on ME 103, go east for almost 2 miles and turn right onto Chauncey Creek Road. Proceed 0.5 mile and then take another right onto Pocohontas Road, following it 1.2 miles until there is an obvious right into the park. The fee is $10 per vehicle. To launch a kayak, take a left toward the windsurfing and scuba beaches, then a right to the windsurfing beach. Hand carry to the beach. There are bathrooms opposite a concrete tower at the second turn, where the road splits off to the windsurfing beach. Questions? Contact the gate (439-2182) or Kittery Recreation Department (439-8000).

2: Pepperrell Cove, Portsmouth Harbor. Expect exposure if there is a south wind, some mud at the bottom of the tide, and very limited parking at the wharf, where most of the slots are private, restricted in time, or reserved for town residents. Spaces at the small lot at the top of the hill go for $10 per day Monday through Thursday and $15 Friday through Sunday. Free parking is available at a nearby school when the school is not in session.

From I-95 in Kittery, take exit 2 onto Route 1 and follow signs to ME 236. From the rotary, go 1.2 miles and turn left onto ME 103. Follow ME 103 about 1.5 miles, going over a bridge and past Fort McClary on the right. With the Post Office on the left and Frisbee's Market on the right, turn right onto Bellamy Lane, which leads directly to the Kittery wharf and launch ramp. The harbor master's building on the wharf has a bathroom.

The fee lot is opposite Frisbee's Market (pay at the market). The free lot is at the Mitchell School; from Bellamy Lane, turn right on ME 103, go 0.2 mile, and turn left into the lot.

3: Back Channel, Kittery. Follow directions as for Pepperrell Cove, except follow ME 236 for 1.2 mile and turn right onto ME 103. In just 0.1 mile turn left at Traip Academy. Go to the far end of the parking lot (almost behind the school) to the launch ramp. Although there is no parking at the ramp, paddlers may use the school lot on weekends, holidays, and from June 16 to August 31. During the school year, parking is allowed after 3 PM.

4: Piscataqua River, South Eliot. The town of Eliot has a large recreation area that includes a launch ramp and small beach. Kayakers may launch from the beach at no charge. From I-95, take the Kittery exit; from the traffic circle in Kittery, take Route 1 south 0.7 mile and turn right onto Eliot Road/ME 101. Go 2.9 miles to the shore access sign and turn left onto Hammond Lane. At the recreation area, go left for the launch ramp and lower parking lot. To the right is a pavilion, an upper parking lot, and an area for ball games. Bathrooms are located next to the upper parking lot.

5: Salmon Falls River. A small picnic area, parking lot, and launch ramp on ME 101 provide access to the Salmon Falls River. From Kittery, take ME 236 northwest 6 miles and then turn left onto ME 101. (From South Berwick, go about 4 miles south on ME 236, then turn right onto ME 101.) Go 1.1 miles to the Salmon Falls River launch site.

6: Counting House Park, Salmon Falls River. The Town of South Berwick has created a park and hand-carry launch just below the dam. From the south, take ME 236 into town, turn left onto ME 4, and go 0.3 mile; from the north, take ME 4 and stay on it until just before the bridge into New

Windsurfers' beach at Fort Foster

Hampshire. In both cases, take a left on Liberty Street just before the Customs House, a large brick building. The park is on the right.

A sign warns paddlers that rocks in the river not far below the dam are passable 2 hours on either side of high water. At other times, you may have to scrape by. (High water here is about 2 hours after Portland, or 1 hour 40 minutes behind Portsmouth Harbor). Also, water may rise or fall rapidly, depending on the flow of water through the hydropower station.

Launch sites in New Hampshire. There are also ramps on Witch Creek at Odiorne Point State Park; Hilton Park, located on Dover Point; and two marinas located on Little Bay.

Points of Interest

Brave Boat Harbor. The land around Brave Boat Harbor is owned and managed by the U.S. Fish and Wildlife Service as part of the Rachel Carson National Wildlife Reserve. Although ME 103 skirts the upper reaches of the harbor at the town line between Kittery and York—and the pull-out on the right suggests a hand-carry launch site—the small "parking" area is privately owned, and refuge managers request that boaters not launch here.

Fort Foster, Gerrish Island. Fort Foster, the southernmost point in Maine, guards the eastern entrance to Portsmouth Harbor. The World War II bunkers and observation towers provide a backdrop for a large park operated by the town of Kittery. The park has a beach for each activity—swimming, windsurfing and sea kayaking, and scuba diving. Pier Beach is reserved for swimming; there are also picnic tables.

Shipwrecks were common in the treacherous area bounded by the entrance to the Piscataqua River, Cape Neddick Nubble to the north, and Boon Island, 6 miles to the east. The six men who drowned when their ship, the Hattie Eaton, foundered on Gerrish Island lie in a graveyard on Kittery Point. The most famous shipwreck along this section of coast occurred on a stormy day in December 1710. The Nottingham Galley out of England smashed against Boon Island. Although the survivors could see ships going in and out of Portsmouth Harbor, they were unable to attract attention. The grisly story is recounted in *Boon Island*, one of Kenneth Roberts's many historical novels about Maine.

The Great Round Gerrish Island Race. Started in 1975, this event draws more than a hundred human-powered small boats; the limiting factor is the culvert through which each boat must pass to get into the marsh north of Chauncey Creek. There is more fun and less competition than at other races.

Whaleback Light. This conical gray tower is located on Whaleback Reef at the eastern entrance to Portsmouth Harbor; its light is 59 feet above water. Nearby Wood Island is the site of an abandoned lifesaving station.

Brave Boat Harbor, inside (top) and outside (below)

Fort McClary. This fort is named in honor of Major Andrew McClary, a local patriot who died at Bunker Hill. Formerly named Fort William, the site was fortified from colonial times through World War II. The octagonal blockhouse dates from the mid-1800s. The fee to visit Fort McClary is $2. For more information, call 384-5160 (summer).

Fort Point, New Castle Island, New Hampshire. Fort Point is the location of Portsmouth Harbor (New Castle) Light, which shines 52 feet above the water; a Coast Guard station and lookout tower; and Fort Constitution. The original fort was built in the 1600s to provide protection from pirates, and the British Fort William and Mary followed. At the beginning of the Revolutionary War, American patriots overwhelmed the British defenders—the first armed conflict of the war—and sent captured gunpowder and other armaments to the troops at Bunker Hill. The fort was rebuilt in the early 1800s and remained in service through World War II.

Fort Stark, New Castle Island, New Hampshire. Fort Stark, constructed in 1746, was used through World War II. The fort is on the southeast corner of the island.

Odiorne Point State Park, New Hampshire. This park, along with New Castle Island, forms the western shore of the approach to Portsmouth Harbor. In agreeable weather, the sandy beach at Frost Point serves as a nice picnic area. The park also has trails, a visitor center, and interpretive programs. A Scottish fisherman settled here in 1623, starting the first permanent settlement of Europeans in New Hampshire.

Wentworth-by-the-Sea, Little Harbor. The huge building on the eastern shore of Little Harbor is Wentworth-by-the-Sea, a resort.

Portsmouth Naval Shipyard. The shipyard, established in 1806 and also known as the Kittery Naval Shipyard, built half of the submarines that saw action in World War II. The yard was considered so critical to the U.S. war effort that a huge net was stretched from Wood Island to New Castle Island to protect the area from waterborne spies. Ships with a legitimate reason to enter the harbor radioed ahead and the net was dropped. One German submarine, however, managed to evade the barricade and observe the shipyard over the course of three nights before it slipped away into the Atlantic. Today the yard maintains nuclear submarines. The huge white building on the east end of the island was once a naval prison.

Maine and New Hampshire have argued for years over who really owns Seavey Island. So far, the courts have favored Maine's claim.

Portsmouth Harbor has a long history of shipbuilding. Captain John Paul Jones oversaw the construction of and then commanded the *Ranger*, built on Bunker Island (next to Seavey Island) for the fledgling U.S. Navy. The *Ranger* was the first government ship to fly the American flag.

Vaughn Woods Memorial State Park. In 1634, the Pied Cow landed in what was subsequently called Cow Cove along the shores of the Salmon Falls River. The boat brought the first cow and the first sawmill to the area. Cow Cove is now part of Vaughn Woods Memorial State Park. The 250-acre preserve, located 1.5 miles above the Salmon Falls River launch site on the east shore of the river, includes some areas of old-growth pine and hemlock as well as trails and a picnic area. There are no signs announcing the boundaries of the park, but hikers frequent the shoreline trails.

Hamilton House. This 1787 mansion of Georgian design has a view any paddler will appreciate—straight down the Salmon Falls River. The house, set high on the shore immediately north of Vaughn Woods, is carefully landscaped and has a formal garden. The Society for Preservation of New England Antiquities owns and maintains the house and grounds. The mansion is open from June through October 15 (call 384-5269 for the hours of operation; there is an entrance fee).

Salmon Falls. The Native American name for the falls, Quamphegan, means "dip net falls," referring to a time when fish could be caught by climbing out onto the rocky falls and using these simple nets. A dam was later constructed at the site of the falls.

At a Glance: Land in Public or Conservation Ownership
(not including historic sites or sites in New Hampshire)

Fort Foster Park	Town of Kittery; day use
Vaughn Woods Memorial State Park	BPL; day use
USFWS Wildlife Lands	
Brave Boat Harbor	Careful day use

York to Wells Harbor

Paddling along the open coast between York and Wells is sharply limited by frequent surf. The York River, though, provides a chance to explore inland. The river rises in the marshy areas to the west, then flows through pine and oak woods interspersed with homes and into the densely developed area surrounding the harbor. The York was originally called the Agamenticus River, which, according to Fanny Hardy Eckstorm—a singular authority on Native American place-names—means "the little river which lies behind an island in its mouth." The York River lies behind Stage Neck, which was once an island.

To the north, the much shorter Webhannet River is more suited to birding than extensive paddling, and there are a lot of birds to see there. Much of the marshland along the Webhannet River east of Route 1 (and almost 400 acres of marshland behind Moody Beach) is part of the Rachel Carson National Wildlife Refuge, a series of coastal wetlands between Kittery and Scarborough managed by the U.S. Fish and Wildlife Service.

Trip Ideas (weather and experience permitting)

From the Wiggly Bridge in York Village, paddle downriver into York Harbor, which is full of commercial fishing boats and recreational craft (2 miles

---

Charts
Chart: 13283, Cape Neddick Harbor to Isles of Shoals (1:20,000)
Chart Kit: Not available in the Cape Elizabeth to Eastport pack
Maine Atlas locator maps: 1, 2

Tides (hours:minutes relative to Portland; average rise)
York Harbor: 0:03 after; 8.6 feet

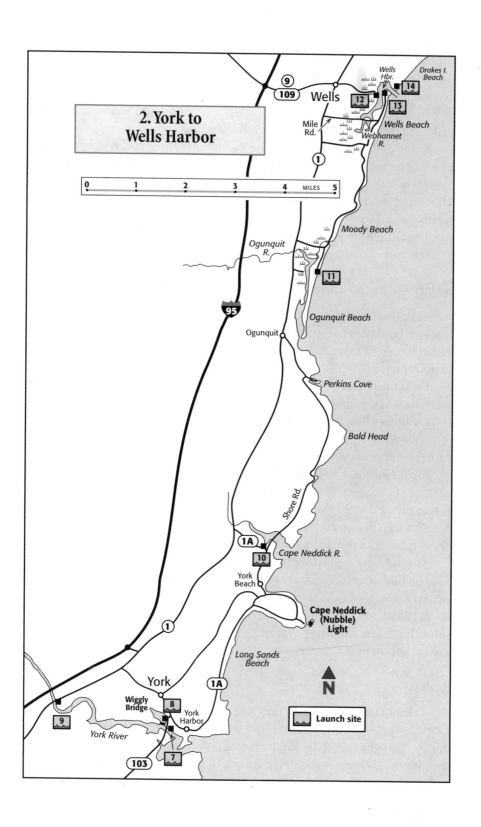

2. York to Wells Harbor

0   1   2   3   4   MILES   5

Wells

9
109

Mile Rd.

1

Wells Hbr.

Drakes I. Beach

14

12

13

Wells Beach

Webhannet R.

Moody Beach

Ogunquit R.

95

11

Ogunquit Beach

Ogunquit

Perkins Cove

Bald Head

Shore Rd.

1A

10

Cape Neddick R.

York Beach

Cape Neddick (Nubble) Light

1

Long Sands Beach

N

York

1A

Wiggly Bridge

8

York Harbor

9

7

York River

103

Launch site

round-trip). Or, paddle upriver. The head of the tide is about 8 miles above the Wiggly Bridge. For the upriver paddle, start on a rising tide and turn around just as the tide begins to ebb.

From the launch site in Ogunquit, with good and stable conditions, paddle in either direction to see coastal beaches.

From Wells Harbor, explore the Webhannet River and nearby marshes. The Webhannet dries to just a channel at low tide, so it is best to paddle on the top two-thirds of the tide. The houses on Wells Beach and the traffic on Mile Road dominate until you start moving away from the village of Wells Beach and into a pretty pocket of salt marsh.

The launch sites at Wells Beach and Drakes Island provide direct access to the ocean.

Safety Considerations, Strong Currents, and Caution Areas

York Harbor. The currents in York Harbor can be strong at narrow sections of the channel; the *Coast Pilot* reports that buoys sometimes tow under. The ebb current from Barrells Mill Pond under the Wiggly Bridge can be surprisingly strong.

Ogunquit River. The entrance to the Ogunquit River can be dangerous, even in calm seas, because swells break there.

Ogunquit Beach. Launching along Ogunquit Beach onto the open ocean often involves a surf launch and surf landing; the prevailing winds in the summer are onshore.

Wells Harbor. The *Coast Pilot* says that swells can break across the harbor entrance even in medium seas; on a rough day, confusing seas can form between the jetties. In these conditions, travel from the harbor to the open ocean can be dangerous. Waves are much smaller by the time they reach the flood-tidal delta that forms within the harbor.

Special note regarding Boon Island. U.S. Navy ships and submarines hold maneuvers in the vicinity of Boon Island, which is almost 6 miles southeast of Cape Neddick. If you encounter navy vessels traveling to or from Boon Island, obey any orders from officers of these vessels, and stay clear of ships that show a red flag or a flag with "NE 2." These flags mean "Be very careful because submarines are located here."

Access

7: York Harbor. Kayakers may launch from the small sandy area at Town Dock 1. York's harbor is small and working boats come and go from the docks. Please be especially careful not to crowd these boats; think of the sign that adorns the rear end of large trucks: IF YOU CAN READ THIS, I CAN'T SEE

Paddlers can launch from the causeway that leads to the Wiggly Bridge.

YOU. Here, if you can't see the boat operator, then the boat operator can't see you. Better yet, launch from the new site along Route 1, described below, and avoid the congestion altogether.

Parking is scarce at Dock 1; half of the spots are reserved for fishermen and lobstermen. There is some parking along the road; obey the signs. There is a portable toilet at the dock.

Follow directions for Barrells Mill Pond (below); continue a short distance south, watching for the town docks on the left.

8: Barrells Mill Pond, York River. It is possible to launch at the Wiggly Bridge, as the pedestrian suspension bridge off Lilac Lane is locally known. At the junction of Route 1A and ME 103 in York Harbor, take Lilac Lane/ME 103 south for 0.1 mile and pull off into the parking area on the left. Carefully hand carry across Lilac Lane, which sees a lot of traffic. Hand boats down from the causeway to water level, launching in Barrells Mill Pond or on the river, depending on the tide.

9: York River at Rice's Bridge. Kudos to Maine's Department of Transportation for including a small parking area and hand-carry, all-tide launch when an MDOT crew worked on that stretch of Route 1. From I-95, take exit 7 and turn south on Route 1. Go about 2 miles. Park parallel to the road on the left, just before the bridge. The Town of York's Goodrich Park is located on the right side of the road.

Note. A hand-carry area immediately south of the York River bridge at Scotland (about 1.5 miles upriver from I-95) has no parking; a few cars can squeeze onto land parallel to the road.

10: Cape Neddick River. The Harborview Oceanside Campground (363-4366) has a launch area that is open to the public; the launch fee is $10. From the south, take exit 7 (York) and get on Route 1, go a little more than 3 miles, and turn right on Route 1A. From the north, take exit 19 (Wells) and head east to Route 1, then go about 10 miles; take a left on Route 1A. The campground is located at the junction of Route 1A and Shore Road, on the south side of the river. Pay the fee at the campground (which, by the way, is for tents and tent campers only); the launch area is next to the Lobster Pound restaurant.

11: Ogunquit. Go almost 2 miles north from the center of Ogunquit on Route 1, then turn east onto Bourne Avenue. Go 0.7 mile and turn right toward the sewage treatment plant. There is a parking lot with bathrooms on the right just before the entrance to the plant. Hand carry across the road to the beach, using a narrow public right-of-way. There is no fee to launch, but a parking fee is sometimes collected.

12: Webhannet River, Wells Harbor. There is a hand-carry site as well as an all-tide ramp on the western shore of Wells Harbor. From the junction of Route 1 and ME 9/ME 109 in Wells, go north on Route 1 and take the first right onto Harbor Road; follow it 0.8 mile to the end.

For the hand-carry site, turn into the parking lot on the right, pass the pavilion, go to the far end of the lot, go behind the playground, and turn left toward the observation deck; carry to the beach. For the all-tide ramp, stay on the road until you come to a wharf; the ramp is on the left. Pay the ramp fee to the harbor master, who has a building on the dock.

13: Wells Beach. The town of Wells runs a parking lot at the northern tip of Wells Beach. You can hand carry to the ocean side of the lot, which lies at the base of the jetty. Parking is by the half day or full day; there are flush toilets. This lot fills up quickly in the summer. From the juncture of Route 1 and ME 9/ME 109 in Wells, proceed south on Route 1 for 1.2 miles. Turn left on Mile Road and continue for 0.9 mile. Turn left on Atlantic Avenue and proceed 1.1 miles to the parking area.

14: Drakes Island. The town of Wells owns a matching (fee) parking lot at the southern end of Drakes Island Beach, opposite the previous launch site. Hand carry across sand on the right. There are flush toilets. This lot, too, fills up quickly. From the junction of Route 1 and ME 9/ME 109 in Wells, proceed north on Route 1 for 1.2 miles and turn right onto Island Beach Road. Go 0.4 mile to the end of the road.

Points of Interest

York River. The York River drains a relatively small area, only 32 square miles. Predominant trees along the river are oak and white pine. During migrations, shorebirds use several tidal flats in York Harbor for feeding.

York Harbor. Stage Neck, which reaches south into the harbor, is named for the stages (wooden drying racks) that fishermen used to dry fish. Immigrants were quarantined on Harris Island.

Wiggly Bridge. There is a small park on the west side of the bridge.

John Hancock Warehouse and Wharf, York River. This historic site is located on the north shore of the York River, to the west of Barrells Mill Pond but before the bridge upriver. The building has exhibits of life in the 1700s, when the man with

Cape Neddick Light

the famous signature (and great penmanship) owned it. At that time, Maine was part of Massachusetts.

Cape Neddick Light. This 41-foot white tower is located not on the mainland but on a small island—Cape Neddick Nubble—barely separated from the shore. The light was built in 1879.

Ogunquit and Moody beaches. Ogunquit and Moody beaches form the largest barrier spit beach, tidal river, and marsh system in the state. Prevailing southwest winds move current north along the shore, but at the end of the Ogunquit spit the swash of swells is the key feature in transporting sand and building beaches. The sand, almost entirely composed of quartz, is dazzling white and fine grained—a product of winnowing by glacial meltwater streams thousands of years ago and by ocean waves more recently.

Moody Beach is the setting for the court case that resulted in the decision that use of the intertidal zone is limited to those who are fishing, fowling, and navigating (see pages 25–26). Keep your map and compass handy.

Wells Beach. Wave action, rather than the pull of currents, is the main factor in sand distribution along Wells Beach.

Webhannet River and Wells Harbor. The river drains only 14 square miles but has a concentration of salt marsh, salt pans, and tidal mudflats that provide excellent feeding and nesting habitat for birds. Great blue and little herons, glossy ibis, and snowy egrets are commonly seen from May through September. Canada and snow geese, green-winged and blue-winged teal, common and red-breasted mergansers, and mallards visit this area in spring and fall migrations, while black ducks can be seen all year. Wells Harbor can also draw in bufflehead, common goldeneye, oldsquaw, and common eider. Many species of shorebirds frequent the marsh on migration.

The Webhannet is a tidal inlet with little or no freshwater input except runoff, so it dries up considerably at low water. Thousands of years ago the inlet was a lagoon behind a barrier beach (what is now Wells Beach), but salt-marsh plants became established as the lagoon filled in.

At a Glance: Land in Public or Conservation Ownership

Rachel Carson National Wildlife Refuge   U.S. Fish and Wildlife Service

---

Kennebunk to Goose Rocks Beach

The Kennebunk River offers beautiful, protected paddling but it is a major challenge to get to the water in the tourist-beset town of Kennebunkport. Paddling opportunities along the dazzling beaches in this area are limited by ac-

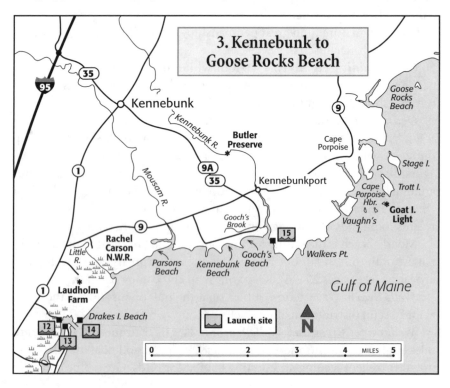

Charts

Chart: 13286, Cape Elizabeth to Portsmouth (1:80,000) with insets of Cape Porpoise Harbor, Wells Harbor, Kennebunk River, and Perkins Cove
Chart Kit: Not available in the Cape Elizabeth to Eastport pack
Maine Atlas locator map: 3

Tides (hours:minutes relative to Portland; average rise)
Kennebunkport: 0:16 after; 8.5 feet
Cape Porpoise: 0:12 after; 8.7 feet

---

cess as well as sea conditions. Cape Porpoise certainly is the prettiest archipelago along this section of the coast, but again access can be difficult.

Trip Ideas (weather and experience permitting)

From Kennebunkport, paddle upstream on the Kennebunk River. The river is tidal above Kennebunk Landing, where a bridge crosses the river; the length of the trip depends on the height of the tide and your interest in paddling (almost 8 miles round-trip from Colony Beach, Launch 15, to the bridge and back. The gazebo on the western shore of the harbor is part of the Franciscans' Saint Anthony Monastery. The harbor is jammed with boats, but above the ME 9 bridge the views improve considerably. The shores are

The harbor in Kennebunkport is small and crowded, but the Kennebunk River above provides lovely, moderate paddling.

lined with oaks and pines rather than condos, and the river provides lovely paddling. Plan to ride the flood tide upriver and catch the ebb tide downriver, as there can be a surprisingly stiff current that takes some effort to paddle against; some paddlers may choose to wait until the current slackens.

From Kennebunkport, head east past Walkers Point to Cape Porpoise Harbor (7 or 8 miles round-trip). If the President is visiting his parents at the Bush compound on Walkers Point, save this trip for another time. For all but the most experienced paddlers, this trip requires calm and stable conditions. Be forewarned that the harbor at Cape Porpoise empties at low tide.

From Kennebunkport, paddle west and explore the Mousam River (11 miles to the head of tide and back). Despite the buffer provided by Rachel Carson Refuge lands, development has inched its way to the shores of the Mousam, and this trip is not as pretty as one on the Kennebunk River. Paddling on the top half of the tide is advisable. Calm and stable conditions are advised for the crossing from the jetties at Kennebunkport and into the mouth of the Mousam.

To explore the Little River, enter on the top half of a flood tide and return on the ebb.

Safety Considerations, Strong Currents, and Caution Areas

Mouth of the Kennebunk River. Storm waves and waves from strong southwest winds will dump at the mouth of the river on an ebbing tide. The *Coast Pilot* reports that when there are heavy seas and wind from the south, it can be perilous to go through the jetties at the mouth of the river. Strong wind and seas can produce surf that makes paddling in this area of the coast difficult and potentially hazardous.

Walkers Point. When George H. W. Bush was president, the U.S. Secret Service set up a security zone around Walkers Point. The restrictions were lifted in 1993. According to a representative of the Secret Service, paddlers may now venture freely in the area: "Currently, the Secret Service does have appropriate security measures in place to protect former President Bush and his family at Walkers Point. However, none of these measures would hinder anyone from kayaking or boating there."

Tighter security restrictions do apply when George W. Bush is visiting Walkers Point. A word of caution is appropriate: Don't push your luck. When Bush senior was in office, the Secret Service picked up a local paddler—outside of the restricted area—and detained him. He did not describe the event in glowing terms.

Cape Porpoise. Numerous ledges outside the Cape Porpoise archipelago contribute to confusing seas whenever there are swells or wind.

Access

15: Colony Beach, Kennebunkport. This beach lies immediately east of the eastern jetty at the mouth of the Kennebunk River. The jetty provides some protection, although the beach is still open to swells from the south. There is a small, public parking lot that immediately fills up in the summer. There is no charge for parking, but there are also no facilities. From the bridge in the center of Kennebunkport, go north on ME 9 for 0.1 mile; take a right onto Ocean Avenue and proceed 0.9 mile. The turnoff is just after the Colony Hotel, where the road curves to the left.

Notes. In Kennebunk, there's a ramp but no parking lot where ME 9 goes over the Mousam River, just north of Parsons Beach. Diligent hunting may turn up a couple of spots where ME 9 is not posted as no parking.

Kennebunkport Marina on the Kennebunk River is geared toward larger boats; the marina charges $15 to launch and another $15 to take out.

A tiny, hand-carry launch site on the western edge of Cape Porpoise has not been included here because it has room for only a few cars and is perpetually overcrowded. Please leave this site to local users. The ramp on Porpoise Cove on the northern edge of the harbor is gated and there is no parking.

Points of Interest

Laudholm Farm: Wells National Estuarine Research Reserve. The major portion of this reserve lies between the Island Beach Road (to Drake's Island) and the Little River to the north. The reserve includes most of Laudholm Beach, a barrier beach; extensive salt marshes; and upland fields and forests. Several times a summer, as part of its education and interpretive tours program, the reserve offers kayak trips on the Little River. The reserve also conducts research on estuarine water quality, clam productivity, fish distribution, salt-marsh restoration, and habitat protection. Laudholm Trust, a membership organization, originally protected the 1,600-acre Wells Reserve and continues to support the reserve's activities.

Little River. This tidal river loops back and forth (and back and forth) through salt marsh and upland woods. Least terns, which nest nearby (and only at a few other sites in Maine), are sometimes visible at the mouth of the river. Piping plover, which are listed as threatened by the federal government and endangered by the state government, nest on Laudholm Beach. If you land on Laudholm, stay within the intertidal zone.

Mousam River Estuary. Parsons Beach, at the entrance to the estuary, is a barrier spit beach that shelters salt marsh along Back Creek. The owners allow the beach to be used by townspeople, but parking is very restricted. Shorebirds congregate at the flats at the mouth of the river during fall migration.

The Kennebunk Conservation Trust has protected many islands in Cape Porpoise Harbor.

From Parsons Beach, the estuary stretches about 3 miles upriver to the head of tide, snaking through salt marshes and mudflats. The marshes have been diked and otherwise altered over the years. A parcel of marshland north of Great Hill, the eastern entrance to the river, as well as land farther upriver form the Mousam River section of the Rachel Carson National Wildlife Refuge.

Butler Preserve, Kennebunk River. This 14-acre preserve is located at a bend in the river just west of the Cape Arundel Golf Course. An exposure of bedrock marks the spot. On the top half of the tidal cycle, there is not much room to land. The current, however, is fairly strong. Perhaps paddlers can best appreciate this preserve as a stretch of protected open space. The Kennebunk Land Trust owns this preserve and several other parcels along the river.

The Kennebunk River Estuary. This estuary, like the Webhannet River estuary in Wells, is a tidal inlet that floods an extensive back-barrier salt marsh. Gooch's Beach is the barrier beach that lies seaward of the marsh. The estuary, from the head of tide to the mouth, is approximately 5 miles long. Gooch's Brook is an arm of the estuary that reaches west from the harbor almost a mile into salt meadow grass, a plant that dominates the high marsh. Whether paddling west or north, birders should take along binoculars, for there are likely to be waders and other birds associated with salt marshes.

Vaughn's Island, Cape Porpoise. This near-shore island offers trails, places to picnic, and a view toward the ocean and into Cape Porpoise Harbor. The 45-acre preserve is owned by the Kennebunkport Conservation Trust.

Goat Island Light, Cape Porpoise. Light keepers operated this station until 1990, when it was finally automated. The white cylindrical tower shows

Immature little blue herons on Stage Island

a light 38 feet above the water. Security officials were stationed here when President George H. W. Bush visited his family home on Walkers Point. The Kennebunkport Conservation Trust, which now owns and manages the island, asks that visitors stay clear of the house, tower, and equipment unless they have the permission of the keeper.

   Other islands in Cape Porpoise Harbor: The Kennebunkport Conservation Trust owns and manages several nearby islands, including Redin's, Cape, Green (a.k.a. President Bush), Bass, Milk, Savin Bush, Trott's, and Pinkham. The trust also owns and manages Bumpkin Island, which lies south of Vaughn's Island. All of these islands except Green (between Vaughn's and Folly islands) are open to the public for careful day use. Green is a wildlife island and so is closed during the nesting season.

At a Glance: Land in Public or Conservation Ownership

Laudholm Farm: Wells National Estuarine Research Reserve	BPL; town of Wells; U.S. Fish and Wildlife Service
Butler Preserve	Kennebunk Land Trust; appreciate as protected land
Bumpkin Island	Kennebunkport Conservation Trust; careful day use
Vaughn's Island	Kennebunkport Conservation Trust; careful day use
Redin's, Cape, Goat, Bass, Milk, Savin Bush, Trott's, and Pinkham Islands	Kennebunkport Conservation Trust; careful day use
Green Island	Kennebunkport Conservation Trust; closed April 1–August 30

The Saco River

A whopping 80 percent of the parking at one of the launch sites on the Saco River is designated for vehicles with trailers, a fact that provides a clear message: The vast majority of recreational users on the Saco are powerboaters en route to the open water. If you want a quieter experience, paddle the Saco during the week or during the off-season. It's a pretty paddle, with trees and a fringe of marsh along the river.

Trip Ideas (weather and experience permitting)

If you like the idea of paddling the length of a tidal river, launch from the Saco ramp and wind your way down to Camp Ellis (10 miles round-trip). Catching a rising tide back to the Front Street ramp makes paddling easier. The river from the head of tide to Camp Ellis is relatively protected, although you will likely catch more wind as you get closer to open water.

You'll want good conditions to paddle outside the mouth of the river and over to Wood Island Harbor. Stage Island is open to the public for day use, so it makes a nice destination, weather permitting (from the Biddeford ramp, 6.5 miles round-trip; from the Camp Ellis ramp, 4 miles round-trip).

If you want to explore the Pool, go in toward the top of the tide—there's more to see when it's full of water—and then go out with the ebbing tide (from Camp Ellis, 8 miles round-trip includes a tour of the perimeter of the Pool). The Pool is all but empty at low tide; it fills up 1 to 3 hours before high tide.

Safety Considerations, Strong Currents, and Caution Areas

The Saco River. From March through May, melting snow and spring floods can raise the water level of the Saco by as much as 8 feet. These high-water conditions can produce dangerous currents.

The outer 0.6 mile of the southern jetty and 0.4 mile of the northern jetty are covered at high tide; beware of breaking waves. The *Coast Pilot* warns small craft against crossing the bar at the mouth of the river when the tide is ebbing and the wind is from the east.

Charts
Chart: 13287, Saco Bay and Vicinity (1:20,000)
Chart Kit: Not available in the Cape Elizabeth to Eastport pack
Maine Atlas locator map: 3

Tides (hours:minutes relative to Portland; average rise)
Wood Island Harbor: 0:02 after; 8.7 feet

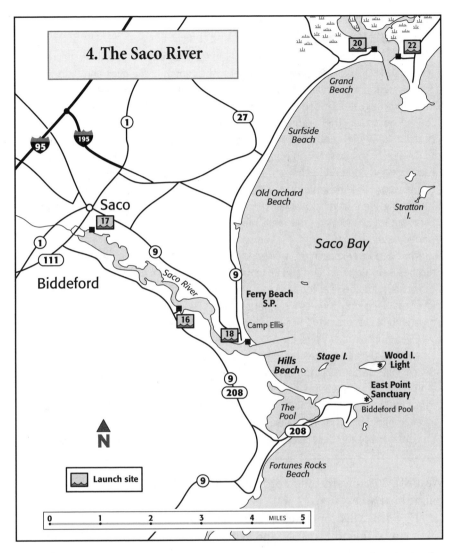

4. The Saco River

Grand Beach

Surfside Beach

Old Orchard Beach

Stratton I.

Saco Bay

Saco

Biddeford

Saco River

Ferry Beach S.P.

Camp Ellis

Hills Beach

Stage I.

Wood I. Light

East Point Sanctuary

Biddeford Pool

The Pool

Fortunes Rocks Beach

Launch site

N

0   1   2   3   4   MILES   5

Biddeford Pool. At their greatest velocity, tidal currents in the Gut at the mouth of the Pool can be quite strong.

Access

16: Biddeford. With two ramps, this launch site on the south side of the river is designed to handle a large volume of powerboats efficiently. On a busy day, kayakers may want to use a shallow area just north of the ramps. There are vault toilets and many parking places, most of which are for vehicles with trailers. From I-95, take exit 32, the Biddeford exit, and then turn left onto ME 111. Go a little more than 2 miles and turn right onto ME 9

The Saco River Estuary

Samuel de Champlain, an early explorer of the Maine coast, sailed into Saco Bay on July 9, 1605, crossed over the sandbar at the mouth of the river, and dropped anchor. He found an established year-round settlement, with Native Americans living in a large cabin surrounded by a stockade. "They plough the soil with a wooden spade," he wrote. "They plant corn in hills with a horseshoe crab for fertilizer and beans to keep the weeds down. They also plant squash, pumpkins, and tobacco."

The Saco was dammed in the early 1800s to produce energy for factories on Factory Island and on the shore. The river continues to produce power today, but the combination of dams and pollution has harmed wildlife and reduced water quality. Historically, there were substantial runs of Atlantic salmon, alewives, and shad in the Saco, but today there are only small numbers of alewives, shad, and nonspawning striped bass.

The Saco River rises in the White Mountains of New Hampshire. By the time it reaches Saco Bay, this river and its tributaries drain 1,700 square miles. In Maine, canoeists value the river for its slow current and beautiful sandy beaches. The Saco River estuary is only 5 miles long, from Cataract Dam to the mouth. Saco simply means "outlet of the river." The river took on the name of its mouth.

Over thousands of years, the Saco carried sand to the mouth of the river, forming an ebb-tide delta. Currents transported sand north to Ferry Beach and south to Hills Beach. In 1938 the U.S. Army Corps of Engineers built a breakwater 6,600 feet long at the mouth, in an attempt to relocate the area of sand deposition and keep the river's mouth clear. Later, another long jetty was built. Attempts to change the character and flow of a river, however, sometimes backfire. Instead of increasing flushing, the jetties made the delta even larger by drawing in sand from flood-tidal deposits.

West/ME 208 toward Biddeford Pool. Proceed 2.5 miles and turn left at the public boat access sign.

17: Saco. This concrete, all-tide boat ramp, maintained by Maine's Department of Inland Fisheries and Wildlife, is located at the head of tide just below Factory Island. The parking lot has slots for 11 vehicles with trailers; there is a portable toilet and a picnic table. From I-95, take exit 36, I-195, toward Saco. At the junction of I-195 and Main Street (Route 1), go west on Main Street for 1.3 miles. Turn left at Pepperell Square and stay right, going under the bridge on Front Street. Continue to the launch area.

18: Camp Ellis. The charge is $10 to park and $5 to launch at the all-tide ramp that is part of the town dock. If you arrive before 9 AM, pay upon leaving. There is a portable toilet. From I-95, take exit 36, I-195, toward Saco. At the junction of I-195 and Main Street (Route 1), go west on Main Street for 1 mile. At the junction of ME 5, ME 112, ME 9, and Route 1, go east on ME 9 (Ferry Road) toward Camp Ellis for 3.9 miles. Take a right on Camp

Champlain's map of the Saco River, showing Native American buildings and garden plots, the sandbar at the mouth of the river, and islands that form Wood Island Harbor

Saltwater and freshwater do not mix thoroughly in the estuary but are highly stratified. As the flood tide pushes saltwater up the channel in a large wedge, freshwater pools at the head of the estuary. When the tide push eases, freshwater escapes on top of the saltwater and out to Saco Bay. This event is even more pronounced during spring floods.

Ellis Avenue and an immediate left on Main (which goes into North). Follow the road to its end at the wharf. Use the small patch of beach opposite the boat ramp to launch, thereby avoiding the congestion of the ramp.

Note. Fishermen use the boat launch at the mouth of Biddeford Pool. As the parking is extremely limited, this site cannot handle additional traffic. Please do not use this ramp to launch kayaks. The Camp Ellis ramp is located nearby.

Points of Interest

Wood Island Light. The Wood Island Light stands at the entrance to the Saco River. The white, conical tower, built in 1808 when James Madison was president, supports a light that is 71 feet above the water. The light was automated in 1986.

Wood Island and Stage Island sanctuaries. The Maine Audubon Society owns these two islands. Several species of wading birds nest on Wood Island

Maine Audubon's Wood Island is a bird sanctuary; it is not open to the public. Instead, visit nearby Stage Island.

(it is also registered with the state's Critical Areas Program), and so the island is closed to the public.

Nearby Stage Island, which has a conspicuous stone monument, gets its name from the drying racks, called stages, that cod fishermen once used to dry their catch. Maine Audubon permits careful day use here. Watch for all three species of black-capped maritime terns—common, arctic, and roseate—and for herons that sometimes mix with gulls along the shore.

East Point Sanctuary. The eastern tip of Fletcher Neck is also a Maine Audubon sanctuary. The 30-acre parcel is a hot spot for birders all year round. Sea kayakers paddling near the sanctuary may spot common eiders, arctic and common terns, and black guillemots during the summer, and northern harriers, merlins, and peregrine falcons during the fall hawk migration. Boaters may land on the small shingle beaches along the shore.

The Pool at Biddeford Pool. Great blue herons, little blue herons, green herons, snowy egrets, black-crowned night herons, and glossy ibises frequent the Pool during spring and summer. There are lots of common terns plus some arctic and roseate terns. Bonaparte's gulls regularly appear in the basin in spring and then from midsummer through fall.

There are two conservation areas on land surrounding the Pool. Maine Audubon's 1-acre M. B. Smith Sanctuary lies on the south shore near the mouth of the Pool, and a 14-acre parcel that is part of the Rachel Carson National Wildlife Refuge is located in the northwest corner of the basin.

Hills Beach. Hills Beach is a barrier spit beach that separates Saco Bay from the Pool. Birders report that common, arctic, and roseate terns feed here in the summer, and many Bonaparte's gulls can be seen here in the fall.

At a Glance: Land in Public or Conservation Ownership

Wood Island Sanctuary	Maine Audubon Society; closed to visitors
Stage Island Sanctuary	Maine Audubon Society; careful day use
East Point Sanctuary	Maine Audubon Society; careful day use

IF&W Wildlife Island

This island is closed during the indicated bird nesting season. After the nesting season is over, the island is limited to careful day use.

Beach Island   April 15–August 31
(0.5 mile S of Biddeford Point)

Scarborough Marsh and Vicinity

Paddling a salt marsh takes patience. It's like hiking switchbacks up a mountain: You go back and forth, back and forth, making a little progress on each pass. Although it is tempting to sneak across what looks like a thin neck of marsh grass, the shortcut generally turns out to be a frustrating dead end, leaving you stuck in the mud. Then it's back to the channel, which would have been faster anyway. With marsh paddling, the destination is less important than the trip—watching a hawk soar on a thermal, listening to grass swish in the breeze, and breathing the sulfur smell of sticky marsh mud.

Trip Ideas (weather and experience permitting)

Put in at any of the launch sites along Scarborough Marsh or the Scarborough River. At high tide the marsh is flooded, and at low tide navigation shrinks to the three shallow creek channels, so planning with the tide in mind (aim for halftide or higher) takes on more than casual importance. Scarborough Marsh is roughly 3 miles across and 2 miles north to south, but in most of the marsh it's hard to paddle in a straight line. Trip length is up to you. The marsh is a fine place for gunkholing and a good choice for paddlers who want a relaxed excursion.

Charts
Chart: 13287, Saco Bay and Vicinity (1:20,000)
Chart Kit: Not available in the Cape Elizabeth to Eastport pack
Maine Atlas locator map: 3

Tides (hours:minutes relative to Portland; average rise)
Old Orchard: 0:00; 8.8 feet
Richmond Island: 0:03 before; 8.9 feet

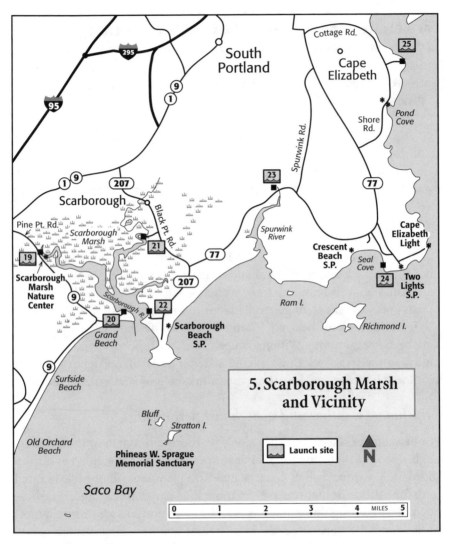

5. Scarborough Marsh and Vicinity

Launch site

N

Saco Bay

A trip to the National Audubon Society's Stratton Island in Saco Bay (from Pine Point or Ferry Beach, 6 miles round-trip) can be delightful in good conditions or an epic if the weather turns against you.

From the Spurwink River site, put in 2 hours or so before high water, paddle against the current to the mouth of the river, then catch the rising tide back to the launch site (4 miles round-trip). This excursion takes you through a section of the Rachel Carson National Wildlife Refuge, so you may see lots of wildlife—egrets, great blue herons, kingfishers, perhaps even least terns (which nest on Higgins Beach) or migrating shorebirds.

From Kettle Cove (Launch 24), visit the beach on the north shore of Richmond Island (2.5 miles round-trip). Even though this is a short trip, be

The high-rise skyline of Old Orchard Beach stands in contrast to surrounding shores.

prepared for swells that may roll in unimpeded from the ocean. The break-water between Richmond Island and the mainland is covered at high water but emerges as the tide ebbs.

Safety Considerations, Strong Currents, and Caution Areas

Mouth of the Scarborough River and Saco Bay. The mouth of the Scarborough River at Pine Point, and Saco Bay in general, can pick up a lot of wind and waves. If you are not sure of your skills, or if the weather promises to deteriorate, consider heading inland to the marsh.

Duck hunting season. Scarborough Marsh is a haven for waterfowl; it is also a favorite area for duck hunters (see pages 20, 77).

Access

19: Scarborough Marsh Nature Center. The Maine Audubon Society runs a small nature center with a boat launch on the west side of the marsh. From the junction of Route 1 and ME 9 (also called Pine Point Road), go south on ME 9 for 0.8 mile; the facility is on the left. The center is open daily from Memorial Day to Labor Day (883-5100). Be prepared: There are no bathrooms.

Note. A short distance south of the Nature Center there is a small, old ramp and dirt pull-off on the left with room for perhaps half a dozen vehicles.

20: Pine Point town landing. The lot here, though large, fills up quickly with commercial fishermen. There is no charge for those who hand-carry over the sand; those who use the ramp must pay $10 (residents) or $20 (non-residents). There are bathrooms on site.

Proceed as if you were going to Scarborough Marsh Nature Center, but continue for another 2.4 miles until the road makes an abrupt turn right at a stop sign. Turn left onto East Grand Avenue and proceed 0.5 mile, following signs for shore access. Take a left onto King Street and follow it to the parking lot.

21: Nonesuch River. This hard-surface, part-tide ramp has room for about a dozen vehicles with trailers. Fishermen do not use this site (they prefer Pine Point), so parking may actually be easier. From the junction of Route 1/ME 9 and ME 207 in Scarborough, proceed south on ME 207 (Black Point Road) for 0.6 mile and turn right onto Clay Pitts Road. Proceed 0.5 mile to the shore access sign. Locally, the site is known as the Clay Pitts ramp.

22: Scarborough Ferry Beach Park. This town park has a concrete, all-tide launch ramp, a swath of sand for beachgoers, and vault toilets. It's a very popular place. From the junction of ME 77 and ME 207 (Black Point Road), proceed south on ME 207 for 1.3 miles and turn right on Ferry Road at the public boat ramp sign. Continue 0.4 mile to the end of the road. The parking fee is $10 per vehicle, and the park closes at 9 PM. The roads in this area are plastered with signs declaring: NO PARKING ALONG ROAD MAY 1–SEPT. 15, so don't even think about leaving cars outside the park.

23: Spurwink River. From Portland, take ME 77 south to South Portland and continue south on Ocean House Road. Take a right on Spurwink Avenue, continue until it runs into ME 77, and turn right. Go less than half a mile, go over the Spurwink River Bridge, and turn right onto a dirt access road. (From Scarborough, take ME 207 south until ME 77 comes in on the left; turn onto ME 77 and continue for about 3 miles; turn left on the dirt road just before the bridge.) Parking is limited to just a few vehicles.

24: Kettle Cove, Cape Elizabeth. Cape Elizabeth has three state parks in a row, from west to east: Crescent Beach, Kettle Cove (on Seal Cove), and Two Lights. The town of Cape Elizabeth has a recreational boat access site adjacent to the Kettle Cove Park. (The park itself has a boat access site that is limited to commercial fishermen, and parking is reserved for the fishermen and for patrons of the park.) Recreational boaters must use the town's access—a beach—both for parking and for launching. A four-wheel-drive vehicle is not necessary for getting onto the beach.

Permits, which cost $5 per day, are required from Memorial Day through Labor Day; town residents can get an annual pass for $25. Permits are available from the Cape Elizabeth Police Station. Take ME 77 over the bridge to South Portland and follow it for a little more than 3 miles. A small shopping center and the Cape Elizabeth Fire Station are on the right. The police station is near the fire station. (Questions? Call Public Safety, 767-3323.)

To reach the launch area, proceed on ME 77 for about 2 miles. Continue past the turn-off for Two Lights State Park and take the next left. Follow this road to Kettle Cove. The town's access site is on the right, immediately before the parking lot. Kettle Cove Park has vault toilets.

25: Fort Williams Park, Cape Elizabeth: See next chapter.

The Birds of Scarborough Marsh

In early spring, Scarborough Marsh looks like a vast three-day beard, with only the stubs of *Spartina* (a marsh grass) left from the winter's ice. But in March, migrating Canada geese, sometimes numbering in the thousands, gather in the marsh to feed on the new shoots. Snow geese are there too, though in smaller numbers. Then come the ducks—American blacks, mallards, common and red-breasted mergansers, blue- and green-winged teals, northern pintails, and others.

By late spring, the wading birds arrive, dressed in their striking hues: great blue herons, little blue herons, and green herons; glossy ibises; and snowy egrets. Cattle and great egrets, tricolored herons, or black-crowned night herons may also appear.

Marsh nesters, meanwhile, stake out their territory and build nests. Red-winged blackbirds, with their brilliant epaulets, are among the most obvious, but there are also ducks (including hooded mergansers), willets, American bitterns, Virginia rails, and several species of sparrows. Ospreys and terns look for fish in the marsh, while northern harriers and Cooper's hawks search for other prey.

Bonaparte's gulls, having dashed through in spring, return in late summer. Shorebirds galore also appear at this time, having already started their long migration south. Geese and ducks follow in the fall. The lush marsh grass turns golden, the days shorten, and winter arrives once again in Scarborough Marsh.

Points of Interest

Scarborough Marsh and the Scarborough River Estuary. The Scarborough River estuary formed when longshore currents, carrying sediments from the southwest, began dropping those sediments at the outlet of the river, partly closing the mouth. The river itself is a truncated affair, hardly more than a harbor. The Dunstan River, which flows in from the west; the Nonesuch River, which flows in from the north; and the Libby River, which flows in from the east form the three backbones of Scarborough Marsh, the largest salt marsh in the state.

Like salt marshes everywhere, the one at Scarborough has been changed over the years. European settlers diked the tributaries and managed the marsh for production of salt-marsh hay. Roadbuilders nipped at its edges, and engineers built a railroad bed straight across it. In the 1940s and 1950s, in an effort to sabotage salt-marsh mosquitoes, sections of the marsh were ditched and drained. Of course, other forms of wildlife were affected as well. Scarborough Marsh is now largely protected from development. Maine's Department of Inland Fisheries and Wildlife owns more than 3,000 acres of the marsh, managing it for waterfowl.

Scarborough. In 1992 and 1993, staff from the Maine State Museum and

National Audubon Society's sanctuary on Stratton Island in Saco Bay

a crew of volunteers excavated bones and teeth from a female mammoth that was apparently washed into the sea some 12,000 to 12,500 years ago. A tusk had been found years before. Research suggests that the mammoth was approximately 35 years old when it met its watery demise. The artifacts are now at the Maine State Museum.

Phineas W. Sprague Memorial Sanctuary. Each summer evening, when the wading birds that have been feeding in Scarborough Marsh turn homeward, one contingent streams south to Stratton Island. Black-crowned night herons, snowy egrets, glossy ibises, little blue herons, and tricolored herons settle into their nests. Common terns, arctic terns, and roseate terns also nest on the island, although predation by a night heron and a mink have reduced tern numbers. Stratton and its companion Bluff lie about 1.5 miles off Prouts Neck in Saco Bay. Together they form the sanctuary owned and managed by the National Audubon Society.

The Audubon Society welcomes visitors between sunrise and sunset but sets out some conditions that embody low-impact use: do not camp or kindle fires; do not remove plants; stay away from nesting areas; and take no dogs to the islands. The small beach on the west side of Stratton, with the Audubon sign and observation deck, is the obvious place to land. Stratton Island must have appealed to Samuel de Champlain, for he anchored here before sailing on to the Saco River.

Scarborough Beach. Scarborough Beach is a *fringing barrier beach*, which means that it is connected to the mainland at both ends. (A *barrier spit beach* like Wells Beach, in contrast, is connected to the mainland only at one end.) Behind the beach at Scarborough lies Massacre Pond, a freshwater lagoon that geologists speculate may once have been a tidal lagoon. Scarborough

Richmond Island

The tranquility of this large but undeveloped island belies its importance in early Maine history. Samuel de Champlain sailed by here in 1605 and saw "many vine-yards bearing beautiful grapes in their season." He was clearly impressed—it was the first time he had seen grapes on this voyage to the New World. He named it the Isle of Bacchus.

In the eyes of fishermen and European settlers, the island was ideally situated. Being an island, it was more easily defended than a mainland site. The land was fertile and close to productive fishing areas. The harbor to the west of the bar (now a breakwater) accommodated deep-draft vessels. An Irishman named John Richmond settled on the island in the 1620s and gave it his name. Walter Bagnall established a trading post in 1628. He cheated the Indians, though, and met his reckoning at their hands in 1631.

John Winter started over in 1633, and the settlement flourished until his death 12 years later. Winter was the agent for the island's owner, Thomas Trelawney. Winter supervised fishermen who caught cod nearby and set up their drying racks on the island. He also established a farm to provide food for the fishermen and other people drawn to the establishment. Winter did well for his employer, but after his death, trade declined, and relations with the Indians, which were never good, worsened. Richmond Island slumped into obscurity for more than 200 years. Then, one day in 1854, a farmer plowed up a pottery crock containing gold and silver coins dating from the 1500s and 1600s. Apparently Walter Bagnall had been careful of his fortune if not of his life.

The Sprague Corporation owns this beautiful, undeveloped island. To visit it, you must first get permission (call John Green at 799-0011). Guidelines for the island's use are posted at a small beach on the northern shore. In addition to following other low-impact practices, visitors are asked not to walk on the dunes and not to go into buildings.

Beach is heavily used as a bathing beach, so it is not a place to launch your kayak.

Spurwink River. More than 300 acres along the Spurwink River are protected as part of the Rachel Carson National Wildlife Refuge.

Crescent Beach. Crescent Beach, a part of which is contained in Crescent Beach State Park, is a small fringing pocket beach. A fringing beach is defined as one that is located at the head of a bay (here, Seal Cove), and it does not have extensive dune fields or an interior lagoon. A fringing beach generally lies next to bedrock or soil.

Cape Elizabeth Light. This bright light, which shines 129 feet above the water with the power of 4 million candles, marks the transition from the southern coast to Casco Bay. There were originally two active lights, built in

1828, but the second one was permanently abandoned in 1924. In 1970, the U.S. Postal Service commemorated Maine's 150th anniversary by issuing a stamp showing Edward Hopper's painting of this light. Cape Elizabeth Light is part of Two Lights State Park.

Two Lights State Park. The bold, steep shore of Two Lights State Park is dramatic and uncompromising. When the surf is up, it's no place to linger. Millions of years ago, marine sediments settled to the bottom of the sea and formed thick layers of clay. Over time, pressure turned the clay into shale. Then, intense heat cooked the shale, turning it into schist, and intense pressure twisted the schist into wild configurations. The pounding surf and other forces have since eroded the rock, exposing its beauty to view.

Robinson Woods. Cape Elizabeth Land Trust owns and manages an 80-acre wooded parcel that includes 1.5 acres on Pond Cove. The shoreline parcel is a triangle of land nestled between Shore Road and the northwest corner of Pond Cove; the balance of the preserve lies on the other side of Shore Road.

At a Glance: Land in Public or Conservation Ownership

Scarborough Marsh	IF&W; open for careful day use
Scarborough Beach	BPL; bathing beach
Stratton & Bluff islands	National Audubon Society; Stratton open for careful day use only at small beach
Spurwink River marshes	Rachel Carson National Wildlife Refuge; shore access restricted
Crescent Beach State Park	BPL; bathing beach
Kettle Cove State Park	BPL; bathing beach
Richmond Island	Sprague Corporation; open for careful day use

2.
Casco Bay

Western Casco Bay: Portland to South Freeport

Casco Bay extends from Cape Elizabeth in the west to Small Point in the east. The bay is loaded with islands, so many that they are called the Calendar Isles—one for every day of the year. (Even counting halftide ledges, though, there aren't quite 365.) The western part of the bay is jammed with places to visit and offers great variety. There are short paddles to Fort Gorges or Basket Island; midlength circumnavigations of Little Chebeague, Cousins, and nearby islands; and strenuous trips to the outer fringes of the bay. Casco Bay has so many moods through the seasons that it's easy to see something new each time you go out.

The western third of the bay, including Portland Harbor, is a very, very busy place. Fishing boats come and go regularly. Tugs accompany large vessels, both domestic and foreign, that carry seafood, petroleum products, paper, and general cargo. The Coast Guard has a station in South Portland on the Fore River; its vessels cruise there frequently. Ferries, water taxis, and excursion boats provide transportation to the islands. Countless recreational boats of all sizes—from sea kayaks to sailboats to cabin cruisers—fill the bay each summer. Traffic is a real consideration when planning a trip in Casco Bay.

Trip Ideas (weather and experience permitting)

A trip to Fort Gorges from East End Beach (Launch 28, 2.5 miles round-trip) is a great introduction to Casco Bay, as it combines protected paddling with local history. The views from the second story of the rampart are superb, so

---

Charts
Charts: 13292, Portland Harbor (1:20,000)
        13290, Casco Bay (1:40,000)
Chart Kit: 59
Maine Atlas locator maps: 3, 5, 6

Tides (hours:minutes relative to Portland; average rise)
Portland: See daily predictions.
Falmouth Foreside: 0:01 after; 9.1 feet

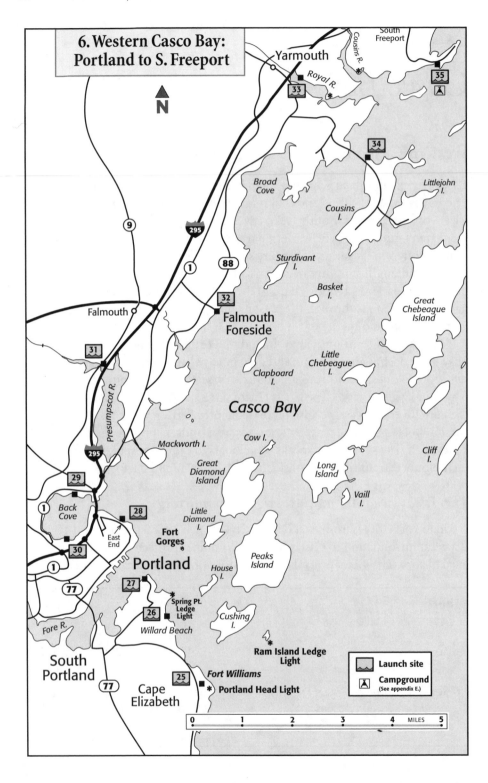

6. Western Casco Bay: Portland to S. Freeport

N

Yarmouth

South Freeport

Cousins R.

Royal R.

35

33

34

Broad Cove

Littlejohn I.

Cousins I.

9

295

1

88

Sturdivant I.

Basket I.

Great Chebeague Island

32

Falmouth

Falmouth Foreside

31

Little Chebeague I.

Clapboard I.

Casco Bay

Presumpscot R.

Mackworth I.

Cow I.

Cliff I.

295

Great Diamond Island

Long Island

Vaill I.

29

1

Back Cove

Little Diamond I.

28

East End

Fort Gorges

Peaks Island

30

1

House I.

77

Portland

27

Spring Pt. Ledge Light

26

Cushing I.

Willard Beach

Ram Island Ledge Light

Fore R.

South Portland

77

25

Fort Williams

Cape Elizabeth

Portland Head Light

	Launch site
	Campground (See appendix E.)

0   1   2   3   4   MILES   5

bring along binoculars if you have them. Allow plenty of time to explore this impressive citadel.

Or, from the East End Beach, paddle around Back Cove (4.5 miles round-trip), a bird sanctuary smack-dab in the middle of the city. (The Back Cove launch sites are perfect for recreational kayakers who want to toot around for an hour or so at the top of the tide.)

Most people see Back Cove from I-295, from Baxter Boulevard, or from an encircling pedestrian path. It's fun to turn things around and see it from the water. Be sure to time your trip with the tide, as Back Cove empties almost entirely.

Paddle to the Presumpscot River from East End Beach (8 miles round trip) or carry your boat down to the water at Walton Park and paddle upstream for 6 more miles, portaging around the riffles/rapids. It's important to plan your trip with the tide in mind, as the area between the mouth of Back Cove and Mackworth Island, and much of the Presumpscot River, turns into mudflats at low tide. Check your chart, too, for the location of the channels.

If you are interested in doing a circumnavigation, check out the two Diamond Islands (7 miles round-trip from East End).

The closest launch ramp to Basket Island is Falmouth Foreside (2.5 miles round-trip), but parking can be a problem. Basket Island is also within paddling range of Sandy Point Park (Launch 34) on Cousins Island (7 miles round-trip).

If you do secure a parking spot at Falmouth Foreside, check out Little Chebeague Island (6 miles round-trip), which is open to the public. A visit to the state-owned Jewell Island (see pages 101-2; 16 miles round-trip) requires cooperative weather for the long haul.

For a trip of moderate length with many different views, circumnavigate

Ferries, cruise ships, cargo ships, and pleasure boats all weave in and out of Portland Harbor. Sea kayakers, using the smallest craft, have to be the most careful.

Cousins and Littlejohn islands from Sandy Point Park (Launch 34), 7 miles. From Sandy Point, it is also possible to visit Little Chebeague Island (9 miles round-trip), or circumnavigate Great Chebeague Island (13 miles).

From the Yarmouth town landing, explore the Cousins River (9 miles to the head of tide and back). Check out the salt marsh that lines the river.

From Winslow Park in South Freeport (Launch 35), explore the Cousins River (10 miles round-trip), circumnavigate Cousins and Littlejohn islands (10 miles), or paddle around other islands to the east.

Safety Considerations, Strong Currents, and Caution Areas

Boat traffic in Portland Harbor and western Casco Bay. Use extreme caution when crossing the main shipping lanes, which enter and leave Portland Harbor from the south between Portland Head and Cushing Island. Crossing from one side of the Fore River to the other in the harbor can be equally hazardous. In addition, strong crosscurrents in the Fore River tend to push vessels toward South Portland.

Smaller commercial vessels often use Whitehead Passage, which runs between Peaks Island and Cushing Island, and Diamond Island Pass, which runs between Peaks Island and the Diamond islands.

Paddlers should take note of an hourly ferry that shuttles from Portland Harbor to Peaks Island and back and a regular ferry between Cousins Island and Great Chebeague Island. Other ferries and cruise vessels use the Diamond Island Pass; one of these stops at Long, Great Chebeague, and Cliff islands.

The Maine Island Trail Association recommends that paddlers launching from East End Beach in Portland who are headed to public islands in Casco Bay (including Little Chebeague, Crow, and Jewell islands—see "Middle Casco Bay" for Crow and Jewell islands) take the following route: Paddle between the two Diamond islands (tide permitting), skirt the north side of Long Island, and then proceed to your destination. A bar forms between the two Diamond islands at low water.

Access

25: Fort Williams and Portland Head Light, Cape Elizabeth. The park at Fort Williams is open from sunrise to sunset; there is no admission fee. Boaters may hand carry to the small beach. From the north, take ME 77 south to South Portland. Turn left on Broadway and then right on Cottage Road, which becomes Shore Road. Go a little more than 2 miles to the sign for Portland Head Light. From the south, take ME 77 north to Cape Elizabeth. At the blinking light, turn right onto Shore Road and go about 2 miles to the sign. For more information, call 299-2661 (cephl@aol.com).

The new launch on the Presumpscot River is a long carry from the parking lot.

26: Willard Beach. Because the beach is so heavily used during June, July, and August, paddlers are now allowed to launch during those months; moreover, the 60-vehicle lot is just about always full. This little pocket of sand is better suited to off-season use. From Portland, take ME 77 south to South Portland. Turn left on Cottage Street. Turn left on Pillsbury and continue to a square. Jog left and continue on Willow Street. Parking is on the right, with the beach straight ahead.

27: Fore River, South Portland. This site, which has two hard-surface, all-tide ramps, is a major artery into Casco Bay. The ramps are part of a park at the Portland Breakwater Light, also called Bug Light. There is a fee to park your vehicle; the park is open sunrise to sunset.

Take ME 77 south to South Portland. Turn left onto Broadway and proceed 1.3 miles. Take a left onto Breakwater (Pickett is the road on the right) and go 0.1 mile. Take a right on Madison and proceed 0.2 mile to the park entrance. The problem with this launch site—and the reason it is not popular with paddlers—is that it opens onto busy shipping lanes.

28: East End Beach, Portland. The noted landscape architect Frederick Law Olmsted designed the spacious Eastern Prom, as it is locally known, to take advantage of the spectacular view from the hill. A launch site along Eastern Promenade provides access to the harbor and islands in western Casco Bay. From I-295 in Portland, take exit 8, Washington Avenue/ME 26 south. Take the first left onto Eastern Promenade and proceed almost a mile. Turn left onto Cutter Street and follow it past a large parking area to a smaller parking lot by the water. There are bathrooms on the right side of the lot; a boat ramp for commercial vessels leading out of the middle of the lot; and a boat ramp for pleasure boats at the far end. Kayaks are not allowed at the middle commercial ramp, and there is a fee for launching at the far ramp, but you can launch at no charge from the beach southeast of the bathrooms. Vehicles may park near the bathrooms for only 5 minutes, so be prepared to drop off boats and gear promptly.

29: North Back Bay, Portland. From I-295, take exit 9, Baxter Boulevard. Go 0.6 mile to a small parking lot on the right, which has a portable toilet. Carry to the water. This area is known as the windsurfers' launch site.

30: South Back Bay, Portland. Continue along Baxter Boulevard from above and park on the large lot on the left when you see a Hannaford store on the right. Or, stay on I-295, take the Forest Avenue exit, take the first right onto Baxter Boulevard, and turn right onto Preble Street Extension. Carry across grass and some rocks to the water. There is a portable toilet at the eastern end of the lot.

31: Presumpscot River, Falmouth. From I-295, take the Bucknam Road exit in Falmouth. Turn right on Bucknam and go 0.4 mile; at an intersection with ME 9, go straight onto Falmouth Road for 1.3 miles. Take a left on Allen Road for 0.2 miles and turn left into Walton Park. The launch is not exactly close to hand. The 200-yard portage goes downhill to a set of steps, a ramp, and a float.

32: Falmouth Foreside. The chances of getting a parking place here are about as slim as winning the lottery. Parking at the landing is by permit only; parking at the lot at the head of the access road is also by permit except for two slots reserved for nonresidents. Perhaps four or five cars of any denomination can be parked parallel to the access road.

From I-295, take exit 10, Bucknam Road, and turn toward Route 1 and Falmouth. Take a left onto Route 1 and proceed for a little more than a mile; turn right at the Johnson Road crossroad. Go 0.8 mile, cross ME 88, and go down the hill (you are now on Town Landing Road) to the launch ramp.

33: Yarmouth Harbor. This launch site in the heart of Yarmouth has two paved ramps, one all-tide and the other part-tide. The charge to launch is $5 for residents and nonresidents alike. From I-295, take exit 17—Yarmouth—then turn south on Route 1. Immediately get into the left lane and turn onto ME 88. Proceed 0.2 mile, take a left onto Bayview Road, and take the first right on Old Shipyard Road. Go 0.5 mile to the landing.

34: Sandy Point Park, Cousins Island. This popular launch site is best used at the top half of the tide, as a large swath across the top of Cousins Island dries out on the ebb. From I-295, take exit 17 and go south on Route 1 toward Yarmouth. Take a left onto ME 88 and follow it through town, going a little less than a mile. Take a left onto Prince Point Road and then another

Portland Head Light has been a beacon to mariners for over 200 years. State Planning Office

left onto Gilman Road (or, if you miss Prince Point, simply take the next left onto Gilman Road). Follow Gilman to the bridge leading to Cousins Island and take the first left after the bridge into Sandy Point Park. There is no ramp; hand carry 100 feet or more, depending on the tide.

35: *Winslow Memorial Park, South Freeport.* Winslow Memorial Park (865-4198), run by the town of Freeport, has a swimming beach, picnic area, campsites, and concrete boat ramp that is good at the top two-thirds of the tide. If you're willing to get your feet muddy, you can use the launch when the tide is low. There is a modest parking fee when using the launch ramp. From the south on I-95, take exit 17 (Yarmouth) and go north on Route 1 for about 1 mile; turn right onto South Freeport Road at the sign for Winslow Memorial Park. Or, from the north, take exit 20 (Desert Road), and follow the signs to Route 1; turn south onto Route 1 and go about 2 miles; take a left onto South Freeport Road. From either direction, proceed 0.5 mile on South Freeport Road, taking the second right onto Staples Point Road; proceed 1.6 miles to Winslow Memorial Park.

Points of Interest

Portland Head Light. Portland Head Light, Maine's very first light, has warned hundreds of vessels off the rocky headland upon which it stands. Construction was begun in 1787, shortly after the Revolutionary War and long before Maine separated from Massachusetts in 1820. President George Washington appointed the first keeper of the light in 1791. The light stands

Fort Gorges and the Many Forts of Western Casco Bay

Western Casco Bay is full of forts and military installations, but Fort Gorges is the most prominent. The fort is a monument to the problems of ever-changing technology. It was begun in 1858, before the Civil War, as part of an effort to protect key ports on the East Coast. The thick granite walls were impervious to the short-range guns that were used previous to that time. But rifled cannon, long-range guns that were capable of dismembering such fortifications, came into use even before the structure was completed in 1864. No troops were ever stationed in the fort, and no shots were fired to defend it.

The fort is beautifully built, with arched bays for the gun emplacements and an interior courtyard. There are wonderful views of the harbor from the second story. There are also rooms designed as living quarters, and large vaults for storage of munitions. The structure is beginning to show its age, however, and some of the brickwork is disintegrating. If you explore, explore carefully.

The city of Portland now owns the structure, which is open to the public during daylight hours. At high water, the fort takes up almost all of the ledge upon which it

T'is the season at Fort Gorges.

101 feet above the water in a white conical tower attached to a house. The former keeper's quarters have been turned into a museum that features lighthouse lenses and various interpretive displays. Admission is $2 per adult.

Fort Williams. In 1894, President McKinley directed that a subpost south of Portland be named Fort Williams. The fort's mission was to protect Portland's harbor. Both infantry and artillery troops were stationed here in World War II, but after that time the post was all but closed.

Spring Point Ledge Light. The light on Spring Point Ledge was built in is built. A small beach and a wharf are located near the entrance to the fort on the north side.

Maine may have been far from the pitched battles of the Civil War, but the tide of the Confederacy did flow into Portland Harbor in 1863. Lieutenant Charles W. Read of the Confederate Navy, an audacious and skillful skipper, captured 20 vessels as he worked his way north from Virginia. He snuck by Forts Preble, Scammell, and Gorges, which were supposed to guard the entrance to the harbor, and into the harbor itself.

There, he took over the *Caleb Cushing*, an armed revenue cutter, quietly towing it away. When the defenders of Portland realized what had happened, they gave chase. Read might have escaped, but he couldn't locate the ship's stash of munitions, which were hidden behind a mirrored door in the captain's quarters. Read was captured, but his daring maneuver alarmed the citizens of Maine, who called for more guns and better protection from the Confederates.

Portland has been guarded by a succession of forts and batteries, including the ones mentioned here:

- Fort Preble, in South Portland, was begun in 1808 and refurbished for the Civil War and the Spanish-American War. The Southern Maine Vocational-Technical Institute now occupies many of the buildings.
- Fort Scammell, on House Island, was also begun in 1808 and was refurbished during the Civil War.
- Fort Allen, built in 1814, was located at the southern end of Eastern Prom. Only earthworks remain today.
- Fort Levett, on Cushing Island, was started in 1894 and was rebuilt in 1903 and 1942. Two observation towers are still visible.
- Fort McKinley, on Great Diamond Island, operated from the 1890s through World War II; it has been redeveloped as condominiums.
- Fort Lyon was situated on Cow Island, north of Great Diamond; today concrete fortifications remain.
- The batteries on Peaks Island date from World War II.
- During World War II, the navy took over the central portion of Long Island to set up an underground fuel depot for ships operating in the Atlantic.

1897 and automated in 1934. A 300-yard-long breakwater connecting the light to the mainland was added in 1951. Spring Point Light shows 54 feet above water in a white conical tower set on a black cylindrical pier.

Portland Breakwater Light. This light with Corinthian columns marks the south entrance to the Fore River. The light was constructed in 1855 and reconstructed 20 years later at the end of a half-mile breakwater. The light was retired after World War II but is now back in use. The building is listed on the National Register of Historic Places.

Circumnavigating Cousins Island may bring you face to face with one of the big guys on the block: An oil tanker unloads at the power plant.

Ram Island Ledge Light and Ram Island. Ram Island Ledge lies south of Ram Island (which is southeast of Cushing Island) and along the northeast side of a major entrance to Portland Harbor. As the ledge is entirely covered at high tide, it is a natural trap for off-route ships. A light was built here in 1905 using gray granite from Vinalhaven. The light, which was automated in 1957, shows 77 feet above the water from a conical tower.

Ram Island is an extremely valuable seabird and wading bird island because of the number and diversity of species that occur here. It is very important that boaters do not land on or linger near this island during the nesting season.

House Island. Now privately owned, this island was once the site of Portland's quarantine station and, during the early 1900s, the city's immigration station. Residents of Peaks Island would visit Maine's version of Ellis Island on Sundays to entertain the people being detained there.

Wrecked ships in Casco Bay. There have been many shipwrecks in the bay, and paddlers can see the hulks of several of them. When the *Thomas Lawson*, a seven-masted schooner, caught fire in Portland harbor, the goal was not to put out the fire—an impossible task—but to get the schooner out of the harbor. The *Lawson* ended up on Diamond Island Ledge, just north of Fort Gorges.

The *Maquoit*, a Casco Bay Lines steamer, and several other vessels lie in the cove between the two Diamond Islands.

During World War II, the military took extensive measures to protect Portland Harbor, including setting up submarine nets and laying minefields.

Browntail Moths and Their Irritating Hairs

Perhaps you stopped at Little Chebeague as you paddled around Casco Bay. You began to itch and developed a rash that looked like you had brushed against poison ivy. It may have gone away after a few hours or it may have lasted for a few days. More seriously, you may have experienced respiratory problems, or a rash that worsened and lingered for weeks. What happened? You may have made contact with the poisonous hairs of the caterpillar of the browntail moth.

In 1897, browntail moths stowed away somehow and made the passage from Europe to Massachusetts. In the 16 years that followed, the species spread all over New England and into Canada. By the 1960s, natural factors caused its territory to diminish to just Cape Cod and a few islands in Casco Bay. But since 1987, the moth has made a resurgence and now infests more than 40 islands in Casco Bay as well as some mainland sites.

Although some people do not react to the caterpillar's hairs, some do. The fact that the hairs become airborne means that there's no way to hide. If you are allergic to the hairs, the best precaution is to avoid paddling in infested areas after the caterpillar makes its yearly debut. The Maine Forest Service reports that June, July, and August are the key months.

To give you an idea of the potential seriousness of the reaction, the agency recommends that sensitive people wear a respirator, goggles, and coveralls tightly closed at the neck, wrists, and ankles when doing something as simple as mowing the lawn. For more information about the browntail moth, contact the Maine Forest Service, State House Station 22, Augusta, ME 04330; 287-4982.

The navy also sunk wrecks off the northern tip of Long Island; these wrecks are visible today.

Cow Island. When Maine Coast Heritage Trust sold 26-acre Cow Island to Rippleffect to be used for youth adventure programs, the trust stipulated that a portion of the island would remain open to the public in perpetuity. Visitors may use the west side of the island throughout the year. In 2005, Rippleffect's web site stated that visitors may use the east side as well (including bunkers, batteries, and gun emplacements) from October through April—when programs are not running. Check the organization's web site (www.rippleffect.net) for current access information. Please stay on established trails.

Andrews Beach, Long Island. This town swimming beach is located on the southern shore of Long Island, opposite Vaill Island. (For Vaill Island, see *At a Glance.*)

Little Chebeague Island. If you stop on Little Chebeague, don't expect a solitary commune with nature. This little island is a popular spot because of its pretty sand and gravel beaches and its proximity to the mainland. On the other hand, stinging nettles and poison ivy proliferate, there's a huge tick population, the old buildings are dangerous, and browntail moths have settled in—maybe you don't want to linger, anyway.

Deep in its past, Little Chebeague was a prosperous farm. In World War II, when so much of the coast was dedicated to the war effort, the navy set up a fire-fighting school. Now, the island is owned by the state and managed by the Bureau of Parks and Lands.

Back Cove. Back Cove is full of mud, but it's not just any mud. When meltwater streams carried silt and clay away from the glacier that once covered Maine, these sediments accumulated. They now show up as the mudflats that emerge at low water along so much of the coast.

Back Cove does not offer vast surprises in terms of paddling, but if you venture here, look for ring-billed, herring, and great black-backed gulls all year long as well as Bonaparte's gulls in May and from August through October. Double-crested cormorants and common terns are regulars in summer. Shorebirds come through on migration in the spring and fall, and ducks are most plentiful in the winter. The Department of Inland Fisheries and Wildlife manages Back Cove, which was designated a preserve for birds in 1915.

Presumpscot River Estuary. The Presumpscot River leaves Sebago Lake in North Windham and snakes almost 27 miles through South Windham and Westbrook before circling north of Portland and emptying into Casco Bay near Mackworth Island. The Smelt Hill Dam at Presumpscot Falls has been removed, opening the way for migratory fish.

The Presumpscot estuary was once a catch basin for untreated paper mill discharge and other pollutants, but efforts to curb pollution have succeeded and the water quality has improved dramatically.

Below the I-295 bridge, the estuary is wide and shallow. Migrating shorebirds use the vast mudflats as they pass through. The Gilsland Farm Sanctuary, which serves as the headquarters of the Maine Audubon Society, is located on the eastern shore. The sanctuary and trails are oriented to pedestrian visitors, and there are no particular attractions for boaters. The prominent buildings at Martin Point, at the western entrance to the river, were formerly a hospital.

Mackworth Island. Governor Percival Baxter presented Mackworth Island to the state of Maine, then donated money to build the Baxter State School for the Deaf. A path that circles the island is open to the public. Paddlers who venture onto the water on the north side of Mackworth Island in April may want to watch for Canada geese. In years past, a flock here has numbered in the hundreds and even thousands.

Mill Creek Preserve. This 20-acre preserve, tucked in along the Falmouth shore about a mile south of Falmouth Foreside (check your chart), is a nice place for quiet paddling. Go into Mussel Cove and under ME 88 into Mill Creek; both the cove and the creek are dry at low tide, so plan accordingly. In the preserve, watch for great blue herons, snowy egrets, and other salt-marsh wildlife. Originally a Nature Conservancy preserve, the area is now owned and managed by the town of Falmouth.

Basket Island Preserve. Basket Island lies a little more than a mile from shore, so it is not surprising that it sees lots of visitors. The 9-acre island has trails and several gravel beaches (watch for poison ivy), including two beaches on the northern shore. The Cumberland Mainland and Islands Trust owns and manages the island.

Cousins Island. The oil-fired power plant on the southwest tip of the island is of note because its stacks can be seen from miles around. In March and April, common eider tend to gather in huge numbers near Sandy Point Beach on the north end of the island.

Royal River Preserve. The Town of Yarmouth owns this 35-acre preserve, which includes woods, wetlands, and half a mile of shoreline near the mouth of the river. Friends of the Royal River, the Trust for Public Land, the Land for Maine's Future program, the federal government, and the town worked together to secure protection for this parcel.

Cousins River Estuary. Travelers on I-295 from Yarmouth to Freeport pass the Cousins River in the blink of an eye—it's the stream that meanders through salt-marsh grass just north of exit 17. While this short river is not a major paddling destination, it does offer a surprisingly pleasant excursion into salt-marsh habitat with its attendant birdlife. If you are a birder, take your binoculars to scout for great blue herons, snowy egrets, black ducks, red-tailed hawks, tree swallows, red-winged blackbirds, and other species. Don't be put off by the roar of traffic on the interstate, which soon drops away to a background hum. Do plan the trip to coincide with the top half of the tide, as the river dries at low water.

Powell Point. This 29-acre preserve graces the north shore of Cousins River. Freeport Conservation Trust owns and manages the property.

At a Glance: Land in Public or Conservation Ownership

Andrews Beach, Long Island	Town park; swimming beach
Little Chebeague Island	Maine Island Trail; BPL
Mill Creek Preserve	Town of Falmouth; careful day use
Basket Island Preserve	Cumberland Mainland and Islands Trust

IF&W Wildlife Islands

These islands are closed during the indicated bird nesting season. After the nesting season is over, the islands are limited to careful day use.

Ram Island	April 15–August 31
(0.5 mi SE of Cushing Island)	
Stepping Stones Island	April 15–July 31
(S of NE end of Long Island)	
Vaill Island	April 15–July 31
(E of S end of Long Island)	
Clapboard Island Ledge	April 15–August 31
(near Clapboard Island)	
Nubbin Island	April 15–August 31
(mouth of Broad Cove, Yarmouth)	

Middle Casco Bay: South Freeport to Harpswell Neck

Middle Casco offers paddling along the protected shores of the Harraseeket River, a trip to the outskirts of Casco Bay, and everything in between. The two most interesting public islands are Eagle, once Admiral Peary's summer home, and Jewell, which has trails and old fortifications. Both islands are part of the Maine Island Trail and both lie southwest of the southern tip of Harpswell Neck, well out in Casco Bay and vulnerable to the weather. The upper bays—Maquoit, Merepoint, and Middle—offer somewhat more protection with several islands to circumnavigate. The heads of these bays turn to mud at low tide, so high-tide trips make the most sense.

Trip Ideas (weather and experience permitting)

From Porter Landing (Launch 38) or Dunning Boat Yard (Launch 37), on the top half of the tide, check out the nicely protected Harraseeket River (4 to 6 miles, depending on the extent of the trip). Almost half of the Harraseeket turns into tidal flats when the tide ebbs, so timing is important.

From Wharton Point, explore the bay (6 miles or so), using the top half of the tide. Or, spot a car at Winslow Memorial Park and travel one way

---

Charts
Chart: 13290, Casco Bay (1:40,000)
Chart Kit: 59, 60
Maine Atlas locator map: 6

Tides (hours:minutes relative to Portland; average rise)
South Freeport: 0:12 after; 9.0 feet
Wilson Cove, Middle Bay: 0:02 after; 9.1 feet
South Harpswell, Potts Harbor: 0:02 after; 8.9 feet

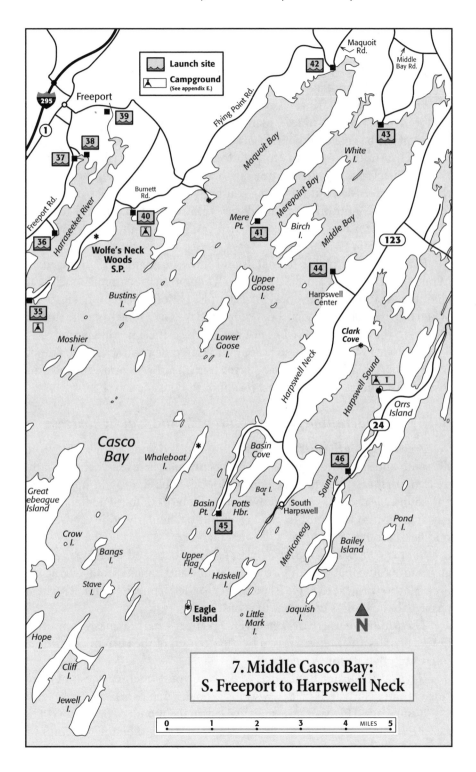

Launch site

Campground
(See appendix E.)

Freeport

Maquoit Rd.

Middle Bay Rd.

Flying Point Rd.

Maquoit Bay

42

White I.

43

Merepoint Bay

Burnett Rd.

Mere Pt.

Birch I.

Middle Bay

123

41

Harraseeket River

Freeport Rd.

Wolfe's Neck Woods S.P.

Bustins I.

Upper Goose I.

Harpswell Center

44

Moshier I.

Lower Goose I.

Clark Cove

Harpswell Sound

Harpswell Neck

Orrs Island

24

Casco Bay

Whaleboat I.

Basin Cove

46

Great ebeague Island

Bar I.

South Harpswell

Pond I.

Crow I.

Basin Pt.

Potts Hbr.

45

Bangs I.

Merriconeag Sound

Bailey Island

Stave I.

Upper Flag I.

Haskell I.

Jaquish I.

N

Hope I.

Eagle Island

Little Mark I.

Cliff I.

Jewell I.

7. Middle Casco Bay:
S. Freeport to Harpswell Neck

0   1   2   3   4   MILES   5

(9 miles). Keep in mind that both Wharton Point and Winslow Memorial Park are part-tide landings. If you launch somewhat before high water, you can paddle during slack water and then ride the current to the park before the tide exposes mudflats at the launch ramp.

From Dolphin Marina, take a spin around Potts Harbor (3.5 miles). Or explore Basin Cove (3 miles), planning to avoid the reversing falls at the mouth of the basin. For either trip, drop by public Bar Island in Potts Harbor for lunch. Another option is to paddle to Upper Goose Island (11 miles round-trip). Catching a rising tide north and a falling tide south will make the trip much easier, but prevailing southerly breezes often kick in. In calm or moderate conditions, Admiral Peary's house on Eagle Island makes a pleasant destination (4 miles round-trip). Allow an hour or so to tour the house and library.

Explore beautiful Whaleboat Island, now permanently protected by Maine Coast Heritage Trust. Set out from Dolphin Marina (4 miles including circumnavigation) or Winslow Park (10 miles including circumnavigation). When touring south of Whaleboat, stop on Bangs any time from the middle of June to the end of March, but not during the critical nesting period.

Harpswell Neck reaches so far out into Casco Bay that when you launch from Dolphin Marina, Jewell Island is relatively nearby (8.5 miles round-trip, instead of 16 miles round-trip from Falmouth Foreside).

Safety Considerations, Strong Currents, and Caution Areas

Prevailing southerlies. The prevailing winds during summer are from the south and southwest. The islands and peninsulas here are oriented southwest to northeast, so when the winds blow, they blow straight up the bays and sounds, leaving less protection than might be desirable. Paddlers should pay attention to the wind in any event, but particularly so in an area like middle Casco Bay.

Boat traffic in Casco Bay. Ferries, fishing boats, and pleasure craft use an inshore route that goes by Great Chebeague and Bangs islands, and across Potts Harbor or next to Eagle Island to get to Merriconeag Sound. It's a busy passage that paddlers may want to avoid.

The Mouth of Harraseeket River. Freeport's harbor master says that novice boaters are often surprised by the strength of the current as it rushes into Casco Bay. Be forewarned.

Harpswell Lobster Boat Race. Make sure your itinerary does not coincide with the Harpswell race (www.lobsterboatracing.com).

Basin Cove. There is a reversing tidal falls at the mouth of Basin Cove. The *Coast Pilot* notes that the mouth is partially obstructed by the remains of a dam and warns that entry is dangerous at any tide level. Sea kayakers require

Be sure to catch the top of the tide when you use the public ramp at Dunning Boatyard.

so little draft that the real problem is the velocity of the water at midcycle. The ideal time to enter Basin Cove is just before or at high-water slack.

Access

35: Winslow Memorial Park. See "Western Casco Bay."

36: South Freeport Town Wharf. This site is not ideal for sea kayakers, especially beginners. It's a small and busy place, with fishermen coming and going. Instead of a ramp, there is a dock (18 inches off the water) accessed by a long walkway. It's difficult to get boats and gear to the water, to get gear and paddlers into the water, and to paddle away through the traffic. The town has considered closing the wharf to kayakers but instead has formed a committee to look at the larger question of shore access.

If you want to launch here despite the challenges, go in spring or fall when there is less congestion. Plan ahead so you can drop boats and gear quickly without blocking the small unloading area. Don't go with a crowd; your and your buddies will inevitably tie up the premises.

Only a few parking spaces are associated with the wharf. You can park at Brewer's Marine next door (the fee will allow you to use the portable toilet as well) or at the Merriconeag School, about half a mile away, on weekends and during the summer.

Coming from the south on I-295, take exit 17 (Yarmouth) and go north on Route 1 for about a mile; turn right onto South Freeport Road at the sign for South Freeport/Winslow Memorial Park. Proceed 1.8 miles, passing the

Merriconeag School and the post office on the right; turn right on Main Street and go 0.4 mile to the town wharf. (From the north, take exit 10, Desert Road, and follow the signs to Route 1. Take a right and almost immediately turn left onto Pine Street. Follow Pine until it crosses South Freeport Road, where it becomes Main Street. Follow Main Street 0.4 miles to the town wharf.)

37: *Dunning Boat Yard, Harraseeket River.* This site has a concrete, halftide launch ramp. From the south on I-295, take exit 20, Desert Road; make a right onto Route 1 and then an immediate left on Pine Street. Go 1.6 miles and turn left on Main Street. Continue 1.5 miles to the launch site. The town ramp is next to a working boat yard.

From the north, take exit 22, Freeport/Durham, and turn right onto Route 1. Proceed into downtown Freeport. With L.L. Bean on the right, take a left onto Bow Street. Then take the second right onto Lower Mast Landing Road and continue for less than a mile to the boat ramp.

38: *Porter Landing, Harraseeket River.* The channel here has water when the Dunning ramp is mud, but at dead low, the channel is mighty narrow and shallow. This site is best used on the upper two-thirds of the tide. From Dunning Boat Yard, continue north for 0.4 mile, take a right on Porters Landing Road, and take the first right on Cove Road, which is dead end. Go 0.2 miles to the Cove Road Waterfront Landing. It's a 30-yard carry; put in from the float or, if there's enough water, from the grass.

39: *Mast Landing, Harraseeket River.* Freeport Conservation Trust owns a small parcel at the head of the river, allowing access to the upper river and to Mill Stream. There is room for two or three vehicles.

Proceed as for Porter Landing, only instead of turning right on Lower Mast Landing Road (also called South Freeport Road), continue straight. Mast Landing is located immediately on the right. Carry to the water, which is lined with mud at low water. This site is best used at the top half of the tide.

40: *Recompense Shore Campsites.* This campground, which is located at the head of the bay formed by Wolf Neck and Flying Point, allows nonpatrons to launch from its shores at no cost. Recompense Shore (865-9307) is a private, nonprofit organization.

There is no ramp, but boaters may launch next to a bridge spanning the Little River. Use it at the top half of the tide—otherwise, there is a great expanse of mud. Follow the directions for Dunning Boat Yard to Bow Street. At the junction of Route 1 and Bow Street (at L.L. Bean), turn left onto Bow Street and proceed 1.5 miles. Take a right on Flying Point Road and proceed 0.8 mile, then another right onto Wolf Neck Road and go 1.8 miles. Take a left onto Burnett Road. There is room for half a dozen cars at the Little River bridge and a few more in a turnout just beyond.

41: Mere Point. Given the state of Brunswick's launch areas (see below), the town clearly needs an all-tide facility with adequate parking. The town and Maine's Department of Inland Fisheries and Wildlife are collaborating to build a ramp on 7.5 acres near the tip of Mere Point. Check progress on the town's web site (www.brunswickme.org, planning department, Mere Point Boat Launch) or call the Planning Department (725-6639).

To get to the ramp when it is constructed, head south from Brunswick on Maine Street until it splits into Maquoit Road on the right and Merepoint Road on the left. Take the left and follow it almost to its end. Just after the left turn to Birch Island Lane—and 500 feet before a gate—turn left and drive down to the water.

42: Wharton Point, Maquoit Bay. Parking is very limited at this site, which has a halftide gravel launching area. Please do not arrive with a dozen buddies. From Main Street (ME 24) in downtown Brunswick, go south toward Bowdoin College; go straight on Main when ME 24 heads left around a church. Pass the college and, later, Parkview Hospital, both on the left. When the road splits 0.3 mile south of the hospital, bear right onto Maquoit Road, following it for 1.9 miles to a landing at the top of the bay.

43: Simpson Point, Middle Bay. Parking is very limited here as well. At the present time, vehicles can park on the shoulder of the east side of the road, but you are likely to find the spaces all taken by locals.

Follow the directions for Wharton Point, except instead of bearing right on Maquoit Road, bear left on Mere Point Road. Go about 1.5 miles, take a left on Simpson Point Road, and follow that road to its end.

Note. The Brunswick town landing at Pennellville on Middle Bay, listed in the first edition, is now posted with no parking signs. Only two or possibly three vehicles can now legally park at this hand-carry site. Instead of launching here, choose one of the other sites in the area.

44: Lookout Point, Middle Bay. This small town launch has tight parking, so definitely carpool. From Brunswick, go south on ME 124 to the flashing yellow light. Continue for 1.9 miles and turn right on Lookout Point Road at Harpswell Center. Go 0.6 mile to a dirt lot.

45: Dolphin Marina, South Harpswell. This marina (833-5343) has a concrete, all-tide ramp; a small beach for hand-carry boats; and a restaurant that provides hearty fare. Fees include $5 to park and $2 per kayak to launch. At the junction of ME 123 and ME 24 in Brunswick, go south on ME 123 for 11.7 miles and turn right at the West Harpswell School onto Ash Point Road. Go 0.2 mile and turn right onto Basin Point Road. Continue for 0.5 mile to Dolphin Marina.

Note. Please do not launch from Stover Cove, which lies at the southern end of Harpswell Sound. Although this cove is marked as a launch site in other

Why Peninsulas Trend Northeast to Southwest

The bays and peninsulas of Casco Bay march across the chart in parallel rows, as if on parade. The alignment is no accident but a product of geological rumblings 400 million years ago.

A: The continental shelf at that time had accumulated layer upon layer of sediments that had coalesced into sedimentary rocks.

B: When forces from within the earth pushed against these layers, the rocks were crushed and crumpled—accordioned into a series of ridges and furrows. Magma welled up through the cracks and crevices.

C: After eons of erosion, the resistant rock remains as ridges and the less-resistant rock was eroded, leaving furrows.

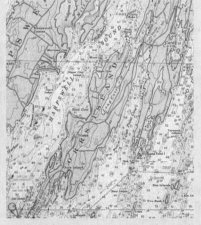

D: The ridges are now peninsulas and islands, the furrows are now the bays.

publications, it is really a local area for swimming, hiking, clamming and—yes—boating. Parking is limited, so leave it for the folks who live here. Harpswell Heritage Land Trust owns this 4-acre parcel.

46: Cribstone Bridge, Orrs Island. See "Eastern Casco Bay."

Points of Interest

Crow Island. Sometimes there are simply too many people for this 2-acre isle that lies just off the eastern shore of Great Chebeague. Nearby islanders have picnicked here for years. Although Crow is part of the Maine Island Trail, MITA advises kayakers to go sparingly, respecting the traditional stewardship and desire for privacy of local users.

A cottage in the middle of the island can be useful if it is raining when you stop for a snack; just close it up when you leave. Be advised that Crow is one of the 40 or so islands infested with the browntail moth (see Part I and page 91).

Bangs Island. Before raccoons invaded this island, Maine's Department of Inland Fisheries and Wildlife managed it for nesting eiders. Now, it is open to public use between June 16 and March 31; the 10-week closure allows for the possibility of renewed nesting. The 55-acre island is replete with ticks and browntail moths, in season, and poison ivy all year long, but if you perch on the edge of shore, it makes a nice stop for lunch or snacks.

Whaleboat Island. Once the site of a fishing community with its own school, Whaleboat is now the largest undeveloped island in Casco Bay. With 3.4 miles of shoreline, the 125 acres could have been the perfect island kingdom. Instead, the Etnier family, which owned it for almost half a century, allowed the public to visit, placed development restrictions on some acreage, and finally sold the island to Maine Coast Heritage Trust for its ultimate protection. The Land for Maine's Future program contributed to the purchase, as did many local donors and donors from as far away as Nebraska. The island is open for careful use.

Upper Flag Island. Admiral Peary's sled dogs would not be welcome on this island today (see Eagle Island sidebar). The U.S. Fish and Wildlife Service bought 30-acre Upper Flag in 1998, chiefly to protect eiders that nest in the low shrubs of bayberry, chokeberry, winterberry, and choke cherry. To protect the birds, the island is closed from April through August. After that time, you may visit; check out the sandy beach near the north end.

Jewell Island. Jewell, once a quiet homestead on the outskirts of Casco Bay, is now a rollicking hot spot. The 186-acre public island is the southernmost island in the Maine Island Trail and it is relatively close to Portland, so it draws more than its share of partygoers. If you're not interested in the blare of boom boxes, visit Jewell early or late in the season.

Jewell has several campsites, four two-seater privies, hiking trails, and lots of sights to see. The protected anchorage on the north side of the island draws sailors and powerboaters, but note that part of the harbor does go dry at low tide.

If you are looking for sand and warm water, try the Punchbowl on the northern end of the island. As the tide recedes, the sun heats water trapped in a natural amphitheater, producing a heated "pool" with lovely sandy shores. The Punchbowl, of course, draws lots of visitors.

Jewell was the logical place for guns and lookout towers during World War II. Jewell's two guns, which were capable of firing shells that reached 15 miles out to sea, were placed along the eastern shore—one at the northern end, the other at the southern end of the island. Observers used the towers near the southern emplacement to look for German U-boats: One was spotted in 1942. These observation towers are still a great place to survey Portland Harbor.

Outer Green Island. After predators wrecked nests on Jenny Island (see the next chapter), the National Audubon Society relocated its tern restoration program to Outer Green, 2 miles southwest of Jewell Island. In 2002, for the first time in 88 years, terns set up housekeeping and raised chicks on the island. In 2004, more than 500 pairs of common terns raised 740 chicks, and 8 pairs of roseate terns raised 13 chicks. The island is closed to visitors.

Cliff Island. If you saw the movie *The Whales of August* with Bette Davis and Lillian Gish, you may recognize the cliffs on this island as the setting for the movie.

The Harraseeket River. The Harraseeket is a saltwater river, filling and emptying with the tide. Mast Landing lies at the river's head. In the 1770s, the landing was a shipping point for masting timbers—the masts themselves, yards, spars, and bowsprits—harvested from Maine's vast woodlands. Now the landing is located less than a mile from bustling downtown Freeport, which is chockablock with L.L. Bean and factory stores. At the mouth of the Harraseeket lie three islands, the center of which is Pound of Tea—reputedly the amount that settlers paid for the tiny piece of land.

Wolfe's Neck Woods State Park. This 218-acre park overlooks both the Harraseeket River and Little River Bay. The park has a long shoreline, 5 miles of trails, panels describing the natural history of Wolf Neck, a picnic area, bathrooms, and lots of great views. Googins Island, on the eastern shore, has long been a nesting site for ospreys; if the nest is active, give the ospreys plenty of space. The rocky shore along Wolf Neck is not particularly inviting to sea kayakers, but it's a delight to be able to paddle along the undeveloped shoreline. The park is not named for Canis lupus, the gray wolf, although wolves once lived in Maine. Instead, the name comes from Henry Wolfe, who

Admiral Peary's House on Eagle Island

Robert Peary was so taken with Eagle Island that he bought it for $500 just four years after graduating from Bowdoin College. He worked for the U.S. Coast and Geodetic Survey, then headed to Nicaragua with the navy to work on a proposed canal. Taking time off for a trip to Greenland in 1886, he found his true calling as an explorer of the far north. He led seven more expeditions to the Arctic. When he was not trekking across the ice, he summered on Eagle Island while his sled dogs stayed on nearby Upper Flag Island. Admiral Peary claimed that on April 6, 1909, he reached the North Pole. Peary's wife, Josephine, didn't hear the news for five more months—she was staying on Eagle Island when she received a telegram on September 6.

Did Peary actually reach the North Pole? Critics questioned his declaration at the time and have continued to question it. The National Geographic Society supported him in 1909. In 1990, in an attempt to quell the controversy, the society hired the Navigation Foundation to use modern technology to cross-check Peary's records. The verdict of the experts: Yes, Peary made it to the top of the world. (Others still have their doubts.)

Peary's house on Eagle Island stands on the rocky ledges of the north shore, looking toward Harpswell, Whale-boat Island, and the interior of Casco Bay. The Pearys had origi-nally built a small structure but en-larged it after the admiral's historic return. The building is a summer cottage

Admiral Peary designed his house and supporting stonework to resemble a ship, with the northern courtyard serving as the prow.

caught in time—full of furniture, furnishings, and personal items from another era. The refurbished library is especially intriguing; it was from here that Peary defended his claim of reaching the North Pole. There is an outhouse, should nature call. Some trails on the island are closed during eider nesting season.

Eagle Island is open to the public from June 15 to Labor Day; there's a collection box near the dock for the modest state park fee. For more information call 624-6080.

Those who would like to see more Peary memorabilia and other artifacts from the far north, including a skin kayak, can stop at the Peary-MacMillan Arctic Museum at Bowdoin College (725-3416).

Great blue herons frequent Maquoit Bay in the summer.
HANK TYLER, STATE PLANNING OFFICE

settled here in the 1600s. (The park is Wolfe's Neck Woods; the neck itself is Wolf Neck.)

L.L. Bean Paddling School. If you see boaters in the vicinity of Little Flying Point, they are likely part of L.L. Bean's paddling school. The school's spacious lawns and shoreline, formerly a campground, are the site of an annual weekend—usually in June—of classes, displays, and general good times.

Maquoit Bay. Viewpoint is everything. Native Americans named the area maquoit, meaning "a low, wet place." The *Coast Pilot* describes Maquoit as a shoal bay obstructed by flats covered 1 to 4 feet. The authors of *A Birder's Guide to Maine* describe it as a productive birding area. Take your pick.

Ducks are the main feature from March through May—mallards, northern pintails, American wigeons, and blue- and green-winged teal—plus large numbers of American black ducks. Shorebirds pass through on migration in both spring and fall. Great blue herons and snowy egrets show up in the summer. Ospreys have settled in here, as they have all along the coast. During fall hawk migration, watch for northern harriers, sharp-shinned hawks, American kestrels, and merlins. Herring and great black-backed gulls are ubiquitous, but also look for ring-billed gulls.

Upper Goose Island. The Nature Conservancy has protected this wildlife area, which is closed to the public from March 15 through August 15. The organization requests that boaters not land or linger offshore. Ospreys nest on the island, and seals haul out on ledges on the southeast shore.

There are no trails on the island, but after August 15 boaters may walk along any part of the shore except for two obvious private-property inholdings, one on the southern end of the island and the other on the western shore. Lower Goose Island is privately owned and is not open to the public.

Bar Island. Bar Island in Potts Harbor is part of the Maine Island Trail. Just barely accessible at low tide, the tiny, grassy island is a handy place to stretch your legs.

Merriconeag Sound. Merriconeag means "lazy portage"—a carry so short that paddlers simply pick up their canoes, cargo and all, and lift them

Little Mark Island Monument Light was built in 1809 as a memorial to shipwrecked mariners. The light sits on a stone pyramid 74 feet above the water. This is a seabird nesting island, so access is restricted.

to the other side rather than carrying canoe and gear separately as in a proper portage. Native Americans used the Merriconeag portage to get into Potts Harbor without paddling around Potts Point. The sound to the east later assumed the name Merriconeag as well.

Clark Cove. This 20-acre public holding with 1,600 feet of shorefront on the west shore of Harpswell Sound serves nicely as a lunch stop.

At a Glance: Land in Public or Conservation Ownership

Crow Island	Maine Island Trail/BPL
Bangs Island	Maine Island Trail/BPL; closed April 1–June 15
Whaleboat Island	Maine Coast Heritage Trust; careful use
Jewell Island	Maine Island Trail/BPL
Wolfe's Neck Woods State Park	BPL; careful day use
Upper Goose Island	TNC; closed March 15–August 15; after that time, careful day use
Eagle Island	BPL; careful day use
Bar Island	Maine Island Trail/BPL
Clark Cove	BPL; careful day use

IF&W Wildlife Islands

These islands are closed during the indicated bird nesting season. After the nesting season is over, the islands are limited to careful day use.

Outer Green Island (2 mi SW of Jewell Island)	April 15–July 31

Junk of Pork (2 mi SW of Jewell Island)	April 15–July 31
Inner Green Island (0.5 mi SW of Jewell Island)	April 15–July 31
Upper Green Island (0.5 mi SE of Moshier Island)	April 15–July 31
Goose Nest Island (0.6 mi N of Bangs Island)	April 15–July 31
West Brown Cow (0.5 mi E of Cliff Island)	April 15–July 31
Little Mark Island (0.4 mi S of Haskell Island)	April 15–July 31
Haskell Island, southern ⅔ (NE of Eagle Island)	Not open to the public
Whale Rock (0.4 mi SW of Little Mark Island)	April 15–July 31
Little Birch Island (almost 0.5 mi SW of Basin Point)	April 15–July 31
Thrumcap (0.6 mi SE of Basin Point)	April 15–July 31
Unnamed island (next to Jaquish)	April 15–July 31
Pond Island	April 15-July 31
USFWS Wildlife Island	
Upper Flag Island	April 1–August 31

Eastern Casco Bay: Harpswell Sound to Cape Small

What are the nicest trips in eastern Casco Bay? Well, it's hard to pare the list. The upper reaches of the New Meadows River provide lovely, protected paddling. Quahog Bay offers protection, too, along with a half a dozen or so pretty islands. Touring around Yarmouth Island lets you look out over a great expanse of water, while a trip around Bailey Island exposes you to the wide-open ocean.

Trip Ideas (weather and experience permitting)

From Launch 46 at the Cribstone Bridge on ME 24 between Orrs and Bailey islands, explore Harpswell Sound (up to 8 miles); Clark Cove makes a nice lunch destination (6 miles round-trip). Skilled paddlers may want to start at the bridge and circumnavigate Bailey Island (6 miles) or Ragged Island

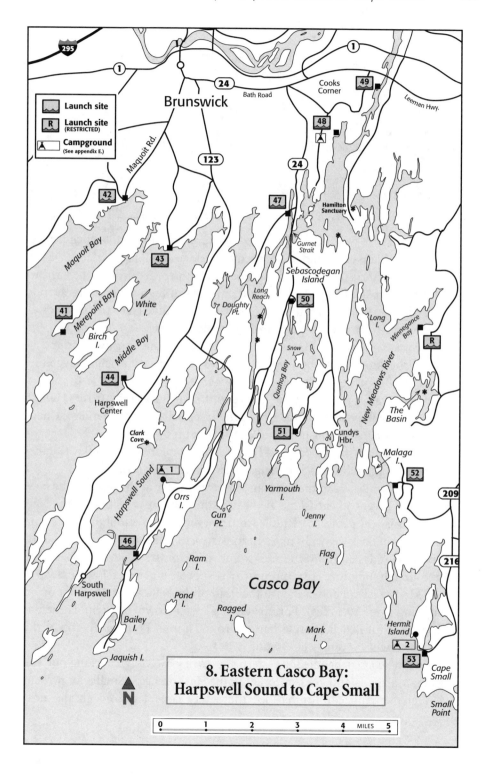

Launch site

R Launch site (RESTRICTED)

Campground (See appendix E.)

295

1

Brunswick

Bath Road

Cooks Corner

49

Leeman Hwy.

24

48

123

24

Maquoit Rd.

42

47

Hamilton Sanctuary

43

Gurnet Strait

Maquoit Bay

Sebascodegan Island

White I.

Merepoint Bay

41

Doughty Pt.

Long Reach

50

Long I.

Winnegance Bay

Birch I.

Middle Bay

Snow

Quahog Bay

New Meadows River

R

44

The Basin

Harpswell Center

Clark Cove

51

Cundys Hbr.

Malaga I.

52

1

Orrs I.

Yarmouth I.

Harpswell Sound

Gun Pt.

Jenny I.

209

46

Ram I.

Flag I.

216

South Harpswell

Casco Bay

Pond I.

Bailey I.

Ragged I.

Mark I.

Hermit Island

2

Jaquish I.

53

Cape Small

8. Eastern Casco Bay: Harpswell Sound to Cape Small

N

Small Point

0   1   2   3   4   5 MILES

Charts

Charts: 13283, Cape Neddick Harbor to Isles of Shoals (1:20,000)
  Chart: 13290, Casco Bay (1:40,000)
Chart Kit: 60
Maine Atlas locator map: 6

Tides (hours:minutes relative to Portland; average rise)
Howard Point, New Meadows River (1.5 miles south of ME 24): 0:05 before;
  9.0 feet
Cundys Harbor: 0:01 before; 8.9 feet
Small Point Harbor: 0:12 before; 8.8 feet

(7 miles). These two trips are exposed to the wind; there's not much protection beyond Jaquish Island or between the bridge and Ragged Island. Or, circumnavigate Orrs Island: Catch the flood tide north, go through the narrows between Harpswell Sound and Gun Point Cove at high water, and return to the Cribstone Bridge with the ebb (8 miles). This route takes you past Lowell Cove, where a humpback whale frolicked one summer.

From Bethel Point (Launch 51), circumnavigate Yarmouth Island (3 miles), check out Quahog Bay (5 to 7 miles), or circumnavigate Ragged Island (11 miles); the trip to Ragged is exposed.

Spot a car at the Cribstone Bridge, put in at Buttermilk Cove (Launch 47), and ride the ebb tide south through Harpswell Sound (10 miles). Check the wind forecast; an onshore breeze can roar up the sound.

From Great Island Boat Yard (Launch 50), explore Quahog Bay (9 miles round-trip, including circumnavigating Yarmouth Island).

It is 8.5 miles from the Leeman Highway bridge at the head of the New Meadows River to Bear Island at the mouth. The upper section of the New Meadows is very protected. Paddle from Sawyer Park to Audubon's Hamilton Sanctuary in Back Cove (10 miles round-trip), to The Basin (16 miles round-trip), to Cundys Harbor (16 miles round-trip), or to whatever looks like an appealing destination. For a one-way trip, spot a car at Casco Bay Boatworks near Malaga Island and launch at the head of the New Meadows River on an outgoing tide (10 miles). For a slightly shorter downriver trip, launch at Thomas Point Beach. Plan to launch from Thomas Point at the top of the tide; otherwise, you may face mud.

From Sebasco, paddle the eastern shores of Casco Bay, checking out The Basin, Malaga Island, and/or Small Point Harbor. Cape Small can present very challenging conditions (see the safety considerations in the next chapter).

Safety Considerations, Strong Currents, and Caution Areas

Gurnet Strait. The *Coast Pilot* reports that the tidal current going through Gurnet Strait is quite strong at maximum velocity, reaching as high as 7 or 8 knots with a 3-foot difference in water level between the cove on the west and water east of the bridge. These reports are for strength of current; at other times the current may be stiff but not necessarily dangerous. The *Coast Pilot* recommends that boats negotiate the strait only at slack water.

Long Reach. The tide floods into Long Reach from both east and west; it ebbs east through Gurnet Strait and west between Prince and Doughty points.

Passage north of Orrs Island. The *Coast Pilot* notes that the passage between Sebascodegan Island and Orrs Island (from Gun Point Cove into Harpswell Sound) can be difficult because of strong currents. Paddling here at high-water slack avoids this problem.

Boat traffic. Mariners use an inside route from Harpswell Sound into Long Reach and through Gurnet Strait into the New Meadows River, so expect traffic along this passage.

Prevailing southerlies. The prevailing winds during summer are from the south and southwest. The islands and peninsulas here are oriented southwest to northeast, so when summer winds blow they blow straight up the bays and sounds.

Access

46: Cribstone Bridge, Orrs Island. S. J. Prince and Son (833-6210) provides a gravel area with all-tide access to Merriconeag Sound, Harpswell Sound, and the waters east of Bailey and Orrs islands. Pay the $5 fee, which covers launching and parking, at the Orrs Island Chowder House (not to the sea kayaking outfitter, as you might think). There is a portable toilet next to the Chowder House. From Cooks Corner, go south on ME 24 for almost 13 miles. Turn right into a lot just before the Cribstone Bridge.

47: Buttermilk Cove. This launch site lies at the head of Buttermilk Cove near Gurnet Strait. The concrete ramp reaches water except for the 3 hours centered on low tide. Clammers use this site at the bottom half of the tide, so park parallel to the road at a reasonable distance from the ramp. From the intersection of Route 1 and ME 24 at Cooks Corner, go south on ME 24 for 3.1 miles and take a right on Prince Point Road. The ramp is immediately on the left.

48: Thomas Point Beach. Paddlers may launch from the sand beach for $3.50 per person. This can be a fun area to putter around in a small boat, but be warned that the beach is dry for the bottom three-quarters of the tide. From Brunswick, take ME 24 (the Old Bath Road) east toward Bath. Immediately past the point at which ME 24 turns south at Cooks Corner, turn right on Thomas Point Road. Go 1.2 miles and then turn right onto Meadow Road. Take an immediate left into the campground. There are lots of toilets.

49: Sawyer Park, New Meadows River. There is an all-tide ramp, a vault toilet, and a large parking lot here. The gate to the entrance of the launch site is closed during the winter months. From Route 1 between Brunswick and Bath, take the New Meadows Road exit and proceed south about half a mile until you come to a T. Take a right onto State Street (also called Leeman Highway) and proceed 0.3 mile to the public boat access sign; turn left into Sawyer Park.

50: Great Island Boat Yard. This boatyard and its ramp are located on Orrs Cove at the head of Quahog Bay. Follow the directions to Buttermilk Cove, except stay on ME 24 instead of turning onto Prince Point Road. Proceed 2 miles south on ME 24; the boatyard is on the left (729-1639). The $5 charge includes parking and launching.

51: Bethel Point. The Bethel Point town landing is an all-tide ramp onto Quahog Bay. Parking at the landing itself is for town residents by permit only. The Bethel Point Boat Yard (725-8145), immediately north of the landing, provides a parking lot and portable toilet; see the owner in the house on the hill. The parking fee is $6 per day. This town landing gets a lot of use from residents, so respect their work-related needs. Give them priority, and unload and move your car to the lot promptly.

From the intersection of Route 1 and ME 24 at Cooks Corner, go south on ME 24 for 4.3 miles and take a left onto Cundys Harbor Road. Go another 4.4 miles and turn right onto Bethel Point Road. Proceed 1.5 miles to the town landing.

Restricted: Painted Point, Phippsburg. This facility is reserved for Phippsburg residents; town landing permits are required.

52: Casco Bay Boatworks, Sebasco. This boatyard allows kayakers to launch from its ramp; there's a $5 parking fee. From ME 209 in Phippsburg, turn right onto ME 217 toward Sebasco Estates. Go 2.1 miles, passing the resort, and turn left on Ridge Road. Take a left onto Gomez and continue 0.2 mile to Casco Bay Boatworks (389-1300, www.cascobayboatworks.com).

53: Head Beach, Phippsburg. Head Beach, a small sand beach on Cape Small next to Hermit Island, looks out onto eastern Casco Bay. Although the privately held recreation area is frequented by beachgoers, it is possible to carry kayaks to the water (there's no ramp) and launch. From the junction of ME 209 and ME 216, travel south on ME 216 for 2.9 miles. Turn right onto Head Beach Road, where there is a small booth that is staffed in the summer; pay the use fee and then proceed 0.2 mile to the beach. The area is open but unstaffed at other times of the year.

The Cribstone Bridge, built of huge granite blocks, is the only bridge of this design in the world.

Points of Interest

Cribstone Bridge. Building a bridge between Orrs and Bailey islands in 1927 involved careful thinking about design. The bridge had to allow free passage of a strong tidal current, accommodate both boats and ice floes, and withstand the corrosive effects of salt. The project engineer came up with a simple yet ingenious design: a bridge constructed of huge granite blocks stacked so that the tide would pass through them. Gravity holds the large blocks in place; there is nothing to corrode. The Cribstone Bridge is the only one of this design in the world.

Ram Island. The U.S. Fish and Wildlife Service purchased this 10-acre island in 1999. Ram is closed from April through August because it provides nesting habitat for common eider, black-crowned night heron, common terns, double-crested cormorants, and great black-backed gulls.

Lowell Cove. In the summer of 1990 a young humpback whale lived in Lowell Cove (just east of the Cribstone Bridge) for a month. The whale slipped around a net that had been set to contain pogies—also called menhaden—that had swum into the head of the cove. Lobstermen use pogies as bait, but the whale ate them, too. The humpback soon became a local attraction. When it twice became entangled in the net, scientists decided that it was time to usher it back to open water. Jane Robinson describes the whale's sojourn in *The Whale at Lowell's Cove*, a charming children's book.

Clark Cove. This 20-acre public holding with 1,600 feet of shorefront on the west shore of Harpswell Sound serves nicely as a lunch stop.

Strawberry Creek Island. At the head of Harpswell Sound, south and east of the bridge over Ewin Narrows, there is a small island by the mouth of Strawberry Creek. Unnamed on the chart but called Strawberry Creek Island, it is part of the Maine Island Trail. The islet is surrounded by mudflats at low tide and does not get much use, as it is far from other islands on the trail, but it is a public island and it does provide a useful stopping place for paddlers touring Harpswell Sound.

Sebascodegan Island. Native Americans called the island Sebascodegan for good reason. The word means "almost through," and a careful look at the map shows that the island has many places where a bay almost but not quite reaches through to the other side.

Doughty Point and Island. The Harpswell Heritage Trust manages 42 acres along the western outlet of Long Reach. Doughty Point can be used for walks and nature observation, but camping and fires are prohibited. Except for its southern tip, the island is closed to visitors from April 1–August 15. Please do not paddle up to or linger near the northern end.

Long Reach Preserve. Harpswell Heritage Land Trust used money from the Land for Maine's Future program and private donations to purchase 99 acres along Long Reach. The parcel has almost half a mile of shoreline, significant wetlands, varied woodlands, and a carefully designed trail system that allows visitors to enjoy the sights. The organization previously protected 217 adjacent acres.

Austin Carey Tree Farm. Although this 250-acre parcel along the eastern shore of Long Reach is far from Katahdin, it is owned and managed by Baxter State Park. It lies adjacent to the Long Reach Preserve.

Little Snow Island. On the chart, the narrow island near the southeastern side of Snow Island in Quahog Bay is unnamed, but it is known as Little Snow. This pretty island is very protected from the wind. Local people have long used the area, and cruising vessels now crowd the waters during July and August. If you want to see Little Snow, consider visiting before or after the height of the season.

Jenny Island. The National Audubon Society ran a successful tern restoration effort here through the 1990s but minks catastrophically destroyed the colony. Most terns left, although a few have since returned. Jenny is still a wildlife island and is closed from April 15 to August 31.

Ragged Island. Poet Edna St. Vincent Millay once had a summer home on this privately owned island.

Mark Island. Five organizations worked together to raise almost $1 million to protect a premier 11-acre nesting island for eider, black-crowned night herons, great blue herons, and snowy egrets. Mark is the northernmost colony in New England of snowy egrets, those birds with long black legs and yellow feet. The island is closed from April through August.

Flag Island. Twenty-seven acre Flag Island is home to 600 or so pairs of nesting common eider, plus smaller numbers of gulls, great blue herons and osprey—plus lots of poison ivy. Flag is closed from April through August.

Indian Point Island. Bombazine Island lies east of Gurnet Strait along the New Meadows River. Indian Point (check your chart) is located to the east, and the tiny, rocky island that lies in between is Indian Point Island. This islet is part of the Maine Island Trail and is available for day use—a good place to eat a snack.

Bombazine Island has an interesting but perhaps incorrect name. Damazee, a Native American, lived near this section of

Head of the New Meadows River

coast in the 1640s. Chief Abomazeen, also called Bombazeen, lived inland at Norridgewalk and was killed by the British in 1724.

Hamilton Sanctuary. This 74-acre Maine Audubon sanctuary is tucked behind Foster Point and White Island on the north side of the New Meadows River. The parcel includes frontage on Back Cove.

Houghton Pond, New Meadows River. The pond itself is not visible, but the rings that once held schooners while they loaded up with ice from the pond can be seen along the steep shore opposite the northern tip of Long Island.

Basin Island. The Basin is located on the eastern shore of the New Meadows River, just south of Winnegance Bay. The chart shows an unnamed island in the Basin; the island is known, naturally, as Basin Island, and it is a stop on the Maine Island Trail. There is a landing on the east side, but be careful not to contribute to soil erosion. A pair of ospreys has set up shop on the southern end of the island; please do not disturb them.

Like Little Snow, Basin Island is hemmed in by cruising vessels during the summer (the anchorage is a hurricane hole, a site of ultimate protection), and it has an inland feel. The Basin is more attractive in the off-season.

Malaga Island. This island, just offshore of Sebasco in the lower reaches of the New Meadows River, is reported to have been a stop on the Underground Railroad and in the late 1800s African Americans established a year-round community here. Maine Coast Heritage Trust purchased the island in 2002.

At a Glance: Land in Public or Conservation Ownership

Clark Cove	BPL; careful day use
Strawberry Creek Island	Maine Island Trail/BPL

Continued on next page

Doughty Point & Island	Harpswell Heritage Land Trust; point open for careful day use; island closed to visitors April–August 15
Long Reach Preserve	Harpswell Heritage Land Trust; careful day use
Hamilton Sanctuary	Maine Audubon Society; careful day use
Little Snow	Maine Island Trail/BPL
Basin Island	Maine Island Trail/BPL

IF&W Wildlife Islands

These islands are closed during the indicated bird nesting season. After the nesting season is over, the islands are limited to careful day use.

Unnamed island (next to Jaquish)	April 15–July 31
Jenny Island (1.5 mi SE of Yarmouth Island)	April 15–August 31
Flag Island	April 1–September 1
Long Ledge (0.7 mi SE of Jenny Island)	April 15–July 31
Two Bush Island (almost 2 mi SW of Yarmouth Island)	April 15–July 31
Hen Island (Winnegance Bay)	April 15–Aug 15
Cedar Ledge (almost 1 mi S of Gun Point)	April 15–July 31
Pond Island	April 15–July 31
Sister's Island (0.7 mi NE of Ragged Island)	April 15–July 31
White Bull Island (0.5 mi SE of Ragged Island)	April 15–July 31
East Brown Cow (1.6 mi WNW of Cape Small)	April 15–July 31
Flash Island (near SW corner of Yarmouth Island)	April 15–July 31
Duck Rock (0.4 mi S of Yarmouth Island)	April 15–July 31
Mark Island (1.6 mi E of Ragged Island)	April 15–August 31

Note: Mark Island is considered one of the most valuable wading bird and seabird nesting islands in southern Maine. It is extremely important that boaters do not land or linger here during the nesting season.

USFWS Wildlife Islands

Ram Island	April 1–August 31

3.

Western Rivers

The Kennebec River: Bath to Cape Small

The relentless current of the Kennebec River dictates downriver excursions. Although it may sound easy to paddle downstream, the swift current (particularly in the spring or following a major coastal storm), strong eddies, complications from onshore breezes, and very tricky currents at the river's mouth all mean that the Kennebec is far from a float trip.

It is possible to circumnavigate Arrowsic Island by going south on the Kennebec and then sneaking north along the Back and Sasanoa rivers, but Upper Hell Gate on the Sasanoa demands absolute respect and careful negotiation.

When Bath Iron Works lets out at 3:30 PM each weekday, the streets of Bath and Route 1 are flooded with vehicles. If you can, avoid going into or out of town around this time.

Trip Ideas (weather and experience permitting)

For a downriver run on the Kennebec, catch the ebb tide and, if an onshore breeze is predicted, start early enough to arrive at your destination before the wind gains strength. There are launch sites at four points along the river, so you can plan a trip to suit your skills and inclinations. Distances between sites are:

North Bath (Launch 54) to Bath, 2.5 miles

Bath (Launch 56) to Morse Cove, 2.5 miles

Morse Cove (Launch 57) to Fort Popham, 4 miles

A trip to isolated Seguin Island (7 miles round-trip from Fort Popham) is a serious undertaking and demands careful consideration and solid skills.

To circumnavigate Arrowsic Island (18 miles), put in at Bath or Morse Cove. Paddle down the Kennebec, then catch the incoming tide up the Back River and the Sasanoa, and take Upper Hell Gate at high-water slack. This trip requires careful planning.

If you're interested in a challenge, circumnavigate the eastern portion of Georgetown Island. Starting at Sagadahoc Bay Campground just before high water on a spring tide, go north on the tidal inlet that drains the salt marsh. When the inlet runs dry, drag or portage about a quarter of a mile over salt marsh grass and through clouds of mosquitos, then pick up water that flows

115

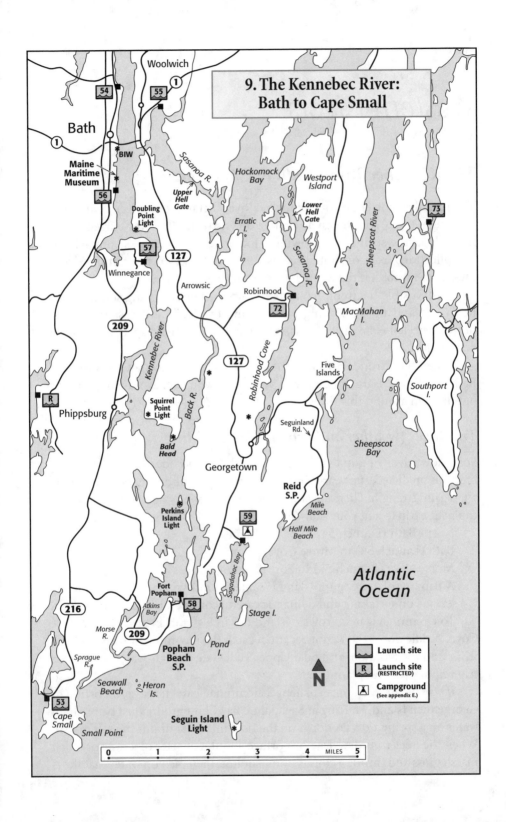

9. The Kennebec River: Bath to Cape Small

Woolwich

Bath

54

55

1

1

*BIW

Maine
Maritime
Museum

56

Doubling
Point
Light
*

Sasanoa R.

Upper
Hell
Gate

Hockomock
Bay

Westport
Island

Lower
Hell
Gate

Erratic
I.

Sasanoa R.

Sheepscot River

73

57

127

Winnegance

Arrowsic

Robinhood

72

MacMahan
I.

Southport
I.

Kennebec River

209

Phippsburg

R

Squirrel
* Point
Light

Back R.

*

Robinhood Cove

127

*

Five
Islands

Seguinland
Rd.

Sheepscot
Bay

Bald
Head
*

Georgetown

Perkins
Island
Light

59

Reid
S.P.

Mile
Beach

Half Mile
Beach

Sagadahoc Bay

Atlantic
Ocean

216

Fort
Popham

58

Atkins
Bay

Stage I.

Morse
R.

209

Sprague
R.

Popham
Beach
S.P.

Pond
I.

Seawall
Beach

Heron
Is.

53

Cape
Small

Small Point

Seguin Island
Light
*

	Launch site
R	Launch site (RESTRICTED)
▲	Campground (See appendix E.)

N

0 1 2 3 4 MILES 5

Charts

Chart: 13293, Damariscotta, Sheepscot, and Kennebec Rivers (1:40,000)

Chart Kit: 61

Maine Atlas locator map: 6

Tides (hours:minutes relative to Portland; average rise)

Bath: High 1:01 after, low 1:17 after; 6.4 feet

Phippsburg: 0:26 after; 8.0 feet

Fort Popham: 0:09 after; 8.4 feet

Mill Point, western Hockomock Bay: High 0:35 after, low 0:43 after; 8.8 feet

Upper Hell Gate, Sasanoa River: High 1:11 after, low 1:31 after; 7.0 feet

into Robinhood Cove. Continue north to the Sasanoa River. Being careful of the swift midtide currents on the Sasanoa and the Little Sasanoa (between MacMahan Island and Georgetown Island), head south on the Sheepscot and return to Sagadahoc Bay. By then, the bay will be partly dry, so slog through the mud to the launch site.

Although the salt marsh portion is a now a grunt, it used to be smooth sailing. Eric Kosalka, proprietor of the campground, says than when his grandmother was a child in the 1880s, there was a saltwater inlet all the way north to Robinhood Cove; boats sailed to a store on the east shore of the inlet to unload.

Safety Considerations, Strong Currents, and Caution Areas

Current in the Kennebec River. The current between Bath and the mouth of the Kennebec runs fast and strong, normally reaching 2 to 4 knots at maximum velocity. Velocities of up to 6 knots have been observed, and during spring floods and after heavy freshets the current speed is even higher. The water barrels past Bath down Long Reach, turns abruptly east at Fiddler Reach, then turns south again. Powerful eddies can form at both of these turns.

Wind can complicate paddling conditions because the narrow corridor tends to funnel wind either straight upriver or straight downriver. Onshore breezes can create a tricky chop on an ebb tide.

Mouth of the Kennebec River. At the mouth of the Kennebec, a complex array of currents come into play as fresh- and saltwater mix, and as water pours around Fort Popham and nearby islands. The *Coast Pilot* reports the strong tidal currents and warns that an ugly chop may form when the current and wind are opposed.

The Maine Island Trail Association (MITA) notes that there may be times when it is simply impossible to make headway against the current. One

The currents at the mouth of the Kennebec River—at Fort Popham (above) and beyond— demand extreme caution.

strategy for dealing with the swift current at Fort Popham is, simply, to wait for the current to diminish and for conditions to improve. Local paddlers say that you can almost always paddle against the flood by sticking to the western shore at the mouth of the river, but this assumes that you can handle whatever awaits beyond.

MITA describes the section from the mouth of the Kennebec to Cape Small as a danger area "deserving of extreme caution and the highest respect." Sea kayakers who paddle in this area need both the skills and judgment to assess conditions. Even a short paddle in adverse conditions can be devastating. In 1991, two sea kayakers set out for a small island located less than 1,000 yards offshore. The paddlers were unaware of or ignored the small craft warning that the Coast Guard had posted that day. Both paddlers capsized; one managed to reach an island and was eventually rescued, but the other was carried out and north, and died.

Cape Small. Cape Small itself demands careful attention. The long, rocky shoreline is fully exposed to ocean swells. MITA recommends that boaters heading east should start around Cape Small early (before the wind rises) and plan to arrive at the mouth of the Kennebec at high-water slack. MITA similarly recommends that boaters heading west start early, leaving the mouth of the Kennebec at high-water slack and then using the ebb tide to round Cape Small. The association warns: The passage from Small Point through the mouth of the Kennebec "calls for a considerable amount of experience and good judgment and should not be attempted by persons new to saltwater boating."

Paddlers should be aware that the current continues to ebb for 1.5 hours after the time of low-water slack.

Seguin Island. Paddlers wishing to visit Seguin Island should be aware that when a southerly wind meets an ebb tide, sizable breakers form at Pond Island Shoal, located south and east of Pond Island.

Upper Hell Gate. When the Sasanoa River leaves the Kennebec at the northern tip of Arrowsic Island and turns to the southeast, it runs though Upper Hell Gate, which is less than 200 feet wide. The current can race through this pinch at 8 knots or more, creating dangerously strong eddies, huge standing waves, and threatening boils for several hours in both flood and ebb tide cycles. On summer weekends, this area is made even more dangerous by the constant procession of powerboats—some quite large—that sprint to and from the ocean. In theory, sea kayakers have the right-of-way, but in fact far too many powerboaters give little or no consideration to their wake or its effect on small boats.

Upper Hell Gate is best paddled at high-water slack, which occurs somewhat after the tide reaches its highest point at the falls; at high tide, water is still pouring into Hansen Bay. If you arrive a little early, pull over and enjoy the view while waiting for safe conditions.

If you paddle at low-water slack, be aware of an unusual phenomenon. After low-water slack, the tide starts to rise. But because the tide rises more quickly in the Kennebec River than in Hockomock Bay, water from the Kennebec spills south through Upper Hell Gate into Hockomock Bay. After Hockomock Bay fills, the current stops flowing south and begins to flow northward.

Access

54: Kennebec River, North Bath. The launch site on the north end of town has an all-tide ramp with lots of parking, but the lot does fill up early on busy days. Coming from the west (or south) on Route 1, take the ME 209/High Street exit in Bath, turn left onto High, turn right onto Center Street, and turn left onto Front Street. From the east (or north) on Route 1, cross over the Kennebec on the new Sasanoa Bridge and take the first right onto Front Street. From either direction, follow Front Street about 1 mile and turn right at the boat ramp sign.

55: Pleasant Bay, Sasanoa River. From the eastern side of the Bath bridge, go 1 mile east on Route 1 and take a right onto George Wright Road. The ramp and parking area are immediately to the right. This is a hand-carry site. Kayakers may launch here at any time (subject to the tide and weather, of course), but boats with motors (15 horse-powered maximum) may launch only during October, November, and December. Why the constraints? Shortnose sturgeon, described in the Merrymeeting Bay section, feed in Pleasant Bay between April and November. The horse-power limit is meant to curb disturbance of these prehistoric fish.

56: Kennebec River, Bath. The launch site near Bath Iron Works has an all-tide ramp with a large parking lot (much larger than the parking area in North Bath and at Morse Cove). From the west (or south) on Route 1, take the ME 209/High Street exit in Bath and turn right. Proceed 0.5 mile and turn left on South Street; continue on South until it ends in a T. Turn right onto Washington Street and proceed 1 mile. The launch site is on the left.

From the east (or north) on Route 1, take the Front Street exit in Bath, go left at the V, and continue to the light. Turn left onto Washington Street, going under Route 1. Proceed south on Washington Street for 1.5 miles, passing Bath Iron Works and the Maine Marine Museum on the left.

57: Kennebec River, Morse Cove, Phippsburg. This popular launch site has an all-tide ramp, a vault toilet, and limited parking (only 12 truck-and-trailer slots). From the west (or south) on Route 1, take the ME 209/High Street exit, turn right onto High Street, and proceed about 4 miles.

From the east (or north) on Route 1, proceed as if you were going to the Bath launch ramp only continue on Washington Street until it joins ME 209. Proceed almost 2 miles.

Then, from either approach, turn left onto Fiddlers Reach Road at the sign for public boat access. Continue for 1.1 miles and turn right at a second access sign.

Note. The launch at Cranberry Point in Phippsburg has been closed by the owner.

58: Kennebec River, Fort Popham. Follow ME 209 to its end at Fort Popham Historic Site, which has picnic tables, toilets, and a small parking lot. It is possible to launch and take out on the margin of sand on the Kennebec River just below the fort (carry from the parking lot). This site, however, puts paddlers right into the narrows between Fort Popham and Georgetown Island, at the mouth of the river, where there can be very difficult—or downright dangerous—paddling conditions.

Both the fort and the restaurant next to the fort are popular destinations, so parking is at a premium. Arrive early to ensure getting a space, and carpool when possible.

59: Sagadahoc Bay, Georgetown. The Sagadahoc Bay Campground (371-2014) allows day paddlers to launch at a small hand-carry site for a modest fee. Paddle on the top half of the tide, because at the bottom half the bay turns into acres of mud. From Route 1 in Woolwich, just east of Bath, take ME 127 south onto Arrowsic and then Georgetown Island. From the bridge onto Georgetown, go a little less than 4 miles and turn right onto Bay Point Road. Go 2.2 miles and turn left on Sagadahoc Bay Road, following signs to the campground. Pay at the office; the launch site and toilets are to the left.

Points of Interest

The Kennebec Estuary. The Kennebec estuary, which is essentially a drowned river valley, extends from the river's mouth north to Merrymeeting Bay. The boundaries to the east are hard to define because water flows in and out from both the Sasanoa and the Back rivers.

The estuary provides habitat for seven species of migratory fish: Atlantic salmon, striped bass, rainbow smelt, blue-back herring, alewife, American shad, and shortnose sturgeon. The sturgeon, a huge, ancient fish, is federally listed as endangered. Studies show that in November, sturgeon in the river near Bath generally move upriver to Swan Island in Merrymeeting Bay, where they remain until they move downstream in April.

The salt marshes and mudflats also provide habitat for many species of birds, including ducks, wading birds, ospreys, and bald eagles.

Bath Iron Works (BIW). During the 1800s, Bath was the shipbuilding capital of the world. Many of the vessels were built for local use, but increasing numbers were for world trade. In 1884, Thomas Hyde started Bath Iron Works. The company established a solid reputation, and by 1914 it had become the preeminent builder of destroyers. Following difficult years after the war, it reestablished itself as one of the country's largest boatbuilders and now turns out frigates, cruisers, and destroyers for the U.S. Navy. The huge crane, dubbed Number 11, is the tallest in the Western Hemisphere.

Maine Maritime Museum. During the summer, any of the following vessels may be tied up at the docks of the museum (443-1316), which is located at the former Percy and Small Shipyard about 1.5 miles south of Bath Iron

Bath Iron Works builds frigates, cruisers, and destroyers for the U.S. Navy.

The Kennebec

The Kennebec River begins at its headwaters in Moosehead Lake and is one of three large rivers that drain the interior of Maine. Native Americans and early European explorers used the river as a transportation route, and lumber became the economic mainstay. Shipbuilding and ice were also once important to the area. *Kennebec* is an Abenaki word meaning "long, quiet water," referring to the long flatwater section between Augusta and the Chops at the outlet of Merrymeeting Bay.

The French navigator Samuel de Champlain explored the lower Kennebec River for a week in 1605. His travels took him from Stage Island at the mouth of the Kennebec up the Back River, through Hockomock Bay, and on to an encampment of Native Americans near present-day Wiscasset. He returned to Hockomock Bay, went up the Sasanoa through the cauldron now called Upper Hell Gate, then proceeded up the Kennebec River to Merrymeeting Bay before returning to the mouth of the Kennebec. By the time he left, he had drawn an impressively accurate map of the area. He also noted, "This river Kennebec, for half a league from its mouth, is very dangerous for vessels, because of the shallow water, great tides, and shoals found both inside and outside." The warning holds true today.

Works: *Chance*, a green 31-foot Friendship sloop; *Eight Bells*, a white 28-foot lobster boat; *M&M*, a white 28-foot launch; *Joyce Marie*, a white 80-foot sardine carrier; *Sherman Zwicker*, a black 142-foot Grand Banks fishing schooner; *Elizabeth II*, a white 24-foot launch; and *Maine*, a green and black 40-foot replica of a Pinky schooner. The museum itself includes five of the original Percy and Small buildings, all of which are set up to show how a boat is built. Percy and Small operated from 1897 to 1920, turning out huge wooden sailing ships. In 1909 the shipyard built the *Wyoming*, the largest American commercial cargo schooner. The vessel was 329 feet long and had six masts.

Winnegance. Although there is a Winnegance Bay on the New Meadows River and a Winnegance Creek flowing into the Kennebec, *winnegance* actually refers to the land between and means "short carry." Historically, the short portage allowed Native Americans to move from one river to the other without having to round dangerous Cape Small.

Doubling Point Light, Squirrel Point Light, and Perkins Island Light. These three lights were established in 1898 to aid in the navigation of the lower Kennebec River. The lights, all between 23 and 45 feet above the water, shine from octagonal white towers.

Goat Island. Two-acre Goat Island, located just off the Phippsburg shore, is not very private, but it is on the Maine Island Trail and does give paddlers a place to stop, snack, and stretch.

Bald Head. Bald Head is an imposing sentinel of the lower Kennebec, separating the Kennebec from the Back River. The 296-acre Bald Head Preserve, owned by The Nature Conservancy, includes the headland and salt marsh that lies to the west. (The preserve does not include the obvious inholdings of private property.) Inland Fisheries and Wildlife manages an adjacent wetland. Be prepared: Salt-marsh mosquitos can be ferocious here.

Opposite Bald Head, on the eastern shore of the Back River, the Maine Wetlands Coalition has safeguarded another 125 acres, which are managed by the Department of Inland Fisheries and Wildlife. In addition to protecting birdlife, the purchase helps conserve striped bass and the endangered shortnose sturgeon, both of which feed at the mouth of the Back River.

Back River. The Back River between Hockomock Bay and the Kennebec River is a gorgeous, mostly undeveloped 6-mile stretch of tidewater. The river snakes through salt marshes, so it is a good place to see great blue herons, snowy egrets, and other wading birds as well as bald eagles, ospreys, and migratory waterfowl. About half a mile north of the Arrowsic-Georgetown bridge, on the western shore of the river, Maine's Department of Inland Fisheries and Wildlife manages a 168-acre parcel with about 0.4 mile of shore frontage.

In the last few years, the Land for Maine's Future program has contributed toward the purchase of a 168-acre parcel and set aside funds for several other local purchases. The Lower Kennebec Regional Land Trust has also been active, acquiring 27- and 35-acre parcels. The Maine Wetlands Protection Coalition, which includes the above three organizations as well as seven other groups and agencies, has targeted the Lower Kennebec Estuary—including the Back River—as a key conservation area.

Erratic Island. Erratic is a very tiny public island on the west shore of Hall Bay, which is located at the foot of Hockomock Bay. The island is not named on the chart. This tree-covered isle features a huge boulder, presumably dropped by the glacier thousands of years ago, from which it gets its name. The tide strands the island for 2 hours on each side of low, so if you want to have lunch on Erratic, plan your trip accordingly.

Perkins Island. This 7-acre public island on the Maine Island Trail makes a convenient stop when paddling from Bath to Atkins Bay. The easiest landing is midway down the east side of the island; a trail leads to a scenic picnic area on the west side near Perkins Island Light. It is also possible to land at the north end of the island by the sign. Perkins Island has more than its share of poison ivy, mosquitoes (all summer), and dog ticks (early in the season).

Higgins Mountain. This hill, one of the highest points in Georgetown, will remain undeveloped—and without a telecommunications tower—

because its owner donated the property to the Lower Kennebec Regional Land Trust in 2000. Thus, 42 more acres have been preserved for the viewshed as well as for hiking, birding, and picnicking.

Popham Colony at Sabino Head. On an August day in 1607, Sir George Popham and 119 English settlers aboard the *Mary and John* and the *Gift of God* arrived at the mouth of the Kennebec River. They chose a small hill overlooking Atkins Bay as their new home. After the settlers built a storehouse for provisions, one ship left for England. Then the grim realities of a harsh Maine winter set in, and when the second ship left in December, it carried about half of the colonists. Insufficient supplies, a devastating fire in the storehouse, and the death of Sir George in February taxed the determination of those who stayed.

When Popham's successor decided to return to England in August, almost all of the colonists joined him, thus ending the first attempt at English settlement on the North Atlantic coast. (Humphrey Damerill decided to remain; see "Damariscove Island" on page 159.) During their brief stay, the Popham settlers constructed the 30-ton *Virginia*, the first English boatbuilding effort in the new land. The small hill that the colonists chose as their home is now called Sabino Head and it lies southwest of present-day Fort Popham.

Fort Baldwin at Sabino Head. The military built the three batteries of Fort Baldwin on Sabino Head in the early 1900s. The tower added in 1942 served as a lookout for enemy ships and submarines during World War II. Fort Baldwin and the lookout tower are open to the public.

Fort Popham's interior

Fort Popham. Construction commenced on Fort Popham in 1861. The site has a commanding view of the Kennebec to the north and to the south, and the goal was to protect Bath's thriving shipbuilding industry from Confederate attack. The semicircular stone citadel, however, was never completed. It was garrisoned during the Civil War, the Spanish-American War, and World War I (during which the Kennebec River above the fort was mined). Fort Popham Historical Site is open to visitors from 9 AM until sundown.

Pond Island. In 1996, the U.S. Fish and Wildlife Service and National Audubon Society initiated a seabird restoration program here for common

Popham Beach

Fed by its tributaries, the Kennebec River carries sand downstream and dumps it into a delta at its mouth, forming the largest undeveloped barrier beach system in the state. The first swath of sand includes Coast Guard Beach (adjacent to Fort Popham), Hunnewell Beach, and Popham State Park Beach. The second stretch, Seawall Beach, runs from the Morse River to the Sprague River. The sand in these beaches is not pure white, like that south of Portland, but glitters from flecks of mica derived locally and shows a pinkish hue from small bits of garnet.

These beaches demonstrate some interesting features. One tombolo connects Wood Island and Hunnewell Point, while another connects Fox Island and Morse Point. A *tombolo* is a small beach or bar that runs between two islands or between an island and the mainland. The ones found here are the only large, sandy tombolos in the state. They provide foot access to Wood and Fox Islands at all but high tide. The sandy cuspate forelands where the tombolos attach to the mainland are formed by currents and the refraction of waves around the two islands. As a wave hits each island, it turns inward and converges behind the island, depositing sand there and on shore, thus forming the cuspate (toothed) feature.

Seawall Beach includes the largest undeveloped barrier spit in Maine. A *barrier spit beach* extends partway across a bay mouth and is associated with a long, straight dune field, a tidal inlet (here, the Sprague River), and a salt marsh.

Both the state park and Seawall beaches provide nesting habitat for piping plovers and least terns. Piping plovers are on the state endangered species list and the federal threatened list; least terns here are at the northern edge of their nesting habitat. During the breeding season, from May 15 through August 15, the nests may be marked by string, electric fences, or signs and should not be disturbed.

Great blue herons, snowy egrets, and other waders frequent the salt marsh adjacent to the Morse River. On the ocean, common and roseate terns, double-crested cormorants, herring and great black-backed gulls, common eiders, black guillemots, red-breasted mergansers, and ospreys are commonly seen. Arctic terns appear, but in smaller numbers.

Maine's Bureau of Parks and Lands operates Popham Beach State Park, a favorite with beachgoers. Seawall Beach is privately owned.

and roseate terns. In 1999, for the first time in more than 60 years, common tern chicks fledged from the island. Since then, the population has continued to grow to 429 common terns and 18 roseate terns in 2004. Leach's storm-petrels and common eider also nest here. Alas, great-horned owls and mammals have preyed upon the birds, crimping restoration efforts. Pond Island is closed to visitors from April 1 through August 31, and paddlers should venture no nearer than lobster boats go—that is, no nearer than the buoys that mark the lobster traps.

Thanks to a seabird restoration program, common terns have taken up residence on Pond Island, at the mouth of the Kennebec River. STEPHEN W. KRESS

Pond Island guards the entrance to the Kennebec. Its light, set on a white tower, shines 52 feet above the water. The previous light and other buildings were torn down when the light was automated in 1963.

Heron Islands. The Nature Conservancy owns the Heron Islands, which are located about a mile south of Popham. These islands provide nesting habitat for double-crested cormorants, herring gulls, and great black-backed gulls. The islands are closed to the public from March 15 through August 15.

Seguin Island and Light. Samuel de Champlain described 145-foot high Seguin as a "rather lofty island" and called it Tortoise because of its humped shape. Seguin Light, Maine's second, was built in 1795, rebuilt several times thereafter, and automated in 1985. The granite tower holds the light a full 180 feet above the water, making it the most visible object for miles around. Friends of Seguin, a nonprofit corporation, now owns the windswept outpost; during the summer, caretakers operate a small museum in the light keepers' house. The lens at Seguin is a high-quality (first-order) Fresnel lens thought to be the second oldest in the country.

Stage Island. The privately owned Stage Island, at the mouth of the Kennebec, gets its name from the many *stages*, or fish-drying racks, that were once built there.

Upper Hell Gate, Sasanoa. The dangers of this area have already been described, but it is interesting to note how Samuel de Champlain spoke of the narrow passage in 1605: ". . . we passed a very narrow waterfall, but not without a great deal of trouble, for although we had a fresh, favorable wind, of which we made our sails reap as much benefit as we possibly could, yet we were not able to pass it in that manner and were obliged to attach a hawser to some trees on shore and all to pull thereat."

At a Glance: Land in Public or Conservation Ownership

Goat Island	Maine Island Trail/BPL
Bald Head Preserve	TNC; careful day use
Erratic Island	Maine Island Trail/BPL
Perkins Island	Maine Island Trail/BPL
Fort Popham	BPL Historic Site
Pond Island	U.S. Fish & Wildlife Service; closed April 1–August 31
Popham Beach	BPL swimming beach (not a launch site)
Heron Islands	TNC; closed March 15–August 15; after that time, careful day use
Seguin Island	Friends of Seguin; open in summer for day visitors

IF&W Wildlife Islands

These islands are closed during the indicated bird nesting season. After the nesting season is over, the islands are limited to careful day use.

North Sugarloaf (0.5 mi SW of Fort Popham)	April 15–August 31
South Sugarloaf (0.8 mi SW of Fort Popham)	April 15–August 31

The Kennebec River: Merrymeeting Bay

Merrymeeting Bay is formed by the confluence of two major rivers—the Kennebec and the Androscoggin—and four smaller rivers: the Muddy, the Cathance, the Abagadasset, and the Eastern. Trips in Merrymeeting Bay require thoughtful planning because there are so many elements to consider: the downstream flow of the Kennebec, the downstream flow of the Androscoggin, the wind (onshore breezes often come from the south or southwest on summer afternoons), the delayed tide, and the configuration of Merrymeeting Bay itself. The Chops demands caution because the entire bay pours through a narrow opening and strong currents can form.

Merrymeeting is a delightful place to paddle, a mecca for birds and birders alike. The 5-mile-long bay has broad marshes and, at low tide, extensive mudflats. Another creature that thrives in the marshes of Merrymeeting Bay is the mosquito. At dawn and dusk, or whenever the breeze dies, be prepared to protect yourself from the hungry hordes.

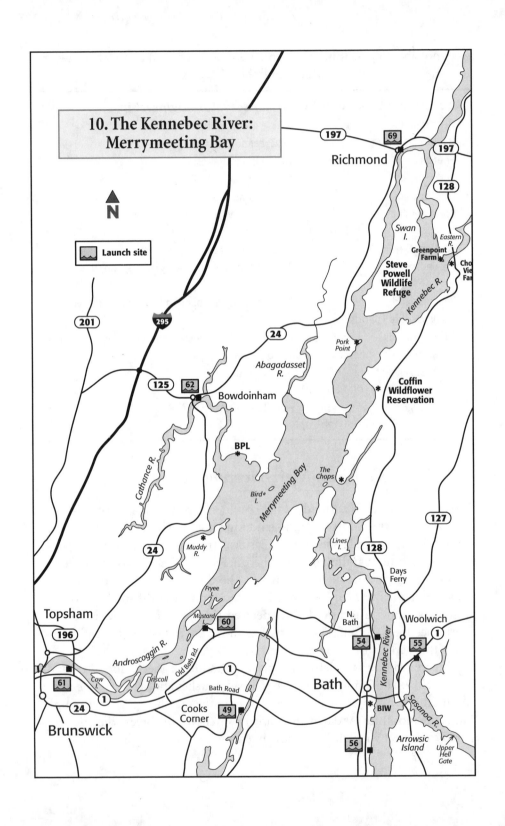

10. The Kennebec River: Merrymeeting Bay

N

Launch site

Richmond

197 **69** **197**

128

Swan I.

Eastern R.

Greenpoint Farm ✳ ✳ Cho Vie Far

Steve Powell Wildlife Refuge

Kennebec R.

201

295

24

Pork Point ✳

Abagadasset R.

✳ **Coffin Wildflower Reservation**

125 **62**

Bowdoinham

BPL ✳

The Chops ✳

Bird I.

Merrymeeting Bay

127

Cathance R.

24

✳ *Muddy R.*

Lines I.

128

Days Ferry

Fryee I.

N. Bath

Woolwich

Topsham

Mustard

60

196

Androscoggin R. *Old Bath Rd.*

54

Kennebec River

1

55

61

Cow I.

1

Driscoll I.

Bath Road

1

Bath

✳ **BIW**

Sasanoa R.

24

1

Cooks Corner

49

56

Arrowsic Island

Upper Hell Gate

Brunswick

Charts

Charts: 13293, Damariscotta, Sheepscot, and Kennebec Rivers (1:40,000)
        13298, Bath to Augusta (1:15,000)
Chart Kit: Not available in the Cape Elizabeth to Eastport pack
Maine Atlas locator map: 6

Tides (hours:minutes relative to Portland; average rise)
Richmond: 2:48 after; 5.5 feet
Cathance River, Bowdoinham: 2:34 after; 5.5 feet
Androscoggin River entrance: High 2:24 after, low 3:26 after; 4.5 feet
Androscoggin River, Brunswick: High 2:35 after, low 4:36 after; 4 feet
The Chops in Merrymeeting Bay: 2:00 after; 5.5 feet

Trip Ideas (weather and experience permitting)

Explore the Androscoggin, which offers quiet paddling in a river chock-full of islands. Put in at Brunswick and paddle as far as you like (to Mustard Island and return, 8 miles) or put in at the mouth of the Androscoggin and catch the flooding tide to the area below the falls and hydropower station in Brunswick (9 miles round-trip).

On the Cathance, venture upstream or out into the bay. The trip upriver is pleasant and protected (9 miles to the head of tide and back). There is little development, and the existing houses are well screened from the river.

For a point-to-point trip, start at Richmond on a falling tide and end in either Bowdoinham (12 miles) or Bath (12 miles). With a rising tide and a breeze from the south or southwest, paddle from Brunswick to Bowdoinham (10 miles), Brunswick to Richmond (16 miles), or Bowdoinham to Richmond (11 or so miles).

Access

50, 55, 56, 57: See pages 106–27.

60: Mouth of the Androscoggin River. This gravel launch is located at the eastern terminus of a biking and hiking trail that runs along the Androscoggin. From Brunswick, follow ME 24 to Cooks Corner. Instead of turning south on ME 24 at the lights, go straight on Bath Road for 0.4 mile. Take a left onto Old Bath Road and proceed 2.2 miles, then turn left onto Driscoll Road at the sign for Bay Bridge Estates. (From Bath, proceed west on Route 1 and take the New Meadows exit. Turn right onto New Meadows Road and travel north 0.8 mile. Take a left onto Old Brunswick Road and proceed 1.3 miles, then turn right onto Driscoll.) Proceed 0.1 mile and turn left onto Bay Bridge Road. Follow this road past a large building on the left and construction machinery on the right to a parking area by the river.

61: Androscoggin River, Brunswick. Brunswick has an all-tide hard-surface ramp quite near downtown. Immediately south of the point at which ME 201 goes over the Androscoggin into Brunswick, go east on Route 1 (Mason Street) and take the first left onto Water Street. Proceed 0.6 mile to the public landing on left. The ramp is just beyond the parking lot.

62: Bowdoinham. The town landing has a hard-surface all-tide ramp on the shore of the Cathance River. There is also a vault toilet (but carry your own toilet paper). At the juncture of ME 125 and ME 24 in downtown Bowdoinham, follow the signs for the town landing.

Safety Considerations, Strong Currents, and Caution Areas

The Chops. Merrymeeting Bay is a large, sprawling bay and when the tide drops, there is an enormous outflow from the bay and the rivers that feed it. Below Bath, the average speed at strength is 2 to 3 knots, and speeds of up to 6 knots have been reported. During spring floods and after heavy freshets, even higher velocities are likely. The *Coast Pilot* does not give figures for the Kennebec above Bath, but it is fair to assume that they are similar to the ones below. The section from the Chops through the narrows at Thorne Head may have strong currents, eddies, and significant chop. Onshore winds, which commonly develop in the afternoon, can delay high and low tide at the Chops by as much as an hour. In some conditions at and below the Chops, the ability to read whitewater is useful.

Points of Interest

Merrymeeting Bay. The bay itself does not fill with saltwater. Instead, the tide backs up freshwater, creating a delayed tidal cycle far inland. The Kennebec (primarily) and the Androscoggin (to a lesser degree) pour fresh water into the bay, while the Chops restricts water from leaving it. As a result, the salinity in Merrymeeting Bay is very low—less than a tenth of a percent—although the exact amount varies according to the strength of the inflowing rivers. Merrymeeting Bay provides an essentially freshwater habitat.

Like other estuaries with a large inflow of fresh water, the Kennebec from Merrymeeting south has a two-layer system. The lighter freshwater flows over the saltwater, creating a wedge of saltwater below. The position of the saltwater wedge depends on the amount and velocity of the freshwater flow and the strength of the tide. Although the forward edge of the wedge usually remains below the Chops, it does sometimes enter Merrymeeting Bay and push as far north as Swan Island.

Another important element in the bay's makeup is that the Androscoggin and to a lesser extent the Kennebec contribute sediment. The bay is an inland delta—a place where sediments are deposited as at the mouth of a river. The constriction at the Chops and diminished effect of the tide mean that much of the sediment stays in the wide, shallow bay, producing extensive

A hike in Merrymeeting Bay: The tide can't always be high.

intertidal flats that stretch across almost half its area. These flats provide excellent feeding and resting habitat for migrant birds.

Merrymeeting Bay is an important stop on the Atlantic flyway. Each spring and fall, migrating Canada geese (sometimes in huge numbers), snow geese (in fewer numbers and mostly in April), American black ducks, northern pintails, green-winged teal, blue-winged teal, wood ducks, common goldeneyes, buffleheads, common mergansers, and other ducks browse in the marshes. Prime migration times are from ice-out in March through April, and in September through October, though duck hunting season makes fall paddling here less appealing (see page 20). The bay also supports nesting American black ducks, both teals, wood ducks, common goldeneyes, and hooded mergansers, as well as many other species.

Bald eagles nest in the bay. Historically, there were 10 to 20 nests, but a variety of factors—including the use of the pesticide DDT—caused a rapid decline. DDT prevents the formation of strong eggshells. In the 1970s, Maine's Department of Inland Fisheries and Wildlife set up a program to bolster the declining numbers. Healthy eggs from nests in the Midwest, where the population was stable, were substituted for cracked eggs in the Merrymeeting Bay nests.

The bay provides habitat for beaver, otter, muskrat, and raccoon. It also supports smelts, alewives, striped bass, Atlantic salmon, and shortnose sturgeon.

Green Point Farm, Choice View Farm, Pork Point. Maine's Department of Inland Fisheries and Wildlife manages these and other areas around the bay for wildlife. Green Point Farm (462 acres) is on the north shore of the Eastern River as it flows in to the Kennebec. Choice View Farm (16 acres) is on the southern shore. Pork Point (40 acres) lies on the west shore of the Kennebec southwest of Swan Island.

Bird Island. This small public island on the Maine Island Trail is located about 400 yards southwest of Brick Island in Merrymeeting Bay. Although it

Sturgeon Delayed $218 Million Expansion at Bath Iron Works

Bath Iron Works (BIW) builds ships for the U.S. Navy, so large, complicated projects are its normal fare. But when the company began moving ahead on a huge expansion, it ran into an unexpected problem. A group of shortnose sturgeon had taken up residence near BIW and just wouldn't go away. Because the shortnose sturgeon is federally listed as an endangered species, the exact whereabouts of these fish were of great importance.

Usually sturgeon move upstream to Merrymeeting Bay in November, but in November 1998, the water temperature was abnormally warm and the sturgeon stayed where they were—too close to the area where BIW wanted to blast and dredge. The company had to get the work done by the end of March, because in April thousands of sturgeon would show up to feed and spawn. The longer the small group lingered, the less time there was to complete this phase of the project.

By February 1999—with sturgeon still in place—BIW got permission to blast as long as none of the sturgeon were in the immediate vicinity. But radio-tagged Sturgeon #12 seemed to favor the targeted area, and when it swam near, progress stopped. Eventually the company was able to complete the underwater work and the expansion moved forward, but the interaction between large company and fish reflected the change in fortunes of shortnose sturgeon.

Sturgeon, an ancient species, are thought to have lived in the Kennebec and Androscoggin rivers for thousands of years. Instead of scales, they have bony plates. Both shortnose and Atlantic sturgeon live in the two river systems. Because it is difficult to differentiate between the two species, it is not known whether the sturgeon taken historically were of one species or both.

Native Americans speared sturgeon in places where fish congregated, such as at the mouth of Cobbossee (also called Cobbosseecontee) Stream in Gardiner. As early as 1628, European settlers fished for sturgeon at Pejepscot Falls in Brunswick. In the early 1800s, a station was set up on what is now called Sturgeon Island at the mouth of Merrymeeting Bay. In 1849, N. K. Lombard set up a business at Burnt Jacket, several miles north of Bath. He was interested in collecting roe for caviar and

is mired in mud at low tide, at other times it serves as a place to snack or stretch your legs.

Mouth of the Cathance River. There are more than 400 public acres, managed by the Bureau of Parks and Lands, to the east of the mouth of the Cathance. The open area along the shore is a pleasant picnic spot at high tide, but it is important to keep an eye on the outgoing tide, which can leave you and your kayak marooned in mud.

Robert P. T. Coffin Wildflower Reservation. This preserve is located opposite and a little north of Abagadasset Point. Owned by the New England Wildflower Society, the reservation is a secluded, quiet area that is used prima-

The shortnose sturgeon is listed as an endangered species by the federal government (from Jordan and Evermann 1902).

processing fish oil. The first year he took in 160 tons of fish; after the second year, the population had dropped so significantly that he discontinued operations.

A New York dealer and Kennebec fishermen set up for business in 1872. Their goal was to collect fish early in the season so that their roe would be black and hard—the best for the market. The flesh was smoked and sold separately. Business declined in five years when fish stocks were depleted. After the 1880s, there were no further attempts at a commercial fishery.

In 1967, the U.S. government listed shortnose sturgeon as an endangered species. A review of the population in the Kennebec and the Androscoggin in the 1990s led the National Marine Fisheries Service to reaffirm the endangered status for those rivers. (Shortnose sturgeon live in other Maine rivers and other rivers along the Atlantic coast.) Scientists estimate that there are about 7,000 individuals in the tidewater portions of both Kennebec and Androscoggin rivers. With the removal of Edwards Dam, sturgeon now have the opportunity to migrate above Augusta. Although it is thought that the fish do not spawn in the Sheepscot, they are present there and in the Sasanoa. Both of these rivers are tidally connected to the Kennebec.

Although they are large—3 to 4.5 feet in length—shortnose sturgeon are mostly invisible to paddlers. But if you are lucky and happen to be in a place where they congregate, particularly at dawn when they are active, you may be able to see them as they jump entirely out of the water—a majestic sight.

rily for birdwatching and studying plant life. Land access is from ME 128, with trails stretching down to the Kennebec River. Its major value to the sea kayaker is that it is a beautiful stretch of shoreline that is secure from development.

Androscoggin River. *Androscoggin* means "place for preparing and curing fish," a testament to the abundant fish populations that once migrated upriver. *Pejepscot*, meaning "long rocky rapids," refers to the rapids at the head of tide in Brunswick; there is now a dam at these rapids.

Cow Island, owned by the Brunswick/Topsham Land Trust, is open to the public. Driscoll is owned by the town of Brunswick. Cornish, an island to the immediate east-northeast of Driscoll, is a public island managed by

Parks and Lands. Care should be taken not to linger around any area that is frequented by bald eagles or ospreys.

The town of Brunswick owns an 8-acre picnic area on the southern shore of the Androscoggin River opposite Driscoll Island. This area is accessible only by boat.

The Chops. Although paddlers may associate the Chops with choppy water and racing currents, the word in older English means "jaws"—and the jaws do nearly close at the outlet of Merrymeeting Bay. To avoid the strong tidal currents at the Chops, Native Americans carried their canoes across the narrow neck between Whiskeag Creek (check your chart) and the bay.

Several parcels south of the Chops are in state or conservation owner-ship. Lines Island, a 157-acre island just south of the Chops, provides habitat for various nesting birds, while shortnose sturgeon use nearby waters. This island was once the site of a brickyard, and discarded bricks still litter the mudflats on the southern shore.

In 2003, Eleanor Burke willed her 125 acres on Chops Creek and Mer-rymeeting Bay to the Lower Kennebec Regional Land Trust. The land is open to the public for hiking, birding, cross-country skiing, and nature appreciation.

Thorne Head. Below Merrymeeting Bay, Thorne Head and Days Ferry squeeze the Kennebec River into an 800-foot narrows. The current sails along at a wicked clip so it's no place to dally, but even a passing glance shows that the 96-acre parcel was worth protecting from trophy homes. Lower Kennebec Regional Land Trust, which owns the parcel (with easements to Maine's In-land Fisheries and Wildlife Department), has developed trails with a terrific view of the bay.

At a Glance: Land in Public or Conservation Ownership

Bird Island	Maine Island Trail/BPL
Coffin Wildflower Reservation	New England Wildflower Society; careful day use
Thorne Head	Lower Kennebec Regional Land Trust; careful day use
Cow Island	Brunswick/Topsham Land Trust; careful day use
Driscoll Island	Town of Brunswick; careful day use
Cornish Island	BPL; careful day use
Picnic area along the river	Town of Brunswick; careful day use
Various Merrymeeting Bay lands	IF&W; careful day use

IF&W Wildlife Islands

These islands are closed during the indicated bird nesting season. After the nesting season is over, the islands are limited to careful day use.

| Freyee Islands, Mustard Island (mouth of the Androscoggin) | February 15–August 31 |
| Lines Island (S of the Chops) | February 15–August 31 |

The Kennebec River: Augusta to Swan Island

You may ask why you should paddle on an inland river when you can paddle on the coast. The options are limited: You can go only upriver or down, and there are no grand island vistas in the distance. But the shoreline is surprisingly undeveloped here, and the river offers sheltered paddling. For boaters who regularly rinse the salt from their gear, a trip on the fresh water of the Kennebec provides a little vacation. Besides, there is an enduring sense of traveling with a companion—the river—whose moods and whimsies are as changeable as your own.

The Kennebec is rich in history, for the Pilgrims traded for furs here, and Benedict Arnold came through on his remarkable assault upon Quebec during the Revolutionary War. There is natural history as well—great blue herons, ospreys, American black ducks, common mergansers, and an occasional bald eagle cruise the river for a meal.

Trip Ideas (weather and experience permitting)

Augusta is 39 miles above the mouth of the Kennebec, and the high tide in Augusta is a full 4 hours later than it is on the coast. Although the tide is fairly benign this far inland, paddlers who want to be as efficient as possible can still factor it in when choosing a launch site. The downriver current is likely to be very strong in the spring, but it lessens considerably during the summer and fall; the flow is controlled by a dam in Waterville. An afternoon upriver wind is common in summer.

Charts

Chart: 13298, Bath to Augusta (1:15,000)
Chart Kit: Not available in the Cape Elizabeth to Eastport pack
Maine Atlas locator map: 12

Tides (hours:minutes relative to Portland; average rise)
Augusta: High 4:03 after, low 5:30 after; 4.1 feet
Hallowell: High 3:54 after, low 5:00 after; 4.3 feet
Gardiner: High 3:43 after, low 4:25 after; 5.0 feet
Richmond: High 2:48 after, low 3:00 after; 5.3 feet

11.
Kennebec River: Augusta to Swan Island

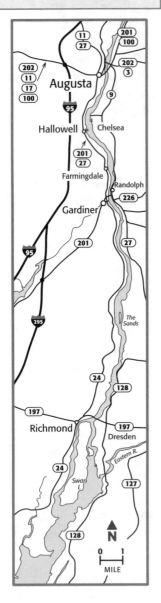

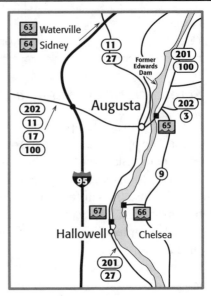

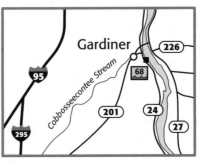

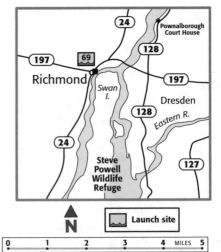

Launch site

Put in at any of the landings for a paddle of a few hours, a half day, or a full day. Paddling from Waterville to Sidney (8 miles one way) or Sidney to Augusta (14 miles one way) puts you on a newly refurbished stretch of the Kennebec. With Edwards Dam in place, the water was merely an impoundment; without the dam, the river has returned to life. Shortly after the dam was removed, a hurricane cleaned out the sediment and bathtub ring, leaving the shoreline free of the usual signs of impoundment. Land along the river is mostly forested or agricultural, making for a pleasant paddle with a rural feel. The stretch between Augusta and Hallowell (5 miles round-trip) is also nice, while the area between Hallowell and Gardiner has more houses (13 miles from Augusta to Gardiner and return). A visit to the Fort Western Museum on the Kennebec, immediately upriver from the Augusta launch site, offers a view of life in the 1700s.

For a downstream paddle, spot a car at Richmond and catch an outgoing tide from Gardiner (11 miles) or Augusta (almost 18 miles). If time allows, stop for a tour of the Pownalborough Court House.

For a pleasant outing from Richmond, circumnavigate Swan Island (10 miles). Or, paddle north of Swan Island and then up the Eastern River as far as time allows.

Safety Considerations, Strong Currents, and Caution Areas

The Kennebec south of Gardiner. The Kennebec River from Augusta to Gardiner is quite protected. From Gardiner south, wind can funnel up the Kennebec valley in a stiff onshore breeze.

Rapids between Waterville and Augusta. Elimination of the Edwards Dam in Augusta has allowed the river to readjust its level, revealing several swiftwater features. Carters Rips (about 2 miles downstream from Waterville), Seven Mile Falls (another 2 miles downstream), Bacons Rapids (4.5 miles south of the Sidney launch), Babcocks Rapid (another 1.5 miles downstream), and Coons Rapid (yet another 1.5 miles downstream) are usually mere riffles but with springtime high water they can be swift indeed. Sea kayaks do not have the maneuverability of river boats, so prudence may be required.

Access

63: Waterville. To reach this launch (not shown on Map 11) from I-95, take exit 127 and turn right on Kennedy Memorial Drive. Go 1.7 miles. Just after crossing Messalonskee Stream, stay right at the fork (Grove Street). At the T, turn right on Water Street and continue to the ball park. Circle around to the launch site, picnic area, and parking area.

64: Sidney. This launch is also not shown on Map 11. From I-95, take exit 113 onto ME 3 and turn north on ME 104. Go about 5 miles, to the center of Sidney; continue about 1.5 miles and turn right on Recreation Drive. Follow this road beyond the ballfield to the water.

65: Augusta. The Augusta boat landing has an all-tide ramp, ample parking, and bathrooms that are not always open. From I-95, take exit 112, Belgrade, and turn south onto ME 27 toward Augusta. Proceed almost 2 miles, then turn left onto Bond Street. At the end of the block, turn right onto Water Street. Take the first left onto Cony Avenue and go over the Father Curran Bridge and past the Augusta city center. Turn south onto Arsenal Street, right onto Williams Street, and left onto Howard Street to the water.

66: Chelsea. This gravel landing is on the east side of the Kennebec River opposite the town of Hallowell. From Augusta, take ME 9 south about 2.5 miles and turn right onto Ferry Road; from Randolph, take ME 9 north about 4 miles and turn left. The landing is at the end of the road.

67: Hallowell. Hallowell's landing, with an all-tide concrete ramp, is located just south of town on ME 201/ME 27. The parking lot is relatively small.

68: Gardiner. The Gardiner landing has an all-tide concrete ramp. From the west end of the Gardiner-Randolph bridge, take ME 24 south past a small shopping center. Take the first left, cross over railroad tracks, and continue to the launch site. (If you miss the turn and wind up at a stoplight, take a left onto River Street and take the first left just past the library.) This is a popular put-in for powerboaters, so the parking lot can fill on busy days.

69: Richmond. The Richmond town landing, which has an all-tide ramp, is located at the downtown waterfront park on ME 24/ME 197, next to an old mill with a brick stack. Just north of the park is a landing owned by Maine's Department of Inland Fisheries and Wildlife for use by people visiting and camping on Swan Island.

Points of Interest

Cushnoc. The colonists of New Plymouth, Massachusetts, may have wanted religious freedom, but they were also interested in making money. They traveled far from their Plymouth base to trade with the Indians. In 1625, they ventured to the headwaters of the Kennebec with a shallop full of corn, which they bartered for 700 pounds of beaver pelts and other furs. Later, they set up trading posts at the mouth of the Kennebec, at Richmond, and at Cushnoc (now Augusta). The Richmond post was soon discontinued, as it became clear that Cushnoc was the ideal conduit for furs from the interior. This lucrative business flourished until the 1640s, by which time fur-bearing animals had been depleted and the Indians were less willing to barter their furs.

Fort Halifax. This fort on the east shore of the Kennebec, just north of the Waterville launch site, was built the same year as Fort Western (see description below). In 1987, flood waters ripped the blockhouse to bits, but several timbers were recovered and incorporated into a new structure.

Fort Western. In 1754, the Plymouth Company built a fort on the Kennebec River near the site of the old trading post (now, just above the launch site) in preparation for the conflict that came to be known as the French and Indian War (1755–1763). Neither the French nor the Indians ever attacked the fort. During the American Revolution, Benedict Arnold used the fort as a staging area before plunging into the wilderness en route to

Pushing the season on the Kennebec River above Augusta

Quebec. After the war, a local merchant lived in part of the fort's garrison house and ran a successful store in the rest of the building. The oldest original fort in New England, Fort Western is a National Historic Landmark. The original garrison house still stands, although the blockhouse and stockade are reproductions.

During the summer, staff members in period costumes represent 18th-century life at the Fort Western Museum on the Kennebec (626-2385). The entrance fee is $4.50.

Edwards Dam. When the Edwards Dam was built in 1837 at a set of rapids that formed the head of tide on the Kennebec River, it profoundly changed the river's habitat and blocked passage of fish that spawned above the rapids. In a groundbreaking decision in 1997, the federal agency in charge of licensing dams put environmental concerns above the production of hydropower. The agency refused to renew the operator's license, paving the way for the dam's removal in 1999. After a 162-year hiatus, Atlantic salmon, sturgeon, rainbow smelt, and striped bass gained access to 17 miles of historic spawning territory.

Bond Brook. Readers of *A Midwife's Tale*, Laurel Ulrich's book about Martha Ballard and life along the Kennebec from 1777 to 1812, will recognize the confluence of Bond Brook and the Kennebec just north of Augusta as the site of a mill that Ballard's husband and son operated from 1778 to 1791. The Ballards lived on the adjacent farm. Despite its now sullied, urban

About a mile north of Gardiner, a string of stone and log cribs extend almost all the way across the river from northeast to southwest. River drivers once linked the cribs with booms and used them to round up pulp logs that had eluded them upriver.

appearance, sea-run salmon still return to Bond Brook to spawn.

Father Curran Bridge. During the April Fools' Day flood that began on April 1, 1987, the Kennebec's churning waters—loaded with downed trees and other debris—pummeled the base of the Father Curran Bridge. This bridge (just above the launch site), normally has a clearance of 27 feet; it was closed until floodwaters receded.

Federal Arsenal. The grey block buildings just south of the high bridge in Augusta were built in 1828. According to *Hayward's New England Gazeteer* [sic], there were "about 2000 stand of arms deposited here, besides cannon and other munitions of war."

Kennebec Rail Trail. You may see walkers, runners, bikers, or birders on this path that runs along the Kennebec from Augusta to Hallowell and Farmingdale to Gardiner. The balance of the path, from Hallowell to Farmingdale, is in the planning stage.

Cobbosseecontee Stream. *Kebasseh* refers to the movement by which sturgeon leap clear of the water and also to the fish themselves. *Kantii* indicates a place of abundance. Thus *cobbosseecontee* means "place where the sturgeon can be found" and describes the mouth of a stream where Native Americans traditionally found and speared large numbers of sturgeon. This stream enters the Kennebec River at Gardiner, just above the town landing.

The Sands. The mudflats in this stretch of the Kennebec attract migrating waterfowl in spring and fall. Canada geese, common goldeneyes, common mergansers, American black ducks, northern pintails, green-winged teal, and blue-winged teal are regular visitors.

The ice trade on the Kennebec. In the latter half of the 1800s, ice was a valuable commodity, and the Kennebec's clear, clean waters provided great quantities of it to the world beyond. It was cut in the winter, stored, and shipped south to be used in iceboxes in warmer climates.

Harvesting ice was hard work. Workers plowed snow from the surface of the ice, laid out fields, scored the surface, then sawed the ice into large blocks. They floated these blocks along precut canals to a conveyer, which carried the ice into a huge icehouse. There they packed the blocks in sawdust to await the coming of spring, when they would be transferred to schooners (later barges) and shipped.

James Cheeseman, a Hudson River ice baron, turned to Maine in 1860 when faced with a warm winter at home. The Union army became one of his customers, and during the Civil War he shipped 200 to 300 schooner-loads of Maine ice to Union hospitals.

Over the years, he expanded his business, and other merchants jumped into the trade as well. Most of the Kennebec icehouses were in Pittston, Richmond, and Dresden, but there were also houses in towns from Augusta south to Bowdoinham. Ice from the Kennebec River dominated the Maine ice trade. In the winter of 1886–1887, over a million tons were harvested from the Kennebec, far surpassing the 238,000 tons from the Penobscot, 31,500 tons from the Cathance, and 512,000 tons from sites along the coast.

Most of the Kennebec ice was shipped to major cities along the East Coast, but some went to distant destinations as well, including Cuba, Panama, South America, India, and New Zealand. The ice trade reached its zenith at the end of the century. In 1890, for example, 25,000 men and 10,900 horses worked the ice fields on the Kennebec. But with the invention of mechanical means to freeze water, there was no need to harvest ice anymore. By 1910, the ice trade had all but melted away.

Pownalborough Court House. John Adams rode circuit here, periodically visiting the courthouse on horseback to represent clients in this far-flung corner of Massachusetts. The upper floor served as the courtroom and is in original condition, with period furnishings, maps, and other documents. A tavern occupied the first floor, providing food and lodging for people with court business. The courthouse, built in 1761 and used until 1794, is visible on a hill on the Kennebec's eastern shore, a little more than a mile north of the Richmond bridge. This historic building is open during the summer (737-2504); an admission fee is charged.

Swan Island. Swan may be short for swango, meaning "bald eagle." Indeed, there is a huge eagle nest on the south end of the island and excellent eagle habitat in Merrymeeting Bay. Swan Island, its neighbor Little Swan, and other parcels in the bay together make up the Steve Powell Wildlife Management Area, which encompasses more than 2,000 acres. In addition to eagles and other wildlife, Swan Island supports a deer herd. Native Americans congregated here for thousands of years to enjoy the abundant fish, fowl, and game. (See *Points of Interest* in "The Kennebec River: Merrymeeting Bay" for

Benedict Arnold's Daring March on Quebec

Although Benedict Arnold later turned traitor to the American cause, at the beginning of the war he was an ardent patriot, and in Maine he is still remembered that way. In 1775, he gathered 1,100 men to attack Quebec City from the least likely direction—Maine. There were no roads, only rivers and little-known Indian trails through what was considered a howling wilderness. (Of course, the Abenakis had lived here for centuries.) Arnold's campaign was a daring military maneuver that involved great privation. "For the boldness of the undertaking and the fortitude and perseverance by which the hardships and great difficulties of it were surmounted, [it] will ever rank among military exploits," a British general subsequently observed.

Ships transported Arnold and his men from Massachusetts to the Kennebec almost as far as Fort Western. There, they gathered supplies and prepared for the daunting trip up the Kennebec and across the Great Carry, a 14-mile portage into the Dead River. They were to ascend to the height of land, drop into the Chaudière River, and make their way downstream to the Saint Lawrence River and Quebec. The fact that *chaudière* is French for "boiler" hints at some of the difficulties to come.

The journey met with one hardship after another. The bateaux, hastily made of green wood, provided poor service. They were heavy, they began to leak almost immediately, and they were of the wrong design. The 400-pound boats were a burden to drag up rapids and carry over portages. It rained so much that the Dead River flooded, and then the rain turned to snow. Provisions that were not lost were spoiled. There were no campsites, no dry wood, and very little food. One of Arnold's officers retreated with disgruntled soldiers. By November 2, Arnold and his remaining men reached the Chaudière in Canada, where the last of their bateaux disintegrated. At last, on November 9, they stood across from Quebec and waited there for reinforcements led by General Montgomery. It was not until December 31, in the teeth of a blizzard, that the Americans attacked the city. But all their privations were in vain. Arnold was injured, Montgomery was killed, and their forces failed to capture Quebec.

more information about the bird life in Merrymeeting Bay.)

In addition to being a wildlife area, Swan Island is a historic district listed on the National Register of Historic Places. Originally part of Dresden, in 1847 the island broke away over the issue of taxes to become Perkins Township, which it is to this day. In the late 1800s, almost a hundred workers lived here, but the population declined in the early 1900s. Several years after the ferry ceased operations in 1936, the state purchased the island.

People may visit or camp on Swan Island by reservation only (547-5322); there is a fee. On the island, naturalists provide visitors with a tour of areas that are otherwise closed because of wildlife conservation.

Eastern River. Not surprisingly, the Eastern River joins the Kennebec from the east, at the southern end of Swan Island. Native Americans called it "the river where the Evil Spirit's rush grows." The Evil Spirit's rush is the cattail, which in myth has certain magical powers. This pretty river provides quiet, low-key paddling.

___

At a Glance: Land in Public or Conservation Ownership

Swan Island	IF&W; by reservation only

___

Wiscasset and the Back and Upper Sheepscot Rivers

There are lots of paddling opportunities in this area. The easiest trips involve exploring a bay or cove: the bay above Wiscasset, Montsweag Bay, and Robinhood Cove. Other ventures along the Sasanoa, Back, and Sheepscot rivers, however, run through tricky and potentially dangerous narrows, so caution is necessary when choosing routes. According to Fanny Hardy Eckstorm, who wrote the definitive book about Native American place-names along the coast, the root words for Sheepscot mean "a place where the river is split into many rocky channels"—certainly an accurate description of this river as well as of the Sasanoa and the Back.

Wiscasset bills itself as the prettiest little village in Maine, but many travelers know it as the prettiest little traffic jam. Route 1, the two-lane road that wanders along Maine's coast, encounters a major bottleneck in downtown Wiscasset. Be prepared to be patient when driving through here. Wiscasset was once a major shipping port—the largest north of Boston—but as the age of sail died so did the commerce. As with many other coastal villages, tourism is now the major economic activity.

Trip Ideas (weather and experience permitting)

Put in at Wiscasset and paddle north to the reversing falls at Sheepscot and back (8 miles round-trip), or to Alna and back (20 miles), catching the tide

___

Charts
Chart: 13293, Damariscotta, Sheepscot, and Kennebec Rivers (1:40,000)
Chart Kit: 62
Maine Atlas locator map: 7

Tides (hours:minutes relative to Portland; average rise)
Sheepscot below the reversing falls: 0:20 after; 9.6 feet
Wiscasset: 0:16 after; 9.4 feet
Lower Hell Gate: High 0:59 after, low 0:23 after; rise not available
Robinhood, Sasanoa River: 0:14 after; 8.8 feet

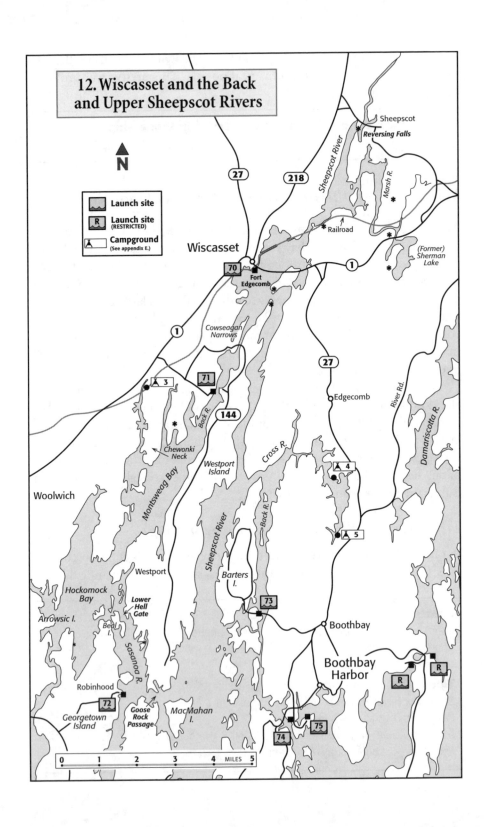

12. Wiscasset and the Back and Upper Sheepscot Rivers

N

Launch site

R Launch site (RESTRICTED)

Campground (See appendix E.)

Sheepscot

Reversing Falls

Sheepscot River

Marsh R.

27

218

Railroad

Wiscasset

1

(Former) Sherman Lake

70

Fort Edgecomb

Cowseagan Narrows

1

27

Edgecomb

River Rd.

3

71

Damariscotta R.

144

Back R.

Chewonki Neck

Cross R.

Westport Island

Back R.

4

Montsweag Bay

Woolwich

Sheepscot River

5

Westport

Barters I.

Hockomock Bay

Lower Hell Gate

73

Arrowsic I.

Beal I.

Boothbay

Robinhood

Sasanoa R.

Goose Rock Passage

72

MacMahan I.

Boothbay Harbor

R

Georgetown Island

R

74

75

0 1 2 3 4 MILES 5

both ways. For the latter trip, plan to arrive in Alna at high water, which means that as you paddle north, you will hit the reversing falls as it flows upstream and as you paddle south you will hit it as it flows downstream. Close to high water, the falls is easily navigable in both directions. (Strong sea kayakers can negotiate the west side of the falls, even at maximum velocity.)

For a point-to-point trip, put in at Wiscasset on a falling tide, paddle down the Sheepscot, and take out near Barters Island (about 12 miles). Unless you encounter a head wind, the trip goes quite quickly because there is a strong current from Wiscasset through the narrow palisades.

For another point-to-point trip, put in at Wiscasset on a falling tide, paddle down the Back River to Hockomock Bay, go through Lower Hell Gate, and take out at Robinhood Marine Center (12 miles). This trip can also be done in the opposite direction with a rising tide. Because it is impossible to time this trip to paddle both Cowseagan Narrows and Lower Hell Gate at slack water (when they are safest), this expedition demands skill, judgment, and an understanding of the currents and your own paddling abilities.

For a longer day, continue the Wiscasset to Robinhood trip through Goose Rock Passage and across the Sheepscot River to Knickerkane Island (16 miles) or Boothbay Harbor (about 19 miles). The warning above applies here as well, for it is impossible to paddle all three danger areas—Cowseagan Narrows, Lower Hell Gate, and Goose Rock Passage—at slack water. This trip is also complicated by heavy traffic through the Sasanoa and Townsend Gut near Boothbay Harbor. The paddle across the Sheepscot may involve dealing not only with the current, but with stiff winds as well.

Start at Robinhood and explore Robinhood Cove (6 miles to the head of the cove and back). The cove can be paddled at low tide, though it is quite shallow. Or, paddle from Robinhood to Knubble Bay (3 miles to the southern tip of Beal Island and back), keeping in mind that the waters of the Sasanoa can be pushy.

Safety Considerations, Strong Currents, and Caution Areas

Sheepscot Reversing Falls. The reversing waterfall at Sheepscot is just that—a reversing waterfall. The fact that whitewater paddlers frequently come here to play is a clue that sea kayakers should proceed carefully.

Wiscasset Harbor and Sheepscot River along Westport Island. The Sheepscot River smashes into the northern tip of Westport Island, splitting into the Back River to the west and the Sheepscot to the east. The current can run 5 knots or more, strong enough to tow under a buoy that marks Seal Rock just west of the northern tip of the island. The deep channel in the Sheepscot takes most of the current, which flows east and then south in a tight S-turn and then south between bold palisades. Note that The Eddy, created in the last curve of the turn, is significant enough to be named on the chart. Paddlers who know how to read and paddle whitewater (including how to ferry and negotiate eddies) will find these skills useful.

Cowseagan Narrows. Cowseagan means "narrows," so Cowseagan Narrows literally means "narrows narrows." The Back River does indeed pinch down here; the flow is forced into a slot about 100 yards wide. This note of caution appears on the chart: "Currents are very strong and erratic in the vicinity of Cowseagan Narrows bridge. Passage should not be attempted without local knowledge and then only at slack tide." Going at high-water slack allows you to avoid the ledges and shoals.

The flood tide reaches the northern lobe of Montsweag Bay before it is turned back by the Back River current, so even at the top of the flood, there is water moving south through Cowseagan Narrows. This current is not insurmountable, however. By paddling along the edge of the river and staying in the lee of Berry Island just south of the bridge, it is possible for paddlers to ascend the river to the harbor at Wiscasset.

Lower Hell Gate. Below Hockomock Bay, the Sasanoa River flows into a narrow channel—Lower Hell Gate—when it passes between Beal (and the long, unnamed island directly north of Beal) and Westport Island. The *Coast Pilot* gives the average velocity of the tidal current at strength as 3 knots on the flood and 3.5 knots on the ebb. It also reports that velocities of up to 9 knots have been observed at The Boilers (the name describes it perfectly) that form where the ebb current goes around the southern lobe of Beal Island.

The Appalachian Mountain Club (AMC), which owns Beal Island, says this of the tide rips at Lower Hell Gate and Goose Rock Passage: "These continue for a period of several hours during each half of the tide cycle. Except for about an hour before and after high- and low-water slack, when these currents subside, only experienced canoeists are to run these waters. They should not be run by anyone at night or in the fog."

A local mariner reports that the biggest danger on the outgoing tide is the strong eddies that form along the shores of the unnamed island north of Beal and Westport Island. A sharp eddy line between the current and the eddies means that it is easy for the eddy to grab the bow and spin the boat around. The even greater risk is not countering the downstream forces on the hull, resulting in a capsize. On the incoming tide, there are three whirlpools in a row just north of the channel marker at the northern end of the unnamed island. If you stay west of the marker, you will miss the whirlpools.

Lower Hell Gate is more safely paddled at or near slack water. Sea kayakers with good boat-handling skills and knowledge of river currents may choose to scout the area, perhaps sneaking along the Westport shoreline at some other water levels.

Goose Rock Passage. Goose Rock Passage carries the Sasanoa into the Sheepscot. The current, averaging 1.8 knots at maximum velocity, has been reported to pull under the buoy near Boiler Rock at the western end of the passage. If there is a stiff wind coming up or down the Sheepscot, paddling can be even more challenging. As with Lower Hell Gate, the AMC recommends passage at high- or low-water slack. Experienced paddlers can use their own judgment.

The Little Sheepscot River is surely the shortest river on the coast, for it is only a mile long. The Little Sheepscot runs between MacMahan Island and the Georgetown mainland, just outside Goose Rock Passage. The tide can tear through here, forming boils and eddies reminiscent of high-volume freshwater rapids.

Boat traffic on the Sasanoa. Mariners use the Sasanoa River as an inside passage. On weekends and summer days, paddlers can expect heavy boat traffic on the Sasanoa (which includes Upper Hell Gate, Hockomock Bay, Lower Hell Gate, and Goose Rock Passage) and across the Sheepscot to Boothbay Harbor.

Access

70: Wiscasset. Wiscasset has an all-tide concrete ramp and flush toilets (bring your own toilet paper), but the parking area fills up early. Going east on Route 1 in Wiscasset, turn right onto Water Street, the last road before the bridge. Go 0.2 mile to the launch site, passing on the right a small municipal parking lot that can be used if the launch parking lot is full. Do not park in the lot that belongs to the Wiscasset Yacht Club or use its launch ramp, which is located next to the public ramp.

71: Back River, western shore. This launch area has two concrete all-tide ramps and a dock. Although parallel parking along the road is limited, there is a large gravel lot on the right as you go back uphill from the ramps. At one time a ferry ran between here and Westport Island. (The small launch site there is a poor choice for boaters because clammers use it heavily and parking is extremely limited.)

From Route 1, go southeast on ME 144 for 0.9 mile. Keep going straight when ME 144 turns abruptly left. Proceed 0.6 mile, keeping defunct Maine Yankee power plant on your right, and turn left when the road splits. Go 0.3 mile to the end of the road. The road makes a J at the bottom of the hill, hiding the dock and the second ramp.

72: Robinhood. Robinhood Marine Center (371-2525) provides access to Robinhood Cove, Knubble Bay, and the Sheepscot River. There is no ramp, but it is easy to hand carry into a tiny cove next to the fuel dock. At low tide, this launch site is a little muddy but is still a better option than the dock. From the Arrowsic-Georgetown Bridge, go south on ME 127 for 0.7 mile and turn left onto Robinhood Road. Proceed 1.6 miles; the road dead-ends at the marina. Drive through the parking lot and past the snack bar to the library. Pay the $8 per car parking fee to the attendant at the fuel dock, which is located behind the library. The attendant will direct you to one of several parking areas. The bathrooms are located in a small building just uphill from the library.

Restricted: Robinhood Cove, Georgetown. The ramp located on ME 127 at the head of Robinhood Cove is for Georgetown residents only. You must have a transfer station sticker to use the site. Parking is extremely limited.

Points of Interest

The harbor at Wiscasset. The large, prominent square brick building near the shore is the old Wiscasset Customs House, a testament to Wiscasset's former glories as a shipping port. The mansion on the hill to the west is Castle Tucker. Judge Silas Lee built the estate in 1807 to please his wife, but after his death it passed through several hands until a sea captain bought it in 1858; the Tucker family still owns the home, which is open for tours. Another landmark, considerably less elegant, is the large brick Mason Station, an oil-fired power plant.

Reachwood Peninsula. Maine's Department of Inland Fisheries and Wildlife holds a conservation easement protecting 4.5 miles of shoreline on a 726-acre peninsula that lies along the Marsh River in Newcastle. The river, which flows from Sherman Lake (or what remains of the lake), curls around the peninsula en route to the Sheepscot River. The area provides valuable habitat for wading birds, waterfowl, eagles, shortnose sturgeon, and wild Atlantic salmon. The easement allows public use, including walking, hunting, and fishing.

The Sheepscot Valley Conservation Association also holds properties in this area. The Wade property lies between Reachwood and Route 1, and the Griggs Preserve overlooks the Sheepscot a few miles to the west. The Sherman Lake and O'Brien preserves, owned by the Damariscotta River Association, include the peninsula on the southwest side of the lake. These properties will be part of River-Link, a hiking and wildlife corridor between the Sheepscot and Damariscotta rivers. Numerous land trusts, towns, state agencies, and a federal agency are working together on this project, which will include Dodge Point (Map 14) on the Damariscotta. The Land for Maine's Future program has contributed to this effort.

Looking northwest into Hockomock Bay, with Beal Island in the foreground
STATE PLANNING OFFICE

Sherman Lake. Heavy rains in October 2005 washed out the dam forming Sherman Lake, leaving 216 acres of tidal mud behind. Maine's Department of Transportation does not plan to rebuild the dam.

Fort Edgecomb. Fort Edgecomb was built in 1808 to protect Wiscasset when it was a major shipping town. The fort consisted of an octagonal blockhouse, earthworks, and 17 guns that could fire through a 180-degree arc. Fort Edgecomb saw no action in the War of 1812 nor in the years following. The blockhouse and earthworks have been preserved as a state historic site (822-7777 in summer), which you can visit for a $1 entrance fee. Paddlers can easily see the fort from the water; it sits high on a hill with a good command of the Sheepscot.

Clough Point Nature Preserve. This 8-acre town preserve (check your chart) is for the birds, so please do not dally nearby.

Maine Yankee. Although the white dome of Maine Yankee is gone from Bailey Point (check your chart south of the Back River launch ramp), other parts of the decommissioned nuclear power plant remain—and remain off limits.

Chewonki Neck and Eaton Farm. Chewonki Neck is home to the nonprofit Chewonki Foundation, which offers a wide range of environmental programs for students of all ages here and at other locations in the state.

In 2005, as part of a rate-case settlement with Maine Yankee, the Federal Energy Regulatory Commission awarded land (the 200-acre Eaton Farm, which lies between Maine Yankee and Chewonki) and $200,000 to the non-profit. The organization's first priority was to construct nature trails; it plans, eventually, to develop a trail system north to Wiscasset.

Chewonki and Maine Coast Heritage Trust worked together to protect a 6-acre island in Montsweag Bay, south of Chewonki Neck, as a nesting area for great blue herons.

Hockomock Bay. This shallow bay lies east of Upper Hell Gate and north of Lower Hell Gate. Although the bay provides relatively benign paddling, the root word for Hockomock means "hell," perhaps referring to its location between two dangerous areas on the Sasanoa River.

Erratic Island. This little island in the southern reaches of Hockomock Bay (if you check your chart, you'll see that it's just east of Flying Point in Hall Bay) offers a place to stretch and munch. Note the large boulder at the center of the isle, thought to be placed there by the receding glacier ten thousand or so years ago. (See "Glacial Geology" in Part III for more about erratics.)

Beal Island. The AMC allows anyone using a nonmotorized boat to land on this island to picnic and see the sights. If you need to use "the facilities," there is an outhouse at the campsite. (Camping, by reservation, is open to AMC and Maine Island Trail Association members.)

Robinhood Cove. Robinhood was a Native American *sachem*, or chief, who lived in the midcoast area. The cove lies south of the Robinhood launch site.

Sasanoa River. When Samuel de Champlain visited what is now Wiscasset in 1605, he met with a sachem named Sasanow, after whom the Sasanoa River was named.

In 2004, the William Bonyun family donated 68 acres along the Sasanoa to the Lower Kennebec Regional Land Trust. The organization plans to develop trails along the property.

At a Glance: Land in Public or Conservation Ownership

Fort Edgecomb Historic Site	BPL; daytime visitation
Erratic Island	BPL; careful day use
Thomas Point, Westport	Lower Kennebec Regional Land Trust; careful day use
Beal Island	AMC; careful day use

IF&W Wildlife Island

This island is closed during the indicated bird nesting season. After the season is over, the island is open for careful day use.

Middle Mark Island	April 15–July 31
(0.3 mi E of MacMahan Island)	

The Lower Sheepscot River and Boothbay Harbor

The lower Sheepscot and the Boothbay Harbor region offer sea kayakers everything from very protected to open-water paddling. For the quietest water, paddle behind Barters Island or investigate the islands to the south. The Boothbay Region Land Trust has several lovely sanctuaries in this area. The Porter Preserve at the southern tip of Barters offers a comfortable beach for landing and lunching, and the trails on Indiantown Island allow a landside view of a coastal island. Unless otherwise noted, the land trust properties are open for careful day use.

With good conditions, experienced paddlers may want to head out to the stark, treeless islands south of Ocean Point—Ram, Fisherman, and Damariscove. While you'll never be very far from the madding crowd—Damariscove is a popular preserve—there are some quiet places to contemplate the universe.

Trip Ideas (weather and experience permitting)

There are two saltwater Back rivers that connect with the Sheepscot. The one described in the previous chapter runs southwest from Wiscasset to the lower Kennebec. The other is located east of Barters Island. This second Back River is nicely protected from the wind that can sweep up or down the Sheepscot.

From Knickerkane Island on the Back River, head north along the Back River, through the Oven Mouth, and into the Cross River (about 12 miles round-trip); this trip needs to be timed to hit the Oven Mouth at an appropriate tide level. If time permits, duck into one or both quiet coves on the southern shore of the Oven Mouth.

Circumnavigate Barters Island (almost 9 miles) or Sawyer, Indiantown, and Isle of Springs islands (5 miles).

From one of the Boothbay Harbor launches or the launch on Southport Island, make a beeline to Burnt Island and its fabulous Living Lighthouse program.

For a point-to-point trip, launch in Wiscasset on a falling tide, paddle down the Sheepscot, and take out at Knickerkane Island (about 12 miles) or Boothbay Harbor (15 miles). Check the safety information below and in the previous chapter.

For a trip that takes you around all points of the compass, circumnavigate Southport Island (13 to 15 miles, depending on how many islands are included in the circumnavigation).

From Ocean Point, paddle to Damariscove Island (10 miles round-trip).

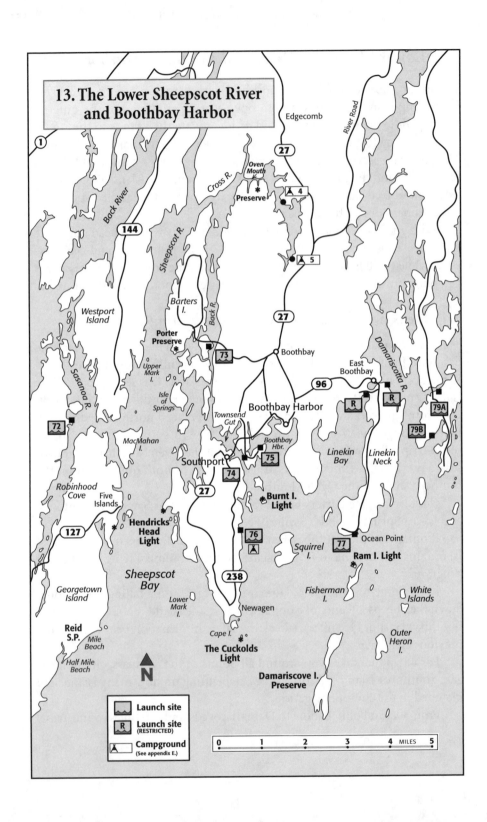

13. The Lower Sheepscot River and Boothbay Harbor

1

Edgecomb

River Road

27

Oven Mouth

Cross R.

Preserve

4

5

Back River

144

Sheepscot R.

Barters I.

Back R.

27

Boothbay

Westport Island

Porter Preserve

73

East Boothbay

Damariscotta R.

Upper Mark I.

96

R

R

79A

Isle of Springs

Sasanoa R.

79B

72

Townsend Gut

Boothbay Harbor

Boothbay Hbr.

R

MacMahan I.

75

Linekin Bay

Linekin Neck

Southport

74

Robinhood Cove

Five Islands

27

Burnt I. Light

127

Hendricks Head Light

76

Ocean Point

77

Squirrel I.

Ram I. Light

238

Sheepscot Bay

Fisherman I.

White Islands

Georgetown Island

Lower Mark I.

Newagen

Reid S.P.

Mile Beach

Outer Heron I.

N

Cape I.

The Cuckolds Light

Half Mile Beach

Damariscove I. Preserve

Launch site

R Launch site (RESTRICTED)

Campground (See appendix E.)

0   1   2   3   4 MILES 5

Charts
Chart: 13293, Damariscotta, Sheepscot, and Kennebec Rivers (1:40,000)
Chart Kit: 61, 62, 18
Maine Atlas locator map: 7

Tides (hours:minutes relative to Portland; average rise)
Cross River entrance: 0:07 after; 9.1 feet
Sheepscot River, Isle of Springs: 0:02 before; 8.9 feet
Boothbay Harbor: 0:06 before; 8.8 feet
Damariscove Harbor, Damariscove Island: 0:09 before; 8.8 feet

Safety Considerations, Strong Currents, and Caution Areas

Sheepscot River. When a south wind blows, it blows straight through Sheepscot Bay and up the Sheepscot River. The force of this wind can be formidable, particularly as there is little protection in the lower reaches of the river.

Oven Mouth. As the Cross River flows past the Oven Mouth northeast of Barters Island, the current is compressed into a 50-yard opening. At maximum velocity—upward of 6 knots—the strong tidal currents on both the incoming and outgoing tide make for tough and possibly dangerous paddling. A paddler who capsizes and comes out of the boat can get pulled underwater for the length of the narrows—and that's a long way to be underwater without a tank, say local divers. The Oven Mouth does not have a huge, frothing falls that says, "Trouble ahead," but this area is hazardous nonetheless. Going in the Oven Mouth near the top of a flood tide and leaving it at the beginning of an ebb tide is ideal. Strong paddlers with river-reading experience can make headway up-tide toward the end of an ebb cycle by using eddies and sticking close to the shore.

Townsend Gut. This narrow thoroughfare that separates Southport Island from the mainland is a busy place, as it is part of the inland passage from Bath to Boothbay. Expect plenty of water traffic. The current can rip right along at midtide, sometimes reaching 5 knots.

Damariscove Island. On an utterly calm day, paddling to this island is like paddling in a pond—but utterly calm days are rare on the coast. Because Damariscove Island is so exposed, solid paddling skills are needed here, as well as sound judgment about when to go and when to choose another destination. There can be a lot of wave action at the mouth of Damariscove Harbor—notice that on the chart "The Motions" lie just outside the harbor. These ledges, which are awash at low tide, deserve a wide berth. The best approach is along the eastern shore, which offers protection from prevailing

Constant wave action at The Motions on the south side of Damariscove Harbor encourages paddlers to enter from the north.

southwesterlies. It can be very difficult to approach the harbor entrance from the west when strong wind-driven waves come from the east or the south.

Southport Island. The southern shore of Southport Island is exposed to winds from the east, south, and west.

Boothbay Harbor Lobster Boat Race. Check the website (www.lobster boatracing.com) to make sure your toot around the area does not coincide with the race.

Access

73: Knickerkane Island in Boothbay. The town of Boothbay maintains two all-tide ramps and a park with a picnic area and outhouse on tiny Knickerkane Island just off Hodgdon Island. The newer ramp, on the east side, is for citizens of Boothbay and their guests only; anyone may use the small ramp to the west. From Route 1, turn south onto ME 27 and then turn right at the monument in downtown Boothbay. When the road forks, veer right onto Barters Island Road and follow it 1.5 miles over the Back River and onto Knickerkane Island.

74: Townsend Gut. A small launch with little parking fronts on the east side of Townsend Gut. (There is much more parking available at the Mc-Known Point ramp around the corner.) Follow the directions to McKnown Point, but when you cross ME 27 onto McKnown Point Road, take the first right onto an unmarked dirt road, which leads to the ramp.

75: Boothbay Harbor. This all-tide ramp lies behind the Department of Marine Resources building that is located at the tip of McKnown Point. There is no parking at the ramp; unload and then park in the lot in front of the DMR building. When the DMR aquarium is open, the adjacent bathrooms are open as well. To reach McKnown Point without driving through downtown Boothbay Harbor, take ME 27 south into Boothbay, turn right at the monument, and at the V veer left onto Lakeside Drive. Go 2.3 miles, then cross ME 27 onto McKnown Point Road and follow it to the end.

76: Gray Homestead Oceanfront Campground, Southport. Kayakers who are not patrons of the campground (633-4612) may launch here for $8 per person and $5 per vehicle; it is an easy carry over the beach. The campground also rents kayaks. Take ME 27 through Boothbay Harbor, cross the bridge onto Southport Island, and take an immediate left onto ME 238. Continue about 2 miles to the campground, which is on the left.

The Town of Boothbay has solved the problem of ensuring access to residents by developing two launch sites side by side.

Restricted: Murray Hill Boat Launch, Linekin Bay. Only citizens of Boothbay and their guests may use this launch.

Restricted: Shipbuilder's Park and Launch, Damariscotta River. Only citizens of Boothbay and their guests may use this launch.

77: Ocean Point. The recreational beach here doubles as a hand-carry launch site. The beach is exposed to southerly winds; high tide and a south to southwest wind can generate tricky surf-launch conditions.

To get to Ocean Point, proceed as to the head of Linekin Bay, only continue south on ME 96 through East Boothbay until the road makes an abrupt right by the edge of the water. The beach is at the bend in the road.

Parking next to the road is limited to Boothbay residents and guests. The Ocean Point Colony Trust has provided an auxiliary lot on the left just before you reach the beach, but it is small, so please do not appear with a fleet of cars. At the beach, unload promptly and do not block the road.

Points of Interest

Ovens Mouth Preserve. The Boothbay Region Land Trust (BRLT) has protected the middle and eastern wooded fingers that reach from quiet backwaters on the southern shore into the swift tidal current of the Oven Mouth. There is a 3.1-mile loop trail on the middle peninsula and a 1.6-mile trail on the eastern peninsula. Great blue herons and ospreys are regulars in the preserve, which includes 146 acres; snowy egrets, bald eagles, and river otters are less frequently seen.

Europeans settled here in the mid-1700s, building wooden sailing ships along the deep waters and protected shores. In early deeds, the Cross River is called Ovens Mouth River. Both British and American ships, in turn, concealed themselves in the river during the Revolutionary War. In the early 1800s, sheep grazed on the middle peninsula, but the land reverted to woods by the middle of the century. When the demand for ice grew, entrepreneurs dammed the cove that lies between the two peninsulas and cut ice from the resulting freshwater pond. Remnants of the dam remain, although the icehouse itself has vanished. The Knickerbocker Ice Works had a substantial enterprise nearby, just opposite the present Knickerkane landing.

Miles Island. Tucked behind Barters Island in the Back River (check your chart), this 17-acre preserve and the outlying mudflats provide habitat for wading birds, migratory seabirds, shellfish, and marine worms. Miles Island is owned and protected by the BRLT; visitors may land, but there are no trails.

Porter Preserve. The beautiful cove on the southern tip of Barters Island makes a nice lunch stop for sea kayakers. The cove is part of the BRLT's 19-acre Porter Preserve. The preserve has a network of trails that snake through spruce, oak, and pine, providing views along both the Sheepscot and Back rivers. Just offshore lies Lydia Ann's Island, which is also part of the preserve.

Coastal Maine Botanical Gardens. These gardens, slated to open in 2006, include 248 acres on the Barters Island Road and along the Back River. If you are interested in plants (or more generally in natural history), stop here after your paddle. For more information, check the web site (www.maine gardens.org).

Upper Mark Island. Hospital Island, the former name for Upper Mark, served as Edgecomb's cholera quarantine station in 1932. This tiny island lies southwest of Barters Island in the Sheepscot River.

Indiantown Island. An archaeological dig at a Native American kitchen midden on Indiantown Island has revealed bone tools, pottery, animal bones, and European trade goods that are between 400 and 2,000 years old. Paddlers may hike the trails on the northern half of Indiantown Island (which the BRLT owns) as well as the southern half of the island (which the BRLT does not own). On the southern half, it is imperative that you stay on the blazed trails and away from the house. The privilege of using this property depends on its careful, low-impact use. Indiantown lies east of the Isle of Springs, next to the mainland.

Ledgewood Preserve, Five Islands. This Nature Conservancy preserve, located just south of the village of Five Islands on Georgetown Island, includes over half a mile of shore frontage extending south to Dry Point and 2-acre Wood Island (check your chart). The beach just south of Five Islands, however, is reserved for residents only, and the estate on the tip of Dry Point is private. Perhaps the best landing spot is on the tidal flats of Wood Island, though this does preclude walking on the rest of the preserve's shoreline.

Guano, not fire, has denuded the trees on Lower Mark Island. The rude odor and rocky shores offer little comfort to paddlers.

Reid State Park. Reid State Park lies on the western side of Sheepscot Bay. Common eiders, black guillemots, double-crested cormorants, and various scoters frequent the offshore waters during summer. Common, arctic, and roseate terns, which nest around the corner in the Kennebec, sometimes make an appearance here as well. It is possible to see laughing gulls throughout the summer; Bonaparte's gulls are regulars from spring through fall, except for early summer. Reid is the northernmost nesting beach for piping plovers and least terns.

Reid State Park has two beaches. A mile-long barrier beach extends from Griffith's Head on the north to Todd's Head on the south. A half-mile long bay-mouth barrier spit beach lies south of Todd's Head. Barrier spit beaches extend partway across a bay mouth and are associated with a tidal inlet (here, the Little River), a salt marsh, and a dune field.

Hendricks Head Light. This light on Southport Island, marking the eastern entrance to the Sheepscot River, began operating in 1829 and was automated in 1951. The square white tower on the headland shows a light 43 feet from the water. The keeper's dwelling is now privately owned.

For many years Rachel Carson, author of *The Sea Around Us*, *Silent Spring*, and other books, summered on Southport Island a little north of Hendricks Head. Her cottage looked across the Sheepscot to Five Islands, and on a foggy day she could hear the lament of the foghorn on Seguin Island. She was listening to that horn when she wrote the final chapter of *The Edge of the Sea*.

Lower Mark Island. Great blue herons, ospreys, eiders, and gulls nest on this island, depositing ample amounts of guano in the process. Guano contains a high concentration of nitrogen and eventually kills the trees on which it lands. Many of the trees on the eastern part of the island have died; when the trees die, the birds move on to new trees. Guano also gives Lower Mark, which is west of Newagen, a distinctly odoriferous character.

The BRLT owns and manages Lower Mark, which is a nationally important seabird nesting area. Paddlers should avoid the island from April 1 through August 1. In any case, the island is not inviting, as it has steep, rocky shores and no harbor.

Cape Newagen. Monarch butterflies migrate past Cape Newagen on their annual trip south to wintering grounds in Mexico.

Cuckolds Islands and Light. The derivation of the name for these two small public islands is not known, but imagination may provide the best story anyway. These islands are home to a light that began service in 1892 and was rebuilt as a 48-foot octagonal white tower in 1907. There was so little room on the island that the light was built on top of the keeper's house. The Cuckolds Light stands 59 feet above the water. Because of nesting seabirds, the islands are closed from April 15 through July 31.

Burnt Island Light. This light marks the way to Boothbay Harbor. Built in 1821 and automated in the 1980s, this white conical tower with a red top shows a light 61 feet above water.

Burnt Island Living Lighthouse. Make a point of visiting this island— the 3-hour tour is jammed with human and natural history. Interpreters portraying Keeper Joseph Muise and his family will show you what it was like to live on a light station in the 1950s; the buildings have been restored to that time and the staff wear period clothing. (Those of you who were alive at that time may wince at the idea that it is now considered history.)

The tour then takes you around the 5-acre island, pointing out plants, animals, and geologic features along the way. The excursion ends at the lantern room and museum, the latter replete with historic photographs. Extracurricular activities include fishing and/or picnicking by the waterfront. Tours are conducted Monday through Friday, from the end of June to early September. Contact Maine's Department of Marine Resources (633-9559, and listen to the entire message) or check the Web site, www.state.me.us/dmr, for exact dates and hours.

Southport Island. A ferry service, begun in the 1830s, shuttled both two-legged and four-legged passengers from the island to the mainland until a bridge was built in 1857. Foot passengers paid 3 cents each except when they were going to church, when there was no fee.

South Boothbay Coast Guard Station. This station is located on Mc-Known Point Road. The launch is not open to the public.

Maine State Aquarium. The Department of Marine Resources operates this modest aquarium, which has displays of extraordinary lobsters, a touch tank with "pettable" dogfish sharks and skates, and exhibits of a wide variety of sport fish. The facility is open daily from Memorial Day through Columbus Day (633-9559). There is a $5 entry fee.

Boothbay Harbor. Like other areas along the Maine coast, the very earliest European activity in the Boothbay region took place on the outermost

Damariscove Island

Stark, treeless Damariscove Island has a vivid history. For hundreds of years, Native Americans canoed to the 210-acre island they called Aquahega ("landing place") to fish and collect eggs. In the 1500s, as European fishermen discovered waters rich in cod, the island's protected harbor and freshwater pond made it a natural station for putting ashore and drying their catch on wooden stages. When the Popham colony failed in 1608, Humphrey Damerill elected to stay in North America rather than return to England. He set up on this island, established a store for the fishing fleets, and became a New World entrepreneur.

Captain John Smith noted "Damerils Isles" in 1614, and the Mayflower stopped here six years later to stock up on cod before heading south to look for a settlement site. Damariscove quickly became a major shipping center (keep in mind that there wasn't much competition in 1620). In 1622, the Pilgrims returned here, asking for and receiving food that they desperately needed; they arrived again in 1624 with a similar request.

Through the years, the island saw almost continuous use for fishing and farming, and a lifesaving station was built in 1896. By the late 1950s, though, the station had closed—its functions were transferred to the Coast Guard station in Boothbay Harbor—and the

The lifesaving station, built in 1896, is now in private hands.

last fisherman had left. Boothbay Regional Land Trust now owns and manages the island as a preserve. Local fishermen and pleasure craft frequent the harbor, and the former Coast Guard lifesaving station is privately owned.

More than 1,500 pairs of common eiders as well as many pairs of black guillemots, herring gulls, and great black-backed gulls nest on Wood End, the northern half of Damariscove. Consequently, Wood End—which has no trails—is closed to visitors from March 15 through August 15.

The trust requests that visitors follow established guidelines (no fires, day use only, no camping). Visitors should not use the stone pier, which is leased to the Fisherman's Coop. A trail system winds around the southern half of this picturesque island, but visitors should beware of the luxuriant stands of poison ivy, some of which are over 6 feet high. The poison ivy is particularly thick on the western side of the island, where prevailing southwesterlies provide difficult growing conditions for other plants, allowing poison ivy to thrive.

islands, in this case, Damariscove. But as the shoreland population increased and ferries and bridges provided access, economic activity shifted toward the mainland. Now, the Boothbay region is a hub for tourists, summer people, and boaters of all kinds. Fishing, charter, sight-seeing, and pleasure vessels crowd Boothbay Harbor and Linekin Bay in the summer, while a regular ferry serves Squirrel Island, a thriving summer resort.

Ram Island Light. This Ram Island, like many other Ram islands, gained its name when farmers used saltwater as a fence to keep the rams from the ewes. The light was built in 1883 and automated in 1965. The gray tower with a white top shows the light 36 feet above the water. Ram Island is just off-shore of Fisherman Island.

The Hypocrites. The Hypocrites lie to the east of Fisherman Island. Although other commentators on place-names offer no explanation for the islands' unusual appellation, Roger Duncan, a naval historian, says this: Fisherman Island itself was once called Hypocris after the Spanish wine that was imported along with Spanish salt used in drying fish. The name mutated to the Hypocrites and jumped to the small islands near Fisherman.

Inner White and Outer White islands. Common eiders, black guillemots, double-crested cormorants, and two species of gulls nest on 5-acre Inner White, which is owned and managed by the Boothbay Region Land Trust. Common eiders, black-crowned night herons, black guillemots, herring gulls, great black-backed gulls, and double-crested cormorants nest on 16-acre Outer White, which is owned by the U.S. Fish and Wildlife Service. Both islands provide an important stopover for migrating birds and monarch butterflies as they head south for the winter. The islands are closed during the nesting season (they have different closure dates—see *At a Glance*), after which they are open to low-impact day use.

Outer Heron Island. Great blue herons no longer nest on Outer Heron, possibly because of predation by bald eagles. The 66-acre island, owned by the U.S. Fish and Wildlife Service, is dominated by red spruce and mixed hardwoods.

At a Glance: Land in Public or Conservation Ownership

Ovens Mouth Preserve	BRLT; careful day use
Miles Island	BRLT; careful day use along shore
Porter Preserve	BRLT; careful day use
Indiantown Island	BRLT; careful day use on blazed trails
Ledgewood Preserve	TNC; careful day use
Reid State Park	BPL; this is a swimming beach
Lower Mark Island	BRLT; closed April 1–August 1
Burnt Island	DMR; careful day use

Inner White Island	BRLT; closed April 1–August 1, then open for careful day use
Outer White Island	USFWS; closed April 1–August 31, then open for careful day use
Damariscove Island	BRLT; south end open for careful day use; north end closed March 15-August 15; harbor available all year

IF&W Wildlife Islands

These islands are closed during the indicated bird nesting season. After the season is over, the islands are open for careful day use.

Middle Mark Island	April 15–July 31
(0.3 mi E of MacMahan Island)	
The Cuckolds	April 15–July 31
(immediately S of Cape Newagen)	

USFWS Wildlife Islands

Outer Heron Island	Closed February 15-August 31

The Damariscotta River

After the complicated tidal rivers and islands of the preceding chapters, the area covered here—Salt Bay, the Damariscotta River, and Johns River—appears relatively straightforward. But like the rivers to the west, the Damariscotta squeezes through several narrow spots that deserve careful attention. The river also offers some gems: a huge Native American shell midden that can be seen from the river, Dodge Point and other riverside preserves, and the spectacular Thread of Life passage. There's also a museum about life in the 1600s right next to a launch site on the Pemaquid.

For short trips, nip into Salt Bay (making sure you paddle with the tide) or paddle up the Pemaquid River. Or, plan to make Dodge Point your destination for a midlength trip on the Damariscotta. The tour around South

Charts

Chart: 13293, Damariscotta, Sheepscot, and Kennebec Rivers (1:40,000)
Chart Kit: 62; Salt Bay is not included
Maine Atlas locator map: 7
Tides (hours:minutes relative to Portland; average rise)
Damariscotta: 0:16 after; 9.3 feet
East Boothbay: 0:02 before; 8.9 feet
Pemaquid Harbor: 0:05 before; 8.8 feet

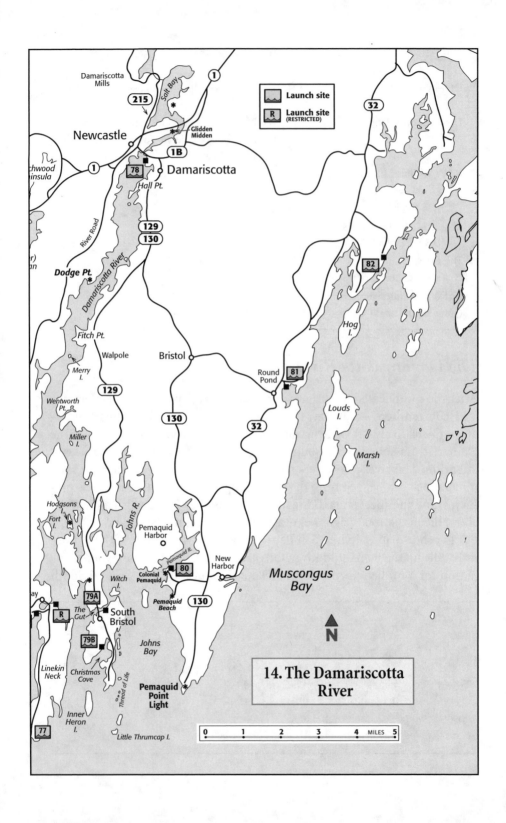

Damariscotta Mills

215

Salt Bay

1

Newcastle

Glidden Midden

1B

32

Launch site

R **Launch site (RESTRICTED)**

78 Damariscotta

1

chwood ninsula

Hall Pt.

r) an

129
130

Dodge Pt.

Damariscotta River

River Road

82

Hog I.

Fitch Pt.

Merry I.

Walpole

Bristol

Round Pond

81

129

Louds I.

Wentworth Pt.

130

Miller I.

32

Marsh I.

Hodgsons

Fort I.

Johns R.

Pemaquid Harbor

Muscongus Bay

Witch I.

Pemaquid R.

New Harbor

Colonial Pemaquid

80

ay

R

The Gut

79A

South Bristol

Pemaquid Beach

130

N

79B

Johns Bay

Linekin Neck

Christmas Cove

Thread of Life

Pemaquid Point Light

14. The Damariscotta River

Inner Heron I.

77

Little Thrumcap I.

| 0 | 1 | 2 | 3 | 4 | MILES | 5 |

Bristol, though not terribly long, offers the most dramatic views—and possibly the most dramatic paddling conditions.

Trip Ideas (weather and experience permitting)

To explore Salt Bay above the town of Damariscotta (about 6 miles round-trip), use the tide to avoid the reversing rapids that form at the Newcastle-Damariscotta bridge and the Route 1 bridge. Start near the top of an incoming tide and paddle north with the current. High tide at the head of Salt Bay is about 1 hour and 45 minutes after high tide in Damariscotta. Time your return to catch the first third of the ebbing tide so that the ebb reversing falls will not be at its maximum velocity. Another factor when considering a visit is that at low water, Salt Bay largely turns to mud.

From Damariscotta, paddle south on the river, exploring as far as your fancy takes you; plan your trip to return on a rising tide. Dodge Point in Newcastle makes a nice lunch stop (7 miles round-trip).

Put in at South Bristol and circumnavigate the island (6 miles including the Thread of Life). Ken Fink, who owns Poseidon Kayak Imports and is a local paddler, recommends doing the trip clockwise—"The views are *much* better that way." Catching an outgoing tide for the paddle south and an incoming tide for the paddle north eases the work both ways. To extend the trip, continue out to the two Thrumcaps (8 miles total). Although the beach on Little Thrumcap has traditionally been a picnic site for people in this area, the island is actually closed from April 1 through August 31. (These dates may vary; check with Maine Coastal Islands National Wildlife Refuge staff, appendix D.) Ken reports that he has seen whales feeding in Johns Bay in summer, and the occasional dovekie and razorbill in the area between Inner Heron and Pemaquid Point in winter.

To explore the lower part of the river, start in South Bristol and paddle west into the Damariscotta (6 miles round-trip to Fort Island; 11 miles round-trip to Miller Island; 15 miles round-trip to Merry Island).

Or, paddle east to tour around Johns River (6 to 8 miles round-trip).

From Christmas Cove, tour the cove and paddle around Inner Heron Island (3.5 miles).

From the Pemaquid launch site, paddle north on the Pemaquid River (4 miles round-trip; the upper section of the river runs dry at low water) or the tidewater Johns River (6 to 8 miles).

For a length-of-the-river trip, spot a car in South Bristol, put in at Damariscotta, and paddle south (about 14 miles). This trip is best done with a falling tide and, for that matter, a breeze from the north. Or, do the trip the other way, catching a flood tide and an onshore breeze.

Safety Considerations, Strong Currents, and Caution Areas

Damariscotta Reversing Rapids. Reversing rapids form at the bridge between Damariscotta and Newcastle and farther upriver. Paddle at or near slack water to avoid the strong current and rapids.

Hall Point. The *Coast Pilot* has received reports of a strong ebb-tide current at the first narrowing of the river below Damariscotta.

Fitch Point. At Fitch Point, north of Mears Cove in Walpole, the river narrows to about 300 feet. Strong ebb-tide currents rush through this section of the river.

The Narrows at Fort Island on the Damariscotta River. Resistant rock at the Narrows east of Fort Island squeezes the channel to about 100 yards. The current can reach 5 knots on an ebb tide, creating boils, swirls, and strong eddies. When the current is at full strength, the buoy at Western Ledge south of Fort Island tows under, and the buoy at Eastern Ledge southeast of Fort Island almost does as well.

Ken Fink says this about Fort Island: "If you are paddling against the ebb, stay close to the shore east of Fort Island to gain the advantage of a very narrow eddy located directly against shore. You will encounter a very strong jet of water flowing from the right as you head north through the narrowest part and clear the last point on the eastern shore. This section can and has capsized paddlers. Lean downstream to your left as you paddle north. You can also use the boat-width eddy directly adjacent to Fort Island on the western side of The Narrows, but there are two short sprints against the full current to avoid two small rocks that force you out. Paddlers should also beware of the reversing rapids behind Fort Island." Although the ebb tide is stronger than the flood, "on some spring tides you'll be looking uphill," he adds.

There are swift currents and swirls on the flood tide in this area and The Narrows demands careful consideration when planning a trip.

The Gut. The narrow passage that separates South Bristol from the mainland gets a lot of traffic, so be patient; this bridge is the second busiest for boat traffic in Maine. The current through the Gut can reach 2 to 3 knots.

South Bristol. Hay Island, Crow Island, the Thread of Life Ledges, and Thrumcap Island provide a surprising amount of protection. It is generally smoother between the Thread of Life, Thrumcap, and Inner Heron Island than it is to the east of the Thread of Life ledges, but boaters should be ready to deal with open-water conditions.

Pemaquid Point. Pemaquid Point ranks high in exposure. The inhospitable, rocky shoreline offers no protection for a long, long way. Waves converge on the headland, concentrating energy there, and waves rebounding from the shore can form a tricky backchop. If you paddle here, stay well off the point. The Maine Island Trail Association lists Pemaquid Point as a danger area and recommends waiting for settled conditions before crossing between Johns Bay and Muscongus Bay.

Pemaquid Lobster Boat Race. Make sure you don't venture into the thick of the Pemaquid Lobster Boat Race (www.lobsterboatracing.com).

Access

78: Damariscotta. The all-tide ramp allows access upriver to Salt Bay and downriver on the Damariscotta River. From Route 1, take the Newcastle/ Damariscotta exit, go through downtown Newcastle following Route 1B, cross the bridge into Damariscotta, and almost immediately turn right at the sign for a boat ramp and parking. The lot serves both the launch site and the downtown, so it fills up quickly. Choose your parking space carefully, as some spots are 3-hour only and others are for boat trailers only.

79A: Bittersweet Landing, South Bristol. There are no public launch ramps on Rutherford Island, and the town docks have extremely limited parking. One alternative is to put in at Bittersweet Landing (644-8731), a private marina on The Gut. From Route 1, take ME 129/ME 130 south and stay on ME 129 when the two roads split. Follow ME 129 onto Rutherford Island (South Bristol), take the first left off ME 129 that is *not* a private lane, and turn left at the sign for the marina. There is a $5 fee to launch.

79B: Coveside Inn and Marina, Christmas Cove. The proprietors at Coveside Inn and Marina (644-8282) allow sea kayakers to launch from their concrete ramp or from their dock at no charge. You do need to plan around the tide, though, as there is only a 4-hour opening when you can get in and out. Drive to Rutherford Island (as to Bittersweet Landing) and stay on ME 129 as it goes up a hill and past a church. Take a right on Coveside Road and continue half a mile to the harbor. All of the marina's buildings are red.

80: Pemaquid River. There is an all-tide gravel ramp with a large paved parking lot at the Colonial Pemaquid State Historic Site. The Colonial Pemaquid Museum has bathrooms that are accessible without going into the museum itself. From Route 1, take ME 129/130 south, and when they split take ME 130 to Bristol. Proceed 5.7 miles and turn right onto Huddle Road, toward the sign for Colonial Pemaquid. Go 1.1 miles to a four corners; take a right on what appears to be Snowball Hill Road but is actually Old Fort Road. Take the first right onto Colonial Pemaquid Drive at the sign for Colonial Pemaquid and Public Boat Access.

Points of Interest

Damariscotta River Estuary. The Damariscotta River, like other rivers along the midcoast, is a drowned river valley. Salt Bay lies at the head of the

A replica of the tower of Fort William Henry at Pemaquid

estuary, at the base of a 50-foot falls flowing from Damariscotta Lake. A narrow ribbon of water then runs through a deep, half-mile-long channel to the mouth of the river at Linekin Neck and the islands south of Rutherford. The river is tidal throughout its length, including Salt Bay.

Salt Bay. Salt Bay has extensive eelgrass meadows, salt flats, and salt marshes. It is one of the northernmost breeding sites—and one of only four breeding sites in Maine—for horseshoe crabs. The horseshoe crab is an ancient animal that dates from the Triassic period, more than 200 million years ago when dinosaurs roamed the earth. Horseshoe crabs move into shallow water in late spring to lay eggs. As they grow, they must shed their shell and grow another.

Salt Bay also provides habitat for two algae, red beard sponge and red chenille algae, that do not otherwise grow this far north.

Eagles nesting in the Damariscotta Mills area often cruise the bay looking for food. Ospreys nesting on an island in the middle of the bay provide paddlers with great displays, even when watched at a discreet distance. Canada geese, ring-necked ducks, and greater scaup feed here on their way north during March and April; American wigeons and common goldeneyes show up in smaller numbers. Great blue herons and green-backed herons are regulars during the summer. Seals sometimes ride the tide into Salt Bay, and river otters can occasionally be seen as well.

Each May, alewives run through Salt Bay and into the upper reaches of the Damariscotta River. A fish ladder, restored by the Damariscotta River Association, affords an opportunity to view the alewife run. The alewife is an anadromous fish that, like the Atlantic salmon, lives in the ocean but ascends rivers to spawn. This area did not originally support an alewife run because few fish could navigate the 50-foot falls blocking upstream passage, but a rock fishway built in 1806 and subsequent stocking program established a healthy run.

Salt Bay Farm Heritage Center. The Damariscotta River Association (DRA; 563-1393) has its headquarters on this 100-acre parcel with a mile of shorefront on Salt Bay. The preserve is open to the public from dawn until dusk. The DRA's mission is to preserve and promote the natural, cultural, and historic heritage of the Damariscotta River, its watershed, and nearby areas for the benefit of all. The organization owns 17 properties and has conservation easements on another 29.

Glidden Midden. Paddling affords the best view of the Glidden Midden, a shell heap located just below the point at which Route 1 crosses the Damariscotta River. It is extremely important not to touch or otherwise disturb the shell heap, which is susceptible to erosion.

Dodge Point. This state-owned day-use property has over 8,000 feet of river frontage with several small pocket beaches tucked in along the shore. Frontage runs from the small point just north of Dodge Upper Cove, which the Bureau of Parks and Lands calls Brickyard Beach, to below Dodge Point. Just south of Upper Cove there is a small sand beach and slightly farther south, a small pebble beach.

The Dodge Point property includes more than 500 acres of woodland plus a 2- to 3-acre freshwater pond. The point by Dodge Upper Cove is the site of a pre–Revolutionary War brickworks; there were 26 brickworks along the Damariscotta estuary. Bricks can still be seen in the mud at Upper Cove when the tide is low. Trails follow the shore and crisscross the property. The parking lot on River Road is almost a mile from the river, so Dodge Point cannot conveniently be used as a launch site. A brochure with a map of the trails is available from the bureau (see appendix D).

Dodge Point is one link in a proposed 10-mile wildlife and hiking corridor between the Sheepscot and Damariscotta rivers and—down the line—a corridor from Whitefield to Boothbay. Properties along the Marsh River (see Map 12), Sherman Lake along Route 1, and the Schmid Preserve in Edgecomb will also be way stations in the River-Link project. A consortium of land trusts, towns, state agencies and federal agencies (including the Land for Maine's Future program) are collaborating on this effort.

Ira C. Darling Center. This oceanographic research facility—the laboratory for the University of Maine School of Marine Sciences—is located on Wentworth and McGuire Points about 7 miles south of Damariscotta.

Fort Island. Fort Webber, built to protect the Damariscotta region

The Biggest Shell Heap

Why is there a huge kitchen midden of oyster shells on the shores of the Damariscotta River, in a place where oysters do not grow today? The answer reaches into prehistory. Several thousand years ago, Salt Bay and the section of the Damariscotta River between the bay and what is now the town of Damariscotta contained fresh water. But as the sea level gradually rose, salt water encroached above Johnny Orr Rapids, formed by a sill located about halfway between the Damariscotta Bridge and the Route 1 bridge, and then Indraft, another sill located at a narrowing of the river above the Route 1 bridge. Oysters moved in, finding the barely saline water an ideal place to grow because their main predator—the oyster drill—needed saltier water.

Perhaps 2,400 years ago, Native Americans began visiting this area of the river, eating the oysters and tossing shells in a heap. The heap grew, shell by shell, for more than a thousand years until sea level rise flooded the sills and increased salinity to the level that supported the clam's marine predators.

By this time the two middens, one on each side of the river, had grown to immense proportions. The Whaleback Midden on the eastern shore is estimated to have extended more than 300 feet inland and almost 400 feet along the shore, to a maximum depth of 15 feet. In 1886, workers set up a mining operation on Whaleback Midden. The shells were crushed and added to chicken feed to increase its calcium content. The Peabody Museum at Harvard hired Abram Gamage to salvage important material as it came to light. Gamage found bones typical of a winter habitation site—white-tailed deer, moose, bear, harbor seal, sea mink; alewife, cod, tomcod, and sturgeon; and loon, eider, and great auk. (Both the sea mink and the great auk are now extinct.) He also found stone axes, potsherds, bone tools, and the partial skeletal remains of 14 Native Americans. Some of the largest oysters were 10 inches long. The commercial venture closed in 1887, having excavated most of the shells.

The Glidden Midden on the south shore has never been mined. It is now the largest surviving prehistoric shell heap on the East Coast. The Damariscotta River Association, a private conservation organization, now owns a 10-acre area that includes the midden. This midden is listed on the National Register of Historic Places.

during the War of 1812, is located on this 37-acre public island managed by BPL. The fort was not an elaborate affair. Six volunteers made up the garrison, and although there was a heavy gun, there were no balls to put in it. The volunteers collected stones instead.

The island has a small beach that is well used as a picnic and camping site, so during the height of the season, expect company (sometimes noisy company). Nature calling? There is a privy near the campsite, just beyond a stone wall.

Menigawum Preserve on Hodgsons (Stratton) Island. Menigawum Preserve, east of Fort Island, is a lovely day-use island that is owned and managed by the Damariscotta River Association. Land on the west side of the island or at Boat House Beach on the northeast; the latter area has a box with preserve guides and a sign-in book. A trail runs along the perimeter and, in the southern section, cuts through the interior. The Damariscotta River Association asks that visitors stay on the trails, leave no waste, leave the flora and fauna undisturbed, avoid the potentially dangerous ruins of an old building, obey caution signs near nesting areas, and make no open fires. The nearby Plummer Point Preserve, owned by The Nature Conservancy, provides important nesting habitat and is closed to visitors.

Tracy Shores Preserve. This preserve, owned by the Town of South Bristol, lies at the head of Jones Cove on the Damariscotta River, less than a mile north of The Gut.

Witch Island Sanctuary. Grace Courtland, who bought the island in 1887, promoted herself as the "Witch of Wall Street"—someone who could predict the future. She won a following, and Wall Street financiers flocked to ask her advice. Her island came to be known as Witch Island.

The island is located at the eastern end of The Gut and thus provides scenic views into Johns River and Johns Bay. Two protected beaches serve as landing and picnicking areas, and a trail around the island weaves through mature pines and oaks. Maine Audubon Society owns and manages this day-use island.

Thread of Life Ledges. The scenery here is stunning. A deep, narrow channel runs alongside bare islets, providing paddlers with superb views to the east, south, and west. A legend holds that a mariner was able to escape pursuit by threading through these islands and finding safety in Johns Bay. To add to the sewing motif, the narrow passage east of Turnip Island is called the Needle's Eye.

Little Thrumcap Island. A *thrum* is a small piece of rope yarn used with canvas to make a protective covering for rigging. A seaman's cap made of pieces of thrum is, naturally, a *thrumcap*. There are six other Thrumcap islands or ledges in Maine.

Little Thrumcap, also called Outer Thrumcap, lies next to Thrumcap Island (and is connected to it at low tide) at the southern tip of the Thread of Life. The U.S. Fish and Wildlife Service purchased this 8.5-acre island in 1995 because in the 1980s roseate, common, and Arctic terns had nested there, along with laughing gulls, herring gulls, and common eider. After monitoring Little Thrumcap for two years—with very little evidence of seabird nesting—the Service opened about half of the island to visitors year-round; the balance is closed from April through August. A small pocket beach on the north

Colonial Pemaquid

Pemaquid Harbor was well-known to fishermen in the early 1600s, and a permanent community had been established by 1626. Archaeological excavations show that there was a tavern, a jail, several homes, a warehouse, and other buildings. The museum displays many artifacts from the excavations, including clay pipes, dishes, men's wig curlers, and even a carving made of elephant ivory from Africa, perhaps carried to the settlement by a sailor. By the 1670s, there may have been 200 people living here. They farmed, fished, and traded with the Abenakis and Micmacs, who hunted and fished here before the arrival of European settlers.

Unfortunately for Colonial Pemaquid, it occupied a political fault line between the English to the west and the French and allied Indians to the east, and the settlement was the site of constant turmoil. A decision by the government to stop selling gunpowder to Native Americans—in conjunction with the ongoing loss of their land—meant that they had an increasingly difficult time securing food. With the encouragement of the French, they attacked and destroyed Colonial Pemaquid in 1676. The British rebuilt the village, but Native Americans destroyed it again in 1689. In 1692, the British responded by building Fort William Henry with 6-foot-thick stone walls, but to no avail. The fort fell to the French and Indians in 1696. Colonel Wolfgang William Romer, a British military engineer, wrote three years later: "The land of Pemaquid is much better than that around St. George's. There was there formerly a

shore offers the best landing site on the upper part of the tide but is difficult to get to at low water. Educational materials at this beach describe which part of the island is affected by the closure.

Johns Bay. This bay and the tidewater river flowing into it were named for Captain John Smith, who sailed through here in 1614. Captain Smith stopped in a cove on Rutherford Island on Christmas of that year, and named it Christmas Cove.

Pemaquid Beach. Pemaquid is a pocket barrier beach, which means that sand has been trapped between rocky fingers or headlands (that's the pocket beach part), and the beach is connected to the mainland at both ends and has a lagoon or salt marsh behind it (that's the barrier part). Pemaquid has a limited amount of sand, so when intense winter storms pull sand from the beach area and deposit it offshore, what remains are underlying stones and pebbles and a sloping layer of freshwater peat. When lower-intensity waves redeposit the sand in spring and summer, the beach is restored.

Stumps of trees that once lived in an ancient swamp can be seen at very low tides. Several thousand years ago, the sea swallowed the swamp and pushed back the land as the sea level rose.

Because this beach is for swimmers and sunbathers, boaters are required to stay well away from the main beach.

village of 36 well built houses on a neck of land, where stood the fort, and there were many farms and farmers in the neighboring country. 'Tis supposed that had peace continued Pemaquid would have been a place of importance because of its fishery, its trade with the Indians and the trade which would have arisen from the productions of the country."

At last the British gave up, abandoning the area until the 1720s, when Colonel David Dunbar tried once again to establish a settlement. Thwarted by conflicting land claims, he too left the area. The remains of Colonial Pemaquid lay dormant until the late 1800s, when John Henry Cartland began excavations. Further work was done in 1923, and then in 1965. The digs, which continue to this day, have yielded thousands of artifacts and fascinating information about the lives of the people who lived in the area 350 years ago.

If you're paddling the Pemaquid River, it's well worth spending an hour at Colonial Pemaquid (677-2423, April to October), which you can visit for a fee of $2. The historic site includes excavated foundations of buildings from the 1600s, a cemetery, a small museum with artifacts from the excavations, the foundations of Fort William Henry and Fort Frederick, and a replica of Fort William Henry's tower. The building foundations, cemetery, and museum are next to the launch-site parking lot, and the fort remains and reconstructed tower are within easy walking distance.

William Henry Memorial Fort. Starting in 1613, three seperate forts were built here and subsequently destroyed. The current building reconstructs the 1692 fortification that was put up during the Second Indian War to protect against French encroachment. The memorial lies southwest of the Pemaquid River ramp.

Pemaquid Point. Four hundred million years ago ocean currents laid down alternating layers of sediments on the ocean floor; these layers subsequently slumped in submarine landslides. The layers eventually became graywacke, a dark sedimentary rock. The thin layers of the remains of minute radiolarian protozoa became limestone. Movement of the tectonic plates later changed the layers dramatically. Molten rock intruded, the layers were folded, and the rocks recrystallized—but the banding survived. At Pemaquid Point, the upturned exposure of this metawacke (metamorphosized graywacke), which has thinly bedded limy quartzite layers and seams of coarse-grained white granite, has been smoothed and beautifully sculpted by wave action.

The Native American word *pemaquid* means "long point" or "a point of land running into the sea." These early paddlers saw no reason to brave the dangers of Pemaquid Point, instead portaging from New Harbor to the Pemaquid River.

Several species of waterfowl are regulars year-round, including common eiders and white-winged, black, and surf scoters. Other water birds that frequent the waters around Pemaquid Point include common loons; double-crested cormorants; black guillemots; herring, great black-backed, Bonaparte's, and laughing gulls; and common, arctic, and roseate terns.

Pemaquid Point Light. The white granite tower that President John Quincy Adams commissioned in 1827 got new life when it appeared on the Maine state quarter. The light rises 79 feet above water level and warns mariners off treacherous Pemaquid Point. The town of Bristol operates a park (with a modest entry fee) that includes a small museum in the former light keeper's quarters. Visitors may also climb the steps to the lantern room; on a clear day, Monhegan Island stands out on the horizon. The American Lighthouse Foundation maintains the tower.

At a Glance: Land in Public or Conservation Ownership

Whaleback Midden	BPL; paddle by but do not stop
Glidden Midden	Damariscotta River Association; paddle by but do not stop
Dodge Point	BPL; careful day use
Fort Island	Maine Island Trail/BPL
Menigawum Preserve	Damariscotta River Association; careful day use
Plummer Point Preserve	TNC; closed to visitors
Witch Island Sanctuary	Maine Audubon Society; careful day use
Little Thrumcap Island	USFWS; closed April 1–August 31
Colonial Pemaquid State Historic Site	BPL; launch site, historic site, museum
Pemaquid Beach	Town of Pemaquid; bathing beach only
William Henry Memorial Fort	BPL Historic Site; day visitation
Pemaquid Point	Town park; no water access

IF&W Wildlife Islands

These islands are closed during the indicated bird nesting season. After the nesting season is over, the islands are limited to careful day use.

New Harbor Dry Ledges (0.7 mi S of New Harbor)	April 15–July 31
Unnamed island in Christmas Cove (southernmost of 3)	April 15–August 31

Western Muscongus Bay: New Harbor to Friendship

Perhaps the most attractive aspect of western Muscongus Bay is the concentration of islands on the Maine Island Trail: Little Marsh, Thief, Crow, Strawberry, and Havener Ledge. These islands, whether snack stops or lunch destinations, allow you to pull up your boat, stroll along the shore, and appreciate the glittering bay from a shoreside toehold.

The open nature of Muscongus Bay, studded as it is with dozens of islands, allows any number of excursions. The Waldoboro and Hockomock Channel launch sites put you into the protected waters of the Medomak River, although the swift currents of The Narrows demand careful attention. The ramp at Round Pond provides access to the beckoning islands of the outer bay.

Two main channels cut through this section of Muscongus Bay: Muscongus Sound, which lies west of Louds Island, and a channel that goes through the center of the bay. Sea kayakers, though, need not stick to these traffic lanes. Indeed, areas that are generally considered shoal and foul provide some of the prettiest paddling.

Trip Ideas (weather and experience permitting)

The Medomak River offers protected inland paddling. At low tide, the river from Waldoboro south to halfway down the Dutch Neck has extensive flats that are nearly bare of water; channel depth at Waldoboro is 3.5 feet and gradually deepens to 5 feet. The best paddling is at the top half of the tide when there is plenty of water. Put in at Waldoboro and gunkhole until you reach a self-appointed turnaround time. Or, spot a car for a point-to-point trip between Waldoboro and Broad Cove Marine (about 8 miles).

From Broad Cove Marine, circumnavigate Bremen Long Island (7 miles). For lunch, stop at Crow Island near the tip of Hog Island or Strawberry Island next to Bremen Long, both of which are open to the public. If Crow is crowded—and it often is—paddle on to a quieter place.

From Round Pond, circumnavigate Louds Island (8 miles), taking a break, if you wish, on Little Marsh. Or, head around Louds for Thief Island, which can be crowded (9 miles). From Round Pond, you can also visit National Audubon's Todd Wildlife Sanctuary on Hog Island (7 miles).

Safety Considerations, Strong Currents, and Caution Areas

Medomak River. The *Coast Pilot* reports strong tidal currents at the mouth of the Medomak River in these areas: the passage through Back River Cove and through Flying Passage (on either side of Hungry Island) and The Narrows (immediately south of Havener Ledge).

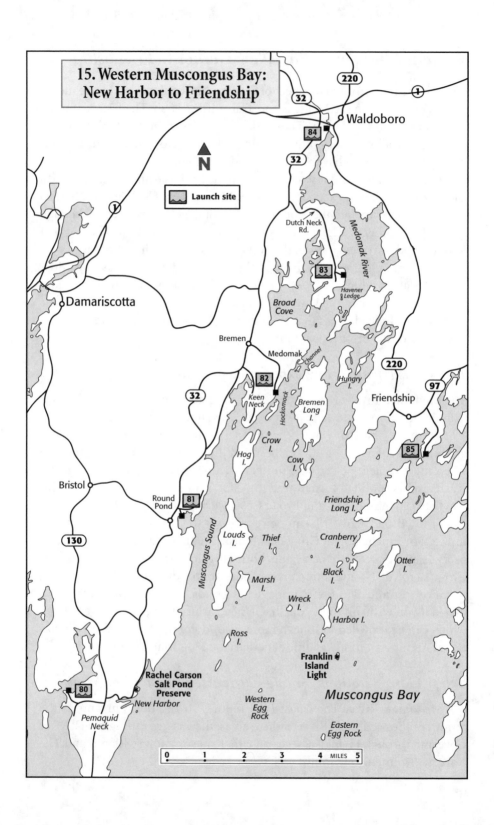

15. Western Muscongus Bay: New Harbor to Friendship

N

Launch site

220

32

1

Waldoboro

84

32

Dutch Neck Rd.

220

97

Damariscotta

83

Havener Ledge

Medomak River

Broad Cove

Bremen

Medomak

Channel

Hungry I.

Friendship

82

Keen Neck

Hockomock

Bremen Long I.

32

Crow I.

Hog I.

Cow I.

85

Bristol

Round Pond

81

Muscongus Sound

Friendship Long I.

130

Louds I.

Thief I.

Cranberry I.

Otter I.

Marsh I.

Black I.

Wreck I.

Harbor I.

Ross I.

Franklin Island Light

Muscongus Bay

80

Rachel Carson Salt Pond Preserve

New Harbor

Western Egg Rock

Pemaquid Neck

Eastern Egg Rock

0 1 2 3 4 MILES 5

Charts
Chart: 13301, Muscongus Bay (1:40,000)
Chart Kit: 63 (does not include north of Havener Ledge)
Maine Atlas locator map: 7

Tides (hours:minutes relative to Portland; average rise)
Waldoboro: 0:16 before; 9.5 feet
Medomak River, Jones Neck: 0:10 before; 9.1 feet
New Harbor: 0:10 before; 8.8 feet
Friendship Harbor: 0:18 before; 9.0 feet

Muscongus Bay. Ken Fink (mentioned under "The Damariscotta River") describes Muscongus Bay this way: "At the ocean end, Muscongus is a 'reverberating bay.' Large swells hit the shores between New Harbor and Pemaquid and various islands and then are strongly reflected. They interact among themselves as well as with new incoming waves. The result is very bouncy, irregular paddling conditions within 2 to 3 miles of the western side of Muscongus until you are near Hog Island. Conditions are slightly better on the eastern side of the bay near Allen Island."

Friendship Lobster Boat Race. Don't get caught in the fun (www.lobsterboatracing.com).

Access

81: Round Pond. This launch site has a small parking lot and all-tide ramp. There is a $2 launch fee per kayak; a small collection box has been set up by the ramp. From ME 32 heading south, take a left onto Back Shore Road and at the fork go right onto Anchor Inn Road. Take the first right onto Landing Road, following the SHORE ACCESS sign. Go 0.1 mile to the parking lot.

82: Broad Cove Marine. A fee of $8 per day per vehicle for parking at this marina (529-5186) gives paddlers access to an all-tide dirt ramp and a measure of reassurance. Take ME 32 from Waldoboro south for 6.9 miles, then turn left onto Medomak Road. Go 1.8 miles to Broad Cove Marine at the end of the road.

83: Dutch Neck, Medomak River. This launch site has a large, paved all-tide ramp and a large dirt parking lot. Reports of vandalism to cars parked here suggest that Broad Cove Marine may be a better place to launch. To get to the Dutch Neck ramp from Route 1 in Waldoboro, take ME 32 south for 2.7 miles to a crossroads. Take a left onto Dutch Neck Road. Proceed another 2.7 miles (staying left when the road splits) and take a left onto an unmarked road. Go 0.3 mile to the launch site.

84: Waldoboro. From the south, at the junction of Route 1 and ME 32, take ME 32 south for 0.4 mile and turn left onto West Main Street. Proceed 0.3 mile and take a right onto Pine Street. Go 0.1 mile to the town landing on the left. From the north, at the junction of Route 1 and ME 220, take ME 220 south for 0.6 mile to downtown Waldoboro. Go straight onto Main Street instead of continuing left on ME 220. Go 0.1 mile and turn left onto Pine Street. Proceed to the landing on the left.

85: Bradford Point, Friendship. Burke and Linda Lynch at Friendship Harbor House B&B allow people who are not staying at the B&B to park there for $5 per day while using the town landing 75 yards down the road. Because parking is limited, paddlers must call ahead to check on availability (832-7447).

To reach the B&B if driving on Route 1 from the south, take ME 220 to Friendship. From the point at which ME 220 becomes ME 97, go 0.2 mile northeast on ME 97 and turn right onto Bradford Point Road. (If driving on Route 1 from the north, turn onto ME 97 a few miles west of Thomaston. Proceed almost 10 miles and, as the speed limit drops to 25 mph, turn left onto Bradford Point Road.) Follow Bradford Point Road for 1.3 miles to the B&B. There is no public parking along Bradford Point Road.

Note about Friendship launch sites. Friendship has several town ramps, but the town owns only the roads to the launch sites, not land along the roads. Land along the roads is all privately owned. Therefore, there is no public parking available at any of these sites. Additionally, Friendship Harbor is a working harbor; Friendship fishermen use a private in-town site. To avoid conflicts with traditional users, please do not attempt to launch in town.

Points of Interest

Muscongus Bay. When Giovanni da Verrazano cruised from what is now Florida to Newfoundland in 1524, he described the islands of Muscongus Bay as "lying all near the land, being small and pleasant to view, high, and having many turnings and windings between them, making many fair harbors and channels, as they do in the gulf of Venice in Illyria and Dalmatia." The islands are still pleasant to view, with many fair harbors and windings between them.

Muscongus, meaning "a fishing place," may originally have referred to a specific area of good fishing but later was generalized to include the entire bay. This relatively shallow body of water provides prime habitat for lobsters, and its waters are crowded with lobster traps and lobster boats as well as pleasure craft.

Rachel Carson Salt Pond Preserve. At low tide, the bedrock here traps salt water in a large pool, creating a microsystem of marine life. Rachel Carson, who summered on Southport Island, visited this salt pond when she was writing *The Edge of the Sea*. This preserve is accessible by water in calm conditions only.

Louds Island. Originally called Muscongus, this privately owned island is supposedly the home and burial site of Samoset, a *sagamore* (a sachem or subordinate Native American leader) who lived during the 1600s.

Little Marsh Island. This 1.5-acre island, also called Thrumcap, lies off the southern tip of Marsh Island, which is itself located east of Louds. Little Marsh is part of the Maine Island Trail.

Thief Island. This 2-acre public island lies northeast of Marsh and Killick Stone Islands. There is a meadow and landing site on the northeast corner. Thief is part of the Maine Island Trail and thus is a popular destination.

Franklin Island. The U.S. Coast Guard maintains the light on Franklin, which shows from 57 feet above the water. The U.S. Fish and Wildlife Service manages the rest of the island for common eiders, black guillemots, herring and great black-backed gulls, black-crowned night herons, osprey, and Leach's storm-petrels. The island is closed from April through August.

Black and Hungry islands. In 2005, the Island Institute agreed to sell Black (southwest of Cranberry) and Hungry (east of Bremen Long) to the Chewonki Foundation. Local folks have long picnicked on both islands, and the Institute had allowed members of the Maine Island Trail Association to camp. With the transfer comes a conservation easement—held by Maine Coast Heritage Trust—to insure ongoing public access.

Black has a small but lovely beach on its north shore. Hungry has two landing areas on the southeastern side and one on the north facing Flying Passage. Hungry has old trails, some by now overtaken by poison ivy and other vegetation—let the walker beware. Chewonki has set aside a small area for its educational activities.

Killick Stone Island. A *killick* is a homemade anchor for a small boat; it is made out of a stone and sometimes enclosed in a wood framework. Killick Stone Island, southwest of Thief, is named for the many broken rocks along the shore that could be used in this way.

Todd Wildlife Sanctuary on Hog Island. Mabel Loomis Todd, an early conservationist, bought part of Hog Island to prevent it from being logged in 1909 and subsequently purchased additional parcels. Her daughter, working with the National Audubon Society, established the 330-acre Todd Wildlife Sanctuary in 1936.

Today, the National Audubon Society runs a popular Audubon Ecology Camp in Maine on Hog Island. The camp welcomes island visitors but requests that boats be kept away from the front of the dock, as Audubon folks frequently travel between the island and the mainland facilities. Sign in at the office, where you can pick up a map of the trail system.

The Sea Parrots at Eastern Egg Rock

Sea parrots are those funny little birds with white faces, black and white body plumage, orange feet, and large, triangular, orange and white bills. Properly known as Atlantic puffins, they spend most of the year far from shore but return to remote coastal areas—including a few islands in Maine—to lay their eggs and raise their young. Unlike many seabirds, which lay their eggs in the open, puffins nest in a burrow in the turf. The female sits on a single egg for about six weeks, then both parents feed the chick for another six weeks. When it comes time for the chick to fledge, the parents are long gone. The chick must fly out to sea by itself, generally under the cover of darkness, to avoid predators like gulls.

During the 1800s, puffins were easy marks for hunters, and the fact that the birds nest in colonies made it easy for egg collectors. As hunting and collecting increased, puffin numbers dropped precipitously. Even after a protective law was passed in the early 1900s, their numbers did not rebound until restoration activities were initiated.

Historically, Eastern Egg Rock was a puffin nesting area, but by 1885 herring gulls had taken over the rocky 7-acre isle. It had been years since a puffin even landed on Eastern Egg Rock when Dr. Steve Kress, of the National Audubon Society and Cornell Laboratory of Ornithology, proposed a program of restoration. Between 1973 and 1986 Kress and coworkers translocated almost 1,000 chicks from Newfoundland to Eastern Egg Rock. They also used puffin decoys and taped bird sounds to give the impression that puffins nested there. Four pairs of puffins nested in 1981, and the numbers have slowly but steadily increased to 25 pairs in 1998.

In addition, some 1,396 pairs of common terns, 144 pairs of roseate terns, 81 pairs of arctic terns, 150 pairs of black guillemots, 575 pairs of laughing gulls, 100 pairs of Leach's storm-petrels, and 25 pairs of common eiders nested on the island that year. These numbers have continued to climb. In 2004, 69 percent of the roseate terns in Maine nested on Eastern Egg.

There is a second trail on Keene Neck. Pull out at the boathouse—again keeping boats out of the way—and walk up the hill to the visitor center, where the trail begins.

The Cora Cressy. The hulk of the *Cora Cressy* lies on a reef between Oar Island and Keene Neck near the Audubon boathouse. The Percy and Small Shipyard in Bath built this five-masted schooner in 1902, at the end of the great schooner era. The ship worked in the coastal trade for many years and retired as a showboat nightclub in the 1930s. In 1938, the *Cora Cressy* was towed to the present location to serve as a lobster pound and breakwater.

Crow Island. Four-acre Crow Island, located east of Hog Island, is part of the Maine Island Trail. Expect company if you land here because this is a popular site. There are pocket beaches on the eastern and western shores.

Strawberry Island. Strawberry is a tiny public island that is part of the

The Puffin Project has changed Eastern Egg Rock from a gull-dominated rock to a highly productive seabird nesting colony. The success here prompted Kress, with help from numerous partners, to develop the Seabird Restoration Program that has since initiated other projects in Maine (on Seal Island National Wildlife Refuge, Matinicus Rock, Pond Island, Jenny Island, Outer Green Island, and Stratton Island) as well as in California, Hawaii, and Canada.

Kress and other Audubon staff continue to monitor breeding efforts on Eastern Egg Rock. Because the birds are sensitive to disturbance,

As a result of the Puffin Project, Atlantic puffins have returned to Eastern Egg Rock.
STEPHEN W. KRESS

the island is not open to unauthorized visitors, and boaters are asked to venture no nearer than lobster boats; if you are among the lobster trap buoys, you are far enough away. Terns don't exactly invite visitors anyway, as researchers can attest. Terns will dive-bomb, defecate upon, and vomit on intruders. If you want to see puffins, sign up for an Audubon-approved puffin tour out of Boothbay Harbor or New Harbor, or tune into the Audubon Web site that carries live video of puffins on Matinicus Rock (www.projectpuffin.org). The best time to watch is morning and early afternoon from June through August.

Maine Island Trail. It lies among the Long Island Ledges, which themselves lie east of Hockomock Channel next to Bremen Long Island. Strawberry is not named on the chart; look for it northeast of the word "Ledges" in "Long Island Ledges."

Havener Ledge. Two-acre Havener (two syllables with a long a) Ledge is also a state-owned island that is part of the Maine Island Trail. The 30-foot-deep channel near Havener Ledge suddenly drops to 90 feet, so this is an area of some turbulence. A small beach at the southern end makes a good landing site. The ledge is mostly rock, with some evergreens at one end and some deciduous trees at the other. Paddlers should ascend near the oak tree, taking care not to loosen soil along the bank.

Medomak River. The Medomak River estuary extends from Waldoboro through the Narrows, where it flows into Muscongus Bay. The upper stretch of the estuary has a two-layer circulation system, with freshwater on top and saltwater below, but the Medomak River provides very little freshwater flow to the system. *Medomak* means "place of many alewives."

Friendship Long Island. Granite from a quarry on the western side of the island provided building material for Grant's Tomb, the New York City Post Office, and other buildings.

Western Egg Rock, Ross Island, and part of Harbor Island. The National Audubon Society owns and manages these islands in the outer reaches of Muscongus Bay. Western Egg Rock is a rocky 7-acre island where gulls, double-crested cormorants, and other species nest. Ross Island (the Edgar B. Mulford Wildlife Sanctuary) is a 10-acre island that supports nesting common eiders, ospreys, and great horned owls. Western Egg Rock and Ross Island are closed to all visitors; the society asks boaters to stay outside the pot buoy zone. The Audubon Ecology Camp uses Ross as a field study station.

The 6-acre Duryea Morton Wildlife Sanctuary on Harbor Island is a nesting area for common eiders, gulls, sandpipers, and other birds. The Audubon Ecology Camp also uses this area as a field study station. Limited visitation is allowed, but prospective visitors must contact the Ecology Camp in advance to make arrangements (see appendix D). Boaters should go no closer than lobstermen; stay among the buoys marking lobster traps.

Wreck Island. In a December storm in 1768, the sloop *Kennebec* lost its way and foundered on this island with the loss of all hands. The island, previously called False Franklin, is presumably named for this tragedy. Great blue herons, ospreys, and eiders nest here; please note closure dates listed under *At a Glance*.

Franklin Island. Even though Franklin Island Light was the third to be built along Maine's coast—it was completed in 1808—it was 40 years too late for the *Kennebec*. The light is set in a white tower and stands 57 feet above the water.

Twelve-acre Franklin Island is owned and managed by the U.S. Fish and Wildlife Service. Over 1,300 pairs of eiders nest on Franklin, making it a significant nesting site for this species. Nesting ospreys and black-crowned night herons join the throng of eiders. The island is closed from April 1 through August 31.

At a Glance: Land in Public or Conservation Ownership

Rachel Carson Salt Pond Preserve	TNC; careful day use
Little Marsh Island	Maine Island Trail/BPL
Thief Island	Maine Island Trail/IF&W
Todd Wildlife Sanctuary	National Audubon Society; day visitation
Crow Island	Maine Island Trail/BPL

Strawberry Island	Maine Island Trail/BPL
Havener Ledge	Maine Island Trail/BPL
Hungry Island	Chewonki Foundation; careful day use
Black Island	Chewonki Foundation; careful day use
Western Egg Rock	National Audubon Society; no visitation
Ross Island	National Audubon Society; no visitation
Harbor Island (northern tip)	National Audubon Society; visitation by prior arrangement only

IF&W Wildlife Islands

These islands are closed during the indicated bird nesting season. After the nesting season is over, the islands are limited to careful day use.

New Harbor Dry Ledges (0.7 mi S of New Harbor)	April 15–July 31
Killick Stone Island (0.5 mi SW of Thief Island)	April 15–August 31
Wreck Island (1.7 mi E of Louds Island)	February 15–August 31
Wreck Island Ledge (immediately N of Wreck Island)	April 15–July 31
Jones Garden Island (1.9 mi E of Louds Island)	April 15–July 31
Crotch Islands (0.4 mi E of Hog Island)	April 15–August 31
Little Marsh Island/Thrumcap Island (S end of Marsh Island)	April 14–July 31
Gull Rock (1.1 mi W of Friendship Long Island)	April 15–July 31
Franklin Ledge (0.4 mi S of Franklin Island)	April 15–July 31
Crotch Island Ledge (0.4 mi E of N end Friendship Long Island)	April 15–July 31
Long Ledge (0.5 mi SE of Franklin Island)	April 15–July 31
Shark Island (3 mi SE of Franklin Island)	April 15–July 31
Eastern Egg Rock (2.1 mi S of Franklin Island)	Closed (see the sidebar "Sea Parrots at Egg Rock")
Old Hump Ledges (1.4 mi SE of Franklin Island)	April 15–August 31

USFWS Wildlife Islands

Franklin Island	Closed April 1–August 31

Eastern Muscongus Bay: Friendship to Port Clyde

The St. George River is the backbone of this area. The river provides very protected paddling from Warren to Thomaston, and from Thomaston south there's a protected shore to hide behind except when the wind howls straight up or down the river. The Georges Islands offer the most allure, but access is difficult and there are only a few public islands, all of which are seabird nesting sites that can be used only after July 31 or later.

Trip Ideas (weather and experience permitting)

Launch in Thomaston, paddle north to Warren, and return (12 miles round-trip). The river winds through a remarkably undeveloped stretch of salt marsh and woods; there are only a few houses between Route 1 and Warren. For the best ride, time your trip to go up on the flood tide and return with the ebb. Watch for great blue herons, ospreys, and bald eagles.

Launch in Thomaston and explore south along the St. George River, using Fort St. Georges as a destination or a snack stop (from Thomaston to Fort St. Georges and back, 7 miles; from Thomaston to the Narrows and back, 14 miles). Be warned, though, that at low tide there are extensive mudflats on either side of the channel above Broad Cove.

Venture into the Georges Islands from Port Clyde (trip length is up to you and the weather).

Charts
Chart: 13301, Muscongus Bay (1:40,000)
Chart Kit: 64 (does not include north of Route 1 in Thomaston)
Maine Atlas locator map: 8
Tides (hours:minutes relative to Portland; average rise)
Thomaston: 0:04 before Portland; 9.4 feet
Otis Cove, St. George River: 0:15 before; 9.1 feet
Port Clyde: 0:11 before; 8.9 feet
Burnt Island, Georges Islands: 0:13 before; 8.9 feet

Safety Considerations, Strong Currents, and Caution Areas

Muscongus Bay. The bay is wide open to wind, so protection along windward shores can be important when traveling here. Also see the general description of Muscongus Bay in the safety section under "Western Muscongus Bay."

Mosquito Head. See *Safety Considerations* in "Tenants Harbor to Owls Head."

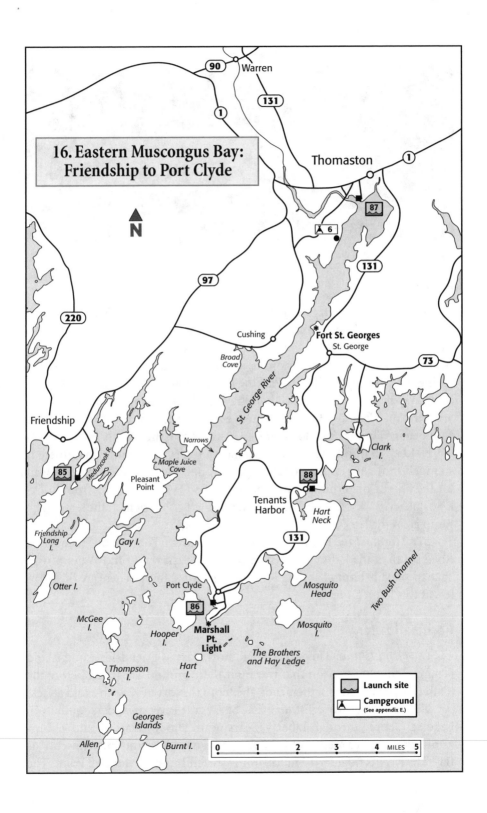

16. Eastern Muscongus Bay: Friendship to Port Clyde

N

Warren
90
131
1

Thomaston
1
87
△ 6
131
97
220
Cushing
Fort St. Georges
St. George
73
Broad Cove
St. George River
Friendship
Narrows
Maple Juice Cove
85
Meduncook R.
Pleasant Point
88
Clark I.
Tenants Harbor
Hart Neck
Friendship Long I.
Gay I.
131
Otter I.
Port Clyde
Mosquito Head
Two Bush Channel
McGee I.
86
Hooper I.
Marshall Pt. Light
Mosquito I.
The Brothers and Hay Ledge
Thompson I.
Hart I.
Georges Islands
Allen I.
Burnt I.

| Launch site |
| Campground |
(See appendix E.)

0   1   2   3   4 MILES 5

The boat ramp at Port Clyde

Access

85: Bradford Point, Friendship. See Access in "Western Muscongus Bay."

86: Port Clyde. Although Port Clyde does have an all-tide ramp, it is less than ideal for sea kayakers. Port Clyde has a busy working harbor that is even busier during the summer months when the town is packed with visitors taking the ferry to Monhegan. Parking is at an absolute premium; you'll find no free spaces. (In years past, there has been vandalism at public parking areas in Port Clyde.) Call ahead to make parking arrangements through the Monhegan-Thomaston Boat Line (372-8848) or the Ocean House (372-6691). Keep in mind that even if you have a reserved parking space, there is so much traffic that it is difficult to get through town easily. Better yet, wait for the off-season. From Thomaston, take ME 131 to its end (or, from Rockland, take ME 73 south until it joins ME 131), turning right at the water. The ramp is on the left.

87: Thomaston. From Route 1 in downtown Thomaston, take Knox Road south at the light, go down the hill, and turn right onto Water Street. Take the next left onto Landing Road to the all-tide ramp. There are flush toilets at this launch site.

Points of Interest

Garrison Island. This small island northeast of Friendship Long Island is named for the garrison that was built there around 1754, just before the Sixth Indian War. Area settlers took shelter in the fort in 1758 to avoid attack.

The St. George River Estuary. The St. George River meanders south from Lake St. George through Liberty, Searsmont, Union, Warren, and Thomaston, where it broadens until it flows past Port Clyde and into Muscongus Bay. The river is tidal for 15 miles, from Warren south to Marshall Point. The salt marshes and intertidal flats in the estuary are important as waterfowl, osprey, wading-bird, and shorebird feeding areas. James Rosier, who accompanied George Weymouth, wrote of the St. George River (and in the spelling of the day), "heere are more good harbours for ships of all burthens. . . . And on both sides every halfe mile very gallant Coves. . . ."

Thomaston. In the 1800s, the major industries in Thomaston were building ships, processing lime to make plaster, and engaging in other aspects of the maritime trade. Today Dragon Cement, using limestone from nearby quarries, is a large employer. Fossils found in the quarries show that this part of Maine was once attached to Europe.

Fort St. Georges. The point 3 miles south of Thomaston has a commanding view of the St. George River, so it was a logical place for a fort. Fort St. Georges was built in the early 1700s and withstood attack during the Fifth Indian War, which ran from 1745 to 1749. Not much remains except earthworks.

Only gulls can find a place to park in Port Clyde Harbor.

Broad Cove on the St. George. In the 1740s and 1750s—and despite the Indian Wars convulsing Maine's coast—Samuel Waldo convinced German families from the Rhineland to settle in this cove along the St. George.

The Georges Islands. In 1605 the English mariner George Weymouth reached Monhegan Island and then sailed north to a chain of islands. He anchored in what he called Pentecost Harbor, now Georges Harbor, just north of Allen Island. Weymouth explored Muscongus Bay for seven weeks and met Native Americans who lived there. Just before leaving, he kidnapped five of them to take back to England and show off as noble "selvages" of the new land. Although several eventually returned to their homeland, the incident put a sour cast on subsequent interactions between Indians and the English.

A lifesaving station was built on Burnt Island in 1892 and a tower added during Prohibition so that the crew could watch for rum smugglers. The station closed in 1972. The Hurricane Island Outward Bound School currently leases the island for use in its programs.

Blubber Island. There was little whaling in Maine. Only one ship each set out from Portland, Wiscasset, Bath, and Bucksport for deepwater whales in far parts of the world. Records show that shore whaling took place on

Mount Desert Island, Winter Harbor, and Prospect Harbor, but there must have been some additional activity because Blubber Island, north of Hooper Island, was once the site of a *tryworks*—a furnace with large pots used to extract whale oil from blubber.

Marshall Point Light. Marshall Point marks the eastern edge of Muscongus Bay. The white tower, built in 1832, shows a light that stands 30 feet above water. The town of St. George now operates the Marshall Point Lighthouse Museum (372-6450).

Hart Island. The U.S. Fish and Wildlife Service owns this 13-acre island, which is located about a mile south of Marshall Point Light. The island is closed for common eider and other nesting birds from April through August.

The Brothers and Hay Ledge Preserve. These Nature Conservancy islands, which provide nesting habitat for black guillemots, double-crested cormorants, common eiders, herring gulls, and great black-backed gulls, are closed during the nesting season (March 15 through August 15). Historically, laughing gulls, common terns, and arctic terns also nested here. There is a landing site on the north shore of Big Brother.

At a Glance: Land in Public or Conservation Ownership

Fort St. Georges Historic Site	BPL; day visitation
The Brothers and Hay Ledge Preserve	TNC; closed March 15–August 15; after that time, careful day use

IF&W Wildlife Islands

These islands are closed during the indicated bird nesting season. After the nesting season is over, the islands are limited to careful day use.

Gunning Rocks (1.1 mi SE of Port Clyde)	April 15–July 31
Shag Ledges (2.8 mi N of Burnt Island)	April 15–July 31
Little Burnt Island (immediately N of Burnt Island)	April 15–July 31

USFWS Wildlife Islands

Hart Island	April 1–August 31

Tenants Harbor to Owls Head

The highlight of this section of the coast is the Muscle Ridge chain, a beautiful archipelago that lies off Spruce Head. With cooperative weather, a trip to these islands makes a rewarding day excursion. For a shorter and more protected trip, explore the Weskeag River (high tide, please, to miss the mudflats) or the islands outside Tenants Harbor. Ugly chop can form at Mosquito

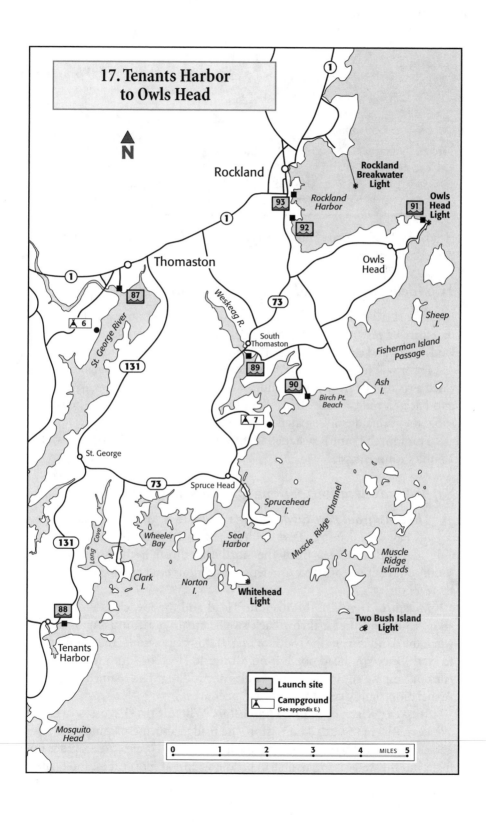

17. Tenants Harbor to Owls Head

N

Rockland

Rockland
Breakwater
Light

93

*Rockland
Harbor*

91 Owls
Head
Light

92

1

Thomaston

Owls
Head

*Sheep
I.*

87

Weskeag R.

73

*Fisherman Island
Passage*

6

St. George River

South
Thomaston

131

89

90

*Birch Pt.
Beach*

*Ash
I.*

7

St. George

131

73

Spruce Head

*Sprucehead
I.*

Muscle Ridge Channel

*Wheeler
Bay*

*Seal
Harbor*

*Muscle
Ridge
Islands*

Long Cove

*Clark
I.*

*Norton
I.*

**Whitehead
Light**

**Two Bush Island
Light**

88

Tenants
Harbor

☐ Launch site

⛺ Campground
(See appendix E.)

*Mosquito
Head*

0   1   2   3   4   MILES 5

> ### Charts
> *Charts:* 13301, Muscongus Bay (1:40,000)
>   13305, Penobscot Bay (1:40,000)
> *Chart Kit:* 64, 65
> *Maine Atlas locator map:* 8
>
> **Tides** (hours:minutes relative to Portland; average rise)
> *Tenants Harbor:* 0:11 before; 9.3 feet
> *Dyer Point, Weskeag River:* 0:10 before; 9.6 feet
> *Owls Head:* 0:16 before; 9.4 feet

Head, south of Tenants Harbor, so caution is advised when paddling along that section of the coast.

Trip Ideas (weather and experience permitting)

For a short trip from Tenants Harbor, investigate Long Cove and the islands that form its eastern border (5 or 6 miles). For a longer paddle, explore the islands north and east to Whitehead Island (9 to 10 miles, depending on route).

For a wildlife tour of the R. Waldo Tyler Wildlife Management Area, catch a rising tide from South Thomaston and paddle up the Weskeag River and back (3 miles round-trip). Plan to launch near the top of the tide to avoid the reversing falls created by the bridge abutments.

From Birch Point Beach, paddle through the Muscle Ridge Islands (8 to 10 miles round-trip).

Safety Considerations, Strong Currents, and Caution Areas

The coast from Port Clyde to Owls Head. (See Map 16, "Eastern Muscongus Bay: Friendship to Port Clyde.") This portion of the coast is vulnerable to wind and seas from the northeast through the southeast and southwest. Waiting for stable, moderate conditions is advisable for trips along this section.

Mosquito Head. Both Mosquito Head and the low cliffs that line the shore to the northeast throw back swells, creating a confusing backchop when the wind is from the south or east. If things go wrong, there is no place to land. Once you head north from Mosquito Head or south from Tenants Harbor, you are committed to 2.5 miles of paddling. The Maine Island Trail Association rightly considers this a danger area.

Weskeag River at South Thomaston. Where ME 73 crosses over the Weskeag River at South Thomaston, the bridge abutments pinch the river and cause the formation of a rapid during both tidal cycles. The rapid is not huge, but the water is impossible to paddle against at most times, and boaters unaccustomed to fast water may not feel comfortable paddling with the current when it is running at maximum velocity at midcycle.

Muscle Ridge Channel. A fast current here runs northeast on the rising tide and southwest on the ebbing tide.

Fisherman Island Passage. This passage has a strong southwesterly current on the ebb tide.

A herring gull speaks its mind.

Access

88: Tenants Harbor. The all-tide concrete ramp at the Tenants Harbor launch site is well protected except from an eastern wind, which can create a chop in the harbor. From Rockland, take ME 73 south until it ends in St. George or, from Thomaston, take ME 131 to St. George. Continue south on ME 131 to Tenants Harbor. Turn left onto Commercial Street and go down the hill to the public boat access site; there is a portable toilet on the right. Parking on the wharf is for 4 hours only. If the wharf is full or if you plan to be out more than the allotted time, unload boats and gear, return to ME 131, go left for a short distance, turn left again on School Street, and park in the lot at the town office (372-6363) on the right. This lot is available all year except for the third week in July, when the town celebrates St. George Days. Please choose a parking spot at the opposite end of the lot from the building. The town office is within a quarter of a mile of the launch site.

89: South Thomaston. The concrete launch ramp onto the Weskeag River has water except when the tide is dead low. From Rockland, follow ME 73 south to South Thomaston. Or, from Thomaston, follow Route 1 east of the town and turn south on Buttermilk Lane just east of Dragon Cement; take a right at ME 73 and proceed for less than a mile to South Thomaston.

90: Birch Point Beach State Park. This is a beach recreation area, but you may launch your kayak as long as you are careful of sunbathers and swimmers. There is no launch ramp, so hand carry from the parking lot to the water. Although the parking area is large, it rapidly fills up on busy summer days. There is an outhouse by the parking lot. The park is open from 9 AM to sunset, and a gate at the entrance means that returning late has a consequence.

Take ME 73 to where it crosses the Weskeag. Go east on Dublin Road for 1.4 miles and turn right on Ballyhoc Road. Go 0.7 mile and turn left into the park. (Or, also coming from the north on ME 73, turn onto North Shore Drive as if going to the Owls Head State Park, but take the first right onto

The Country of the Pointed Firs

"There was something about the coast town of Dunnett which made it seem more attractive than other maritime villages of eastern Maine." Thus Maine author Sarah Orne Jewett begins *The Country of the Pointed Firs* (1896), a book inspired by the author's visits to Tenants Harbor and nearby Martinsville. The fictional Dunnett is a pastoral village of the late 1800s, a place removed from the grime, dislocation, and confusion of the industrial age. The friendships the book's narrator makes with people are like the relationship she develops with Dunnett Harbor itself:

> *Perhaps it was the simple fact of acquaintance with that neighborhood which made it so attaching, and gave such interest to the rocky shore and dark woods, the few houses which seemed to be securely wedged and tree-nailed in among the ledges by the Landing. These houses made the most of their seaward view, and there was a gayety and determined flow-eriness in their bits of garden ground; the small-paned high windows in the peaks of their steep gables were like knowing eyes that watched the harbor and the far sea-line beyond, or looked northward all along the shore and its background of spruces and balsam firs. When one really knows a village like this and its surroundings, it is like becoming ac-quainted with a single person. The process of falling in love at first sight is as final as it is swift in such a case, but the growth of true friendship may be a life-long affair.*

Jewett's longing for a simpler, more intimate time resonates even today. And when the sun begins to penetrate the cool veil of fog that lies thick on the harbor on a quiet August morning, the dark pointed treetops appear as reminders of Dunnett Harbor and a time long ago.

The joy of off-season paddling: a cove of your own (here, Birch Point Beach)

Ash Point Drive, cutting across the head of the peninsula and passing the Knox County Airport. Take a right onto Dublin Road and proceed to Ballyhac Road.) In either case, stay left at each fork, following the signs to the park.

91: Owls Head Light State Park. This access site stretches the limit of "hand carry," so launch from here only if you're ready for a 200-yard haul.

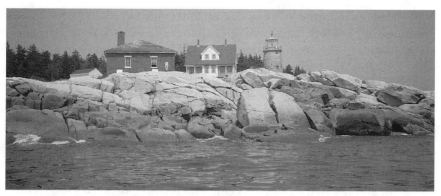

Whitehead Light

The Rockland ramp is only 3 miles away, so it's hard to get too excited about putting in here. To get to the park from Rockland, take ME 73 south about 1.5 miles and turn left on North Shore Drive at the sign for Owls Head Light State Park. Proceed 2.6 miles and turn left onto Main Street at another state park sign. Take a left onto Lighthouse Road and follow it 0.7 mile to the park and Coast Guard station.

Points of Interest

Whitehead Light. The white rock of Whitehead Island was a landmark for seafarers entering or leaving the Muscle Ridge Channel long before the light was established in 1807. A lifesaving station followed in 1874 and operated for 80 years, its crews helping not only mariners in distress but also looking for rum smugglers during Prohibition and enemy vessels during World War II. The 41-foot gray tower holds its light 75 feet above water.

Long Cove and Seal Harbor. High, Clark, Rackliff, Spruce Head, and other areas along this part of the coast were quarried for ornamental and paving granite. Quarries on Clark Island operated for about a hundred years, beginning in the 1830s.

Tommy's Island. This tiny isle, so small that it doesn't have an official name, has long been a popular local picnicking area. It was one of the Georges River Land Trust's first purchases. Tommy's is in Long Cove, west of Clark Island (check your chart) and is mired in mud at low water.

Weskeag River. *Weskeag* is shortened from *wessaweskeag*, which means "tidal river." At the head of the Weskeag lies the R. Waldo Tyler Wildlife Management Area, a 618-acre tract that Maine's Department of Inland Fisheries and Wildlife manages for waterfowl.

The area has gained new life in the last several years. In the 1800s farmers dug wide ditches to drain the marsh so they could cut salt marsh hay for their cattle. A hundred years later, a second round of ditching took place for mosquito control. These activities changed the marsh's ecology, eliminating diversity. Between 1998 and 2001, wildlife managers used new technology to plug the ditches, restore the water table, and lure back species that had long been absent.

Birders will find plenty to see here. During the spring and summer, look for great blue herons, snowy egrets, glossy ibis, and other waders. During spring and fall migrations, Canada geese, mallards, wood ducks, American black ducks, ring-necked ducks, blue-winged teal, green-winged teal, northern pintails, buffleheads, American wigeons, and common, red-breasted, and hooded mergansers come through, as do a variety of shorebirds. Birds of prey including northern harriers, ospreys, American kestrels, red-tailed hawks, and even eagles hunt in the marsh. (Human hunters also hunt here during the fall hunting season; see page 20.)

Birch Point Beach. This pretty state park has a fringing pocket beach with a small freshwater marsh squeezed between the upper rocky ridge and the upland. Otter Point and Birch Point, the rocky headlands, are composed of granite with flecks of black mica and light mica. Common eiders and black guillemots often ride the waves offshore.

Muscle Ridge Islands. "Muscle" is an obscure English variant of "mussel," so the name rightly refers to the blue mussel beds among the islands and not a workout at the gym. This group of islands is, quite simply, stunning. The water is clear and the cottages few. Expect company out here; it's a favorite spot for sailors and powerboaters.

The Muscle Ridge Islands are a mecca for wildlife. The islands and ledges provide prime habitat for harbor seals—about 10 percent of the seals in the Gulf of Maine make this area their home. Gray seals also show up here upon occasion. In early summer, female common eiders watch over nursery groups of young. Throughout the summer, osprey soar and hover overhead, eyeing the prey below. Herring and great black-backed gulls can be seen dropping bivalves onto ledges, breaking the shells so that the tasty contents are more accessible.

Dix, High, and Hewett were all quarrying islands, but Dix was home to the largest enterprise by far. After the Civil War, the widow Mrs. Horace Beals secured contracts for high-quality finished granite, notably for the New York City Post Office. At the peak of operations, almost 2,000 workers lived on the island and worked in one of the eight quarries. There were two gargantuan boardinghouses—Shamrock House accommodated 500 Irish stonecutters, while Aberdeen House accommodated 500 Scot stonecutters—as well as many smaller facilities. The island even boasted an opera house that could seat 450 people. But the granite industry went bust, and in the early 1880s workers fled the island. By 1900, only two families lived on Dix. A large granite wharf, giving mute testimony to an era gone by, remains on the eastern shore. High Island also has a large granite wharf, on its southwest corner.

Two Bush Island. The U.S. Fish and Wildlife Service manages this 8-acre island at the southern end of the Muscle Ridge chain for nesting seabirds. The Coast Guard owns the island and operates Two Bush Island Light. The square white tower, which began operating in 1897, shows a light 65 feet above the water.

Owls Head Light. "Owls Head" is the English translation of a Native American place-name. As seen from the north, the peninsula is supposed to look like the head of an owl. Although the light tower at Owls Head is only 20 feet high, the headland raises the light so that it stands 100 feet above the water. The white conical tower and light were built in 1825.

Owls Head Light State Park. The park is at the same location as the light and is jointly administered by the Maine Bureau of Parks and Lands and the Coast Guard. One path leads to a gravel swimming beach located immediately west of Owls Head Light; the beach has picnic tables and outhouses. Another trail leads from the parking lot past the keeper's dwelling (yes, people live there and no, it is not open to the public) and on to the light, which people may visit. Owls Head Light State Park is open from 9 AM to sunset. There is no entrance fee.

At a Glance: Land in Public or Conservation Ownership

Tommy's Island	Georges River Land Trust; careful day use
Birch Point Beach	Maine Island Trail/BPL; may launch carefully (swimming beach)
Two Bush Island	USFWS; closed April 1–August 31
Owls Head Light State Park	BPL; may carefully launch or visit from water (swimming beach)
R. Waldo Tyler Wildlife Management Area	IF&W; careful day use only

IF&W Wildlife Islands

These islands are closed during the indicated bird nesting season. After the nesting season is over, the islands are limited to careful day use.

Seal Island (immediately NE of Whitehead Island)	April 15–July 31
Yellow Ridge Island (0.7 mi E of Whitehead Island)	April 15–July 31
Garden Island (0.7 mi NE of Sprucehead Island)	April 15–July 31

USFWS Wildlife Island

Two Bush Island	April 1–August 31

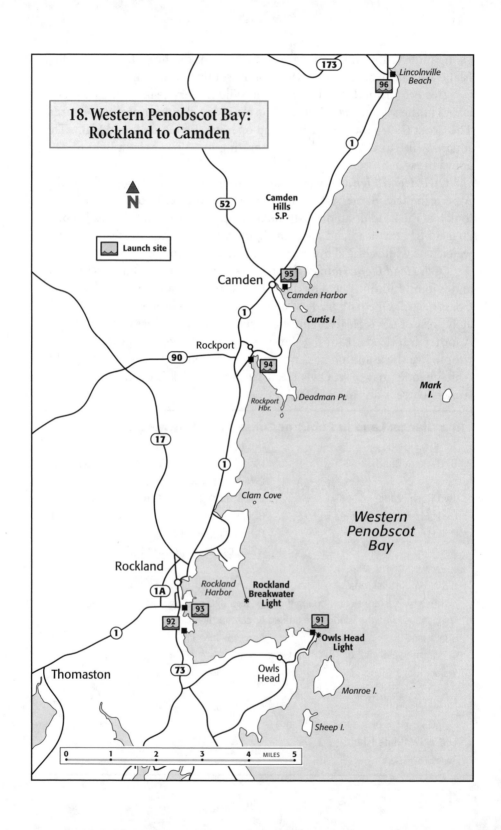

18. Western Penobscot Bay: Rockland to Camden

N

Launch site

173

96 Lincolnville Beach

1

52

Camden Hills S.P.

Camden

95

Camden Harbor

Curtis I.

1

Rockport

90

94

Rockport Hbr.

Deadman Pt.

Mark I.

17

1

Clam Cove

Western Penobscot Bay

Rockland

1A

Rockland Harbor

Rockland Breakwater Light *

93

91

Owls Head Light *

92

1

73

Owls Head

Monroe I.

Thomaston

Sheep I.

0   1   2   3   4   MILES   5

4.
Penobscot Bay

Western Penobscot Bay: Rockland to Camden

Native Americans called Lermond Cove, a section of Rockland Harbor, the Great Landing Place because it was a hub for travel in western Penobscot Bay. By landing at Lermond Cove and traveling overland to the St. George River, they avoided the more difficult trip around Owls Head and Port Clyde.

Today, Rockland still serves as a major harbor. Although the lime and fish-processing industries have given way to more genteel commerce, and tourism is gaining a place as an important part of the economy, Rockland retains its working waterfront. Both the North Haven and the Vinalhaven ferries dock here.

Camden, a picture postcard town with its hills as a backdrop, wooden schooners in the harbor, and Curtis Island at the harbor's mouth, has long been a mecca for tourists and summer people. Half a dozen windjammers—refitted cargo and fishing schooners—take visitors on half-day, full-day, or multiday trips to see the splendors of Penobscot Bay.

Trip Ideas (weather and experience permitting)

Put in at one of the Rockland launch sites and tour the perimeter of Rockland Harbor (6 miles) or paddle east to Owls Head (6 miles round-trip), where you can stop at a gravel beach that is part of Owls Head Light State Park; be careful when landing, as it is also a swimming beach.

Camden's inner harbor is packed with boats and people, but if you have patience (and if you can stay out of the way of vessels in transit), you may enjoy threading through the moored boats to the head of the harbor, where

---

Charts
Charts: 13305, Penobscot Bay (1:40,000)
          13307, Camden, Rockport, and Rockland Harbors (1:20,000)
Chart Kit: 65, 68A, 20
Maine Atlas locator map: 14
Tides (hours:minutes relative to Portland; average rise)
Rockland: 0:08 before; 9.8 feet
Camden: 0:12 before; 9.6 feet

Andre, who used to live and perform in Rockport's harbor, immortalized the boat launch.

the Megunticook River tumbles down a stair-step waterfall (2 miles includes a tour of the inner harbor and Curtis Island).

For point-to-point or round trips, use these one-way numbers: from Rockland to Rockport, 8 miles; from Rockland to Camden, 10 miles; from Rockport to Camden, 5 miles.

Safety Considerations, Strong Currents, and Caution Areas

Exposure. The launch site in Camden's outer harbor is open to the east, so wind and waves from that direction can make launching difficult. Except for the harbors, the shoreline from Rockland to Lincolnville is fairly straight and is vulnerable to wind from the northeast, southeast, and southwest.

Access

91: Owls Head Light State Park. See Access in "Tenants Harbor to Owls Head."

92: Snow Marine Park, Rockland. Snow Marine Park has an all-tide ramp, a large parking lot, and a portable toilet. There is no charge for hand-carried boats. To get to the park from downtown Rockland, take ME 73 south 0.7 mile, then turn left onto Mechanic Street at the PUBLIC BOAT LAUNCH sign. Proceed a short distance to the park on the right.

93: The Waterfront, Rockland. Technically, the tiny, unattractive ramp wedged into the waterfront is available to kayakers, but the ramp at Snow Marine Park is so much better (more parking, less boat traffic) that it's hard to see why anyone would want to launch here.

Nevertheless, if you are determined to put in your boat here, travel north on Route 1 into Rockland. (Traveling south, stay on Route 1 into Rockland—do not take Route 1A—and continue south on Union Street. Take a left on Route 1/Park Street.) From either direction, take a right on ME 73 instead of turning left onto Main Street. Turn left immediately into a large parking lot. The ramp is on the left just beyond a restaurant; there are bathrooms in the building to the right that houses the Chamber of Commerce and harbor master. Park carefully, as there are various designated time limits (and if you exceed them, you will get a parking ticket). During various festivals on the waterfront, parking is at a premium and Snow Park looks even more attractive.

94: Rockport. The town has built a new harbor master's office (with flush toilets, a laundry room, and showers), added a small beach for hand-carry boats, enlarged the parking lot, and generally transformed a formerly drab corner of the harbor into an appealing little park—complete with a sculpture of Andre the seal. The launch fee is still $1 for Rockport residents and $2 for nonresidents; put the green stuff in a collection can located at the front of the parking lot or hand it over to the harbor master on the way to the bathroom.

To get to the marine park from the junction of Route 1 and ME 90, go east on West Street (the apparent extension of ME 90). In 0.3 mile turn left on Pascals and after another 0.3 mile, turn right at the PUBLIC BOAT ACCESS sign onto Andre Street. You may launch at the ramp to the left or the beach behind the office, but on weekends you'll appreciate the beach, which gets much less traffic.

95: Camden. Although there is a town dock in Camden's inner harbor, it is not an optimal place to launch kayaks. Parking is limited to 2 hours, and the inner harbor is very crowded. There is, however, an all-tide ramp on Sea Street that overlooks the outer harbor. From the blinking yellow light at the junction of Route 1 and ME 52, go north on Route 1 for 0.1 mile and turn right on Sea Street. Go 0.3 mile onto Sea (this includes a left turn) and turn right onto Steamboat Landing Drive. There is room for only a few vehicles at the launch site. Spillover parking on Avey Avenue is within easy walking distance. Go back to Sea Street and take a right. The road will curve to the left; the lot is on the left.

Points of Interest

Rockland Harbor. In the harbor, look for ring-billed, Bonaparte's, and laughing gulls. Beyond the breakwater, keep an eye out for double-crested cormorants, great blue herons, laughing gulls, common terns, bald eagles, common eiders, and black guillemots.

Maine Lighthouse Museum. In 2005, the museum moved into its own quarters and opened its doors on Park Drive—downtown—even before it was finished. The official opening is scheduled for 2006. If you are a lighthouse buff, check the hours and see what's on display (www.mainelight housemuseum.com or 594-3301).

Rockland breakwater. The granite breakwater that protects Rockland Harbor, begun in 1888 and completed in 1902, stretches out from Jameson Point for 0.7 mile. After each segment was completed, the navigation light

Rockland Breakwater Light with the Camden Hills in the background

was moved southward. The present light was built in 1902 and renovated in 1990. The square white tower shows a light 39 feet above water. The 17-foot wide breakwater is open to the public as a park.

Rockport Harbor. This harbor was once a center for the lime industry. Lime was shipped from nearby quarries on a narrow-gauge railroad to large ovens that baked the lime so that it could be used in cement. Paddlers who launch from the boat ramp can see a lime kiln and a steam locomotive left over from the heyday of this industry. Indian Island Light, situated at the eastern entrance to the harbor, is privately owned and no longer functions as a navigational aid.

Camden Harbor. The focus in Rockport and Camden is definitely on the summer trade. The harbors of both towns are full of pleasure craft, and Camden is home to a small fleet of schooners dating to the late 1800s. The beautiful lines and bold sails of these windjammers allow modern mariners to catch a glimpse of the era when wind prevailed.

The Megunticook River, which flows into Camden Harbor, teems with elvers in the spring. Elvers are baby eels that migrate from the Sargasso Sea to the Megunticook and other rivers along the North Atlantic. Because eels are prized in Asian cuisine, an elver fishery has developed in the Megunticook and other small rivers and streams along Maine's coast. The inch-long eels are caught in nets stretched across the mouth of each river and then shipped live to Asia to be raised until they are adults. The fishery has fluctuated according to the economy in the Far East and elver stocks.

Curtis Island. When a pair of bald eagles moved onto Curtis Island at the mouth of Camden Harbor, suddenly everything changed. From the beginning of March through mid-July, boaters can neither visit Curtis nor paddle within 300 feet of its shore. In years that the eagles are not rearing young, the island will be opened. In either case, look for a prominent sign at the small landing site on the western end of the island. (Caretakers are allowed on the island, so human presence does not mean that you can land.)

Curtis Island is named after Cyrus Curtis, a philanthropist and publisher of *The Saturday Evening Post.* A light tower and keeper's house are located on the southeast end. The light was established in 1836 and rebuilt several times. Even when the island is open to visitors, the light and house are not.

Camden Hills. The hills of Camden provide a scenic backdrop for the busy harbor. Mount Battie, which has a stone tower on its summit, stands not far from the head of the inner harbor. Mount Megunticook, behind Battie, presents a long, flat profile. At 1,385 feet, Megunticook may not be high by mountain standards, but it is the second highest point—after Cadillac Mountain at Acadia—on the Atlantic coast. The name, which is thought to mean "big mountain harbor," originally referred to the harbor and only later was generalized to the mountain and river as well.

Edna St. Vincent Millay, a Pulitzer prize–winning poet, loved to climb in the Camden hills. She started "Renascence," one of her best-known poems, with a description of the view from the summit of Mount Battie. Her "three long mountains" are likely Megunticook, Ragged, and Bald. And her "three islands in a bay"? They are perhaps Islesboro, North Haven, and Vinalhaven.

Mark Island. Mark Island, which lies 5 miles southeast of Camden, is a Nature Conservancy preserve. The 36-acre sanctuary provides habitat for ospreys and other birds; historically, great blue herons nested here. The island was never settled, perhaps because it lacks a good harbor and has little level ground. There are no trails. The island is closed to visitors from February 15 through August 15, the duration of the nesting season.

At a Glance: Land in Public or Conservation Ownership

Curtis Island	Town of Camden; closed March 1–July 15; after that time, careful day use
Mark Island	TNC; closed February 15–August 15; after that time, careful day use

IF&W Wildlife Islands

This island is closed during the indicated bird nesting season. After the nesting season is over, the island is limited to careful day use.

Goose Rocks (E of Rockport)	April 15–July 31

Northern Penobscot Bay: Lincolnville to Belfast Bay

Between Camden and Lincolnville, the coast is rocky and uninviting. Indeed, the Native American name for Lincolnville, *Mag-win'-teg-wak*, means "choppy seas," and locales in Northport have names such as Great Spruce Head, Temple Heights, and Bluff Shore Road. Captain John Smith, sailing through this area in the early 1600s, got the terrain right when he noted the "high Mountains of Pennobscot, against whose feet doth beat the sea." The high mountains are the Camden Hills, and their feet form the uncompromising shoreline north toward Belfast, against which the sea does beat.

Trip Ideas (weather and experience permitting)

With favorable weather, launch from Lincolnville and circumnavigate Warren Island and Seven Hundred Acre Island (10 miles). If you have a yearning to stop in Islesboro, there is a town launch ramp just east of the ferry dock on Grindel Point. Otherwise, Warren Island, a state park, provides an agreeable lunch site; take money for the day-use fee.

The Passagassawakeag River winds its way south from Lake Passagassawakeag in Brooks to Belfast Bay. The tidal section offers protected paddling along surprisingly undeveloped shores (about 6 miles round-trip from Belfast). Start when a rising tide is near its height to get the most water, and watch for ospreys and bald eagles along the way.

For a point-to-point trip between Lincolnville and Belfast, spot a car in one place and launch from the other (12 miles). You could head in the other direction, from Lincolnville to Camden (6 miles one-way), but this option is less inviting because the shore does not have as much variety.

Safety Considerations, Strong Currents, and Caution Areas

Exposure. The launch sites in Lincolnville and Belfast are largely exposed to winds from the east. The rocky shore between Camden and Lincolnville and the high bluffs of Northport offer few landing sites.

Charts
Chart: 13309, Penobscot River (1:40,000)
Chart Kit: 20, 66
Maine Atlas locator map: 14

Tides (hours:minutes relative to Portland; average rise)
Belfast: 0:08 before; 10.0 feet

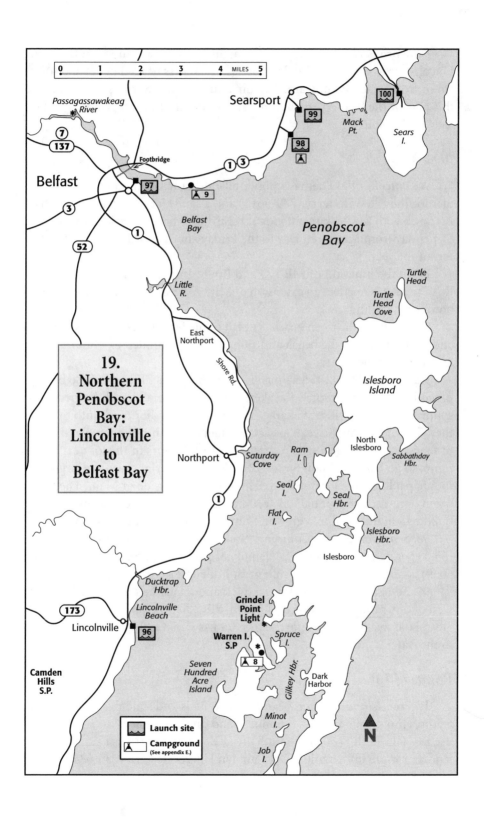

0   1   2   3   4 MILES 5

Passagassawakeag
River

Searsport

100

99

Mack
Pt.

Sears
I.

7
137

Footbridge

98

1 3

Belfast

97

9

3

Belfast
Bay

Penobscot
Bay

1

52

Little
R.

Turtle
Head

Turtle
Head
Cove

East
Northport

Shore Rd.

19.
Northern
Penobscot
Bay:
Lincolnville
to
Belfast Bay

Islesboro
Island

Northport

Saturday
Cove

Ram
I.

North
Islesboro

Sabbathday
Hbr.

1

Seal
I.

Seal
Hbr.

Flat
I.

Islesboro
Hbr.

Islesboro

Ducktrap
Hbr.

173

Lincolnville
Beach

Grindel
Point
Light

96

Lincolnville

Warren I.
S.P

Spruce
I.

Camden
Hills
S.P.

Seven
Hundred
Acre
Island

8

Gilkey Hbr.

Dark
Harbor

Minot
I.

Launch site

Campground
(See appendix E.)

Job
I.

N

Islesboro Ferry. The ferry runs straight across West Penobscot Bay from Lincolnville to Grindel Point. Freighters and tankers headed north and south (to or from Mack Point Cargo Terminal in Stockton Springs) also travel in this part of the bay. When crossing, stay well out of the ferry's path and be alert for big ships.

Access

96: Lincolnville. There is a public all-tide launch ramp just north of the pier for the Islesboro ferry (789-5611) and a sandy launch area just south of it. Check with the parking attendant regarding where to park; parking costs $7 per day from Memorial Day to the Friday after Labor Day and is free the rest of the year.

From the junction of ME 173 and Route 1 in Lincolnville, take McKay Road (which is in effect an extension of ME 173) a short distance to the Islesboro ferry landing.

The Lincolnville town beach is north of the ferry terminal. Between 7 AM and 5 PM, parking at the beach and along Route 1 is limited to 4 hours. There are portable toilets here.

97: Belfast. The all-tide launch ramp in Belfast is a busy place, so be prepared to unload promptly. Kayakers can use the small beach immediately south of the ramp without charge. Take any of the major roads into the city; they all lead to Main Street. Go east on Main Street through town and down to the waterfront. Parking is restricted to 1 or 2 hours in the lot next to the ramp, so go back up Main Street 0.1 mile and turn right into the large, free municipal lot; there is another free lot on the other side of Main. The bathrooms are located about 100 feet up the hill from the harbor master's building, on the right in a gray building next to the boat access sign.

98: Searsport Shores Camping. Nonpatrons may launch from the beach ($5.00 per person, subject to availability of parking). The campground (548-6059) is on the right about 5 miles east of Belfast on Route 1.

99: Searsport. Searsport has a dock and an asphalt all-tide ramp. Just west of downtown, traveling on Route 1/ME 3 in Searsport, turn south onto Steamboat Avenue at the PUBLIC BOAT ACCESS sign. Go 0.3 mile down the hill to the water.

Points of Interest

Warren Island. Warren Island is the only island state park in Maine. It features trails, a picnic area, outhouses, and campsites; there is a modest day-use fee. The landing site is about halfway down the northeast side of the island. For more information, call Camden Hills State Park (236-0849).

Grindel Point Light on Islesboro. This light marks the entrance to Gilkey Harbor. It was built in 1851, rebuilt in 1874, deactivated in 1934, and reactivated in 1987.

Belfast. Belfast has gone through several incarnations. In the early 1800s it was a bustling shipping port, and in the 1900s it became a major chicken processing center. As waste material from the poultry plants was discharged directly into the harbor, water quality plummeted. With the closing of those plants in the 1970s and the recent opening of a huge credit card service center (and the attendant rise in employment), Belfast has reinvented itself once more. The cleaned-up harbor is home to fishing boats as well as a growing number of recreational vessels.

If you are paddling in Belfast Harbor and are enveloped by a large bubble with a foul smell, don't panic. The bottom of the harbor is the site of craters thought to be created during the process of anaerobic decomposition. The theory is that large deposits of some kind—perhaps peat from a time when the sea level was lower, or sawdust discarded from area mills over the years—lie below the mud in the harbor. As this material decomposes, it releases hydrogen sulfide and methane. Every now and then, bubbles of these gases burst from the mud, creating pits, and rise to the surface. Most of the pits are less than 500 feet in diameter and 50 feet deep.

The Footbridge. After years of neglect, the crumbling footbridge over the Passagassawakeag River has been transformed into a safe pedestrian walkway.

The Passagassawakeag River. The name of this river is a Maliseet word meaning "sturgeon's place" or "place for spearing sturgeon by torchlight." Traditionally, Native Americans used bonfires on the shore and birchbark torches to blind sturgeon to spear them. The area at the river's mouth came to be known for the great fish that lived there.

The Passagassawakeag River estuary is only 3 miles long, starting from the head of tide beyond City Point and ending in Belfast Bay. The water is stratified above the Route 1 bridge, with freshwater on top and saltwater below.

The Coastal Mountains Land Trust is the owner of two properties—the Knowlton-Swanson-Stephenson (KSS) Preserve and the Stover Preserve—that are part of a projected greenway on the western shore of the Passagassawakeag River. The KSS Preserve overlooks the river about three-quarters of a mile north of Route 1 and the second preserve lies almost 2 miles upriver.

City Point on the Passagassawakeag River. The rows of logs embedded on the north side of the Passagassawakeag at City Point are the remains of wharves that used to line this section of the river. Until 1839, when the bridge was built, scows made their way to City Point to unload and pick up goods.

At a Glance: Land in Public or Conservation Ownership

Warren Island State Park   BPL campground and picnic area

IF&W Wildlife Island

This island is closed during the indicated bird nesting season. After the nesting season is over, the island is limited to careful day use.

Flat Island   April 15–July 31

(2 mi SE of Northport)

The Lower Penobscot River: Searsport to Bucksport

The dominating feature of the Penobscot River is its relentless current. Flowing south from Bangor, it twists past Fort Knox, funnels down the main channel west of Verona Island, and speeds past Fort Point. Here at last the current decreases as it becomes diffused in the open waters north of Islesboro.

There are only two islands in this section of the coast and both are fun to circumnavigate—Sears Island as a half-day trip and Verona Island as a full-day trip. If the wind is blowing and you are looking for a protected area, check out the South Branch of the Marsh River, which is managed by Maine's Department of Inland Fisheries and Wildlife.

If you'd like a bird's-eye view of your trip, take an elevator to the top of the observation tower on the Fort Knox end of the new Penobscot River bridge. The tower is scheduled to open in the fall of 2006.

Trip Ideas (weather and experience permitting)

From Searsport Harbor (see previous chapter), circumnavigate Sears Island (9 miles). This route crosses south of the Mack Point cargo facility, so be aware of ship traffic; the route also includes a portage across the causeway. Or, circumnavigate the island starting from the island's causeway (5 or 6 miles).

From Fort Point State Park or Sandy Point Beach, explore Fort Point Cove (6 to 7 miles), keeping in mind the potentially strong current that flows in the main channel past the beach and Fort Point.

Charts

Chart: 13309, Penobscot River (1:40,000)

Chart Kit: 67

Maine Atlas locator map: 14, 15, 23

Tides (hours:minutes relative to Portland; average rise)

Penobscot River, Fort Point: 0:06 before; 10.5 feet

Bucksport: High 0:26 before, low 0:08 before; 11 feet

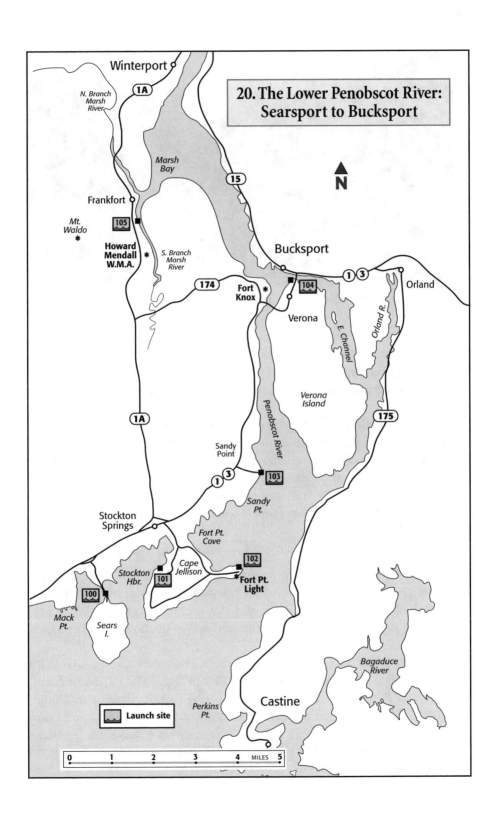

20. The Lower Penobscot River: Searsport to Bucksport

N

Winterport

1A

N. Branch Marsh River

Marsh Bay

15

Frankfort

Mt. Waldo *

105

Howard Mendall W.M.A. *

S. Branch Marsh River

174

Fort Knox *

Bucksport

1 3

Orland

104

Verona

E. Channel

Orland R.

1A

Penobscot River

Verona Island

175

Sandy Point

1 3

103

Sandy Pt.

Stockton Springs

Fort Pt. Cove

102

Cape Jellison

* Fort Pt. Light

Stockton Hbr.

101

100

Mack Pt.

Sears I.

Bagaduce River

Launch site

Perkins Pt.

Castine

0   1   2   3   4   MILES   5

Paddling north from Belfast on the Passagassawakeag River

The current is an important element when circumnavigating Verona Island (11 miles). As the main channel is the deepest and carries the most water, it makes sense to go south on the west side of the island. At low tide, there are extensive mudflats in the Eastern Channel, but they do not prohibit navigation by shallow craft.

The South Branch of the Marsh River flows into the Penobscot at Frankfort. This river encompasses a lovely, quiet area that is relatively protected and therefore a good choice when the wind is strong. If possible, put in on the top half of a rising tide so there is enough water to explore the inner reaches of the river (6 or 7 miles round-trip). The North Branch of the Marsh River is shorter, more built-up, and less inviting.

Safety Considerations, Strong Currents, and Caution Areas

Penobscot River. The Penobscot River and its tributaries drain about one-quarter of Maine and contribute one-fifth of all fresh water that enters the Gulf of Maine. In March, April, and May the Penobscot's flow is twice the amount (and can reach five times the amount) of the flow at other times of the year.

According to the *Coast Pilot*, currents of 3 knots are not unusual in the Penobscot River between Orrington and Odum Ledge west of Verona Island. The *Coast Pilot* has received reports of spring runoff currents reaching 5 knots and higher. When the current is at maximum ebb, it can pull buoys under. Also, these fast currents can create large, strong eddies along the shores of the main channel west of Verona Island. During times of high runoff, the river may carry logs and other debris that could prove dangerous to paddlers.

When a powerful river current meets the incoming tidal surge—especially with a strong onshore breeze—paddling conditions in the main channel between Verona Island and Fort Point can become hazardous.

Sears Island. Because Sears Island is flanked by two industrial facilities— Mack Point cargo terminal west of Sears Island and a mooring platform east of Sears Island—paddlers should exercise caution when paddling in the vicinity of the island or near the ships that use these facilities.

Searsport Lobster Boat Race. Stay out of the action by checking the date (www.lobsterboatracing.com).

New Fort Knox Bridge. Expect the Coast Guard to restrict access to any stretch of river below construction. The new bridge from Prospect to Verona is scheduled to be completed in the fall of 2006.

Access

100: Sears Island Causeway. Maine's Department of Transportation, under whose jurisdiction Sears Island falls, has sometimes allowed and some-times disallowed access to the causeway. At the time of this writing, the no parking signs have been removed and boaters are allowed to park along and launch from the causeway. From downtown Searsport, proceed north on Route 1/ME 3 for 2 miles, passing Hamilton Marine—where you can get flares, wire to fix the rudder, reflective tape, and thousands of other handy items. Turn right at a green maintenance shed onto Sears Island Road. (Or, from Stockton Springs, drive south on Route 1/ME 3 for about 2 miles. Pass the turnoff for Kidder Point and take the next left by a green shed.) Go 1.1 miles to the end of the road. Carry boats through the gate and down to the water.

101: Stockton Harbor. This is a working harbor, with a wharf, floats, ramp, harbor master's office, and bathroom. There's plenty of beach for kayakers, making it easy to stay out of the way. From Route 1/ME 3 in Stockton Springs, turn south onto Cape Jellison Road at the sign for Fort Point State Park. Proceed 0.9 mile; at the split in the road, go right, following signs for Stockton Harbor. Go 1.2 miles and turn right on Cape Docks Road. Go straight to the launch area.

If you'd like to view an aerial shot of the harbor, grab a 2005 copy of *Down East* magazine and turn to the spread on Stockton Harbor town-houses. Just six years ago, the harbor was a quiet, secluded place. Now, a string of brand new townhouses stretching half a mile dominates the shore, which is quiet no more.

102: Fort Point State Park. This is not a particularly easy place from which to launch because there is a long carry—about 100 yards—and no ramp. Proceed as above, but after 0.9 mile turn left at the sign for the park. Follow this road for 1.5 miles and turn left into the park. Proceed 1 mile

Ospreys Make a Comeback

On coastal wildlife maps of Maine made by the U.S. Fish and Wildlife Service in the early 1980s, every osprey nest was marked—and there weren't many. Today, if you don't see an osprey when you're paddling, you probably need to get your glasses checked because ospreys are everywhere. What happened?

Principally, pesticides like DDT were banned. A breakdown product of DDT prevented ospreys and other top-of-the-food-web birds like eagles from absorbing

and using calcium. Eggs cracked easily. Reproduction plummeted. Birds vanished. People wondered if ospreys—and eagles— would disappear from Maine altogether.

After Rachel Carson wrote *Silent Spring*, illuminating the problem of pesticides, there was a wave of conservation action aimed at setting a new course. And, over the long run, osprey (and eagle) populations have

Ospreys have a dark eye stripe and banded tail. Conservation measures have restored their population so that there are now more than 2,000 nesting pairs in Maine. JEAN HOEKWATER

bounced back, establishing themselves on inland lakes and rivers as well as coastal shores and islands. Now there are more than 2,000 nesting pairs in Maine.

After a winter sojourn in South America, ospreys arrive in Maine in early April, the female a few days after the male. Year after year, they occupy the same nest, a huge treetop structure built out of large sticks. The female generally lays three mottled brown-on-beige eggs, one day apart in the third week of April.

The female incubates the eggs, occasionally taking a short exercise break while the male sits on the nest. The eggs hatch 1 day apart in mid-May; if food is scarce, the oldest chick gets priority. For the first 10 days the young lie in the nest, then they sit up and begin to move around. By the fifth and sixth week, they are able to eat by themselves and begin wing exercises. As the summer lengthens, they begin flying and fishing with their parents. Parents

Osprey nest on navigational aids, in tree tops, and—occasionally—on sea stacks. (In contrast, eagles nest about one-third of the way down a tree.)

and young migrate south together in mid-October. Immature ospreys remain in South America until they are ready to mate, build a nest, and raise their own young.

along the access road. Pay the entrance fee of $1 per person and follow the loop past the earthworks and picnic parking area back to the fee station. Then take the first dirt road on your right and follow it to a parking lot. Carry down the path from the far end of the lot to the pier, then down the embankment. Or, if one of the picnic sites between the lot and the water is free, carry to the water that way. The park (941-4014) is open from Memorial Day through Labor Day, 9 AM until sunset. As the property is gated, be mindful of closing time.

103: Sandy Point Beach. There is no ramp at Sandy Point Beach, but paddlers can hand carry to the water. About 2 miles east of the junction of Route 1 and Route 1A in Stockton Springs, turn at the sign for the Hershey Retreat Center. Go straight at the crossroads and continue down the hill to the water.

104: Verona Island. This popular launch site, which has a concrete, all-tide ramp, is located on the northern tip of Verona Island facing Bucksport. Traveling north on Route 1/ME 3, go over the Penobscot River, cross the island and take a left onto Admiral Perry Lane. (Or, from Bucksport, take the first right on Verona Island.) Take the first right to the launch. If the ramp is stacked up with trailered boats, hand carry right of the ramp. The launch area has a portable toilet.

105: South Branch Marsh River in Frankfort. This site provides access to the Howard Mendall Wildlife Management Area. There is a concrete ramp, a large parking lot, and several picnic tables. At the junction of Route 1A and ME 174, go north on Route 1A for 2.7 miles to the well-marked picnic and boat access area on the right.

Points of Interest

Northern Penobscot Bay and Penobscot River. The Penobscot River has a two-layer circulation system, with less-dense freshwater floating over denser saltwater. Lobsters are caught as far north as Bucksport, so the leading edge of a wedge of saltwater must move at least that far north. In spring, the plume of freshwater—about 15 feet deep—flows by Sears Island and Islesboro and along the western side of the bay as far south as Owls Head.

Sears Island. Henry Knox, a leader in the Revolutionary War and this nation's first secretary of war, owned the island in the late 1700s, but it passed from him to his creditors. The Sears family owned it for most of the 19th century. Commercial development picked up when the Bangor and Aroostook Railroad acquired the property in the early 1900s and built Penobscot Park, a resort complete with a dance hall and an amusement park. The resort folded just before the Depression, as the automobile supplanted the train and changed the habits of vacationers.

Fort Knox was ideally located to guard Bangor, but technology rendered it outmoded before it was even completed.

There was little activity until the 1970s, when the island was proposed as a site for a nuclear power plant. That plan was abandoned, as was a proposal for a fossil fuel power plant. The State of Maine began pushing for a cargo terminal in the 1980s and proceeded with preliminary work without permits and broke several environmental laws; when the terminal flunked environmental review, politicians at last shelved the idea. For the time being, Sears Island remains a beautiful, undeveloped wooded island, but the specter of commercial development looms large.

Stockton Harbor. There is an offshore platform with a mooring facility between Sears Island and Cape Jellison (check your chart). A pipeline connects the platform with Kidder Point.

Fort Pownall at Fort Point State Park. Fort Point has a commanding view of the lower reaches of the Penobscot River and the Castine peninsula. The British built the fort in 1759, during the French and Indian War. Later, during the Revolutionary War, the British twice burned the structure to prevent it from falling into American hands. Only the earthworks endure at this state historic site from which paddlers may launch (see *Access*) as well as stop by on a downriver trip.

The sailing ships that once carried lumber and other cargo from Bangor were often captive to the wind. With the upriver breeze that prevailed in the summer, the ships were frequently stuck in port. With the advent of steam, steamboats came to the rescue, towing rafts of sailing ships down the Penobscot, past Bucksport, and around Fort Point to open water. These rafts were sometimes as large as 10 rows of ships with 3 abreast.

Fort Point Light. This light, which is located on the south shore of Fort Point, is housed in a square white tower and stands 88 feet above the water. It was built in 1836, rebuilt 21 years later, and automated in 1988. The bell tower is on the National Register of Historic Places.

Sandy Point Beach. Sandy Point Beach lies on the western shore of the Penobscot River between Fort Point and Verona Island. The 100-acre recreation area, managed by the town of Stockton Springs, includes an extensive sand and gravel beach that is used for swimming, sunbathing, picnicking, and other water-related activities. Sea kayakers may launch or visit from the water if they do so carefully.

Verona Island. The *Roosevelt*, the vessel that Robert Peary sailed north on his expedition to reach the North Pole, was built on this island in 1905.

Fort Knox. Tensions between the United States and England lasted through the Revolutionary War and into the War of 1812, when the British sailed up to Bangor and captured the prosperous, timber-rich city. When a border war with Canada broke out in northern Maine in 1839, Americans feared that British ships would return. Bureaucracy prevailed, however, and Fort Knox was not even started until 1844. It was, alas, obsolete by the time it was completed 25 years later. Although troops were quartered at Fort Knox during both the Civil War and the Spanish-American War, those soldiers saw no action. The fort is named for Major General Henry Knox, who once owned Sears Island. The entrance fee to this state historic site (469-7719) is $3 per person.

Waldo-Hancock Bridge. When the old bridge showed signs of dangerous disrepair, planners tweaked its technology and then set out to design a new bridge. Officials broke ground in 2003 and plan to have the structure in operation by October 2006. Paddlers and others may then take an elevator to the bridge's observation tower, which stands 420 feet above the water and will offer stunning views of the region. Access for the tower lies on the western shore.

Prospect Ferry. The village of Prospect Ferry lies immediately north of Fort Knox. The stone foundation of the ferry landing that can be seen at low tide is a reminder of the time when ferries, not bridges, carried travelers across the state's waterways.

Bucksport. Bucksport is home to the Champion International paper mill, the second largest in the state. The mill makes paper for *Sports Illustrated*, *Good Housekeeping*, Victoria's Secret, and other publications and catalogs.

Howard Mendall Wildlife Management Area. This 221-acre area along the South Branch of the Marsh River provides habitat for bald eagles, water-fowl, wading birds, shorebirds, and other birdlife. Striped bass, Atlantic salmon, alewives, and other fish use the river and tributary streams in season.

At a Glance: Land in Public or Conservation Ownership

Sears Island	Maine Department of Transportation; careful day use
Fort Point State Park	BPL; launching and careful day use
Sandy Point Beach	Town of Stockton Springs; launching and careful day use
Fort Knox Historic Site	BPL; careful day use
South Branch, Marsh River	IF&W; careful day use

The Penobscot River: Bangor to Winterport

The river between Bangor and Hampden is urban and industrial; paddling here gives you a unique perspective on a bustling city. The prettiest part of the Penobscot lies between Hampden and Winterport, where the shoreline is steep—almost but not quite a gorge—and mostly undeveloped. This territory is great habitat for ospreys and eagles. Below Winterport, the river widens and is more vulnerable to onshore breezes.

Trip Ideas (weather and experience permitting)

For a point-to-point trip, spot a car and paddle downriver. Distances between launch sites are:

Bangor to Hampden, 3.5 miles

Hampden to South Orrington, 6.5 miles

South Orrington to Verona Island, 10 miles

If you paddle below Winterport, note that the current sweeps along the outside shore by Frankfort and jumps from Bowden Point to the opposite bank. Frankfort Flat (check your chart), a large shallow area on the eastern shore, is essentially a huge, slow eddy.

If you plan to take out at the same place that you put in, time your paddle so that the incoming tide will help carry you back to the launch site.

Safety Considerations, Strong Currents, and Caution Areas

Current. According to the *Coast Pilot*, currents can reach 3 knots (5 knots and higher when the river floods in the spring) at and below South Orrington. When the river is in flood, it often carries logs and other debris that can be dangerous to small craft.

Large ships. Bangor has an industrial waterfront, with oil and asphalt being the primary commodities. Give ships a wide berth.

Charts

Chart: 13309, Penobscot River (1:40,000)

Chart Kit: 67

Maine Atlas locator map: 23

Tides (hours:minutes relative to Portland; average rise)

Winterport: High 0:25 before, low 0:05 before; 11.7 feet

Bangor: High 0:30 before, low 0:04 after; 13.1 feet

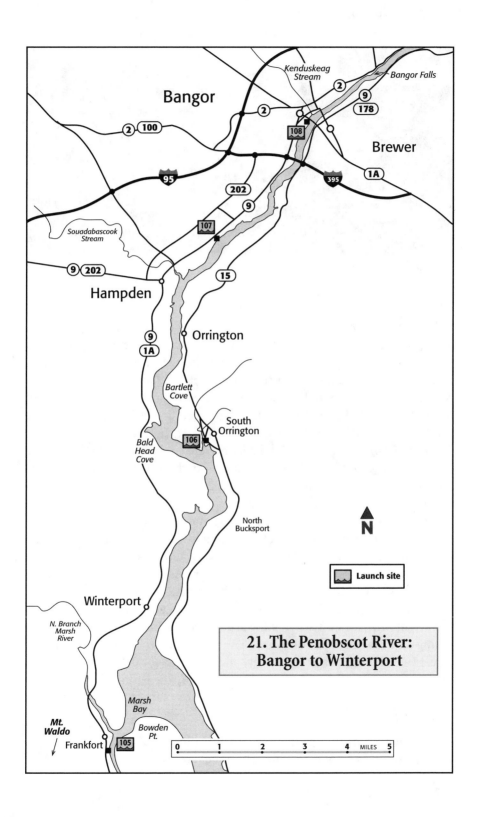

Kenduskeag
Stream

Bangor Falls

Bangor

2

2

9

178

2 100

108

Brewer

95

1A

202

395

9

Souadabascook
Stream

107

9 202

15

Hampden

9
1A

Orrington

Bartlett
Cove

South
Orrington

Bald
Head
Cove

106

North
Bucksport

N

Launch site

Winterport

N. Branch
Marsh
River

21. The Penobscot River:
Bangor to Winterport

Marsh
Bay

Mt.
Waldo

Bowden
Pt.

Frankfort 105

0 1 2 3 4 MILES 5

Hampden boat launch

Access

106: South Orrington. Although the Bureau of Parks and Lands calls this a part-tide ramp, sea kayakers can launch from the concrete ramp at all but the lowest tides. This is a pretty area, with no houses in view, and can double as a picnic area on a downriver trip. From I-395 in Bangor, take exit 4 onto ME 15 and proceed south for 7.2 miles. At the sign for shore access, turn right onto Blake Road. Proceed 0.2 mile, jogging left across Settlers Way. Drive down the hill to the launch area.

107: Hampden. The public boat launch area in Hamden has two all-tide concrete ramps, toilets, and picnic tables. From the junction of ME 9 and US 395 in Hampden, go south on ME 9 for 2.4 miles. Turn left onto Marina Road at the sign for Turtle Head Marina.

108: Bangor. The Bangor Landing is not an ideal place for sea kayakers to launch. You can carry your boat to the point where the Kenduskeag Stream meets the Penobscot (but there is a steep bank and rock riprap), or you can launch from a dock (but it is high off the water). Ask the harbor master about which dock to use; the office is in the railway station replica.

From I-395, take exit 3 onto Main Street in Bangor. Proceed 0.5 mile and turn right onto Route 1A/ME 9 toward Brewer and Bar Harbor. Instead of taking an immediate left on Route 1A and ME 9, go straight on Railroad Street (which becomes Front Street) and continue for 0.2 mile. Turn right into the waterfront area. There are bathrooms by the parking lot.

Points of Interest

Bangor. Rumors of gold enticed early explorers to the New World, and even the stern, rockbound Northeast was believed to harbor a secret place of riches. Norumbega, a City of Gold, was said to lie along a great river in the north. When Samuel de Champlain sailed up the Penobscot in 1604, instead of gold he found an Indian camp at what is now Bangor. Unlike other European explorers, who treated the "savages" with disrespect, Champlain feasted and traded with Bessabez and Cabahis, two sachems, and other members of their group.

The encampment, located at the head of tide, grew into a bustling rendezvous point for trade in the interior and shipping from the rest of the world. Bangor became the queen city of lumber. Lumberjacks cut trees all winter and stacked them on the shores of innumerable rivers and streams; at iceout they knocked out the supports, and the lumber flushed downriver on the crest of the spring flood. At one point, Bangor shipped more lumber than any other city in the world. In 1860 alone, it sent out 2.5 million feet of long lumber. That same year, an average of 14 ships a day arrived and left the city during the eight months or so that the river was free of ice.

American Folk Festival. If you feel like paddling the Penobscot River in Bangor, don't plan a trip for late August because this exciting event spreads across every inch of the waterfront (www.americanfolkfestival.com).

Bangor Falls. The tide reaches about a mile above the city to Bangor Falls. A dam used to span the river here, but now only the Waterworks, a complex on the north shore, remains. Native Americans called the falls *Pemjeedg'-e-wock*, "current raggedly dropping down," a fit name for a rapids.

Mount Waldo. This 1,064-foot hill comes into view in the straightaway below South Orrington. Granite from Mount Waldo was used to built Fort Knox.

Northern Penobscot Bay: Castine and the Bagaduce River

Holbrook Island Sanctuary has a beautiful launch or landing site along with sand beaches, undeveloped shores, and a 120-acre island. Smith Cove is a place for quiet paddling and birding, while the Bagaduce River has very fast currents that demand attention and river-paddling skills.

Trip Ideas (weather and experience permitting)

From Castine or Holbrook Island Sanctuary, explore Smith Cove (4 to 6 miles, depending on your inclination).

From either place, extend the tour to include the Holbrook Island area (7 to 9 miles); on a clear day there are great views of Islesboro and the Camden Hills to the west. To make a circle trip, portage across Indian Bar,

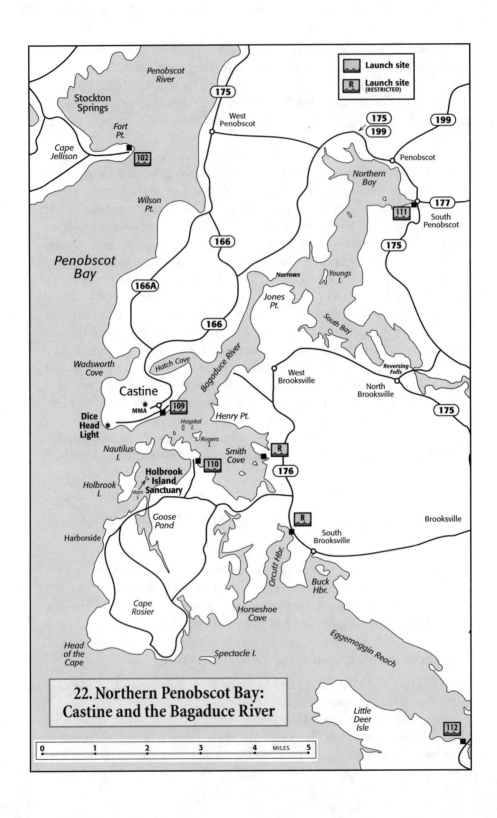

22. Northern Penobscot Bay: Castine and the Bagaduce River

Legend:
- Launch site
- R Launch site (RESTRICTED)

Penobscot River

Stockton Springs

Fort Pt.

Cape Jellison

102

175

West Penobscot

175
199

175
199

199

Penobscot

Northern Bay

177

South Penobscot

111

Wilson Pt.

166

175

Penobscot Bay

166A

166

Narrows

Youngs I.

Jones Pt.

South Bay

Reversing Falls

Wadsworth Cove

Hatch Cove

Bagaduce River

West Brooksville

North Brooksville

175

Castine

MMA

109

Henry Pt.

Dice Head Light

Hospital I.

Rogers I.

Nautilus I.

Smith Cove

R

176

Holbrook I.

110

Holbrook Island Sanctuary

Ram I.

R

Brooksville

South Brooksville

Harborside

Goose Pond

Orcutt Hbr.

Buck Hbr.

Cape Rosier

Horseshoe Cove

Eggemoggin Reach

Head of the Cape

Spectacle I.

Little Deer Isle

112

0 1 2 3 4 MILES 5

Chart

Chart: 13309, Penobscot River (1:40,000)

Chart Kit: 66

Maine Atlas locator map: 15

Tides (hours:minutes relative to Portland; average rise)

Castine: 0:04 before; 9.7 feet

---

the sandy neck between Smith Cove and the islands; look for a 500-foot trail on the south end of the bar. The northern half of the bar and the land beyond are privately owned. Watch for ospreys, eagles, terns, and sea ducks on this trip.

From Castine or Holbrook Island Sanctuary, paddle up the Bagaduce, around Youngs Islands, and return (10 to 11 miles). Or, paddle to Bagaduce Falls (16 to 17 miles), a reversing falls that forms under the ME 176 bridge. See *Safety Considerations* for both the Narrows and Bagaduce Falls.

From South Penobscot, at the top of the tide, explore Northern Bay (7 miles round-trip to Youngs Islands). Be careful not to get stranded when the tide goes out; a substantial portion of Northern Bay turns into mudflats.

Safety Considerations, Strong Currents, and Caution Areas

Bagaduce River. The current in the Bagaduce River is swift throughout the river's length, but it is particularly fast at the Narrows at Jones Point, a few miles northeast of Castine. The average maximum current here, both

The Maine Maritime Academy's ship State of Maine *dominates the waterfront in Castine.*

Bagaduce Falls on the Bagaduce River

flood and ebb, is over 4 knots. These currents form strong eddies, whirlpools, and boils. The *Coast Pilot* recommends passage only at slack water, but skilled paddlers can make their own choice. The logical way to paddle the Bagaduce is with the current. Start up through the Narrows on a rising tide and return after the tide begins to ebb.

Upriver, the abutments of the ME 176 bridge squeeze the Bagaduce, creating a reversing falls. Whitewater kayakers and canoeists sometimes practice in this narrow rapid, so sea kayakers may want to turn around below the bridge. The bridge is a dividing line for tidal current; when the tide is dropping in the Bagaduce, water is still pouring south under the bridge. Because there is no public portage around the bridge, if you decide to run under it, you may be stuck there for a while.

Access

109: Castine. The all-tide launch ramp is located on the north end of the public parking lot on the waterfront. Parking is limited to 3 hours from May through October, and 4 hours from November through May, so you'll have to find on-street parking if you plan a longer excursion. Although the sign at the wharf directs overflow to the Steven Road parking lot—four blocks back on Main Street and to the left—you need a permit to park there.

From Route 1/ME 3 in Orland, take ME 175 south to West Penobscot, then follow ME 166 south (the ME 166A variation is more scenic) into Castine. The road bends left, putting you on Main Street. Follow signs to the downtown and/or Dennets Wharf Restaurant. When you see water, continue straight to the harbor. There are bathrooms on the south side of the parking lot.

110: Holbrook Island Sanctuary, Cape Rosier. Holbrook Island Sanctuary (326-4012) includes a beautiful sand beach—an elegant launch site—that overlooks Smith Cove. There are also picnic tables and a vault toilet.

Holbrook Island Sanctuary

Anita Harris loved Holbrook Island, which had been in her family since 1893. In the 1960s, while summering in the big house there, she decided to protect forever the wildlands on the Cape Rosier peninsula and Holbrook Island itself. She began acquiring land in Brooksville and, in 1971, donated 1,230 acres to the state of Maine as a wildlife and natural area "to preserve for the future a piece of the unspoiled Maine that I used to know." When she died in 1985, she left the 115-acre island and 5 more acres to the state, as well as funds for the maintenance of the sanctuary and for research.

The sanctuary is a gem in the state park system. Eight miles of hiking trails lead through woodlands of spruce, fir, and hardwoods. A sandbar offers views of Smith Cove to the east and Holbrook Island to the west. River otter, beaver, mink, muskrat, porcupine, white-tailed deer, moose, coyote, red fox, bobcat, and bear frequent the sanctuary. Over 200 species of birds have been sighted in the woods, wetlands, and meadows and along the shore. Osprey, great blue herons, and bald eagles nest here in the summer, while spring and fall migrants offer great birding.

The sanctuary maintains an ambitious nature-walk series in July and August, covering wildflowers, trees, insects, local history, animal tracks, and other topics.

For further information about the sanctuary—including a map, a checklist of birds, a list of nature walks, and a brochure about resident mammals—contact the Park Manager, Holbrook Island Sanctuary, P.O. Box 280, Brooksville, ME 04617 (326-4012).

From West Brooksville, take ME 176 south and turn right onto Cape Rosier Road at the sign for Holbrook Island Sanctuary. (From South Brooksville, take a left onto this road.) Proceed 1.6 miles and take a right onto Back Road, also called Lawrence Hill Road, at another sign for the sanctuary. Go 0.8 mile and turn right onto Indian Bar Road, which leads in almost a mile to the sanctuary headquarters, picnic area, and parking lot; there is an entrance fee of $1 per person. The beach is just beyond the parking lot; drop boats and gear, then return your vehicle to the lot. This day-use area is open from 9 AM to sunset, year-round.

Restricted: Smith Cove, West Brooksville. This site is limited to individuals with Brooksville registration stickers on vehicles and boats. (Note: There is no boat launch at the end of Wharf Road, which runs to the Bagaduce River about 2 miles north of the Smith Cove launch.)

Restricted: Orcutt Harbor, South Brooksville. This site is also limited to individuals with Brooksville registration stickers on vehicles and boats.

111: South Penobscot. South Penobscot has a part-tide concrete ramp and a small parking lot. The site is just off ME 175 in the center of town. Take ME 175 south from Penobscot for almost a mile, passing Northern Bay

Market on the right. Take the first right (0.1 mile south of the market) onto Town Landing Road. Continue to the end of the road.

Points of Interest

Castine. Castine was the site of early and ongoing activity in the New World. Samuel de Champlain sailed by here in 1604 and James Rosier, a companion of Weymouth, ventured up the Bagaduce in 1605. Captain John Smith explored the area in 1614. By the late 1620s, the Plymouth Colony had set up a post to trade for furs with the Indians. The British and the French (and, briefly, the Dutch) traded Pentagoët, as Castine was then called, back and forth for the rest of the century.

Baron Jean Vincent de St. Castin was stationed here when the fort was in French hands and returned after he was discharged from the French army in 1667. He married the daughter of a Penobscot sachem and set up a trading post. He represented French interests and had considerable influence with the Penobscot Indians. In 1696, he gathered 200 warriors and they paddled in canoes to Pemaquid, where they joined the French in attacking the fort there.

Things were quiet in Pentagoët until the Revolutionary War. The British held on to the fort in Castine—even when attacked by a much larger American force—and did not turn the town over to the Americans until 1783, well after the peace treaty had been signed. British forces recaptured Castine during the War of 1812 but left for good three years later.

Dice Head Light. There are two lights on the northern entrance to the Bagaduce River at Castine. The prominent white stone tower and keeper's house were built in 1829; the town of Castine now owns the property. The active Coast Guard tower stands nearby, 27 feet above the water.

Maine Maritime Academy. The Maine Maritime Academy (MMA), founded in 1941, offers training at undergraduate and graduate levels in marine engineering, transportation, and management as well as ocean sciences. The academy also offers preparation for those who want to join the U.S. Merchant Marine and branches of the military. MMA has a fleet of nearly 100 vessels, including the training vessel *State of Maine*, the tug *Pentagoet*, the barge *Central*, the research vessels ARGO *Maine* and *Friendship*, the historic schooner *Bowdoin*, and dozens of smaller craft. Some combination of the larger vessels can be seen at the MMA wharf next to the public parking area on the waterfront, and many smaller vessels are kept in the Bagaduce River.

Bagaduce River. Bagaduce means "big tideway river." The Bagaduce is a *neutral embayment*, meaning that it is an extension of Penobscot Bay rather than a river with a major source of fresh water. Neutral embayments typically have a few freshwater streams, but the salinity remains constant and high. There are also usually large areas of mudflats and marsh.

The name *Pentagoët*, which through history was variously applied to the Bagaduce River, Castine, and the Penobscot River, means "falls of the river" or "at the falls." The term likely referred to the tidal falls at the Narrows.

Native American canoe routes. The Penobscot Indians called Castine Neck "where they waited for the tide" because it was easier to portage the neck at high water than to paddle around it. To canoe from Castine Neck to Eggemoggin Reach, they took "the many directions route" up the Bagaduce to Walker's Pond (not shown on map), where a short portage led to Eggemoggin Reach. To avoid Cape Rosier, canoeists went "where it is very narrow," heading south through Goose Pond and portaging to Weir Cove.

Hospital Island. In his book about the islands of Penobscot Bay, Charles McLane reports that the chart incorrectly locates Hospital Island. The large island at the mouth of Smith Cove is Rogers; Hospital lies west of Rogers. McLane writes that Hospital Island probably served as Castine's quarantine station.

Shipwreck in Smith Cove. The remains lie off Henry Point.

Nautilus Island. A battery on this (now private) island served to protect or bombard Castine, depending on whose hands it was in during the Revolutionary War. A fish-curing business was later set up in the cove on the north side of the island.

Ram Island. This island, which lies east of Holbrook Island (check your chart), is open to the public for enjoyment of its natural beauty. The Conservation Trust of Brooksville, Castine, and Penobscot owns and manages the island.

Goose Pond. To avoid paddling around the exposed perimeter of Cape Rosier, Native Americans portaged from the head of the creek flowing into Goose Pond to Weir Cove to the south, a distance of less than a mile. The Native American name for this carry means "where there is a very narrow place." There is a reversing tidal falls at the outlet of Goose Pond.

At a Glance: Land in Public or Conservation Ownership

Ram Island	Conservation Trust of Brooksville, Castine, and Penobscot; careful day use
Holbrook Island Sanctuary	BPL; careful day use

Eastern Penobscot Bay: Little Deer Isle

The islands immediately south of Cape Rosier and Little Deer Isle are some of the prettiest along the coast. For a grand tour, circumnavigate Little Deer Isle and some of the islands to the south. If conditions, skills, or time dictate a shorter trip, explore Eggemoggin Reach. With available launch sites, the

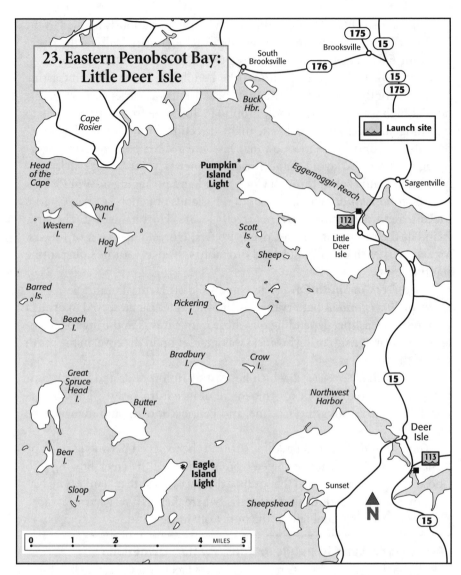

23. Eastern Penobscot Bay: Little Deer Isle

islands west of Deer Isle and north of North Haven are at the outer fringes of a day trip for many paddlers.

Trip Ideas *(weather and experience permitting)*

From Eggemoggin Landing, paddle to the western end of Little Deer Isle (5 miles round-trip), to Buck Harbor (8 miles round-trip), or to Pond Island, which belongs to Maine Coast Heritage Trust (12 miles round-trip). Or, paddle in the other direction to Sedgwick (9 miles round-trip; see page 238). The tide in Eggemoggin Reach, which is only moderate in strength, floods

Charts

Chart: 13305, Penobscot Bay (1:40,000)
Chart Kit: 68B
Maine Atlas locator map: 15

Tides (hours:minutes relative to Portland; average rise)
Little Deer Isle: 0:06 before; 10.0 feet
Northwest Harbor, Deer Isle: 0:12 before; 10.1 feet

northwest and ebbs southeast. The reach does funnel wind, though, so beware of northwest and southeast breezes.

Several trips involve circumnavigating Little Deer Isle and portaging across the causeway. A simple circumnavigation (9 miles) takes you past Scott Islands and The Nature Conservancy's Sheep Island. For a longer trip, take in Pond Island and paddle by Pickering Island before heading back to the causeway (15 miles). The causeway between Little Deer Isle and Deer Isle is bordered by mudflats at low tide, so time your portage accordingly. Mudflats are more extensive at the west end of the causeway than at the east end.

From Mariner's Park, tour Long Cove and Southeast Harbor (3 to 6 miles, depending on your energy). Plan to paddle during the top half of the tide.

Safety Considerations, Strong Currents, and Caution Areas

Exposed conditions. The islands in Eastern Penobscot Bay are sufficiently far apart that wind and seas can be an issue when crossing from one to another.

Evening on Eggemoggin Reach

Access

112: Eggemoggin Reach, Little Deer Isle. Eggemoggin Landing, a marina on the southern shore of Eggemoggin Reach, was put up for sale in late 2005, and will be closed through 2006. The sandy waterfront is a perfect place to launch boats, so it's worth making inquiries (perhaps through the Chamber of Commerce) at a future date regarding any new business that might occupy this site.

113: Mariner's Park. Kayakers may launch at the Deer Isle Garden Club's 30-acre park, which lies at the head of Long Cove. Take ME 15 to the village of Deer Isle, turn left on the Sunshine Road, and take the first right onto Fire Road 501. Paddlers are advised to go out with and come back with the tide; fast water in a nearby narrows can be quite challenging. At the bottom of the tide the launch turns to mud.

Note. Causeway Beach, at the eastern end of the causeway between Little Deer Isle and Deer Isle, looks like it would be a perfect launch site. Alas, it is not. The Causeway Beach Network, a citizens' group, purchased the beach in 2004 and gave it to the Island Heritage Trust to be used for "traditional public use and enjoyment" such as walking, watching wildlife, clamming, and gathering seaweed for gardening.

The trust asks that no unattended vehicles be left there, which rules out boating. The causeway has another drawback as well: it is stranded in mud when the tide is low, providing less than ideal access.

In 2004, the trust announced a purchase and sale agreement for 26 acres on Eggemoggin Reach. From the southern end of the causeway, and north of ME 15, the two parcels stretch east. Plans for the site feature a boat launch, recreational beach, picnic area, and walking trails.

Note. Island Guide, published by the area Chamber of Commerce, shows public boat launches in North Deer Isle (onto Eggemoggin Reach from the old ferry landing), the village of Deer Isle (onto Northwest Harbor from a pull-out along the main road), and Sunset (onto Southwest Harbor; not to be confused with the Deer Isle Yacht Club on Sylvester Cove). The problem with each is that there is very little parking—room for a couple of vehicles at the most. As a further drawback, the launch from the village looks out onto mud at low water. Please leave these cramped sites to local users.

Points of Interest

Eggemoggin Reach. Eggemoggin means "fish weir place." The name probably referred to a specific area where Native Americans set up a weir to catch fish; the place-name was later generalized to include the entire reach.

Pumpkin Island Light, built in 1854 to mark the west end of Eggemoggin Reach. The light was extinguished in 1934 and is in private hands.

Pond Island. The Maine Coast Heritage Trust allows picnicking and other day-use activities on this island, which is nestled between Western and Hog islands south of Cape Rosier. John's Head at the northwest end of the island, which appears to be a separate island at high tide, is a seabird nesting area for guillemots, eiders, gulls, and—occasionally—terns; this area is closed from March 15 to July 15. The spit on the southeast end of the island, which generally has bank swallows, is also closed at this time. Native Americans used to frequent this island, and they left behind shell middens dating back some 2,000 years. Despite rumors of lost treasure, no riches have yet been found. The island is a popular one, so you are likely to have company.

Unlike many of the rock-bound islands sprinkled along the coast, Pond Island is composed of sand and gravel that once flowed from a glacial river. These sediments form a cuspate barrier beach on the southeast end of the island. A cuspate ("tooth-shaped") barrier beach usually forms when wave trains bend around an island and then converge behind it, dropping sediment. In the case of Pond Island, the Penobscot's ebb current and the nearness of Hog Island are as influential in the formation of the beach as the wave trains.

Crow Island. Ten-acre Crow is a nesting island and so is closed from April 1 through August 15. After that time, this lovely public island is open for day use. There is a pretty meadow with roses and other wildflowers in the center of the island. Expect company on Crow, as it is popular.

Bradbury Island. This Nature Conservancy island, which lies several miles west of Northwest Harbor on Deer Isle, is closed to the public from

February 15 through August 15 because it is a nesting area for ospreys and other species. There are no trails and visitation after that time is limited to the shoreline. TNC warns boaters to beware of strong currents around this island.

Sheep Island (near Little Deer Isle). The Nature Conservancy owns and manages this island, which is a nesting site for ospreys; common eiders nest on offshore ledges. The island is open to the public, though the shore is for the most part steep and uninviting and there are no trails.

Scott Islands. The children's writer Robert McCloskey set *One Morning in Maine, Time of Wonder, Blueberries for Sal*, and other classic stories on these privately owned islands that lie to the south of Little Deer Isle.

East Barred Island. East Barred is provisionally open for careful use and is part of the Maine Island Trail. West Barred is an osprey and seabird nesting island; the Maine Island Trail Association requests that boaters refrain from visiting this island year-round. Access to East Barred will continue if the nesting birds on West Barred remain undisturbed. West Barred is managed by the Department of Inland Fisheries and Wildlife; East Barred is managed by the Bureau of Parks and Lands. Note that these two Barred Islands are located west of Beach Island; they should not be confused with the Barred Islands west of Butter.

Great Spruce Head Island. Eliot Porter took many of the photographs for *Summer Island: Penobscot Country* on this island, which lies to the west of Butter Island. Spruce is privately owned and not open to visitors.

Eagle Island Light. This light, on the northeastern end of the island, was built in 1839. The light stands 106 feet above water in a white granite tower. Both Eagle Island and Butter Island supported thriving resorts from the late 1800s until World War I, when the increasing use of automobiles diminished interest in vacation spots accessible only by ferry.

At a Glance: Land in Public or Conservation Ownership

Pond Island	Maine Coast Heritage Trust; careful day use; both ends closed for nesting seabirds March 15–July 15
Crow Island	BPL; closed April 15–August 15, then open for careful day use
Bradbury Island	TNC; closed February 15–August 15; after that time, careful day use
Sheep Island	TNC; careful day use (steep shore)
East Barred Island	Maine Island Trail/BPL; provisionally open for careful day use

IF&W Wildlife Islands

These islands are closed during the indicated bird nesting season. After the nesting season is over, the islands are limited to careful day use.

Thrumcap Island   April 15–July 31
(0.9 mi NW of Little Deer Isle)

Buck Island   April 15–July 31
(2 mi NW of Little Deer Isle)

Green Ledge   April 15–July 31
(0.9 mi W of Pond Island)

Two Bush Island   April 15–July 31
(2.4 mi ESE of Pond Island)

Colt Head Island   April 15–July 31
(2.9 mi SW of Pond Island)

West Barred Island   April 15–July 31
(near Beach Island)

Eaton Island Ledge   April 15–August 31
(N of Pickering Island)

Grass Ledge East   April 15–July 31
(0.7 mi SW of Eagle Island)

Hardhead Island   April 15–July 31
(0.8 mi NE of Eagle Island)

Sloop Island   April 15–July 31
(1.4 mi W of Eagle Island)

Sloop Island Ledge   April 15–July 31
(W of Sloop Island)

Grass Ledge West   April 15–August 31
(1.4 mi SW of Great Spruce Island)

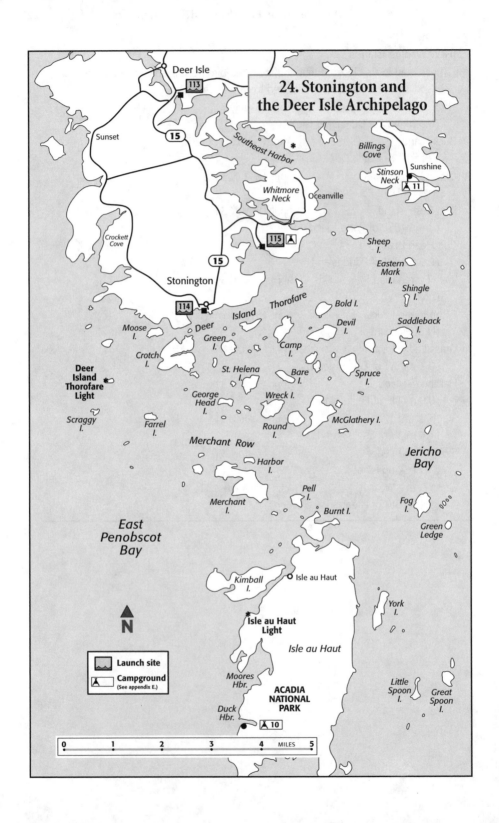

24. Stonington and the Deer Isle Archipelago

Deer Isle

113

15

Sunset

Southeast Harbor *

Billings Cove

Stinson Neck   Sunshine

11

Whitmore Neck

Oceanville

Crockett Cove

115

Sheep I.

Eastern Mark I.

Shingle I.

15

Stonington

114

Island   Thorofare

Bold I.

Devil I.

Saddleback I.

Moose I.

Deer   Green I.

Camp I.

Crotch I.

St. Helena I.

Bare I.

Spruce I.

Deer Island Thorofare Light

George Head I.

Wreck I.

McGlathery I.

Scraggy I.

Farrel I.

Round I.

Merchant Row

Jericho Bay

Harbor I.

Pell I.

Fog I.

Merchant I.

Burnt I.

Green Ledge

East Penobscot Bay

N

Kimball I.

Isle au Haut

York I.

Isle au Haut Light

Isle au Haut

Launch site

Campground
(See appendix E.)

Moores Hbr.

ACADIA NATIONAL PARK

Little Spoon I.

Great Spoon I.

Duck Hbr.

10

0   1   2   3   4   MILES   5

5.

Stonington and Mount Desert Island

Stonington and the Deer Isle Archipelago

It is no wonder sea kayakers flock to Stonington. The Deer Isle archipelago is an island lover's paradise: Isle after beautiful isle stretches across the glimmering sea. But beauty attracts people, and great numbers of people detract from beauty. Given the number of cruising vessels, small craft, schooners, and paddlers in this area, there are barely enough islands available for public use—and there are more here than on any other part of the coast. Plus, you literally need a scorecard to keep track of which islands are open to the public and which are closed during the summer nesting season.

Trip Ideas (weather and experience permitting)

A major difficulty here—as in other parts of Deer Isle—is the limited number of launch sites. Once you get on the water, there are many places to explore. Most of the islands north of Merchant Row are packed into an area roughly 5 miles by 2 miles, and a trip of 10 miles allows for a generous tour. A trip of only 6 or 7 miles will take you through an array of dazzling islands open to the public. The trip straight out to Isle au Haut is about 5 miles.

Safety Considerations, Strong Currents, and Caution Areas

Deer Island Thorofare. Deer Island Thorofare lies just south of Deer Isle, linking East Penobscot Bay on the west with Jericho Bay on the east. The

---

Chart
Chart: 13313, Approaches to Blue Hill Bay (1:40,000)
Chart Kit: 69
Maine Atlas locator maps: 9, 15

Tides (hours:minutes relative to Portland; average rise)
Stonington, Deer Isle: 0:18 before; 9.7 feet
Oceanville, Deer Isle: 0:18 before; 10.1 feet
Isle au Haut: 0:23 before; 9.3 feet

Fog on Merchant Row: Stay out of boat travel lanes; never assume someone else can see you; use your compass and (solid) navigation skills; listen for other boats and reposition accordingly.

Stonington fishing fleet uses this passage, as do many small craft. The passage is, in some places, only 300 feet wide and fairly shallow. In the middle of the summer, there can be so much traffic that paddling across the thoroughfare is a feat of timing. In addition to using the eastern route shown on the chart, boats sometimes enter the passage from the southeast, cutting between Shingle and Saddleback Islands, then heading between Bold Island and Bold Island Ledges.

In an interesting quirk of the sea, wind affects the direction of tidal currents in Deer Island Thorofare. Normally, the tide floods east and ebbs west, with the tide continuing almost an hour past high and low waters. When the wind blows strongly from the east, both the flood and ebb are to the west; when the wind blows strongly from the west, both the flood and the ebb are to the east.

Merchant Row. Merchant Row lies 2 to 4 miles south of the thoroughfare. It also connects Penobscot Bay and Jericho Bay, but it is much wider and deeper throughout. Larger vessels with a deeper draft choose this passage over the narrower and more difficult passage northward.

Fog. Stonington is known for fog and because there is so much boat traffic, the utmost caution is required. For more about fog, see part I.

Stonington Lobster Boat Race. Consult www.lobsterboatracing.com for the race date.

Access

114: Stonington. The only place to launch in Stonington is at a ramp that is tucked behind the ferry service. (The town landing next to Bartlett's Market is no longer available, so please do not go there except perhaps to use the portable toilets.) From Main Street, turn onto Bayview, which runs between Ocean View House and the funeral home. When you reach the ferry parking area, turn right (past a restaurant) and then left behind the ferry building, where you will find a narrow all-tide ramp. There is very little space here and parking is limited to 30 minutes. Unload promptly and whisk away your vehicle.

Parking spaces on Main Street are for 2 hours only. The town parking lot is likely already full. The ferry parking lot is for people using the ferry. Do everyone a favor and take advantage of a handy parking service. Linda Pattie and Carol Este (Island Taxi and Tours, 845-688-2134; lpattie@hvc.rr.com) provide a place to park and will shuttle you to—and from—the waterfront.

115: Buckmaster Neck. Old Quarry Charters (266-7778) encourages sea kayakers to use their all-tide launch dock that fronts on Webb Cove. There is a small parking fee. You can also rent kayaks here; arrange for a registered guide to take you out; sign up for a powerboat backup for emergencies or re-supplies; camp; or rent an ocean-view house. From downtown Deer Isle, go south on ME 15 for a little more than 3 miles. At Ron's gas station, turn left toward Oceanville. Proceed almost a mile and turn right onto Fire Road 22. Follow this road to its end at the water.

Points of Interest

Deer Island Thorofare Light. This light, also called Mark Island Light, is located on the west side of Mark Island, which lies at the western entrance of Deer Island Thorofare. Built in 1857, the light stands 52 feet above the water in a white square tower.

Weir Island. Weir Island is unnamed on the chart, but it is part of the Maine Island Trail. It is the westernmost of the two tiny islands located northwest of Moose Island, which itself lies just off the southern shore of Deer Isle. The banks of the island are wearing away, and visitors are asked to be careful not to contribute to the erosion.

Crotch Island. It's impossible to miss big, sprawling Crotch Island, which lies just off the Stonington shore. Native Americans visited often, leaving shell middens in their wake. Although the first business on the island was a sawmill in the late 1700s, it was granite that gave Crotch Island fame. A quarry opened in 1870, producing beautiful pink granite that was used at the Boston Museum of Fine Arts and for other noteworthy projects. Crotch was not the only island to see quarrying, though. Almost every isle in the vicinity shows signs of activity—a stone wharf, a pile of discarded stones, a square-cut ledge at water level, or a flat-topped rocky outcrop.

The granite business did not fail spectacularly here, as it did on islands in Penobscot Bay, but after 1910 activity diminished substantially. Many years later, Crotch Island provided 1,500 blocks of Sherwood Pink granite for President John F. Kennedy's memorial in Arlington Cemetery. The derricks on

Discarded granite blocks on Granite Island, which lies immediately south of Stonington

Crotch Island fell silent for a time, but in the early 1980s they started up again, to provide stone to buildings on the eastern seaboard.

Sand Island. In 2006, Maine Coast Heritage Trust announced the purchase of Sand Island, a 10-acre island (not labeled on the map) located at the southeast corner of Crotch Island. The island's owners had long allowed the public to picnic there and decided to sell to MCHT to ensure continuing access.

Russ Island. The Chewonki Foundation agreed to buy this 50-acre island, which lies immediately south of the Thorofare, from the Island Institute in 2005. A small area has been set aside for the nonprofit's educational programs. Be aware that sailors and schooner groups have long used the beach on the southeast, and don't be surprised if you get company there. A trail leads from the eastern point to a cove on the western side, and also south to the beach.

Hells Half Acre. Despite its name, Hells Half Acre is neither a half acre in size—it's 2 acres—nor is it a place of torment. On the contrary, its sloping granite shores are rather lovely; it's one of the few places that offer excellent access for paddlers who use a wheelchair. This island (unnamed on the chart) lies north of Devil Island and halfway between Camp and Bold islands. Because it is a public island in a popular place, Hells Half Acre gets a lot of use.

Millet Island. Millet is a nature preserve. Day-use visitors are welcome to picnic and walk the perimeter—there are no trails—but should leave dogs at home and make no fires. A beach on the northwest side of the island is the best place to land; the island itself lies west of Saddleback. Margaret Hundley, an ornithologist, gave the island to The Nature Conservancy, which later transferred it to the Island Heritage Trust.

Saddleback Island. Thanks to its Campaign for the Coast, Maine Coast Heritage Trust was able to scoop up 78-acre Saddleback Island soon after it was listed for sale in late 2004. The organization has been developing a management plan that will include public day use.

Eastern Mark Island. Maine Coast Heritage Trust bought this 14-acre island in 2003 to protect its great blue heron rookery; the island is open to the public from September 1 through April 14. The Coastal Maine Islands

National Wildlife Refuge lists Eastern Mark as an island to be acquired.

Little Sheep Island. This isle tags after Sheep Island, which is located east of Buckmaster Neck on the eastern side of Deer Isle. At 1.5 acres, there's not much to see except grass and one tree, but it is on the Maine Island Trail and open to public use.

Steves Island. Steves is the westernmost in a row of four islands (including the next three), all of which are open to the public for day use. Unnamed on the chart, it is the 2-acre isle that lies between George Head Island and Wreck Island. Steves is on the Maine Island Trail.

Wreck Island. Inside the fringe of spruce along the shore, Wreck Island has a tranquil grassy field. The Island Heritage Trust, which owns and manages the 40-acre island, allows careful day use. Landing beaches flank the thumb on the north shore of the island; there is a sign at the eastern beach. There are no trails, but it is easy to walk across the field and bedrock outcroppings. Be careful around the old fences and foundations.

Round Island. Wreck and Round islands are a study in contrasts. While Wreck is open, Round is thickly vegetated. Although the Island Heritage Trust allows careful day use, there are no paths into the interior. There is a beach on the east side, opposite McGlathery Island, and another on the southern shore.

McGlathery Island. McGlathery Island, owned by Friends of Nature, is open to the public for careful day use. Charles McLane, author of *Islands of the Mid-Maine Coast: Penobscot Bay*, recounts an unverified story that the newly married Lindberghs, Charles and Anne, spent part of their honeymoon hiding here from reporters and photographers. They are said to have anchored their boat along the north-shore cove and then camouflaged it with spruce boughs.

Water and granite, Merchant Row

Whatever secrets the island harbored in 1929, today it is open to all visitors, and they all do visit—sailors, paddlers, skippers and their crews, captains and their windjammers full of guests. The favored anchorages are between Round and McGlathery, and in the cove of Lindbergh fame. Sea kayakers (and others) find the beach on the west side and the sandy bar on the northeast corner the most welcoming places to land. Note that No Man's Island, to the northeast, is managed by Maine's Department of Inland Fisheries and Wildlife and is closed during spring and summer.

Harbor Island. Eleven-acre Harbor Island, which lies south of Merchant Row and north of Merchant Island, is part of the Maine Island Trail. Harbor has inviting little beaches and meadows plus a good anchorage on the south side, so it draws a large audience. The schooner crowd goes ashore on the beach on the south side, so if you are looking for solitude, look elsewhere.

Bill's Island. In 2006, Maine Coast Heritage Trust accepted the donation of 12-acre Bill's Island (located not quite half a mile north of Pell Island, but not shown on the map). The island is open to the public.

Wheat Island. Wheat is the 4-acre island just off the northern tip of Burnt Island, which itself lies at the northern end of Isle au Haut. The sandy spit on the western side is the natural landing site. Wheat is part of the Maine Island Trail.

Doliver Island. Doliver is only 7 miles, as the crow flies, from Stonington, but as it lies on the east side of Isle au Haut (and off the northwest tip of York Island) it seems far away, indeed. This 2-acre island on the Maine Island Trail is open for day use only.

Isle au Haut. Both Samuel de Champlain and Captain John Smith noted this high island (*haut* is French for "high") that forms the eastern boundary of Penobscot Bay. The highest "peaklet" in the island's ridge rises to 543 feet. The northern half of the island and land all along the eastern shore are privately held; most of the rest is part of Acadia National Park. The park maintains hiking trails and a very small campground at Duck Harbor (see appendix E for contact information for the campground).

Isle au Haut Light. This light was built on Robinson Point on the western shore of Isle au Haut in 1907. The light stands 48 feet above the water, showing from a two-tone tower. The keeper's house is now a B&B.

Deer Isle. Because of historic use patterns, Deer Isle (the island) developed two quite different faces. Early settlement involved the northern three-quarters of the island. There was a village at Deer Isle, a port at Oceanville, and farms throughout. Activity in the inhospitable southern quarter picked up only with the establishment of granite quarries at Green's Landing (later called Stonington, for obvious reasons) and on numerous islands to the south. Stonington also developed into the port for the fishing fleet. This division continues today. The town of Deer Isle includes Little Deer Isle and everything north of a line drawn from Crockett Cove to Inner Harbor and Southeast Harbor, while the town of Stonington includes the southern section of the island and all the islands north of Merchant Row. Isle au Haut became its own town in 1874.

Polypod Island. The Island Heritage Trust owns this 4-acre wooded isle in Southeast Harbor (not named on the chart).

Edgar M. Tennis Preserve. This state-owned preserve, managed by the Island Heritage Trust, fronts on Southeast Harbor about a mile east of Polypod Island.

At a Glance: Land in Public or Conservation Ownership

Weir Island	Maine Island Trail/BPL
Sand Island	Maine Coast Heritage Trust; careful day use
Russ Island	Chewonki Foundation; careful day use
Hells Half Acre	Maine Island Trail/BPL
Millet Island	Island Heritage Trust; careful day use
Eastern Mark Island	MCHT; April 15–August 31
Saddleback Island	Maine Coast Heritage Trust; careful day use
Little Sheep Island	Maine Island Trail/BPL
Steves Island	Maine Island Trail/BPL
Wreck Island	Island Heritage Trust; careful day use
Round Island	Island Heritage Trust; careful day use
McGlathery Island	Friends of Nature; careful day use
Harbor Island	Maine Island Trail/BPL
Bill's Island	Maine Coast Heritage Trust; careful day use
Wheat Island	Maine Island Trail/BPL
Doliver Island	Maine Island Trail/BPL
Polypod Island	Island Heritage Trust; careful day use

IF&W Wildlife Islands

These islands are closed during the indicated bird nesting season. After the nesting season is over, the islands are limited to careful day use.

Moose Island Ledge (0.4 mi W of Moose Island)	April 15–July 31
Scraggy Island Ledge (immediately S of Scraggy Island)	April 15–July 31
No Man's Island (0.7 mi NE of McGlathery Island)	February 15–August 31
Rams Island (0.4 mi N of McGlathery)	February 15–August 31
Shabby Island (1.5 mi SE of Stinson Neck)	April 15–July 31
Hardwood Island (0.2 mi W of Merchant Island)	February 15–August 31
Sparrow Island (1.8 mi WNW of Merchant Island)	April 15–July 31
W. Halibut Ledge (1.2 mi W of Merchant Island)	April 15–July 31

Continued on next page.

So. Popplestone Island (2.4 mi NE of Isle au Haut)	April 15–August 31
Southern Mark Island (2.7 mi NE of Isle au Haut)	April 15–July 31
Fog Island Ledge (1.4 mi NE of Isle au Haut)	April 15–July 31
Great Spoon Island (2.2 mi E of Isle au Haut)	April 15–August 31
White Ledge (2 mi E of Isle au Haut)	April 15–July 31
Green Ledge (SE of Fog Island)	April 15–July 31
The Cow Pen, both isles (1 mi E of Isle au Haut)	April 15–July 31
White Horse Island (2 mi E of Isle au Haut)	April 15–July 31
Black Horse Island (1.6 mi E of Isle au Haut)	April 15–July 31
USFWS Wildlife Islands	
Little Spoon (1 mi E of Isle au Haut)	April 1–August 31

Eggemoggin Reach and Blue Hill Bay

Naskeag, which means "the end" or "the extremity," correctly describes this neck of land that lies at the extreme southeast of the massive Blue Hill peninsula.

Trip Ideas *(weather and experience permitting)*

Explore the islands between Naskeag and Deer Isle (up to 10 miles, depending on route) or the islands east of Naskeag (8 to 10 miles, depending on route).

Charts
Chart: 13316, Blue Hill Bay (1:40,000)
Chart Kit: 71
Maine Atlas locator maps: 15, 16

Tides (hours:minutes relative to Portland; average rise)
Sedgwick: 0:11 before; 10.2 feet
Naskeag Harbor: 0:16 before; 10.2 feet

Safety Considerations, Strong Currents, and Caution Areas

Wind. The area covered here is vulnerable to the wind from almost any direction, and paddlers need to assess carefully the conditions, the weather forecast, and their own skills.

Casco Passage and York Narrows. The busy Casco Passage, which lies north of Swans Island and joins Jericho and Blue Hill bays, floods east and ebbs west with a current that reaches less than a knot. York Narrows, however, has currents that can run quite strong. York Narrows branches off the western end of Casco Passage, just north of Buckle Island.

Access

116: Naskeag Harbor, Brooklin. To get to this all-tide gravel launch, which has a portable toilet and a new wharf, turn south from ME 175 in Brooklin onto Naskeag Point road. Continue for 3.6 miles.

Restricted: Benjamin River, Sedgwick. The town of Sedgwick owns and manages this site for the use of town residents.

117: South Blue Hill. See next chapter for description.

Points of Interest

Campbell Island. In 2005 the Chewonki Foundation, which offers a variety of educational programs focusing on natural history, signed a purchase and sale agreement for Campbell with the Island Institute. The island lies within the embrace of Deer Isle's Oak Point and Greenlaw Neck. More than a hundred years ago, the Smithsonian Institute sent an ethnological team to Campbell. The team found two burial sites; in one of them lay a European wearing armor, possibly dating from the early 1600s.

Little Hog Island. This island, not named on the chart, is joined at low tide to the privately owned Hog Island; Hog Island forms the southern side of Naskeag Harbor. Little Hog is on the Maine Island Trail, as are the next three islands.

Sellers Island. Two-acre Sellers Island, which has a small beach that serves as a great snack or lunch site, lies to the east of Hog Island.

Potato Island. Two-acre Potato lies across Eggemoggin Reach, a little more than a mile southwest of Hog Island.

Apple Island. Apple Island is a tiny wedge of land in Fish Creek (north of Stinson Neck). Be forewarned that Apple is mud-locked at low tide.

Smuttynose Island. Captain William Owen, in a narrative of his travels in the 1760s and 1770s, wrote that Smuttynose is "a remarkable white, rocky, tufted island ... and pretty bold, too." It is now managed by Maine's Department of Inland Fisheries and Wildlife.

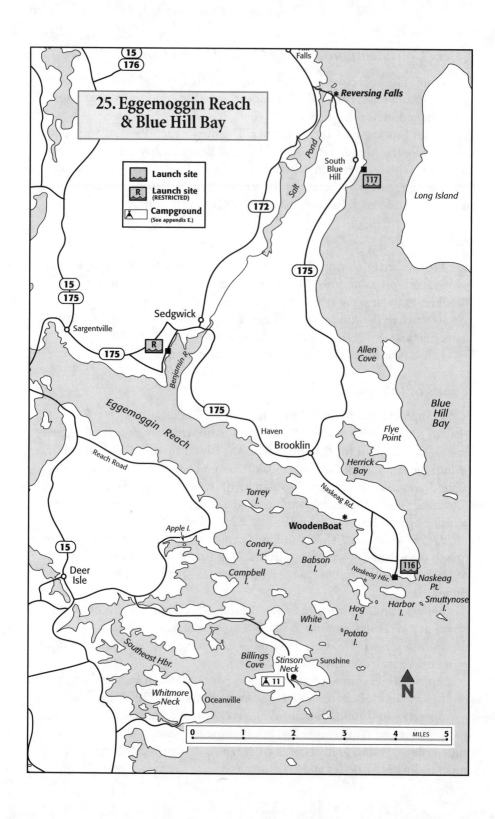

25. Eggemoggin Reach & Blue Hill Bay

Launch site

R Launch site (RESTRICTED)

▲ Campground (See appendix E.)

15
176

* Reversing Falls

Salt Pond

South Blue Hill

117

Long Island

172

175

15
175

Sedgwick

Sargentville

175

R

Benjamin R.

175

Allen Cove

Eggemoggin Reach

Haven

Brooklin

Blue Hill Bay

Flye Point

Reach Road

Herrick Bay

Naskeag Rd.

Torrey I.

WoodenBoat *

Apple I.

Conary I.

Babson I.

116

Naskeag Pt.

15

Campbell I.

Naskeag Hbr.

Harbor I.

Smuttynose I.

Deer Isle

Hog I.

White I.

Potato I.

Southeast Hbr.

Billings Cove

Stinson Neck

Sunshine

▲ 11

N

Whitmore Neck

Oceanville

0   1   2   3   4   MILES   5

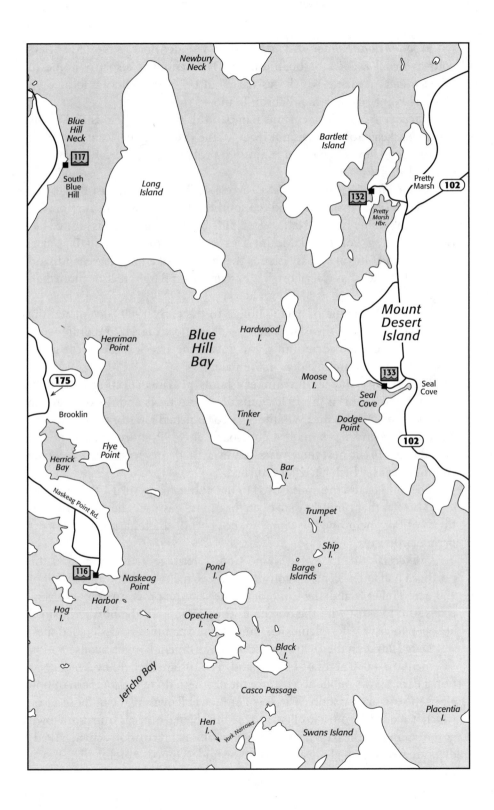

WoodenBoat School of Boatbuilding. WoodenBoat (359-4651) offers courses in all aspects of boatbuilding. The school is also the home of *WoodenBoat* magazine, which was started in 1974. The school is located on Naskeag Point, just north of Babson Island.

Opechee Island. The curious name of this privately held island to the east of Naskeag Point comes not from Maine's Native Americans, but from one of Longfellow's poems. In *Hiawatha*, a robin—an *opechee*—begs not to be shot by Hiawatha.

Ship Island Group. Trumpet (3 acres), Ship (11 acres), East Barge, and West Barge (each 0.5 acres), and the southern half of Bar Island are part of the Coastal Maine Islands National Wildlife Refuge. The group is located between Naskeag Point and Mount Desert Island in Blue Hill Bay. Bar, Trumpet, and Ship are grassy islands that are part of a long gravel and sand deposit that likely has glacial origins. East and West Barge are little more than ledges.

Until an epidemic of avian cholera in the early 1980s decimated the seabirds that lived on the islands here—killing more than 1,700 common eiders, double-crested cormorants, and gulls—the area was the third largest nesting site for common eiders in the state.

Historically, Ship and Trumpet islands provided nesting habitat to common terns, but in the 1930s gulls destroyed nests and drove away the nesters. The U.S. Fish and Wildlife Service launched a restoration effort on Ship in 1993 and terns made a comeback; in 1999, more than 500 pairs nested there. In the next three years, however, predators again drove away the common terns, which have not returned.

The Ship Island group is closed to the public from April 1 through August 31. After that time, they are open for careful day use. The northern two-thirds of Bar, including the camp, are not part of the refuge; please respect private property.

Tinker Island. In 1991, Maine Coast Heritage Trust purchased the northern half and accepted a conservation easement on the southern half of 430-acre Tinker Island; the Land for Maine's Future program granted a generous sum to assist with the purchase. The 235 acres of the northern parcel are open to visitors for picnicking, hunting, and camping at designated sites.

Long Island. In the 1990s, the federal government bought a conservation easement on 4,000 acres of Long Island. The easement, held by Acadia National Park, allows public access from the northern tip to the southern thumb along the east-facing shore. The Town of Blue Hill owns many of those acres, which it acquired from a tax lien. For the time being, officials from both town government and the park favor allowing traditional recreation activities. Paddlers are free to stop along any part of the undeveloped shoreline. The beach at the northern tip, and Dunhams and Fogg Coves (check your chart) along the southeast offer good landing areas. These areas provide a spectacular view of Mount Desert Island. The rest of the eastern shore is rocky with woods.

Hen Island. Hen Island, not shown on the map on page 239, is a 2-acre public island linked to Swans Island at low water. On the chart, look for Seal Cove on the northwest side of Swans Island. Hen is about half a mile south of Buckle Island, in the eastern side of Seal Cove. Hen, which is managed by the Bureau of Parks and Lands, has a luxuriant stand of poison ivy on the northwest side; raccoons feast on unattended food.

At a Glance: Land in Public or Conservation Ownership

Campbell Island	Chewonki Foundation; careful day use
Little Hog Island	Maine Island Trail/BPL
Sellers Island	Maine Island Trail/BPL
Potato Island	Maine Island Trail/BPL
Apple Island	Maine Island Trail/BPL
Hen Island	Maine Island Trail/BPL
Tinker Island (northern half)	Maine Coast Heritage Trust; careful day use
Long Island (eastern side)	Town of Blue Hill with Acadia National Park easement; careful day use

IF&W Wildlife Islands

These islands are closed during the indicated bird nesting season. After the nesting season is over, the islands are limited to careful day use.

Shabby Island (1.5 mi SE of Stinson Neck)	April 15–July 31
Green Island Ledge (1.6 mi NE of Naskeag Point)	April 15–July 31
Smuttynose Island (0.4 mi S of Naskeag Point)	April 15–July 31

USFS Fish and Wildlife Islands

Ship Island Group	Closed April 1–August 31

Upper Blue Hill Bay and the Union River

The Union River is a small gem in the rough, offering a half-day or evening tour with lots of wildlife. If you paddle on weekends and holidays, you are sure to be accompanied by powerboaters heading for open waters. So if you value quiet, plan accordingly. You can also set out from Blue Hill to explore the upper reaches of Blue Hill Bay. It's fun to paddle by (but not necessarily through) the tidal falls that forms at the mouth of Salt Pond.

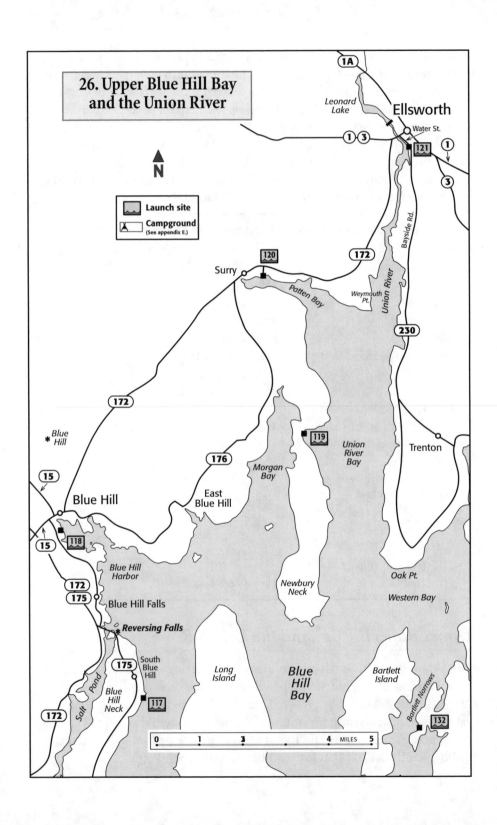

26. Upper Blue Hill Bay and the Union River

N

Launch site
Campground
(See appendix E.)

1A

Leonard Lake

Ellsworth

Water St.

1 3

121 1

3

172

120

Surry

Patten Bay

Weymouth Pt.

Union River

230

172

Blue Hill

15

176

Morgan Bay

119

Union River Bay

Trenton

Blue Hill

East Blue Hill

15

118

Blue Hill Harbor

172

175

Blue Hill Falls

Reversing Falls

Newbury Neck

Oak Pt.

Western Bay

175

South Blue Hill

Salt Pond

Blue Hill Neck

117

172

Long Island

Blue Hill Bay

Bartlett Island

Bartlett Narrows

132

0   1   2   3   4   5
MILES

Chart

Chart: 13316, Blue Hill Bay (1:40,000)
Chart Kit: 71, 72
Maine Atlas locator maps: 15, 16

Tides (hours:minutes relative to Portland; average rise)
Union River: 0:09 before; 10.4 feet
Blue Hill Harbor: 0:13 before; 10.1 feet
Allen Cove, Blue Hill Bay: 0:12 before; 10.3 feet

Trip Ideas (weather and experience permitting)

From Ellsworth, Surry, or Newbury Neck, paddle the Union River (8 miles from Ellsworth to Weymouth Point and back). The shoreline is a mixture of rural homes, woodland, and fields. Watch for bald eagles, ospreys, double-crested cormorants, and common terns. Seals swim surprisingly far up the Union River.

From South Blue Hill or Blue Hill, explore Blue Hill Harbor (mileage depends on how far you want to go). For a longer trip, circumnavigate Long Island, an island in private ownership (17 to 19 miles, depending on launch site). Note that the Blue Hill ramp fronts on mudflats during the lower part of the tide cycle.

Safety Considerations, Strong Currents, and Caution Areas

Blue Hill Falls. A reversing tidal falls forms at the mouth of Salt Pond, several miles south of Blue Hill. When the current is at its greatest, this is a serious rapid, one that whitewater kayakers and canoeists have used to hone their skills. The Coast Pilot notes its strength and turbulence. The Maine Island Trail Association recommends scouting the rapids and passing at or near slack water.

Blue Hill Harbor. Sculpin Point and Harbor Point divide the inner from the outer harbor at Blue Hill. When the tide is running at its greatest velocity, a stiff current pours between these points.

Access

117: South Blue Hill. This site has a concrete all-tide ramp and a gravel parking lot. From the junction of ME 15 and ME 172/ME 175 west of Blue Hill, take ME 175 south. From the reversing falls, continue for 1.5 miles and turn left onto a dirt road. Local fishermen use this launch site, so please do not clog the ramp or fill up the parking lot.

118: Blue Hill Harbor. This launch site has a small parking lot and a

Sea kayakers should approach Blue Hill Falls only at slack water.

part-tide concrete ramp. The ramp has water at and above halftide. From the north, take ME 15 into Blue Hill, following it as it makes a right turn in town. Turn left onto Water Street at the hospital sign and proceed 0.1 mile. The launch is behind the Fire Station. (Blue Hill Town Park, on the same road, has public rest rooms.)

Note. Blue Hill Falls does not have a launch site. Parking is not allowed along the road at Blue Hill Falls, where ME 175 crosses the mouth of Salt Pond, and the adjacent land is privately owned.

119: Carrying Place Beach, Newbury Neck, Union River. From Surry, take ME 176 (also called the Morgan Bay Road) southeast for 2.8 miles and turn left onto Cross Road. Go 0.8 mile and at the T turn right onto Newbury Neck Road. Go 1.6 miles to where a gravel/cobble beach lies on the left and a small parking area on the right. Paddlers may launch anywhere along the beach.

120: Patten Bay, Surry. From Surry, take ME 172 east for less than a mile. Turn right on Wharf Road to arrive at the Patten Bay boat ramp and dock, where there is a ramp, dirt parking lot, and granite tables and benches.

121: Union River, Ellsworth. This launch site has an all-tide concrete ramp, flush toilets, and a large parking lot. From the intersection of Route 1/ ME 3 and ME 230 in Ellsworth, go south on ME 230 for 0.5 mile and turn right at the public boat access sign. This launch is popular with powerboaters because it serves as a conduit to Blue Hill Bay and beyond.

Points of Interest

Blue Hill. The hill after which the town and bay are named is a modest 934 feet high.

Twin Oaks Island. This half-acre public island in the inner section of Blue Hill Harbor is open to visitors for careful day use. Twin Oaks is about

200 yards southwest of the island that lies directly between Peters and Parker Points (check your chart).

Traditional inside passage. Instead of paddling around Naskeag Point, Native Americans followed a route through Salt Pond, across Great Meadow, and into the Benjamin River. Aerial photos suggest that this route now involves some portaging.

At a Glance: Land in Public or Conservation Ownership

Twin Oaks Island	BPL; careful day use

Northern Mount Desert Island and Frenchman Bay

Frenchman Bay is drop-dead gorgeous. The Porcupine Islands, prickly with spruce and fir, march across the horizon. Black guillemots dive for fish while common terns flit and scream. Laughing and Bonaparte's gulls, with their distinctive black heads, stand out from their ever-present herring and great black-backed cousins. Bald eagles and ospreys soar over the water, keeping a keen eye out for food below. Harbor porpoise, the smallest of the marine mammals along this coast, swim by quietly. Sometimes, if the seas are calm and you are quiet, you can hear them breathe when they surface.

Frenchman Bay is the center of activity for northern Mount Desert, but there are other inviting places to paddle as well. For quieter waters, turn to Eastern Bay, where sea caves and an arch grace the southern shore, and Mount Desert Narrows. Or, explore some of the pretty areas—such as the Skillings River, Sullivan Harbor, and Flanders Bay—that lead into Frenchman Bay.

Frenchman Bay is not necessarily a paddler's best friend. Wind, waves, and fog can turn a pleasant day sour or worse. The granite shore, fir-tipped islands, and powerful flanking bays deserve careful consideration and respect.

Charts
Charts: 13318, Frenchman Bay and Mount Desert Island (1:40,000)
          13316, Blue Hill Bay (1:40,000)
Chart Kit: 72, 73, 74
Maine Atlas locator maps: 16, 24

Tides (hours:minutes relative to Portland; average rise)
Mount Desert Narrows: 0:08 before; 10.5 feet
Salsbury Cove: 0:15 before; 10.6 feet
Bar Harbor: 0:22 before; 10.6 feet
Sullivan: 0:10 before; 10.5 feet
Sullivan Falls: High 1:10 after, low 1:35 after

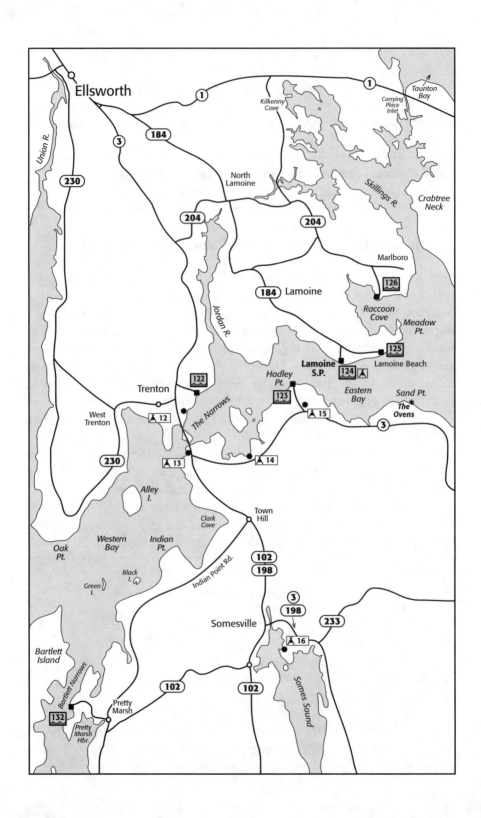

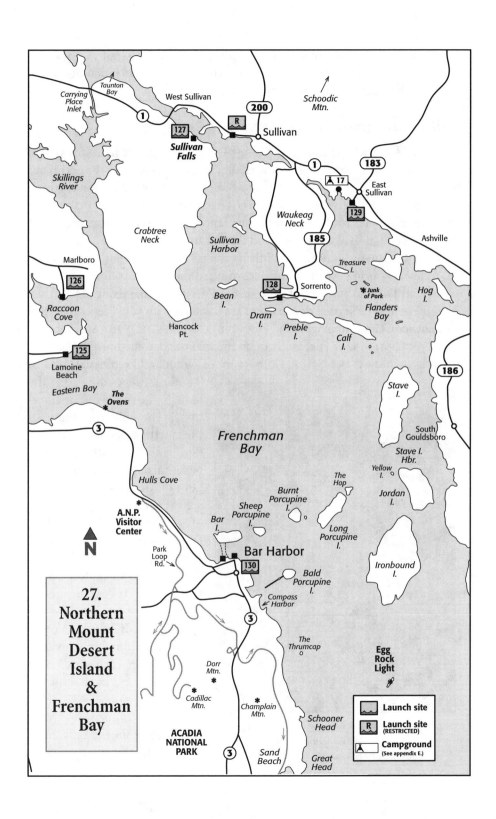

Taunton Bay
Carrying Place Inlet
West Sullivan
200
Schoodic Mtn.
1
R
Sullivan
127
Sullivan Falls
1
183
▲ 17
East Sullivan
Skillings River
129
Crabtree Neck
Sullivan Harbor
Waukeag Neck
Ashville
185
Marlboro
Treasure I.
126
Bean I.
128
Sorrento
✳ Junk of Pork
Hog I.
Raccoon Cove
Dram I.
Preble I.
Flanders Bay
Hancock Pt.
Calf I.
125
Stave I.
Lamoine Beach
186
Eastern Bay
The Ovens ✳
Frenchman Bay
South Gouldsboro
3
Stave I. Hbr.
Hulls Cove
The Hop
Yellow I.
Jordan I.
A.N.P. Visitor Center ✳
Burnt Porcupine I.
Sheep Porcupine I.
Long Porcupine I.
Bar I.
Park Loop Rd.
N
Bar Harbor
Ironbound I.
130
Bald Porcupine I.
Compass Harbor
27. Northern Mount Desert Island & Frenchman Bay
3
The Thrumcap
Egg Rock Light
Dorr Mtn. ✳
Cadillac Mtn. ✳
Champlain Mtn. ✳
Schooner Head
ACADIA NATIONAL PARK
3
Sand Beach
Great Head

	Launch site
R	Launch site (RESTRICTED)
▲	Campground (See appendix E.)

The area is so beautiful that it draws millions (yes, millions) of visitors each year. Dodging traffic, both on the water and off, can be as much of a challenge as the elements themselves.

Trip Ideas (weather and experience permitting)

To explore the waters north of Mount Desert Island, put in at any of the launch sites—Trenton, Lamoine, or Hadley Point—and paddle the perimeter of Mount Desert Narrows and Eastern Bay (11 to 12 miles covers everything from the bridge at Trenton to the Ovens just east of Sand Point; or, you can pick out a shorter route that suits your fancy). This area is more protected than Frenchman Bay when the wind is from the north or the south.

For a point-to-point trip, paddle between Trenton and Bar Harbor (9 or 10 miles), choosing the direction according to the tide and wind.

From Bar Harbor, explore the scenic Porcupine islands. It's fair to say that there may be several dozen other sea kayakers with you; Frenchman Bay is a hot spot. Circumnavigate the Porcupines (8 miles) or plan a shorter trip.

From Sorrento or East Sullivan on the mainland, tour through the local islands, including The Nature Conservancy's Dram and Preble islands (4 to 9 miles, depending on the launch site and your inclination). The bald mountain to the north is Schoodic Mountain. To the southwest, in a beautiful display, are the mountains of Mount Desert.

Carrying Place Inlet at low water, showing why it's important to pay attention to the tide when circumnavigating Crabtree Neck.

When planning a trip out of Sullivan Falls, it is important to consider tidal flow, river current, and wind. Launch above Sullivan Falls to explore Taunton Bay (7 miles) or below them to poke around Sorrento and its islands (up to 13 or so miles, depending on your destination). In each case, plan to go there and back with the tide.

To circumnavigate Crabtree Neck from the falls, head north with the tide, arrive at

Carrying Place Inlet at high water (it is dry at low water), and paddle south. The flow may initially be against you—water in the inlet ebbs north—but as soon as you reach "Old Pond" (check your chart) you can ride the ebb south to Young's Bay and the Skillings River. The current on the river is strong on the ebb, and you can expect chop if the wind is from the southwest. From Hancock, round back to the falls (13 miles round-trip).

Safety Considerations, Strong Currents, and Caution Areas

Mount Desert Narrows. Mount Desert Narrows is the northern thoroughfare between Blue Hill Bay and Frenchman Bay. The current floods westward and ebbs eastward. At the bottom of the tide, the Narrows is mostly mud and the channel nearly dry. At maximum velocity, the current can move right along—the *Coast Pilot* calls it "turbulent."

Frenchman Bay. Boat traffic is a very real consideration in Frenchman Bay. Numerous vessels, from cruise ships to schooners to yachts to all manner of smaller boats make their way to and from this summer hot spot. *The CAT*, a high-speed ferry that runs between Bar Harbor and Yarmouth, Nova Scotia, sends out a huge wake—a wake that would be a veritable tidal wave to a kayaker. *The CAT* docks just north of Bar Harbor. Although it slows down as it nears its destination, there have been instances when its wake caused injuries to individuals and damage to boats.

Also, when fog visits, it's no fun to be the smallest and most vulnerable boat in the crowd.

A local mariner notes that once or twice a summer, squalls sweep through Frenchman Bay. These squalls, which advance from the north and usually last less than half an hour, may bring winds of 60 knots that kick up large, confused seas. Often, but not always, the wind is accompanied by heavy rain. If you see a black line of clouds with a white line at water level, find shelter promptly.

Even without a squall, wind is a consideration in Frenchman Bay. Although the islands do offer some shelter, there is still plenty of exposure.

Bar Harbor. The end of the breakwater that extends from Bald Porcupine Island to within 250 yards of the shore is marked by a light; the breakwater is not entirely covered at high tide. Although the breakwater does offer some protection, seas can develop inside the line of rocks.

Dorr Point and southern coast. The shoreline from Dorr Point south is bold and rocky, with few safe havens. Dorr Point is located at the southern end of the town of Bar Harbor just south of Compass Harbor.

Long Porcupine. When the wind is from the south, the cliffs on the south side of Long Porcupine can throw back swells to create a confusing chop.

Launch ramp, Trenton

Jordan Island. When the tide and wind are opposed, a vicious chop can develop in the area of the shallow underwater bar that connects Jordan Island to the mainland on the east side of Frenchman Bay. In addition, at some stages of the tide, strong tidal currents can run through the passage between the island and the mainland.

Sullivan Falls. Sullivan Falls is a reversing falls that forms at the head of Sullivan Harbor. The *Coast Pilot* is effusive in its warning: "Tidal currents are swift and dangerous. . . . There is a great turbulence whenever the current is running at strength. . . . Tidal currents through the falls are dangerous at strength. . . . Navigation through the falls is safe only at slack water."

Experienced sea kayakers may choose to run through the narrows with the current some time before or after slack. When it is high tide in Sullivan, the water through the falls is fast and pushy but runnable for people who understand the dynamics of whitewater and who are comfortable with fast currents.

Now that kayakers can launch at the falls, putting in either above or below the rapids, there's no reason to court danger in the falls unless you have the skills and desire to do so.

Winter Harbor Lobster Boat Race. Make sure you're not competing for elbow room with the big boats. Check www.lobsterboatracing.com for the date of this race.

Access

122: Mount Desert Narrows, Trenton. This is one of the most user-friendly launch ramps on the coast of Maine. The extra-wide ramp is made of huge granite blocks that can handle everything from sea kayaks to seaplanes; the parking is more than ample; and the view of Mount Desert Island is worth the trip. The ramp is all-tide except during the very lowest of spring tides. From Ellsworth, take ME 3 south toward Mount Desert. Note the mileage as you pass the junction of ME 3 and ME 204; proceed a little more than 3 miles and turn left onto Caruso Drive at the sign for the Hancock County–Bar Harbor Airport. Go 0.3 mile and turn right onto Ramp Road. Follow this road to its end at the Hancock County boat and seaplane launch site.

It is possible to launch from the picnic area at nearby Thompson Island (by the bridge onto Mount Desert) but the mudflats at the bottom of the tide and the general congestion at that site make the Trenton launch a better bet.

123: *Mount Desert Narrows, Hadley Point.* This is a lovely sand-beach site far from the bustle of Bar Harbor, but it can be crowded on a warm summer day. In 2005, the Town of Bar Harbor talked about putting in a paved ramp and turning nearby land into a parking lot, but so far that plan hasn't come to fruition. There is a portable toilet and very little parking at high water; make sure your vehicle is safe if you are going to be away during that time.

Take ME 3 onto Mount Desert and go 3.2 miles. At the top of a hill, take a left onto Hadley Point Road and follow it 0.6 mile to the end. Hand carry to the water.

124: *Lamoine State Park.* This park (667-4778) has an all-tide gravel launch ramp, picnic area, camping area, and vault toilets. The entrance fee is $3 per person. Take Route 1 through the town and continue on it when ME 3 goes straight to Acadia. In a little more than a mile, bear right on ME 184 and follow it 7.9 miles. State Park Road will be on the right.

125: *Lamoine Beach.* Go to the state park and keep on driving for almost a mile. When it looks like you're going to drive into the sea, stop. This town beach has an unpaved parking lot, an outhouse, and a hard-surface, all-tide ramp.

126: *Raccoon Cove.* There's not much to recommend this hand-carry site. Parking is on ground that is not quite high enough during storm surges, yet the entire cove—except for a channel that does not reach the launch area—goes dry at low water. Sea kayakers tend to favor maintained sites on The Narrows and Eastern Bay that are closer to boating destinations. From Route 1 east of Ellsworth, go south on ME 184 for 3 miles. Turn left at the Lamoine Town Hall onto ME 204. Go 4 miles to Raccoon Cove Road. Turn right and go 0.7 mile to Marlboro Beach. Turn right to the launch area.

127: *Sullivan Falls.* Before the Frenchman Bay Conservancy bought this 4-acre parcel, a large fence prevented anyone but restaurant customers from viewing the dramatic tidal falls. Now, the fence is gone and you may hand carry above or below the falls, depending on your inclination. Sullivan Falls

Bar Harbor's harbor is crammed with vessels of all sizes, including cruise ships, The CAT (an international ferry), pleasure yachts, and paddle craft. Here, a cruise ship dwarfs the Porcupine Islands.

is both beautiful and instructive; if you've ever wanted to see how rapids change as the water level goes up and down, this is the place to do so.

In July and August, the little restaurant still sells lobster rolls, with the proceeds going to the land trust. The Land for Maine's Future program contributed funding to this project, and an easement to the Department of Conservation guarantees permanent public use.

From Ellsworth, drive east on Route 1 until ME 182 comes in on the left. Go 4 more miles, passing Carrying Place Inlet, and turn right on East Side Road. In less than a mile, turn left on Tidal Falls Road and go down the hill.

Restricted: Sullivan Harbor. Only residents, their guests, or individuals lodging in Sullivan may use this ramp. The Sullivan Falls site provides access just a few miles away.

128: Sorrento Harbor. This site, which looks out onto Sorrento Harbor, is well used during the summer. There is room for less than two dozen vehicles; the lot is often full. At the junction of Route 1 and ME 185 east of Sullivan, go south on ME 185. When the road splits, go left onto East Side Road (called Pomola at the other end) and at the T-intersection, take a left on Kearsarge. Proceed 0.5 mile to Ocean Avenue. Turn right on Ocean and go 0.1 mile to the town pier and parking lot, which are on the left. Hand carry to the beach next to the parking lot or—at high water—launch promptly from the ramp 100 yards west of the lot. There is a portable toilet behind the gray fence.

129: Flanders Bay, East Sullivan. This small launch site has a gravel ramp and gravel lot that holds about eight cars. The ramp is dry at dead low tide. Going east on Route 1, pass through Sullivan. From the point at which ME 185 comes in from the right, go 1.5 miles and turn right onto Town

A Thumbnail History of Mount Desert Island

Native Americans lived here for thousands of years. Giovanni da Verrazzano noted the island on his voyage of exploration in 1524, and Samuel de Champlain described it as *L'Isle des Monts Desert*—island of the barren mountains—in 1604. The Jesuits founded a mission in 1613 but it didn't last long. Antoine Laumet, who called himself Antoine de la Mothei sieur de Cadillac, obtained rights to the island and 6 square miles along the coast in 1688. Although he and his bride arrived with the intent of settling, in the long run his plan didn't work and he moved westward, eventually starting a trading post in 1701. The post grew into Detroit, and therein lies the connection between Mount Desert's Cadillac Mountain and the American luxury car.

The bay east of Mount Desert Island was called *Douaquët*, but on English maps, at least, a different name appeared by the end of the 1600s. Charles McLane, the chronicler of the history of Maine's islands, suggests that the English wanted to name it themselves; because many French expeditions to harass the British were organized here, they chose Frenchman Bay.

The French held Mount Desert—and Frenchman Bay—through the 1700s but lost Canada and their Acadian lands after the fall of Quebec. England gained control in 1763 but passed Acadia on to the Americans after the Revolution.

Life hummed along until the mid-1800s, when nature-loving rusticators began discovering the beauties of Bar Harbor and its deserted mountains. These vacationers included the Rockefellers, Carnegies, Vanderbilts, Fords, and others who built "cottages" (most would call them mansions) overlooking the sparkling waters of Frenchman Bay. These wealthy families also led the effort to protect portions of the island. By a stroke of the pen in 1916, President Woodrow Wilson created Sieur de Monts National Monument. Three years later, the monument became Lafayette National Park, and in 10 more years, the park gained its final name—Acadia.

Acadia is Maine's only national park and it is a popular one: The park logs 3 million visits each year.

Landing Road (across from where ME 183 joins Route 1). Proceed 0.3 mile to the water.

Note. Fishermen use the ramp in South Gouldsboro and there's not much room left over for kayakers to park.

130: Bar Harbor. Theoretically, it is possible to launch from the all-tide launch ramp or beach next to it at the town pier, but given the crowds, it's not worth the effort. Should you wish to try, as you follow ME 3 east into Bar Harbor, take the first left onto West Street, which leads to the town pier, ramp, and bathrooms. Secure a recreational boater parking sticker from the harbor master. Parking in Bar Harbor is at best challenging and at worst impossible. Be aware that a brisk easterly wind can make launching difficult.

Duck into the Ovens only when the water is calm.

Paddlers sometimes launch from Bridge Street, which leads to the bar to Bar Island. When you turn onto West Street, as if you were going to the town pier, go 0.3 mile and turn left on Bridge Street. Parking is no better here.

Points of Interest

The Ovens. The Ovens are sea caves located east of Sand Point on Eastern Bay. The rock, called tuff, is formed from compacted fragments of volcanic ash. There are about 75 feet of cliffs here. Waves continually erode and undercut the rock, which breaks off along fracture lines, and a considerable amount of debris is visible along the bottom of the cliff at low tide. (*Note:* Rock falls on sunny days as well as stormy ones.) The arch, visible at low tide, is called Cathedral Rock. The set of stairs that leads up from the arch is private.

Bar Island. Bar Harbor gets its name from this island, which Acadia National Park now owns in its entirety. Bar is open to and quite popular with visitors. As a paddler, you'll get a little more privacy at high tide.

Compass Harbor. This small cove lies between Ogden Point and Dorr Point just south of Bar Harbor. Dorr Point and the land along the cove (but not including Ogden Point) are part of the park and are available as a snack or lunch stop.

Burnt Porcupine. The glacier that covered Maine thousands of years ago flowed over everything it encountered—mountains, hills, and domes of granite alike, including the dome that later became this private island. The massive sheet of ice ground down the near side of each projection, but as it flowed up and over, it plucked bedrock away from the far side, leaving a characteristic shape: a gradual rise on the north flank and a rocky face on the south. This geologic feature is called a *roche moutonnée,* or "sheepback rock," and this private island is an excellent example of it. Look for this feature on other islands in Frenchman Bay and along the Maine coast.

Burnt Porcupine has another interesting geologic formation, the Keyhole, a notch 2–3 feet wide with a small "room" at the end. The corridor is so narrow that those who enter find that they have to back out. Logic suggests that testing the Keyhole, on the island's western side, is best done when seas are absolutely calm.

Long Porcupine, Sheep Porcupine, and Bald Porcupine. All three of these wildlife islands,

Glaciers once plucked blocks from the south side of Long Porcupine, creating a steep face and a sea arch.

which stud Frenchman Bay east of Bar Harbor, are part of Acadia National Park. Bald Porcupine is open for careful day use; the other two are closed from the middle of February through the end of August, unless the park biologist posts them otherwise. Look for closure dates at www.nps.gov/acad/regulation.htm and its link to more detailed information.

Ospreys, black guillemots, and other species nest on Long Porcupine. Guillemots use the cliffs on the southwestern side of the island for their "nests," which are no more than flat rock ledges. There are no trails to entice visitors; the thick growth of spruce and fir is fairly impenetrable. Long Porcupine, like Burnt Porcupine, shows the effects of glacial plucking on its south side. This area also features a sea arch that stands about 40 feet above the water. This arch formed thousands of years ago when sea level was much higher.

The Hop. This small island on the northern end of Long Porcupine is part of Acadia. The bar that extends southwest at low tide is a regular lunch stop for kayakers; The Hop is open to visitation.

The Thrumcap. This Fisheries and Wildlife Island, located south of the Porcupines, has been transferred to Acadia. It is now closed from April 1 to July 21 or as posted.

Junk of Pork Island

Egg Rock and Egg Rock Light. Sieur de la Mothe Cadillac recorded in his journal in 1692 that he found 600 dozen eggs on this 12-acre island, which is low and mostly bare of vegetation. Although sailing vessels managed to negotiate Frenchman Bay, the advent of summer ferries in the mid-1800s prompted the U.S. government to build a light and a keeper's dwelling on Egg Rock in 1875. The square light tower, built on top of the house to conserve space, is 40 feet high; the light it holds shines 64 feet above the water. As any mariner would expect, over the years fierce storms have pounded both the island and its light station.

Black guillemots, Leach's storm-petrels, common eiders, herring gulls, and black-backed gulls nest on the Island, and seals use it as a haul-out area. The U.S. Fish and Wildlife Service owns and manages Egg Rock as part of the Maine Coastal Islands National Wildlife Refuge. The island is closed from April through August.

Yellow Island. If you see this island in late-afternoon or evening light, its rocks look yellow—or red, which was the island's previous name.

Jordan Island. Let the fog-enshrouded paddler beware: The authors of the *Coast Pilot* note that they have received accounts of compasses veering as much as 3 degrees from normal in the vicinity of this island. Jordan is privately owned.

Junk of Pork. This little island east of Sorrento has an intriguing name. Three of the definitions of "junk" in the *Oxford English Dictionary* are: a piece or lump of anything; an old rope; the salt meat used as food on long voyages, often compared to pieces of rope. Perhaps the unusual appearance of this island—a cone of sand and gravel rather than a rocky dome like the

Porcupines—prompted a mariner to describe it in terms of a none-too-favorite mainstay of sea life. Thrumcap, Little Calf, the east end of Calf, and Junk of Pork—all of which are composed of sand and gravel—are likely glacial deposits of some kind.

Dram and Preble islands. These two Nature Conservancy islands lie immediately south of Waukeag Neck and form Sorrento's harbor. Dram came to the conservancy in a most unusual way. A vacationing minister had purchased the 6-acre island at a town tax sale in the 1940s. Twenty-some years later, when he desperately needed an organ for his church in Wyoming, he decided to sell the island to a company that intended to strip its timber. When word got around the summer community in Sorrento, one of its members bought an organ and traded it for the island; he then gave Dram—plus Preble next door—to the conservancy.

Historically, these islands have provided eagle nesting habitat, and ospreys nest there now. Visitors may land on the islands—there are several nice cobble beaches on the south side of Preble—but are asked not to linger near the nests. There are no trails on either island.

Dram and Preble, like the northern end of Mount Desert Island, are of volcanic origin. Here, too, wave action has eroded the heavily jointed rock, creating sea caves.

At a Glance: Land in Public or Conservation Ownership

Lamoine State Park	BPL; boat launch, picnic area, camping area
Lamoine Beach	Town of Lamoine; swimming beach and boat launch
Dram Island (Sorrento)	TNC; careful day use
Preble Island (Sorrento)	TNC; careful day use
Black Island (Western Bay)	Maine Coast Heritage Trust; not open for visitation

USFWS Wildlife Islands

South Twinnie (Mount Desert Narrows)	Closed February 15–August 31

Acadia National Park Lands and Islands in Frenchman Bay

Bar Island	Careful day use
Compass Harbor	Careful day use
Sheep Porcupine Island	Closed February 15–August 31 or as posted
Bald Porcupine Island	Careful day use
Long Porcupine	Closed February 15–August 31 or as posted
The Hop (E of Long Porcupine)	Careful day use
Thrumcap (1.9 mi NW of Egg Rock)	Closed April 15–July 31 or as posted

Southern Mount Desert Island

Great Head and Schooner Head stand as sentinels, while a harsh, bold coast stretches around to Bass Harbor. Thunder Hole booms with the rising tide. Spectacular, steep-shored Somes Sound reaches into the very heart of the island. The island's stark mountains—Cadillac, the Beehive, Gorham, Pemetic, Penobscot, Sargent, Bernard, and others—roll across the horizon. The Cranberry Isles stand offshore, inviting or rebuffing depending on the weather. And the waves crash, eternally it seems, against the staunch shore. Indeed, the south side of Mount Desert Island is striking.

In terms of birds and marine mammals, look for the species that frequent the rest of Mount Desert Island: black guillemots, double-crested cormorants, various gulls (herring, great black-backed, laughing, and Bonaparte's), common terns, bald eagles, ospreys, harbor seals, and harbor porpoises. Gray seals occasionally show up on haulout ledges, and sometimes minke whales venture north into Blue Hill Bay. If you're paddling near Great Head on the eastern side of Mount Desert, you might be lucky enough to see peregrine falcons, which nest on cliffs along Champlain Mountain.

Trip Ideas (weather and experience permitting)

For a point-to-point trip, paddle between Seal Cove and Trenton (13 miles), picking the direction according to the tide. Be warned that Bartlett Narrows can be thick with sea kayakers.

From the picnic area on the shores of Somes Sound, paddle either north (5 miles round-trip to Somes Harbor) or south (4 miles round-trip to Valley Cove). Valley Cove is a nice stop for lunch and a short hike up Flying Mountain, which has a rewarding view.

From Manset or Southwest Harbor, circumnavigate Greening Island (3 miles), paddle the lower half of Somes Sound (6 to 8 miles round-trip), or

---

Charts
Charts: 13316, Blue Hill Bay (1:40,000)
          13318, Frenchman Bay and Mount Desert Island (1:40,000)
Chart Kit: 71, 74
Maine Atlas locator map: 16

Tides (hours:minutes relative to Portland; average rise)
Pretty Marsh Harbor: 0:13 before; 10.2 feet
Bass Harbor: 0:18 before; 9.9 feet
Southwest Harbor: 0:22 before; 10.2 feet
Somes Harbor: 0:16 before; 10.6 feet

paddle the entire length of the sound (14 miles round-trip). The sound is impressive, with mountains rising on both shores. If possible, go in with a flooding tide and out with an ebbing tide. At the very least, plan your trip so you are not paddling against the mid-cycle tide, particularly at the Narrows. Also factor in the wind, which can be a formidable adversary.

From Manset or Southwest Harbor, paddle to the town of Islesford on Little Cranberry (7 miles round-trip) or Baker Island (11 miles round-trip). These trips can also be done from Northeast Harbor, with a slight adjustment in mileage. From Seal Harbor, visit Islesford (4 miles round-trip) or Baker

Steep granite cliffs mark the southern shore near Hunters Beach Cove.

Island (8 to 9 miles round-trip). Although the Cranberry Isles may seem like they are a friendly puddle-hop away, when the wind rises the crossings take on a sharper edge.

To circumnavigate Mount Desert Island (46 to 49 miles depending on the exact route), choose legs that are in accord with the tide and weather conditions. This is where day trips shine: in 3 or 4 days spread over time—several weeks, a summer, or several summers—you can pick the right day for each leg and paddle with wind and tide in your favor. Paddlers undertaking trips on the exposed southern shores of Mount Desert need to have solid skills and good judgment. Bass Harbor Bar, for example, can be difficult for lobster boats and tour boats as well as sea kayaks when conditions are adverse.

Safety Considerations, Strong Currents, and Caution Areas

Bartlett Narrows. At its greatest velocity, the tidal current runs through the narrows at about 2 knots.

Bass Harbor to Dorr Point. The Cranberry islands provide some shelter for the southern coast of Mount Desert Island, and there are several

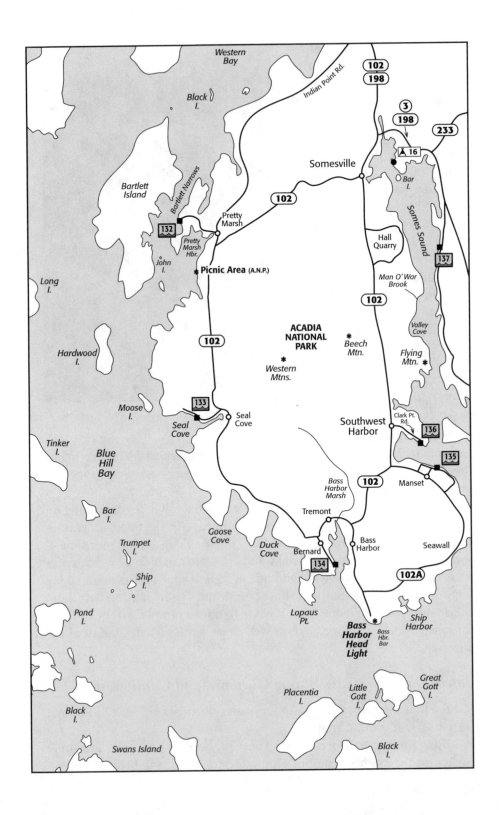

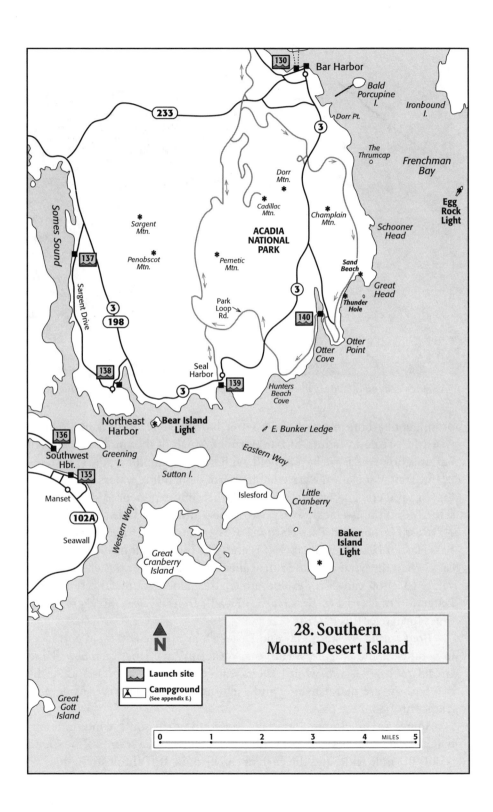

Bald
Porcupine
I.

Bar Harbor

130

Ironbound
I.

233

Dorr Pt.

3

The
Thrumcap

Frenchman
Bay

Dorr
Mtn.
*

Egg
Rock
Light

Cadillac
Mtn.
*

Champlain
Mtn.
*

Schooner
Head

Somes Sound

Sargent
Mtn.
*

ACADIA
NATIONAL
PARK

137

Penobscot
Mtn.
*

Pemetic
Mtn.
*

Sand
Beach
*

Great
Head

Sargent Drive

3

Thunder
Hole

198

Park
Loop
Rd.

3

140

Otter
Point

Otter
Cove

138

Seal
Harbor

139

3

Hunters
Beach
Cove

Northeast
Harbor

Bear Island
Light

E. Bunker Ledge

136

Greening
I.

Eastern Way

Southwest
Hbr.

Sutton I.

135

Islesford

Little
Cranberry
I.

Manset

102A

Western Way

Baker
Island
Light
*

Seawall

Great
Cranberry
Island

28. Southern
Mount Desert Island

N

Launch site

Campground
(See appendix E.)

Great
Gott
Island

0   1   2   3   4   MILES   5

Swells and surf can threaten paddlers along the exposed shores of Mount Desert Island.

prominent harbors and coves in the stretch from Bass Harbor counterclockwise to Dorr Point (south of Bar Harbor). Much of the shoreline between harbors, however, is rocky and bold, with little margin for error. The Maine Island Trail Association warns that these are demanding waters, particularly for sea kayakers. The association advises that only experienced skippers—in settled conditions—tackle a traverse of the southern and eastern shores.

Bass Harbor Bar. Bass Harbor Bar is an underwater bar that connects Bass Harbor Head and Great Gott Island. The tide here floods west and ebbs east. When the wind and tide run against each other, a serious chop can develop. (A chop can also develop, under the same circumstances, at Long Ledge, 1.6 miles east of Bass Harbor Head.) In heavy seas, breakers sometimes form over this bar.

Boat traffic. Western Way and Eastern Way are the two main entrances to Southwest and Northeast Harbors. Western Way lies between Sewall and Great Cranberry Island, while Eastern Way lies north of Sutton Island. As the two harbors are major fishing and yachting centers, there is considerable traffic through these passages.

Somes Sound. Somes Sound is exposed to north-south winds and vulnerable to downdrafts that spill off the mountains. At the Narrows, the sound is only 0.2 mile wide, and the current can be quite stiff at full strength.

Somes Sound

Somes Sound is a major feature on Mount Desert because it all but splits the island in half. The sound is considered the only fjord in Maine, and some geologists say it is the only fjord on the East Coast. A fjord is a deep, high-walled, glacially carved valley that has been flooded by the sea. This drowned valley is indeed deep. From its lowest point, 152 feet below sea level, to the top of Norumbega Mountain, 852 feet above sea level, is a total rise of more than 1,000 feet.

Somes Sound has its share of history. In 1613, two French priests arrived and started a colony, St. Sauveur, on Fernald Neck at the mouth of the sound. A skirmish with the English forced them to abandon the attempt; Jesuit Spring marks the site. During the protracted French and Indian Wars, ships gathered in Valley Cove, a wide cove on the west shore that effectively hid vessels from view from the mouth of the sound. A short trail from the pebble beach at the southern end of Valley Cove leads up Flying Mountain. Although a mere 284 feet high, the summit provides good views of the sound to the north and the Cranberry islands to the south.

About a mile north of the trail, Man o' War Brook plunges down Acadia Mountain, forming a chain of waterfalls over the terraced rock. The deep anchorage at the base of the brook provided ships easy access to critically important fresh water. Just beyond the brook there is a plaque honoring the Reverend Cornelius Smith and his wife, Mary Wheeler, who—the plaque says—pioneered a summer colony at Northeast Harbor in the late 1800s and early 1900s. (Mount Desert must have been considered quite a wilderness to need pioneering.) The couple donated Acadia Mountain to the public.

Hall Quarry, farther north, offered up its granite to the Library of Congress, the U.S. Mint in Philadelphia, and other well-known public buildings.

Bar Island, at the entrance to Somes Harbor, is part of Acadia National Park. The island provides habitat for bald eagles and mariners should not stop or linger by the island. Somes Harbor is shallow and very protected from wind.

Somes Sound HANK TYLER

Cranberry and Baker islands. When tide and wind are contrary, a nasty chop can develop over the bar between Little Cranberry and Baker islands.

Access

132: Bartlett Landing. In the summer this small all-tide site is so heavily used that it's hard to find parking in the tiny lot and hard to get away from the crowd of paddlers. A better option is to launch from nearby Trenton or Seal Cove. To get to Bartlett Landing, at the junction of ME 3 and ME 198/ME 102, follow ME 198/ME 102 for 2 miles and turn right onto Indian Point Road. Continue for 5.6 miles and turn right at Pretty Marsh onto Bartlett Landing Road. Continue 1 mile to the end of the road. There is a portable toilet.

133: Seal Cove. Seal Cove has a concrete all-tide ramp plus two places to hand carry to a gravel beach. Follow ME 198/ME 102 to Somesville. When ME 102 splits, take the western road toward Pretty Marsh. Almost 4 miles after Pretty Marsh, having passed Seal Cove Pond on the left, turn right onto Cape Road. (If you miss the turn, you will immediately come upon Kelly-town Road on the left.) Proceed 0.5 mile to the launch site. Parking is along the road; there is a portable toilet.

134: Bernard. This concrete ramp provides access to Bass Harbor and the southwest side of Mount Desert Island. Bass Harbor is a working harbor with a large lobstering fleet, so be prepared to give way if the launch site is busy. The ferry to Swan's Island and Frenchboro leaves from the opposite shore, in the town of Bass Harbor.

There is a portable toilet in back of the building on the dock. Although there is an auxiliary lot, parking is still tight; please don't show up with a fleet of cars. To get to this launch site, take ME 102 south through Southwest Harbor. At the junction of ME 102 and ME 102A, stay right on ME 102 (Bass Harbor Road) for 2.7 miles. Take a left toward Bernard and go 0.6 mile (passing a parking lot on the right) to Steamboat Wharf Road; take another left and drive down to the dock.

Restricted: Bass Harbor. There is virtually no parking at the tiny stretch of gravel that leads to the water. Please leave this area for local people.

135: Manset. Manset has an all-tide ramp, but the gravel beach next to the ramp may be more convenient for sea kayakers. There is a portable toilet at the ramp. Proceed south on ME 102 through Somesville and Southwest Harbor. Take ME 102A when it bears left and proceed 0.9 mile, turning left onto Mansell. Follow the road downhill and bear left at the water. The launch site is almost immediately on the right.

136: Southwest Harbor. This launch site is extremely congested and there is very little parking. Spaces available to the public have a limit of 3

Peregrines in Valley Cove

Peregrines raised chicks in Valley Cove until 1947, after which the cries of a chick were not heard for many years. In 1970 the federal government listed peregrines as endangered and scientists began a reintroduction program. By 1975, the eastern subspecies of the peregrine falcon had become extinct. Only a hundred individuals of the western subspecies remained in the wild. (A tundra subspecies still thrived in the far north.)

Fast-forward to the mid-1980s, when 23 peregrine chicks were released at Jordan Cliffs in Acadia. One of those birds returned to Acadia in 1997 and in 1991 a pair raised chicks on The Precipices. Gradually other birds took up residence at Jordan Cliffs and Somes Sound.

Park naturalists keep telescopes trained on The Precipice and in 2005 noted events in an online diary (www.nps.gov/acad/pere_update.htm): Four eggs hatch one day apart, May 6–10, on a high ledge. The parents begin feeding them small birds caught on the wing. By June 13, the nest-bound chicks are almost as large as their parents. The youngsters exercise in the nest, building wing muscles. By June 20, two birds take the big leap; their siblings soon follow.

By the end of the month, the fledglings hang out at the top of the cliff—flying, stooping, and grabbing—developing skills to feed themselves. Gradually the parents provide less food. By July 4, the young are acrobatic masters of the sky and expand their range daily. A month later, they and their parents leave to winter in the sunny south.

Paddlers might spot The Precipice peregrines north of Schooner Head, and the Valley Cove birds in southern Somes Sound. At a distance, look for a powerful, rapid beat of sharp-pointed wings—the tail is generally short and narrow in flight—and listen for a fierce scream that is variously described as "rehk, rehk, rehk" or "kek, kek, kek" or—from the eyrie—"we'chu, we'chu." If the birds get close enough, the dark cap and mustache are striking.

When peregrines are nesting in Somes Sound, the trail along Valley Cove north to Man o' War Brook is closed. (The trail from Valley Cove to Flying Mountain is still open.) If the birds are unsuccessful, the park biologist may post an early opening of the trail.

hours; spaces with a longer limit are reserved for fishermen. This site might be useful in spring and fall, but avoid it in summer when Southwest Harbor is crowded with visitors.

From the center of Southwest Harbor on ME 102, turn east at the light onto Clark Point Road. Proceed 0.2 mile and stay right when the road splits. Go 0.5 mile to the end of the road. The concrete all-tide ramp is on the right beyond the Coast Guard station. The site has portable outhouses.

Note. It may look like the area behind Port in a Storm Bookstore in

High water at Otter Cove

Somesville is a launch site, but it's not. Please don't fill up the store's parking lot.

137: Sargent Drive, Somes Sound. The picnic area along Sargent Drive does not have a launch ramp, but it is possible to put in along the shore. From the junction of ME 198, ME 3, and ME 233 near the head of Somes Sound, take ME 198/ME 3 south fo 1.2 miles. Turn right onto Sargent Drive and continue 0.8 mile. Turn right onto a road with the gate open. There may or may not be a sign announcing the picnic area.

138: Northeast Harbor. The harbor is full of vessels, large and small. From ME 198/ME 3, go south on ME 198 for 0.7 mile. Take a left onto Harbor Drive at the sign for a marina. Proceed 0.8 mile to a large parking complex. The all-tide ramp is in the far corner, past the harbor master's building (which includes bathrooms). If you unload your boat and carry it to the ramp, you do not have to pay the $5 launch fee. If you pull onto the ramp or block the ramp in any other way, then head back to the harbor master and plunk down your money. Be warned that although the day parking area is large, many people use it and the lot is often full.

139: Seal Harbor. Where ME 3 skirts Seal Harbor in the town of the same name, park next to ME 3 and hand carry to the beach at the head of the harbor. This strip of sand is the town's beach, so the area is heavily used, and the lot holds only 25 vehicles. To park here, go in the off-season or start very early in the morning.

140: Otter Cove. It is possible to launch from the head of Otter Cove. The shore of the cove is sand, rock, or mud, depending on the level of the tide. Otter Cove opens directly to the south, so launching or landing with a stiff south wind can be problematic; a chop can develop at the mouth of the cove.

Take ME 3 going south from Bar Harbor. From the turnoff to Sieur de Monts Spring, continue for a little more than 3 miles, then turn left onto Otter Creek Road. Turn at the second right into the Fabbri Memorial (which has bathrooms) and then take a right onto the Loop Road. Go 0.3 mile to the head of the cove. Parking is permitted in the right lane of the two-lane road. The carry to the water can be long when the tide is low. A launch site on the eastern shore of the cove is reserved for fishermen.

Note. The National Park Service asks that paddlers not launch from Sand Beach and discourages landings except in emergencies. The beach is often crowded with visitors.

Points of Interest

The Hub. The Hub is a tiny public island—mostly ledge—located next to the northern tip of Bartlett Island. Seals use the Hub during pupping, so please avoid this island during May and June. If you are paddling through Western Bay (northeast of the Hub), stay north of Black Island and near Alley Island (check your chart), far away from seals and seal ledges on the shore.

Black Island. Give Black Island a wide berth during nesting season; Maine Coast Heritage Trust owns this 14-acre nesting island.

John Island. John is another tiny public island, but it lies near the southern end of Bartlett Island, just outside Pretty Marsh Harbor. This low, grassy, day-use island does not command much privacy. If you stop, be careful not to contribute to the bank erosion. Both the Hub and John Island are on the Maine Island Trail.

Pretty Marsh Harbor. North of Bass Harbor Head, the only national park land on the west side of the island is a picnic area in Pretty Marsh Harbor. Paddle into the harbor and look for a set of steps and a gazebo on the eastern shore directly across from West Point. These steps lead to picnic tables.

Hardwood Island. The Cleveland Museum of Natural History operates a biological field station and ecology camp on this private island.

Ship Island Group. See *Points of Interest* in "Eggemoggin Reach and Blue Hill Bay."

Bass Harbor Head Light. This light, built in 1858, is set in a white tower and shines 56 feet above the water. The dwelling is privately owned. The land along the shore, from Bass Harbor Head to about half a mile west of Seawall Point, is part of Acadia National Park.

Bear Island Light. In 1891, buoys replaced this light, which was built in 1839 to mark the entrance to Northeast Harbor.

Little Cranberry Island. Great and Little Cranberry islands get their name from the wild fruit that once grew in abundance in a 200-acre bog on Great Cranberry. Little Cranberry offers a pleasant stop, complete with museum, public rest rooms, and restaurant. The southernmost of the three docks on the waterfront is the town dock; paddlers may land on either beach flanking this dock.

The restaurant and National Park Service museum are located near the waterfront on the northwest corner of the island. The museum has furnishings, photographs, and other artifacts of early island life. There is no fee to enter the museum (244-9224 in summer), which is open from mid-June through the end of September, 10 AM to 4:30 PM, every day of the week.

Baker Island. A path leads from the grassy northwest corner of the island to Baker Island Light. A white stone tower 43 feet tall houses the light, which reaches 105 feet above the water. A side path branching off to the right leads to the Dance Hall Floor, flat ledges that used to resound to tunes from a Victrola and the stamp of feet when Cranberry islanders came here for picnics and dancing. Most of Baker Island is part of Acadia National Park; the private property is on the eastern part of the island.

Hunters Beach Cove to Oak Hill Cliff. The eastern half of Hunters Beach Cove eastward to Oak Hill Cliff (just short of Schooner Head), as well as a half-mile stretch north of Schooner Head, are part of Acadia.

Thunder Hole. When large waves race into this sea cave about 3 hours before high tide, they trap air in a chamber and force it out of a narrow opening in an explosion of noise and water. At most other times, Thunder Hole is thunderless.

Sand Beach. Sand Beach is tucked into the head of Newport Cove, on the southeast side of Mount Desert Island. Not surprisingly, the beach is a magnet for visitors. About 70 percent of the sand here is composed of shell fragments from sea urchins, mussels, and other animals; the remaining 30 percent is from eroded bedrock. Shells break down easily in cold water, but there is always an ample supply of shells to replenish the beach.

Anemone Cave. Anemone Cave is a sea cave located immediately south of Schooner Head on the east side of Mount Desert. Be careful about paddling into the cave when swells are running; you could get plastered onto the ceiling.

At a Glance: Land in Public or Conservation Ownership

The Hub	Maine Island Trail/BPL; avoid May and June
Black Island	MCHT; closed February 15–August 31

John Island	Maine Island Trail/BPL
Ship Island Group	USFWS; closed April 1–August 31
Acadia National Park	
Pretty Marsh Picnic Area	Acadia National Park; careful day use
Valley Cove	Careful day use
Bar Island in Somes Sound	Closed February 15–July 31
Baker Island	Careful day use
Sand Beach	Swimming beach

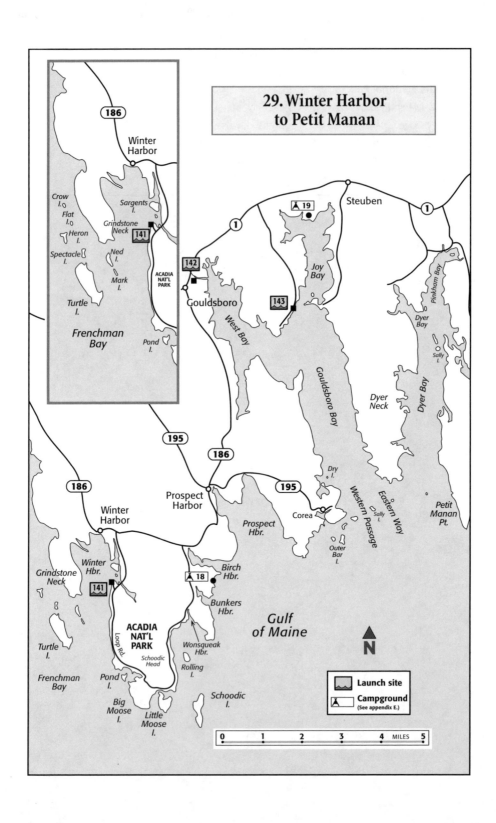

29. Winter Harbor to Petit Manan

186

Winter
Harbor

Crow
I.
Flat
I.

Sargents
I.

Heron
I.

Grindstone
Neck

141

Spectacle
I.

Ned
I.

ACADIA
NAT'L
PARK

Mark
I.

Turtle
I.

Frenchman
Bay

Pond
I.

▲ 19

Steuben

1

142

Joy
Bay

Gouldsboro

143

West Bay

Dyer
Bay

Pinkham Bay

Sally
I.

Gouldsboro Bay

Dyer
Neck

Dyer Bay

195

186

Prospect
Harbor

195

Dry
I.

Corea

Sally
I.

Western Passage

Eastern Way

Petit
Manan
Pt.

186

Winter
Harbor

Prospect
Hbr.

Outer
Bar
I.

Grindstone
Neck

Winter
Hbr.

141

Birch
Hbr.

▲ 18

Bunkers
Hbr.

Gulf
of Maine

Turtle
I.

ACADIA
NAT'L
PARK

Loop Rd.

Wonsqueak
Hbr.

N

Frenchman
Bay

Pond
I.

Schoodic
Head

Rolling
I.

Big
Moose
I.

Little
Moose
I.

Schoodic
I.

Launch site

▲ Campground
(See appendix E.)

0   1   2   3   4 MILES 5

6.

Downeast

Winter Harbor to Petit Manan

Big, brazen Schoodic Peninsula dominates this stretch of Maine's coast. Unless you head for open water, boating opportunities are limited (by geography and launch sites) to a tour of Winter Harbor and environs or a paddle down Gouldsboro Bay, with its string of islands at the bay's mouth. Driving to and from the launch site offers its own reward. Both state and federal governments have touched three roads with the magic wand that makes them the Schoodic Scenic Byway. The suddenly scenic byway includes Route 1 from the Hancock-Sullivan Bridge to West Gouldsboro; ME 86 from West Gouldsboro to Winter Harbor; the park road from Winter Harbor to Birch Harbor; and ME 186 north to Prospect Harbor.

Trip Ideas (weather and experience permitting)

Tour Winter Harbor (3 to 4 miles) or paddle among the islands outside the harbor (5 or 6 miles). Or, explore Gouldsboro Bay, taking in the Sally islands. Note that Winter Harbor is vulnerable to seas from the south. The launch site in Gouldsboro Bay, though more protected, is still vulnerable to winds coming from the north or south. The head of West, Joy, and Dyer bays are dry at low tide.

Safety Considerations, Strong Currents, and Caution Areas

Schoodic Point. The French called Schoodic Point *cap enragé*, which translates as "enraged cape"—an apt description for this finger of land that juts far into the sea. It is easy enough to see how dangerous paddling conditions can build up here. The Maine Island Trail Association notes that Schoodic is well-known for its rough waters, where waves crash into and rebound from the steep rocks. "Schoodic must be respected under the best of conditions. . . . Only skilled boat operators should attempt its challenges," the association warns. The risk is high enough that some through-paddlers choose to avoid the point itself by portaging along the road from West Pond to a picnic area on Arey Cove.

Gouldsboro Bay. There are two passages through the Sally islands and into Gouldsboro Bay. The current through Western Passage, which cuts

Charts

Charts: 13318, Frenchman Bay and Mount Desert Island (1:40,000)
          13324, Tibbett Narrows to Schoodic Island (1:40,000)
Chart Kit: 74, 75
Maine Atlas locator map: 16, 17

Tides (hours:minutes relative to Portland; average rise)
Winter Harbor: 0:23 before; 10.1 feet
Corea Harbor: 0:25 before; 10.5 feet
Garden Point, Gouldsboro Bay: 0:23 before; 10.8 feet
Pinkham Bay in Dyer Bay: 0:23 before; 10.9 feet

between Sheep and Sally islands, can reach 2 to 3 knots at greatest velocity. Eastern Way, which lies between Bald Rock and Eastern Island, has strong tidal currents that flow at an angle to the channel. The *Coast Pilot* recommends that small craft not attempt to use Eastern Way when the tide is ebbing, especially with winds from the south and east.

The passage that runs from Gouldsboro Bay to Dyer Bay north of the Sally islands also has strong tidal currents, reaching 2 to 3 knots at strength.

Access

141: *Frazer Point Picnic Area, Winter Harbor.* It's a long carry to the water and there is no ramp, but there is ample parking (as well as bathrooms and picnic tables) at this picnic area just inside Acadia National Park. From Route 1, take ME 186 south to Winter Harbor and then continue 0.6 mile to the sign for the Schoodic unit of Acadia National Park. Proceed 1.5 miles to Frazer Point Picnic Area on the right. Hand carry across a lawn and picnic area to a dock, then down a cobble beach to the water. The carry from lot to dock is about 250 feet.

Breakers on Schoodic Point

Schoodic Peninsula

Schoodic Point can be a dangerous place to paddle, but it ranks high in scenic views and natural history. If you have a little extra time after paddling in Winter Harbor, turn your car onto the one-way park loop and see the sights. The southern portion of Schoodic Peninsula, Pond Island, Little Moose Island, and Schoodic Island form the eastern outpost of Acadia National Park. Big Moose Island is the site of a U.S. Navy base.

At Schoodic Point, great slabs of red granite, cut by black basalt, reach out into the sea. Millions of years ago, magma forced its way into cracks and seams in the overlying granite, forming dikes; this magma, now cooled, is the basalt. A variety of birds can be seen in this area in summer: common loons, black guillemots, double-crested cormorants, all three scoters (white-winged, surf, and black), common eiders, red-breasted mergansers, herring gulls, great black-backed gulls, Bonaparte's gulls, laughing gulls, common terns, and—occasionally—arctic terns. Ospreys and bald eagles nest nearby.

Two plants, jack pine and crowberry, are of special interest. Jack pine, which grows in only a few places in Maine, forms healthy stands on the Schoodic Peninsula. The needles of jack pine are about ¾ inch to 1½ inches long and appear in clusters of two. The other scrubby-looking pine that grows along the coast is pitch pine; its needles are 1½ to 5 inches long and appear in clusters of three. Both white pine and red pine generally grow straight and tall.

Crowberry also has evergreen needles, but it is a low-growing, rock-hugging arctic-alpine plant that grows here because of particular maritime conditions. The cold Nova Scotia current sweeps down the coast, creating frequent fog, cooler temperatures, and poor growing conditions in early summer. Although the effect is felt all along the Maine coast, it is most marked between Mount Desert and Lubec. Plants like crowberry and mountain cranberry, which moved south ahead of the continental ice sheet, remained in this sea-cooled coastal strip (and on high mountains like Katahdin) after the ice receded.

142: West Bay, Gouldsboro. This hand-carry gravel launch site at the head of West Bay can be used only at the top half of the tide, so it does not see a lot of traffic. There is a small area for parking. From the junction of Route 1 and ME 186, go east 0.3 mile on Route 1 to an unnamed dirt road on the right. Follow this road to the launch area.

143: The Narrows at the head of Gouldsboro Bay. This launch site has a concrete all-tide ramp and a small parking area. If you plan to paddle from here with friends, please carpool. From Gouldsboro, go almost 3 miles northeast on Route 1 and turn right on Gouldsboro Point Road. Go 2.4 miles to a gravel parking lot on the left.

Note. Some publications show a hand-carry site in the middle of town in Winter Harbor. This site is a patch of rough beach along the main road, and with space for one or two vehicles pulled parallel to the road. The town wharf, to the west, does not have a ramp either.

Points of Interest

Turtle Island. Great blue herons nest in the interior of this island, seals haul themselves out onto the ledges at the south end, and tide pools form on the eastern shore. Perhaps it is just as well that this 136-acre preserve, which lies just outside Winter Harbor, is off the beaten track in Frenchman Bay. The island came into the hands of The Nature Conservancy in 1963, after a cutting operation had begun to mow down the island's forest.

Although the interior of the island is closed from March 15 through August 15, mariners may walk along the shore. The best landing site, weather permitting, is on the north tip of the island. Please avoid the seal ledges at the south end of the island.

Little Crow. This Maine Island Trail ledge west of Crow Island—both are west of Grindstone Neck—works as a day stop when seas are calm, but you'll want to be far away when rough waves cascade over it. Crow Island to the east is privately held; please be considerate of anyone staying there.

Mark Island. Mark Island Light, which marked the entrance to Winter Harbor, has been abandoned. The light and dwelling are now privately owned.

Little Moose Island. This rocky island is joined to the mainland at low water. If you go ashore, please stick to the rocks or obvious trails to avoid stepping on little plants that cling to life.

Schoodic Island. This island, east of Little Moose, is closed for bird nesting from February 15 to August 31. The Acadia biologist may open the island earlier if no nesting occurs.

Rolling Island. Acadia's small, wooded isle in Schoodic Bay is also closed from February 15 to the end of August.

Sheep Island. The owner of this 8-acre, wooded island—who traced his family's ownership back 129 years—gave it to Maine Coast Heritage Trust to protect it from development. Sheep provides nesting habitat and so is closed from February 15 through the end of August.

Gouldsboro Division of Maine Coastal Islands National Wildlife Refuge. This section includes 607 acres on the eastern shore of West Bay, from Williams Point (check your chart) to the salt marsh a little more than one mile to the northwest. The upper half of the parcel is dry at low water.

Sally Island. This one-acre Sally (not to be confused with the larger, private Sally Island that lies at the mouth of Gouldsboro Bay between Corea and Dyer Neck) is part of the Maine Coast Islands National Wildlife Refuge; it lies in the northern half of Dyer Bay. This bird nesting island is closed from

February 15 to the end of August. If no nesting occurs, signs on site will alert paddlers that they may visit after May 15.

Dry Island. This tiny, grassy, public island at Long Mill Cove north of Corea is part of the Maine Island Trail. The island provides a place to stretch and snack, but shoreside houses overlook the island and there is nary a tree, so it is not exactly private.

The Sally islands. This little archipelago stretches across the mouths of Gouldsboro and Dyer Bays. The islands, all privately owned, are havens for seabirds and seals. Please do not paddle near these islands during the seabird nesting and seal pupping season.

At a Glance: Land in Public or Conservation Ownership

Little Crow	Maine Island Trail/BPL
Turtle Island	TNC; closed March 15–August 15; after that time, careful day use
Sheep Island (near Outer Bar)	MCHT; closed February 15–August 31
Dry Island	Maine Island Trail/BPL
Acadia National Park	
Heron Island (NW of Turtle Island)	Closed April 1–July 31
Schoodic Peninsula	Careful day use
Pond Island	Careful day use
Little Moose Island	Careful day use; stay on trails
Schoodic Island	Closed February 15–August 31 or as posted
Rolling Island	Closed February 15–August 31; after that time, careful day use
USFWS Wildlife Islands	
Sally Island (Dyer Bay)	Closed March 15–August 31 or as posted

The Narraguagus and Pleasant Rivers and Their Bays

The jewels of Narraguagus and Pleasant Bays are Bois Bubert, Shipstern, and Flint islands. Most of Bois Bubert is wild and undeveloped. Shipstern is bold and unapproachable, a haven for eagles and ospreys. Flint offers two landing sites, bare toeholds on this island where crinoids—lilylike animals that lived some 420 million years ago—have been preserved in the bedrock.

But these three islands lie on the outer edge of the outer bays, so when conditions are unfavorable (or if you are still honing your skills), they are islands for another day. There are sheltered rivers to explore—like the lovely Pleasant River—and more protected islands to circumnavigate in the inner reaches of the bays.

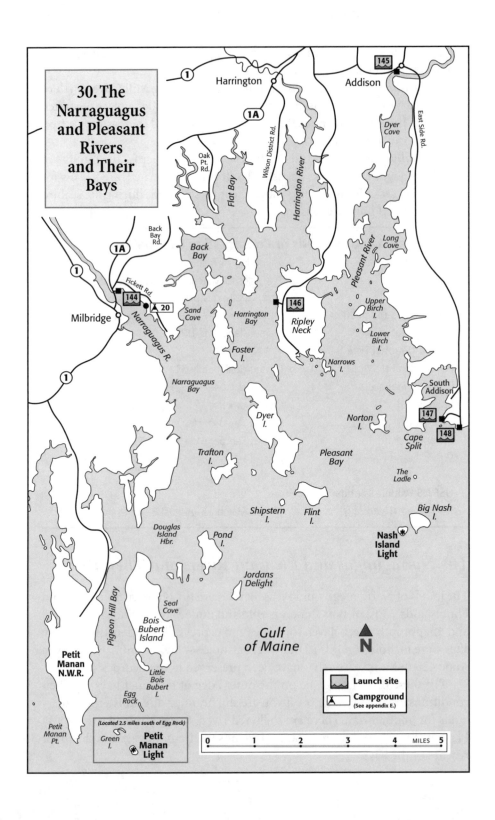

30. The Narraguagus and Pleasant Rivers and Their Bays

1

Harrington

Addison

145

1A

Oak Pt. Rd.

Wilson District Rd.

Harrington River

Dyer Cove

East Side Rd.

Flat Bay

Back Bay Rd.

1A

Back Bay

1

Fickett Rd.

144

▲ 20

Milbridge

Narraguagus R.

Sand Cove

Harrington Bay

146

Ripley Neck

Pleasant River

Long Cove

Upper Birch I.

Lower Birch I.

Foster I.

1

Narraguagus Bay

Dyer I.

Narrows I.

South Addison

Norton I.

147

Cape Split

148

Trafton I.

Pleasant Bay

The Ladle

Big Nash I.

Shipstern I.

Flint I.

Nash Island Light ✳

Douglas Island Hbr.

Pond I.

Jordans Delight

Pigeon Hill Bay

Seal Cove

Bois Bubert Island

Gulf of Maine

N

Petit Manan N.W.R.

Little Bois Bubert I.

Egg Rock

Launch site

Campground
(See appendix E.)

Petit Manan Pt.

(Located 2.5 miles south of Egg Rock)

Green I.

Petit Manan Light ✳

0 1 2 3 4 MILES 5

Charts
Chart: 13324, Tibbett Narrows to Schoodic Island (1:40,000)
Chart Kit: 75, 76
Maine Atlas locator map: 17, 25

Tides (hours:minutes relative to Portland; average rise)
Pigeon Hill Bay: 0:21 before; 11.1 feet
Milbridge, Narraguagus River: 0:20 before; 11.3 feet
Trafton Island, Narraguagus Bay: 0:23 before; 11.1 feet
Addison, Pleasant River: 0:00; 11.8 feet
Gibbs Island, Pleasant River: 0:20 before; 11.3 feet

Trip Ideas (weather and experience permitting)

For an excursion with some protection, put in at Addison and paddle south on the Pleasant River (trip length is up to you). A point-to-point trip between Addison and South Addison takes you from a sheltered coastal river to the mouth of an open bay—or vice versa (almost 10 miles).

The trip from Milbridge to Bois Bubert is long and vulnerable to wind and weather (15 miles to Seal Cove and back, 20 miles to circumnavigate Bois Bubert). Planning the trip to take advantage of the tide is definitely in order. A shorter trip to the vicinity of Trafton Island (8 miles round-trip) or Flint Island (13 miles round-trip) provides views of Bois Bubert but will still put you into open water.

Flint Island is relatively near the launch site in South Addison, but paddlers must cross open water to get there (7 miles round-trip).

Safety Considerations, Strong Currents, and Caution Areas

Petit Manan Point. The underwater bar from Green Island to Petit Manan Point presents several dangers. Strong, swift tidal currents flow over the bar, flooding northeast and ebbing southwest. With a swell or heavy weather, breakers pound the bar's entire length. Wind, whether against or with the tide, can further complicate the paddling scene. The Maine Island Trail Association calls Petit Manan "one of the wildest and most exciting places on the Trail . . . a place to be treated with greatest of caution." The association warns that only skilled boat people should paddle here; with a small boat, the quickest and safest route is through the channel called Inner Bar (check your chart), just south of Petit Manan Point.

Fog. The fog signal on Petit Manan Island gets a workout, as the island averages more hours of fog from June through September than any other station in Maine. July is the peak, with an average of 275 hours, the equivalent of 11.5 straight days of fog. The outer bays—Pigeon Hill, Narraguagus, and

Launching from Addison on the Pleasant River

Pleasant—are sometimes clear when Petit Manan is shrouded in fog.

Outer bays. The inner bays and the Narraguagus, Harrington, and Pleasant rivers are largely protected; the outer bays are much more exposed to swells, wind, and—in general—the weather.

Access

144: Milbridge, Narraguagus River. This all-tide concrete ramp has a large parking lot but no facilities. From the junction of Route 1 and Route 1A in Milbridge, go north on Route 1A for 0.3 mile. Turn right onto Bayview Street and go 0.3 mile to the launch site on the right.

145: Addison, Pleasant River. This launch site has a concrete all-tide ramp and a dirt parking lot. From the junction of Route 1 and Route 1A east of Harrington, go north on Route 1 for 1.9 miles. Turn right onto an unmarked road just past Delia's Store; the road is very hard to see. Go 2 miles to an intersection where you can see the Pleasant River off to your left. Go left and proceed less than a mile to the launch site, which is on the right.

Note. The launch site shown on Ray Point (Back Bay, Milbridge) in some sources is next to a private home; there is no parking.

146: Harrington, Ripley Neck. Clammers use this concrete all-tide launch site, wharf, and dock, and parking is tight during the bottom half of the tide. If clammers are lined up and waiting for the magic tide moment, bide your time until they have launched. At the junction of Route 1 and Route 1A east of Harrington, go north on Route 1 for 0.7 mile. Turn right on Marshville Road and proceed 7.4 miles. Turn right at the town boat landing sign and go to the end of the road.

The launch sites at Milbridge and South Addison, although less well positioned for the Dyer, Flint, and Shipstern group, offer better parking.

147: South Addison, Eastern (Cape Split) Harbor. South Addison has found the perfect balance between recreational and working waterfront interests: It has two launch sites. The first, on Cape Split Harbor, consists of a wharf, floats, ramp, vault toilet, and paved parking suited to trucks and trailers. The second, described below, is a quiet, hand-carry area well removed from marine businesses.

To reach the harbor, proceed as above, but continue past the Addison boat launch and through the town (the Historical Society lies on one side of the road and the Grange on the other). Stay on East Side Road, which hooks around to the south and parallels the Pleasant River. After 6 or 7 miles, at a fork in the road, go right onto Mooseneck Road. Just past the area from which you see open water, continue straight on The Narrows Road. Go 0.8 mile, where the road splits; one sign points left to the beach, the other right to the town ramp.

148: South Addison, opposite Marsh Island. At the split, above, turn left and proceed for 0.3 mile to the beach. Drop gear by the water and park back in the field. The launch is nicely protected by Marsh Island. If you need facilities, use the vault toilet at the other launch site.

Points of Interest

Coastal Maine Islands (formerly Petit Manan) National Wildlife Refuge: This refuge, administered by the U.S. Fish and Wildlife Service, includes most of Petit Manan Point, most of Bois Bubert Island, all of Little Bois Bubert Island, part of Nash Island, and all of Petit Manan Island—as well as many islands along the rest of Maine's coast.

Petit Manan Point: More than 10 miles of shoreline and 2,000 acres of this peninsula are protected. The shoreline is rocky with some cobble beaches and saltwater marshes. Red and white spruce predominate, but there are also stands of mixed hardwoods as well as jack pine. Raised peatlands, an unusual bog formation, can be found back from the shore.

Bois Bubert Island: Visitors may explore any part of Bois Bubert except the private holding that lies on the northwestern shore. Seal Cove, on the eastern shore, has a grassy area that makes a nice picnic spot. Birds are plentiful. Watch for common loons, double-crested cormorants, black guillemots, surf scoters, bald eagles, and ospreys as well as great black-backed, herring, ring-billed, Bonaparte's, and laughing gulls. Common eiders and other species nest on Bois Bubert, while arctic, common, and roseate terns as well as great blue herons nest nearby. Keep an eye out for peregrine falcons, which are occasionally seen in this area. Bois Bubert has great storm ridges and overwash fans, a testament to the violent weather than can sweep along the coast.

The name "Boisbubert" appears on maps made before the Revolutionary War. Although it is not known for certain, the island may be named for Sieur de Boishebert, a French naval officer who fought against the British in New Brunswick. Locally, the island is called "Bo Bear."

Little Bois Bubert Island: This island is closed from April 1 through the end of August.

Petit Manan Island: Petit Manan Island lies 2.5 miles south of Petit Manan Point. A light was established in 1817 and the present tower, 119 feet

Crinoids

Four hundred and twenty million years ago, a shallow sea covered what is now Flint Island. Plantlike animals called *crinoids* lived in this sea. Crinoids are echinoderms, a group of radially symmetrical marine animals that also includes starfish, sand dollars, brittle stars, and sea urchins. Crinoids have roots that attach to the seabed; a long, jointed stem; and a cup with many undulating feeding tentacles at the top.

Gradually, sediments fell to the bottom of this sea and over millions of years the sediments turned into rock—and some crinoids were preserved as fossils in the bedrock siltstone on Flint Island.

A few species of this ancient animal still exist, living at depths of 100 feet or more. Sometimes the skeletons of crinoids are transported to the surface and are washed up on Maine's beaches. Remarkably, these fragile-looking skeletons can wash up intact. If you see a lot of kelp on shore, look for crinoids. Sometimes crinoids grow right in the *holdfast,* the point at which kelp attaches to the seafloor, and sometimes they are simply washed up with the holdfasts.

Crinoids like this one (Botryocrinus) lived on the bottom of shallow seas 420 million years ago (from Bather 1910 in Kummel 1970).

high and showing a light 123 feet from the water, was built in 1855. It is Maine's second tallest light.

This 9-acre treeless island has long been an important colonial seabird nesting island. After more aggressive herring and great black-backed gulls displaced nesting laughing gulls and several species of terns in the late 1970s, the U.S. Fish and Wildlife Service took steps in 1984 to reduce the competition. As terns, common eiders, black guillemots, and laughing gulls returned, Atlantic puffins also took up residence.

Nash Island: The northern 5 acres of this island are part of the refuge. (A separate description of Nash follows).

Green Island: Green Island, which is barred to Petit Manan Island at low water, is an IF&W seabird island that is closed to visitors year-round. Both Green and Petit Manan islands are well protected by distance, fog, and the fast currents that flow between Green Island and the mainland.

Pond Island. The light on Pond Island went into service in 1853 but was deactivated in 1934, replaced by a lighted bell buoy east of the island. The light station is now privately owned.

Shipstern Island. Eagles wheel and soar over this unassailable island in Narraguagus Bay. The rocky perimeter of this 95-foot-high island is so uninviting that Shipstern was never inhabited; most mariners don't even try to visit. The island gets its name from the south side's rocky bluff, which rises directly from the water like the poop deck of a galleon. Part of the island is protected as a Nature Conservancy preserve, and Shipstern is closed to the public during nesting season—February 15 through August 15. Please do not land (a demanding maneuver anyway) or linger near the island, which provides habitat for eagles and other birds.

Flint Island. Although the two islands are side by side, Flint and Shipstern are very different. Flint has a lower, more gradual profile. There are fields and alder swamps among the spruce and fir woods. Sheep used to

The imposing silhouette of Shipstern gives the island its name.

graze here, and there are two landing sites—one on each side of the peninsula that hangs off the western shore. Flint Island does not have flint on it. The island gets its name from the siltstone that somewhat resembles flint.

Flint Island is a Nature Conservancy preserve. Ospreys and other species nest here; seals haul out on nearby ledges. Visitors are allowed from August 15 through February 15, but there are no trails.

Little Nash Island and Light. Terns, common eiders, and gulls make their summer homes on 16-acre Nash. Nash Island Light, built in 1838 and discontinued in 1981, was replaced with a lighted buoy that lies west of the island. Friends of Little Nash Island Light now own the small plot of land upon which the light rests, and maintain the building.

Jenny Cirone, daughter of Nash's lighthouse keeper, knew this island intimately. She grew up there, then kept sheep on the treeless isle for 8 decades, inviting friends to both Nash and Big Nash to lamb and shear the woolly critters. When she died at age 91, she left her share of the island to friends, who then sold it to Maine Coast Heritage Trust. (The Coastal Maine Islands refuge includes 5 acres on the northern end of the island.) Because sheep still inhabit the island, dogs are not permitted there at any time.

The Ladle. Maine Coast Heritage Trust acquired this striking 2-acre island in 2005. It's easy to see how the isle got its name: rock rises steeply on all sides but one, where the "handle" trails as low rocks and half-tide ledges.

Jordan's Delight: A Delight Once More

In 1985, when I first paddled past the lump of rock known as Jordan's Delight, birds swarmed over the 60-foot cliffs and bare summit, their cries mingling in the wind. The island sat on the edge of the great beyond; Spain lay on the other side of the sea.

When I paddled toward it twelve years later, I could see even at a great distance that it had changed. The exoskeleton of a huge building squatted on the treeless ridge. The view was wrenching.

I arrived at the island just as a huge powerboat drew up. The owner said that my husband and I could eat lunch there and took us to a small building on the southern end. On the way, he gave us a tour of his mansion-to-be. The view from the picture windows was stupendous.

I asked if he had encountered any problems getting permits. Oh yes, he said. He almost hadn't been able to build there. They—the legions of bureaucrats—had hassled him no end. He had to promise that he would do this and that and a long list of other things. It was hard enough building on an island, but to have to build around the life cycle of sea birds—that was asking too much.

Later I talked with some local people, who were horrified at the prospect. The island had always been wild. No one had ever lived there. But what could they do? What could anyone do?

Marsh Island. Great Auk Land Trust secured this 11-acre island (along with the salt marsh opposite, on shore) with the help of Maine Coast Heritage Trust and the Coastal Maine Islands National Wildlife Refuge. Marsh lies between Cape Split and the mainland, and is connected to the mainland at low water. Please give this a go-by from April 15 through the end of August.

Pleasant River. The Pleasant River from the head of tide below Columbia Falls to Seavey and Guard Points (just north of the two Birch Islands) has been designated as an "A River" under the Maine Rivers Act. This designation means that the river segment is afforded extra protection from pollution and development. The estuary provides nesting and feeding habitat for bald eagles, and it supports runs of several important species of anadromous fish. The salt marsh located in and north of Dyer Cove is the largest in the region.

Upper Birch Island. Upper Birch lies in the upper reaches of Pleasant Bay, just east of Ripley Neck. Great blue herons have nested here for more than 40 years. This Nature Conservancy preserve is closed to visitors from March 15 through August 15; please do not land or linger nearby. The island has no trails.

Mink Island. The northern tip of this tiny public isle (located northwest

When the man from New Jersey ran out of cash, he put the island up for sale. That's when the equivalent of the Tooth Fairy stepped in. A family foundation purchased Jordan's Delight, then turned around and donated all but a few acres to the Maine Coast Heritage Trust. The foundation put those few acres, including the little shelter on the southern tip, under a conservation easement that prohibits development.

The story wasn't quite over. In 2001, Maine Coast Heritage Trust took down the 3,000-foot-square house—every beam, board, and picture window. Black guillemots, storm petrels, eider ducks, and gulls rule the rock once more.

Jordan's Delight before (house in saddle, left) and after

of Upper Birch and southwest of Raspberry—check your chart), provides a convenient lunch stop when exploring the Pleasant River.

Mary's Island. Great Auk Land Trust owns this 4-acre island east of Pinkham Island (both at the mouth of Back Bay; Mary's is not named on the chart). Also called Kemp's Folly, Mary's Island offers bird nesting habitat and so should be avoided from February 15 through the end of August 15. After that time, you may picnic on its shores, but beware: Most of Back Bay, including Pinkham and Mary's, is dry at low water. There are no trails on this isle.

At a Glance: Land in Public or Conservation Ownership

Jordan's Delight	Maine Coast Heritage Trust; closed April 1–August 31
Shipstern Island	TNC; closed February 15–August 15
Flint Island	TNC; closed February 15–August 15
Little Nash Island	Maine Coast Heritage Trust; closed April 1–August 31
The Ladle	Maine Coast Heritage Trust; closed April 1–August 31
Marsh Island	Great Auk Land Trust; closed April 15–August 31
Upper Birch Island	TNC; closed March 15–August 15
Mink Island	Maine Island Trail/BPL
Mary's Island	Great Auk Land Trust; closed February 15–August 15

IF&W Wildlife Islands

These islands are closed during the indicated bird nesting season. After the nesting season is over, the islands are limited to careful day use.

Green Island (NW of Petit Manan Island)	Closed to visitors
Egg Rock (1 mi S of Bois Bubert)	April 15–July 31
Pot Rock (1.3 mi SSW of Cape Split)	April 15–July 31

USFWS Wildlife Lands

Petit Manan Point	Shore and trails open for careful day use
Petit Manan Island	Closed April 1–August 31
Bois Bubert Island	Maine Island Trail
Nash Island	Closed April 1–August 31

The Great Wass Archipelago

The Great Wass archipelago is awe-inspiring and majestic, a world of granite cliffs and crashing seas, of auks and bird's-eye primrose. The Nature Conservancy has protected about a third of the islands in the archipelago, either by outright ownership or through easements.

For the paddler, all this protection from development means miles of shoreline of great granite slabs and tight-packed forests of spruce and fir. Swells crash on the exposed rocky shores, and the outer islands offer little comfort to paddlers who seek shelter. Almost all trips in this area involve crossing open water and rounding exposed points. Even Eastern Bay, which lies in the center of the archipelago, is not entirely sheltered when the weather gets heavy. The archipelago is also a magnet for fog—and yes, wind and fog can coexist. Whether a paddle here is thrilling or frightening depends entirely on the condition of the sea and the competence of the paddler.

Trip Ideas (weather and experience permitting)

From South Addison, head east to Stevens, Drisko, and the three Sands (6 to 8 miles round-trip).

From Jonesport, explore Eastern Bay and Mistake Harbor (10 miles round-trip) or circumnavigate Steele Harbor Island (11 miles). Mistake Island can serve as a lunch site and turnaround point, conditions permitting. For a paddle on the wild side, circumnavigate Great Wass and Beals islands (15 miles).

Charts
Chart: 13326, Machias Bay to Tibbett Narrows (1:40,000)
Chart Kit: 77
Maine Atlas locator map: 17, 25, 26

Tides (hours:minutes relative to Portland; average rise)
Jonesport, Moosabec Reach: 0:23 before; 11.5 feet
Steele Harbor Island: 0:28 before; 11.6 feet

Safety Considerations, Strong Currents, and Caution Areas

Stevens, Drisko, and the Sands islands. Although the distance is not great, paddlers heading to this chain have to cross open water to get there, and the islands themselves are quite exposed. Both judgment and skill are necessary for this trip.

Great Wass. The steep, rocky southern shore of Great Wass Island and the adjacent smaller islands are open to the brunt of swells, wind, and fast currents; rebound waves can leave the seas confused, and safe havens are scarce. There are almost always waves breaking on the treeless Man islands at the mouth of Head Harbor. Paddling in the Great Wass archipelago demands solid skills, sound judgment, and good, stable conditions.

Moosabec Reach. Because it is the inside alternative to rounding the Great Wass chain, Moosabec Reach is well traveled, mostly by fishing boats (larger sailboats cannot duck under the relatively low bridge). The reach, however, has its own concerns. The causeway for the bridge narrows the area through which water can flow, and the tidal current here can reach 6 to 8 knots. In addition, strong eddies can form on both sides of the bridge. The current floods east and ebbs west, and when a wind from the southwest hits the ebb current, an undesirable chop can develop. Once each summer, boats

Paddling along Main Channel Way south of Steel Harbor Island

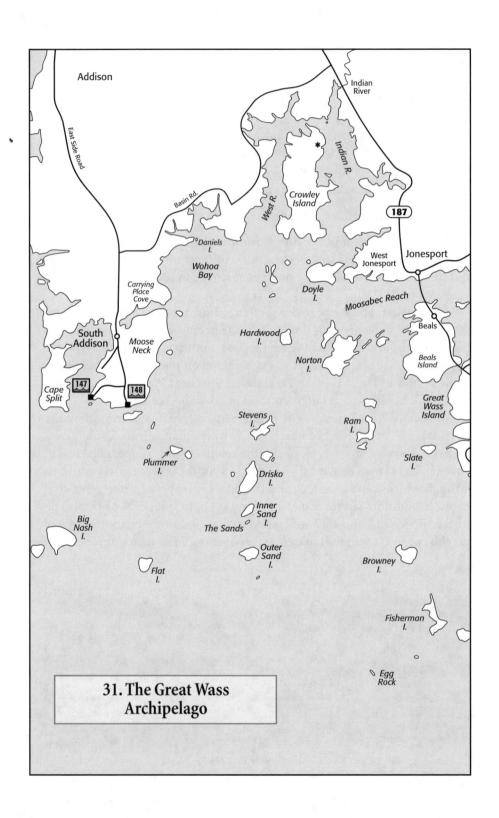

Addison

Indian
River

East Side Road

Indian R.

Basin Rd.

West R.

Crowley
Island

*

187

Daniels
I.

West
Jonesport

Jonesport

Wohoa
Bay

Doyle
I.

Moosabec Reach

Carrying
Place
Cove

Beals

South
Addison

Moose
Neck

Hardwood
I.

Beals
Island

Norton
I.

Cape
Split

147

148

Great
Wass
Island

Stevens
I.

Ram
I.

Slate
I.

Plummer
I.

Drisko
I.

Inner
Sand
I.

Big
Nash
I.

The Sands

Outer
Sand
I.

Browney
I.

Flat
I.

Fisherman
I.

Egg
Rock

**31. The Great Wass
Archipelago**

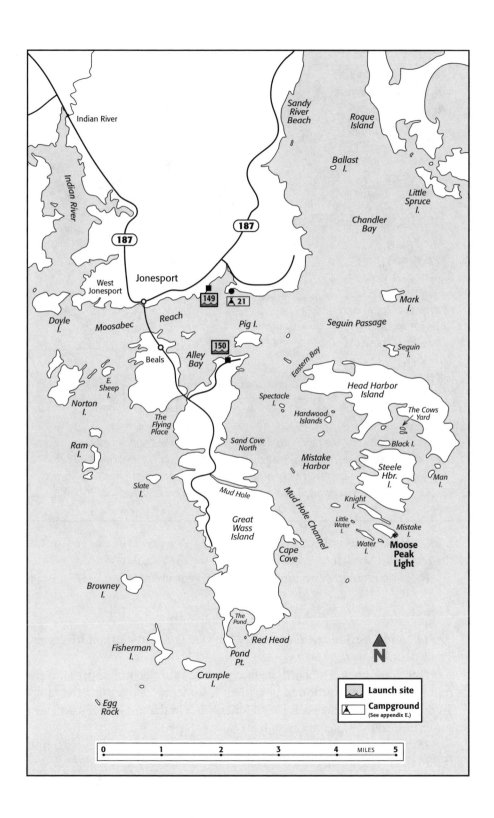

Indian River

Indian River

Indian River

187

187

Sandy
River
Beach

Roque
Island

Ballast
I.

Little
Spruce
I.

Chandler
Bay

Jonesport

West
Jonesport

Mark
I.

149

21

Reach

Moosabec

Pig I.

Seguin Passage

Seguin
I.

Doyle
I.

150

Beals

Alley
Bay

Eastern Bay

Head Harbor
Island

The Cows
Yard

E.
Sheep
I.

Spectacle
I.

Hardwood
Islands

Black I.

Norton
I.

The
Flying
Place

Sand Cove
North

Mistake
Harbor

Steele
Hbr.
I.

Man
I.

Ram
I.

Slate
I.

Mud Hole

Mud Hole Channel

Knight
I.

Little
Water
I.

Mistake
I.

Great
Wass
Island

Water
I.

**Moose
Peak
Light**

Cape
Cove

Browney
I.

The
Pond

Red Head

N

Fisherman
I.

Pond
Pt.

Crumple
I.

Egg
Rock

Launch site

Campground
(See appendix E.)

0   1   2   3   4   MILES   5

Natural History of the Great Wass Archipelago

Three areas of Great Wass Island are of particular interest to the naturalist: Red Head, with its unusual array of deepwater invertebrates in the intertidal zone; a jack pine stand in the interior of the island; and two uncommon forms of bogs, also on the interior of the island. While these features are not readily apparent to the sea kayaker—Red Head is fairly inaccessible at the very southern extremity of the island—the plants on the shores of Great Wass and neighboring islands are themselves intriguing. These plants are characterized by their ability to live in a challenging oceanic microclimate where ocean breezes and fog make the summer growing season cool and short. Black crowberry grows here, just as it does in the

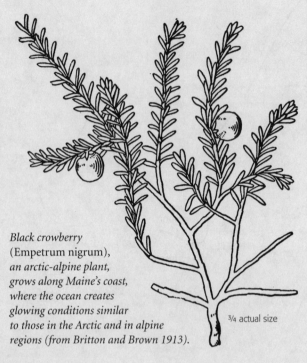

Black crowberry (Empetrum nigrum), an arctic-alpine plant, grows along Maine's coast, where the ocean creates glowing conditions similar to those in the Arctic and in alpine regions (from Britton and Brown 1913).

¾ actual size

line up for the Moosabec Lobster Boat Race; it's a good time to stay out of the reach (see www.lobsterboatracing.com for the race date).

Fog. Fog regularly envelops the islands in summertime.

Access

147 and 148: South Addison. See "Narraguagus and Pleasant Rivers and Their Bays."

149: Jonesport. The hard-surface all-tide ramp at Jonesport is in the midst of a working harbor, so be patient if someone else is using the ramp. To get to the harbor, take ME 187 to Jonesport. On the east end of town, turn south toward the water at the sign for Sawyer Square.

150: Great Wass Island. Go onto Great Wass and take a left; go 0.9 mile (past Hixie Head Road on the left) to a float with a very long ramp.

subarctic and Arctic. Beach head iris, bird's-eye primrose, roseroot, oysterleaf, and other maritime and northern plants can be found as well.

The normal complement of birds can be seen in and around Great Wass—common loons, double-crested cormorants, black guillemots, American black ducks, common eiders, herring gulls, great black-backed gulls, laughing gulls, Bonaparte's gulls, common terns, arctic terns, bald eagles, and ospreys. A fortunate paddler might, in late August, see razorbills or even puffins, both of which are alcids that prefer the open waters along the outer shores of the outer islands.

The bedrock of the archipelago is either light or dark. The light is pink granite, and it is showcased on Crumple, Great Wass, Mistake, Steele Harbor, and other islands. The dark is metavolcanic or metasedimentary rock, meaning that the original volcanic or sedimentary rocks were changed (metamorphosed) by heat and pressure. This bedrock is evident on the Head Harbor islands.

Roseroot (Sedum rosea) *grows sparingly along rocky shores Downeast. The plant has purplish or yellowish flowers and fleshy leaves.* HANK TYLER, STATE PLANNING OFFICE

Points of Interest

East Plummer Island. This Nature Conservancy island, which lies southeast of Cape Split, is a nesting island and is therefore closed to visitors from February 15 through August 15. After that time, paddlers may land—the best bet is on the bar between Plummer and East Plummer—and walk along the shore; there are no trails.

The Sands. The Sands is a smidgen of ledge and sand that lies between Inner and Outer Sand Islands. But it's a beautiful smidgen, with Petit Manan Point in the distance to the west and Great Wass Island a looming presence to the east. The little chain of islands that unfolds around the Sands is crammed with seabirds and seals—to the extent that paddlers should be careful not to disturb hauled-out seals or nesting birds. The Sands does have its drawbacks, though. It is open to any weather, and the highest tides sweep

Cetaceans sometimes wash up on Great Wass; here, a whale skull showing eye orbits.

right over the island. It's a nice place to visit when the seas are calm. Land on the beach on the north side.

Inner Sand Island. This 18-acre seabird-nesting island joined the Maine Coastal Islands National Wildlife Refuge in 1999. The island is predominantly spruce/fir, with some shrubs and meadowland. Inner Sand is closed during the nesting season, April 1 to August 31.

Stevens Island. Very rarely do entire islands come into public hands these days for the sole purpose of recreation, but Stevens defied the odds. Maine Coast Heritage Trust brokered the deal and provided two-thirds of the funding; the Maine Outdoor Heritage Fund provided the balance. This 31-acre island, fringed with sand beaches and rocky shores and thickly wooded on the interior, is now on the Maine Coast Trail. The best landing is in the cove on the northeast side of the island.

Hardwood Island. This privately owned island on the western end of Moosabec Reach still has the trappings of a granite quarrying island—stone wharf, tailings, and stranded machinery. The quarry here operated intermittently from the late 1890s until 1957. There were quarries on a few other islands, but the main business of Jonesport has been fishing, boat building, and related trades.

Daniels Island. This 2-acre public island is located off Bare Point in Wohoa Bay. If you visit, you'll probably have Daniels to yourself. It's off the beaten path and accessible only at the top half of the tide.

Crowley Island. The Pleasant River Wildlife Foundation owns two sizeable parcels on Crowley, including 100 acres in the northeast corner and 312 acres in a band in the southern half (in the area covered by "Crowley Island" on Map 31). The shoreline of the protected area is open for traditional uses such as clamming, worming, and recreation. Note that during low water,

Crowley and Indian River islands (below) are surrounded by mud. Only a narrow channel of the West River and a slightly wider channel of the Indian River remain navigable.

Indian River Island. This small, wooded island at the mouth of the Indian River (between the west shore of the river and Crowley Island) falls into the same category as Daniels. It's a public island, it is dry at low tide, and it is not a huge draw as a destination island.

Moosabec Reach. The origin of the name is not definitely known, but it may be connected with a Native American myth about a moose—a "moose rump" hill at Cape Rosier is called Moosekatchik. The reach has had a variety of names over the years, including Mispecky, Moose à Becky's Beach, and Mrs. Becky's Reach.

The Jonesport town pier and launch ramp are located in Sawyer Cove toward the eastern end of the reach and are protected by a large breakwater. This breakwater does not show on the chart.

Jonesport Coast Guard Station. This station is located on Moosabec Reach, west of the bridge to Beals Island.

Browney Island. Life-saving crews once set out from Browney to save ships in distress, but these days the island quietly provides nesting habitat for seabirds. The Great Auk Land Trust acquired Browney, which is open for walking and picnicking, in 1996. Separated as it is from the islands in the Stevens Island chain—and from other islands as well—it sees little traffic.

Little Water Island. This tiny, grassy, public isle is located between Water and Green Islands, just west of Mistake. It is a favorite of harbor seals, who often haul out—with pups—on the nearby ledges. Beach head iris grows here along with other maritime plants like roseroot. Little Water makes a nice, if exposed, lunch stop on an exploration of Eastern Bay, but the abundance of seals through midsummer means that it should be visited after that time. Please take care to stay on the rocks and spare the erodible banks and the unusual flora.

Great Wass Island Archipelago. The Nature Conservancy (TNC) has protected part or all of the following islands:

Great Wass Island Preserve: Of TNC's islands in the archipelago, only Great Wass has trails. If you would like to take a break from paddling, head for the Mud Hole trail, which runs along the south shore of Mud Hole. Paddle to the head of Mud Hole, secure your boat, and scramble up and to your left to the trail. Just south of Mud Hole Point, where the trail ends, there is a series of basins called Taft's Bath. After a steady rain, fresh water splashes and leaps down through these basins. As the name indicates, Mud Hole does revert to mud; on an average low tide, about 1,500 feet of the inner inlet is dry.

Crumple Island Preserve: High, bare Crumple Island—located southwest of Great Wass—apparently gets its name from the crumpled look of its outer cliffs.

Mistake Island Preserve: The Nature Conservancy, which owns 21 acres on this island, requests that visitors stay on the boardwalk or along the rocky shore to avoid trampling vegetation. Beach head iris, roseroot, blueberry, and raspberry can be found here, along with bog plants like leatherleaf, lambkill, and Labrador tea. TNC bought this lovely parcel from the grandson of the last keeper of Moose Peak Light.

The Coast Guard, which owns the remaining 4 acres at the east end of Mistake, provides a boardwalk from the landing area (near the bar to Knight Island) to Moose Peak Light. The light, built in 1827, refurbished sixty years later, and automated in 1970, is housed in a white tower and stands 72 feet above the water. To the north, the austere granite shore of Steele Harbor Island along Main Channel Way is nothing short of stunning.

Little Hardwood Island Preserve: Little Hardwood in Eastern Bay is far distant from (big) Hardwood, which looks south onto Western Bay. Little Hardwood, a TNC preserve, is closed to visitors from February 15 through August 15.

Mark Island: This island, which is covered with spruce and fir and has no trails, is closed from February 15 through August 15. Mark is located north of Head Harbor Island.

Other TNC islands: Man Island lies at the mouth of Head Harbor; it is bare, windblown, and uninviting. Black Island is snuggled deep in Head Harbor; it is forested with spruce and fir. If you go ashore on these islands, stay close to the shore.

At a Glance: Land in Public or Conservation Ownership

East Plummer Island	TNC; closed March 15–August 15
The Sands	Maine Island Trail/BPL
Stevens Island	Maine Island Trail/BPL
Daniels Island	Maine Island Trail/BPL
Indian River Island	Maine Island Trail/BPL
Browney Island	Great Auk Land Trust; careful day use
Little Water Island	Maine Island Trail/BPL
Great Wass Island Archipelago	TNC
Great Wass Island	Careful day use
Crumple Island	Careful day use
Mistake Island, western half	Careful day use
Man Island	Careful day use, but uninviting
Black Island	Careful day use along shore

Mark Island	Closed February 15–August 15; after that time, careful day use along shore
Little Hardwood Island	Closed February 15–August 15; after that time, careful day use along shore.

IF&W Wildlife Islands

These islands are closed during the indicated bird nesting season. After the nesting season is over, the islands are limited to careful day use.

Baston Ledge (0.9 mi SE of Drisko Island)	April 15–July 31
Stanley Ledge (1.3 mi S of Drisko Island)	April 15–July 31
Little Drisko Island (NE of Drisko Island)	April 15–July 31
Inner Goose Island (2.8 mi N of Drisko Island)	February 15–August 31
Little Ram Island (0.7 mi SW of Beals Island)	February 15–August 31
Curlew Rock (1 mi SW of southern tip of Great Wass)	April 15–July 31
Crumple Island Ledge (near S tip of Great Wass)	April 15–July 31
Freeman Rock (1.1 mi SW of Mistake Island)	April 15–July 31

USFWS Wildlife Islands

Inner Sand	Closed April 1–August 31

Chandler and Englishman Bays

Englishman Bay is one of those breathtakingly beautiful places that makes people say, "I wish I lived here!" Even though most of the islands are privately owned and off-limits to visitors, sea kayakers can paddle around the bay to take in its charm. There are several access points, the best of which—when the wind is manageable—is Roque Bluffs State Park, a secluded pocket barrier beach that overlooks the bay. From here, it's a short hop to Halifax Island, the only island in the Roque Island archipelago that is open to visitors.

Trip Ideas (weather and experience permitting)

The paddle from the Chandler River launch site to Englishman Bay and back (5 miles) is quite protected, though you do have to use the top two-thirds of the tide or risk being caught in the mud.

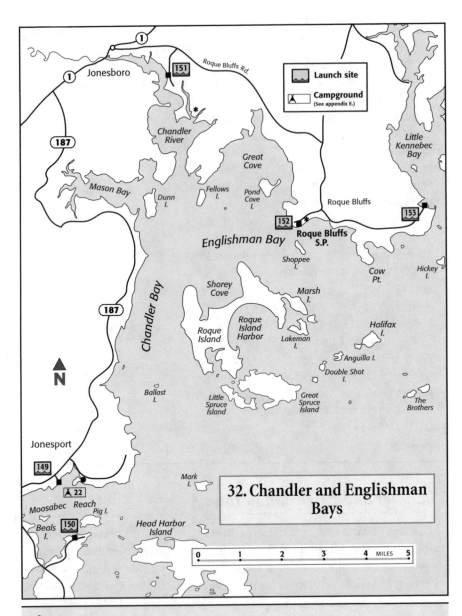

Jonesboro

Roque Bluffs Rd.

151

Chandler
River

Great
Cove

Little
Kennebec
Bay

Launch site

Campground
(See appendix E.)

Mason Bay

Dunn
I.

Fellows
I.

Pond
Cove
I.

Roque Bluffs

152

Roque Bluffs
S.P.

153

Englishman Bay

Shoppee
I.

Cow
Pt.

Hickey
I.

Chandler Bay

Shorey
Cove

Marsh
I.

Halifax
I.

Roque
Island

Roque
Island
Harbor

Lakeman
I.

Anguilla I.

Double Shot
I.

N

Ballast
I.

Little
Spruce
Island

Great
Spruce
Island

The
Brothers

Jonesport

149

Mark
I.

22

Moosabec Reach
Pig I.

Beals
I.

150

Head Harbor
Island

32. Chandler and Englishman Bays

0 1 2 3 4 MILES 5

Charts

Chart: 13326, Machias Bay to Tibbett Narrows (1:40,000)
Chart Kit: 77, 78
Maine Atlas locator map: 26

Tides (hours:minutes relative to Portland; average rise)
Shoppee Point: 0:23 before; 12.1 feet
Roque Island Harbor: 0:28 before; 12.3 feet

From Roque Bluffs, visit Halifax Island (about 6 miles round-trip) or circumnavigate the Roque Island archipelago (13 miles).

From the mouth of Little Kennebec Bay, explore northward. While Little Kennebec catches some wind, there is more protection here than there is outside.

From Jonesport, take in the broad sweep of Chandler and Englishman Bays by circumnavigating the Roque Island archipelago, stopping on Halifax (19 miles).

Safety Considerations, Strong Currents, and Caution Areas

Halifax Island. The *Coast Pilot* reports that the current can boil over the underwater bar that stretches from Halifax Island to Green Island and urges caution when crossing the bar. Green is the island between Halifax and The Brothers.

Access

149: Jonesport and 150: Great Wass Island. See "The Great Wass Archipelago."

151: Chandler River, Jonesboro. This ramp provides access to the Chandler River. Shortly after Route 1 crosses the Chandler River going northeast, take a right onto Old US 1, which becomes Roque Bluffs Road. After 1.5 miles, turn right onto Evergreen Point Road. Go 0.5 mile, then turn right toward the wharf and ramp.

152: Roque Bluffs State Park. The state park (255-3475 in summer) does not have a ramp, but paddlers can launch from the sand. There is often wind here, however, so be warned that surf can pound the southeast-facing beach. Shortly after Route 1 crosses the Chandler River going northeast, take a right onto Old US 1 (which becomes Roque Bluffs Road) and go 5.5 miles until it ends in a T intersection. Take a right and proceed 1.7 miles (staying right at the Roque Bluffs town hall) to the park. The use fee is $3 per person; facilities include vault toilets, a bathhouse, and a picnic area. The park is open from May 15 through October 1, from 9 AM until sundown. Be aware that the parking lot is gated.

Note. If you drive past the park to the end of the road, you'll find a ramp on the right, with very little parking, at the tip of Shoppee Point. Do not use the wharf (on the left) that belongs to Roque Islanders. The state park beach has plenty of parking and is a better launch site except in surf.

153: Little Kennebec Bay. There is a gravel ramp at the mouth of Little Kennebec Bay, which lies east of Englishman Bay. Proceed toward Roque Bluffs State Park, but turn east at the Roque Bluffs town hall and follow the

View from Roque Bluffs beach, looking east

road to its end. The small parking lot lies next to the river, just beyond a house. The dirt road leads steeply to the river; hand carry your kayak to the water.

Notes. There is no ramp at the end of Duck Cove Road, about 2 miles north of the site described above, and parking is limited to a few vehicles pulled parallel to the road. The southern site is a better choice.

Although some sources show a pair of launch sites on the peninsula west of Dunn Island on Englishman Bay, local inspection shows that one is posted as private property and the other does not have a parking area.

Points of Interest

Ballast Island. The name suggests that mariners picked up cobblestones from this island to serve as ballast on top-heavy ships. This island is managed by Maine's Department of Inland Fisheries and Wildlife; please respect the closure dates.

Roque Island Archipelago. This stunning set of islands includes Bar, Marsh, Lakeman, Roque, Great Spruce, Little Spruce, Double Shot, Anguilla, and Halifax islands. Joseph Peabody bought Roque Island in the early 1800s and, except for a few years when it went out of family ownership, his descendants have lived on or used the island ever since. Aside from Halifax, all of the islands in this group are privately owned by the Gardner and Monks families. (Isabella Stewart Gardner, an ancestor, was a Boston society matron, art collector, and artist.)

The owners of Roque Island are adamant about not wanting boaters of any kind on or near their islands; all of the islands are prominently posted with NO TRESPASSING signs. Saying that scientific studies may be underway at any given time, the family corporation would prefer that paddlers stay outside of Roque Island Harbor and at least a mile offshore their islands. Alert paddlers, however, might notice numerous sailboats in the harbor; no Coast Guard regulation prohibits boaters of any kind from these waters.

Halifax Island. The southwest finger of Halifax, a grassy island with rocky shores on the eastern end of the Roque Island archipelago, is part of the Maine Island Trail. Paddlers may land at the cove on the north side of the neck or along the western shore of the cove on the south side of the neck (but beware of getting trapped in the south cove if the wind comes up). The rest of the island is closed; it is the site of a raised bog, an unusual feature that occurs (in the U.S.) only in a narrow coastal band between Acadia and West Quoddy Head. Access to Halifax Island depends on its careful use. The island is managed by the U.S. Fish and Wildlife Service.

Eastern Brothers Island. Because common eider, black guillemots, great black-backed gulls, herring gulls, and Leach's storm-petrels nest on this far-flung, 17-acre island, it is closed from April 1 through the end of August. The U.S. Fish and Wildlife Service owns Eastern Brothers and its state counterpart owns Western Brothers. The two islands are joined at low water.

Shoppee Island. The U.S. Fish and Wildlife Service also owns Shoppee, an 18-acre, forested island immediately offshore and barred to the mainland at low water. In the Revolutionary War, Anthony Shoppee served first as a redcoat and then in the Continental Army. He settled here thereafter and bequeathed his name to the island and the point northward.

Roque Bluffs Beach. The beach at Roque Bluffs is a pocket barrier beach that encloses a freshwater pond. It is likely that a spit built west across a saltwater lagoon and cut the lagoon off from the tide. Both the beach and the freshwater pond are part of the state park; the pond is used for swimming. Roque Bluffs Beach may have the northernmost stand of American beach grass on the U.S. Atlantic coast. Common eider and other sea ducks as well as bald eagles frequent this area.

The yellow bluffs at the mouth of the Englishman River to the east give this area its name. The bluffs are part of a moraine, a glacial feature that forms when rock material is brought forward to the outer edge of glacial ice and deposited in a ridge. The beach is composed of eroded material from the bluffs.

Tide Mill Creek. Great Auk Land Trust purchased this 220-acre tract after a furious fund-raising campaign. Paddlers can explore this stream, which feeds into the Chandler River, at high water or simply thank trust members for protecting an important wildlife area.

At a Glance: Land in Public or Conservation Ownership

Halifax Island	Maine Island Trail/USFWS; southwest finger only open for careful day use
Roque Bluffs Beach State Park	BPL; careful day use
Mark Island	TNC; careful day use along shore

IF&W Wildlife Islands

These islands are closed during the indicated bird nesting season. After the nesting season is over, the islands are limited to careful day use.

Ballast Island (1 mi W of Roque Island)	April 15–July 31
Green Island (1 mi SE of Halifax Island)	April 15–July 31
Pulpit Rock (1 mi S of Halifax Island)	April 15–July 31
West Brothers Island (1.4 mi SE of Halifax)	April 15–August 31

USFWS Wildlife Islands

Halifax Island	Closed year-round except southwest finger
Eastern Brothers Island	Closed April 1–August 31
Shoppee Island	Closed February 15–August 1 or as posted

Machias Bay

Machias Bay is an utterly beautiful area of rocky shores and wide landscapes. The big draw is the islands in midbay, which provide some protection while allowing views seaward of Cross Island, the Libby Islands, and the open ocean. The Machias River and the inner bay south of Machiasport offer more sheltered paddling. Stone Island, a Nature Conservancy preserve at the western entrance to Machias Bay, is not a destination island because there is no place to land.

Because all the launch sites are located on the western side of Machias Bay, paddlers have to undertake a substantial crossing to reach Cross Island at the east entrance to the bay. A trip from Bucks Harbor, the nearest launch site, involves an open-water crossing of 3 miles each way.

You can expect to see double-crested cormorants, black guillemots, common eiders, herring gulls, great black-backed gulls, terns, ospreys, and bald eagles in Machias Bay. A multitude of migrant shorebirds, Canada geese,

Charts

Chart: 13326, Machias Bay to Tibbett Narrows (1:40,000)
Chart Kit: 78
Maine Atlas locator map: 26

Tides (hours:minutes relative to Portland; average rise)
Stone Island, Machias Bay: 0:20 before; 12.4 feet
Machiasport: 0:17 before; 12.6 feet

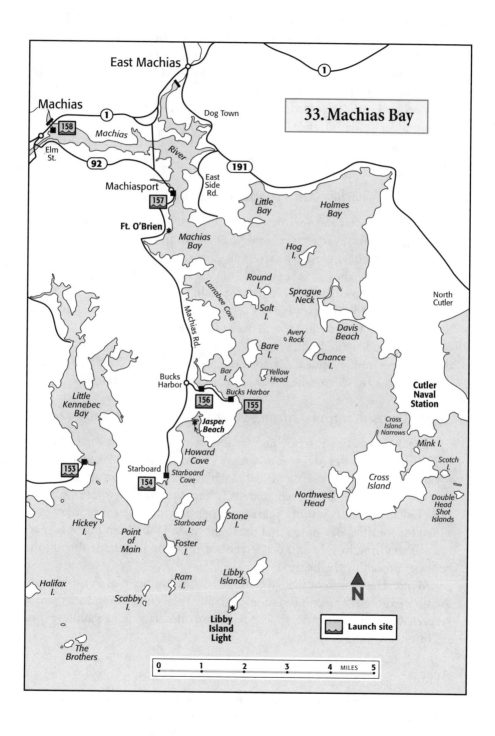

East Machias

Machias

Dog Town

33. Machias Bay

158
Machias

Elm
St.
92

River

East
Side
Rd.
191

Machiasport
157

Ft. O'Brien

Machias
Bay

Little
Bay

Holmes
Bay

Hog
I.

Round
I.

Sprague
Neck

North
Cutler

Larrabee Cove

Salt
I.

Avery
Rock

Davis
Beach

Bare
I.

Chance
I.

Machias Rd.

Bar
I.
Yellow
Head

Bucks
Harbor

Cutler
Naval
Station

Bucks Harbor
156
155

Little
Kennebec
Bay

Cross
Island
Narrows

Mink I.

Jasper
Beach

Scotch
I.

153

Howard
Cove

Cross
Island

Double
Head
Shot
Islands

Starboard
154

Starboard
Cove

Northwest
Head

Hickey
I.

Point
of
Main

Starboard
I.

Stone
I.

Foster
I.

Halifax
I.

Ram
I.

Libby
Islands

Scabby
I.

N

Libby
Island
Light

Launch site

The
Brothers

0   1   2   3   4 MILES 5

and black ducks use shallow Holmes Bay as a foraging area; Holmes Bay lies at the northeast corner of Machias Bay. Peregrine falcons and merlins occasionally zero in on the concentrated prey, and raptors use Cross Island as a migration stop. Harbor seals frequent many haulout ledges and harbor porpoise course quietly through the water.

Machias Bay has three prominent navigation points: Libby Island Light in the middle of the entrance to the bay; two domes (formerly part of a radar station) on Howard Mountain on the west side of the bay; and a cluster of radio towers on the east side of the bay.

Trip Ideas (weather and experience permitting)

On windy days, take cover on the Machias River, which is great eagle-watching territory, as several pair nest nearby (round-trip between Machias and Machiasport, 6 miles). The river has carved a deep channel through the mudflats and marshes, so it is possible to paddle at any stage of the tide, but there is more elbow room during the top half.

To take in the midbay islands with a midday low tide, paddle from Machiasport to Bucks Harbor and back (10 miles).

With a midday high tide, start at Bucks Harbor and head north around the midbay islands (9 miles). Or, for a longer trip with the same tide pattern, start at Starboard Cove, take in the islands, and return (13 miles).

Safety Considerations, Strong Currents, and Caution Areas

Fog. Machias Bay is renowned for fog. Two examples, unearthed by island historian Charles McLane, may serve as a warning. In 1890, an inspector for the Lighthouse Service described Machias Bay as "a region abounding in fog, not exceeded, it is believed, in density and duration anywhere along the New England coast." Seventy years later, opponents to an oil refinery proposed for Machias Bay noted that the foghorn on Libby Island blew 87 percent of the time in July and 63 percent of the time in August during the summer preceding the hearing.

Wind. The mouth of the bay and the islands southeast of Point of Main are very exposed. The combination of strong tidal currents and stiff winds (especially when the two are opposed) can provide challenging paddling conditions in any part of the bay.

Access

154: Starboard Cove. From Route 1 in Machias, follow ME 92 east and south through Machiasport and Bucks Harbor, proceeding a little more than 10 miles. The paved road ends at Starboard Cove. Hand carry to a cobble

Razorbills

Razorbills spend most of their lives at sea, wintering in the North Atlantic and coming to shore only to mate and raise young. In Maine, they make their temporary homes

Razorbills "billing," a greeting and courtship behavior

JEAN HOEKWATER

on four islands, including Matinicus Rock near Matinicus Island and Old Man Island near Cutler. Razorbills also breed in eastern Canada, Greenland, Iceland, and some coastal areas of Europe.

Razorbills return to the same site every year, arriving in late February and pairing up in April. The courtship behavior includes synchronized flying with "butterfly" wing beats. On the water, the male circles the female, calling to her and opening his mouth so she can see his bright yellow *gape*, the line along the upper and lower bill.

In May, the female lays a single egg on a narrow ledge or in a protected crack in the rock. The egg is noticeably pointed at one end—when it rolls, it merely rolls in a circle rather than plummeting off the cliff. The female and male take turns incubating the egg; incubation lasts about thirty-four days. The chick requires about fifteen days to fledge. It generally alights from the cliff around dusk to avoid predators, flies to the water, and starts swimming—with an adult—out to sea. Chicks are vulnerable to gull predation during fledging, hence the short span of time they remain in their rocky nest.

Of the three alcids that nest in Maine, the razorbill is the largest—about the size of a small duck. The bird's bill is thick, long, and blunt, and has a thin white vertical stripe; another white line runs from the bill to the eye. The razorbill is a striking bird, with black plumage above and white below. In the summer, its head is completely black. On the water, it appears double-bowed, with cocked head and an upturned tail. In flight, it has a chunky body with a back that is noticeably arched; the trailing edge of the wing is white.

---

beach on the east side or launch in the inlet on the west side. This is a busy launch area, so make sure that your car is parked so it does not block traffic.

155: Pettigrow Beach, Bucks Harbor. When owners of Pettigrow Beach, who had long allowed free use to the maritime community, decided to sell, it seemed certain that access would disappear. With the help of Maine Coast Heritage Trust and a grant from the Land for Maine's Future program, the Town of Machias was able to purchase the 1.5-acre beach and ensure continued access to salt water.

Native American Petroglyphs

Petroglyphs in several locations in Machias Bay show humanlike figures with arms, legs, headdresses or horns, and—in one instance—an *atlatl* (spear thrower). Although it is not known exactly when bow and arrows replaced atlatls in North America, archaeologists believe that the changeover occurred some time before A.D. 1000. Some researchers estimate that the petroglyphs are 3,000 years old.

In 1999, sea kayakers from Machias Bay Boat Tours and Sea Kayaking discovered a new site with 70 petroglyphs including a ship—similar to ships that European explorers used 400 to 500 years ago—causing great excitement among archaeologists.

Maine has only three known petroglyph sites: in Embden on the Kennebec River, along Grand Lake Stream, and in Machias Bay. The Machias sites are by far the most extensive.

On a more sobering note, in some places along the coast from Machias Bay to Eastport, land is being lost to the ocean by as much as 2.5 feet per century. The rest of Maine's coast is being inundated at a rate only half that much. The difference, believes Harold Borns, a retired geology professor from University of Maine in Orono, is that the plate underneath southern Washington County is flexing, and the land is actually sinking while the global sea level is rising. One landowner in Bucks Harbor that Borns interviewed said that he once planted crops on 200 acres; almost all of that land is now covered by salt water.

Follow ME 92 south to Bucks Harbor, then take the first left onto Pettigrow Point Road. Go 1.1 miles, passing Finn Beach Road and the town wharf along the way. The ramp is on the left and parking on the right; there's a portable toilet back at the town wharf. Kayakers can launch from the cobble beach.

156: Finn Beach, Bucks Harbor. If the Pettigrow lot is full, try Finn Beach (see directions, above).

157: Machiasport. There is a small, hand-carry site behind the Gates House, a historic building on the Machias Road in Machiasport. Take ME 92 from Machias to Machiasport and pull in behind the Gates House.

Note. At Jasper Beach, hearty boaters may haul gear up and over the berm, then out to the water, but it's more fun to paddle to this lovely place and have lunch there.

158: Machias River. The town of Machias has an all-tide concrete ramp with ample parking. Proceed northeast to Machias on either Route 1 or Route 1A. The launch site is on the right, just after the two roads join.

Points of Interest

Libby Islands. Libby Light is located on the southern island. It shows 91 feet above the water in a conical granite tower. The light, built in the 1820s, was sorely needed. Treacherous fog and driving storms caused many wrecks here—35 between 1856 and 1902 alone. The U.S. Fish and Wildlife Service manages this island for nesting seabirds; it is closed to visitors from April 1 through August 31. Maine's Department of Inland Fisheries and Wildlife manages Big Libby for nesting seabirds; the island is closed from April 15 through August 31.

Stone Island. The steep, rocky shores of Stone Island have discouraged human settlement, but the island provides excellent nesting habitat for great blue herons, ospreys, and other species. As of the late 1980s, there were more than 100 great blue heron nests on Stone. The island is covered with spruce and fir, except at the northern end where the herons have nested. Heron guano is full of nitrogen and kills trees over time.

In the 1960s, Occidental Petroleum and several other companies proposed building an oil refinery on Point of Main and using Stone Island as the docking station. Tankers would have landed at a quarter-mile-long pier projecting from Stone, and oil would have been pumped to the refinery and back in huge pipes. The project met with wide and strong opposition. A major strike against the idea was the fog that regularly covers the bay. After a 10-year struggle, the oil companies finally lost interest. The Landguard Trust, which staunchly opposed the project, bought the island and eventually it became a Nature Conservancy preserve.

There are aquaculture pens just north of Stone Island, a cruel temptation to the ospreys living there. From the air, the birds can see fish jumping in the pens, but when they streak down to strike, they are stopped short by the nets that keep the fish in—and ospreys out.

Jasper Beach. Jasper is a lovely, crescent-shaped beach that lies at the head of Howard Cove. It is a *spit barrier beach*, with one end attached to the mainland and the other end forming a spit that extends partway across a small bay to the north. Most of the small, polished stones are from igneous bedrock: red-colored rhyolite, dark green and dark gray basalt, and light green syenites and dacites. The beach is called "jasper" because the rocks are

The polished stones at Jasper Beach, which look like jasper but are actually of volcanic origin, give the beach its name. Hank Tyler, State Planning Office

similar in coloration to true jasper, which is an opaque red, brown, or green quartz. The Nature Conservancy worked with the town of Machiasport to secure access to this unusual feature.

Avery Rock. The federal government built a lighthouse on this tiny 1.6-acre island, and keepers lived there from 1876 to 1933. For lack of room, the light was built on top of the house. In one storm, when waves smashed against the structure and threatened to push it into the sea, the keeper opened the doors and windows to allow the towering waves to pass through and thus saved the building. A light buoy and bell later replaced the light. The island is owned by the public, but access is atrocious and there is nothing to visit.

Salt Island. James Lyon, the first minister in Machias, built a saltworks and house on Salt Island in the late 1770s or early 1780s. In 1983 The Nature Conservancy bought the western half of the island (the eastern half is privately owned). The sanctuary is closed to visitors from March 15 through August 15. Please do not land on the island or linger offshore during the nesting season.

Fort O'Brien. Fort O'Brien, on the point of the same name just south of Machiasport, is not a port of call for sea kayakers, but it does represent some of the area's history. The men of Machiasport seized a British ship in 1775, marking the first naval action of the Revolutionary War. Although military strategists never actually planned an attack on Nova Scotia, rumors that Machiasport might be used for such an effort prompted the British to destroy Fort O'Brien in 1777. The fort was later rebuilt, and the British destroyed it again during the War of 1812. Only the rather unexciting breastworks remain.

The Bold Coast

The Bold Coast is not included in this book as a sea kayaking area because access is problematic. Although Lubec has a public boat ramp, the town-owned ramp at Cutler is so small that it is unsuitable for wide public use; the next public access to the south is in Machias Bay.

Moreover, the 22-mile section between Cutler and West Quoddy Head is called the Bold Coast for good reason. The long, straight coastline is exposed to winds and waves from the southwest, southeast, and northeast. There are only a few coves for protection. The shoreline is rocky and steep, providing the opportunity for rebound waves and confusing seas to develop. The *Coast Pilot* notes, "A rough sea builds up quickly when the wind is contrary to the tidal current and small craft may find themselves beset and unable to make the shelter of the coves without assistance." In addition, passage through Lubec Narrows is difficult due to very strong tidal currents and eddies.

An impressive amount of land has been protected along the Bold Coast. Quoddy Head State Park (733-0911 during the summer) includes West Quoddy Head, which is the easternmost point in the United States. Visitors to the bluffs have sometimes spotted humpback, minke, and finback whales. (The park is open for day use; there is a $2 entrance fee.)

The Nature Conservancy owns two headlands with almost 924 acres. The Conservation Foundation has protected 8,900 acres of nonshoreline land north of Cutler. Maine's Bureau of Parks and Lands owns and manages 2,100 acres at one head and 263 acres at another; it also manages two public islands at the mouth of Bailey's Mistake. "Quoddy Trails," a booklet that describes hiking trails along the Bold Coast and Cobscook Bay, is available from the Quoddy Regional Land Trust (see appendix D; inquire regarding cost).

The Bold Coast between Cutler and West Quoddy Head is steep and unforgiving.

Machias. There were transient trading posts in Machias Bay during the 1600s, but European settlers did not come to stay until the 1760s. The chief attractions were timber and a mill site on the river, and lumbering became the main economic activity; lumbering has since given way to blueberry cultivation and fishing. *Machias* is thought to be Micmac for "bad little falls," referring to the steep falls at the head of tide in the town of Machias. There is now an abandoned dam at this site.

Cross Island. This large, stunning island at the eastern entrance to Machias Bay is open for careful day use. The island provides habitat for white-tailed deer, osprey, and many other species. In the 1940s the Cabot family of Boston acquired most of Cross as well as the smaller islands nearby and, eventually, Coast Guard buildings in Northeast Cove. In 1980, Thomas and Virginia Cabot donated the buildings and 19 acres to the Hurricane Island Outward Bound School, which operates a field station there. They kept 20 acres and gave the balance—1,615 acres—plus several nearby islands to The Nature Conservancy, which later transferred ownership to the U.S. Fish and Wildlife Service. Cross and the other islands are now part of the Maine Coastal Islands National Wildlife Refuge.

Lifesaving Station #2 began operating in Northeast Cove in 1874. The captain and half a dozen "surfmen" assisted crews of stranded ships and shipwrecks in the Machias Bay and Cutler area. With the onset of World War I, the Coast Guard took over the station.

Double Head Shot, Old Man, Mink, and Scotch islands. These islands are also all under the management of the U.S. Fish and Wildlife Service. Grasses, thickets, and stunted trees grow on the two Double Head Shot islands, providing nesting areas for common eiders, double-crested cormorants, black guillemots, and Leach's storm-petrels. Old Man Island, east of Scotch, is one of a handful of sites in the Gulf of Maine where razorbills nest. Mink and Scotch Islands provide habitat for bald eagles. These five islands are closed from April 1 through August 31.

At a Glance: Land in Public or Conservation Ownership

Stone Island	TNC; closed March 15–August 15
Jasper Beach	Town managed; careful day use
Avery Rock	BPL; access extremely difficult
Salt Island, western half	TNC; closed March 15–August 15

IF&W Wildlife Islands

These islands are closed during the indicated bird nesting season. After the nesting season is over, the islands are limited to careful day use.

Big Libby Island	April 15–August 31
(entrance to Machias Bay)	

Shag Ledge	April 15–July 31
(0.6 mi SW of Point of Main)	
Hog Island (in the bay)	February 15–August 31
USFWS Wildlife Islands	
Cross Island	Careful day use
Mink Island	Closed April 1–August 31
Double Head Shot Islands	Closed April 1–August 31
Old Man Island	Closed April 1–August 31
Scotch Island	Closed April 1–August 31

Cobscook Bay

Cobscook means "boiling tide waterfalls," an apt description of this large bay and its many arms. Three factors contribute to the boiling tides and water-falls: the tide averages almost 20 feet; a huge volume of water passes into and out of Cobscook; and several peninsulas and one chockstone island substan-tially constrict the water's flow. As a result, dangerous tidal currents rush through the bay, creating huge eddies, whirlpools, and boils. Paddlers who venture into Cobscook Bay must be able to read and deal with strong currents, eddy lines, and eddies. Solid river-paddling skills—and the proficiency to ex-ecute these skills in a boat that is designed to go straight rather than dance through tricky water—are necessary. Paddlers must also be able to judge when to paddle and when to wait, and when to stay out of an area altogether.

For people with less skill, there are opportunities to paddle in side bays like Whiting Bay, but even here there is a wide tide range and the currents are strong. Regardless of the trip, it is imperative to consider the tide whenever you get out of your boat. Water covers a lot of ground quickly and can easily strand you in several acres of mud—or whisk away a boat that you thought was secure on high ground.

Alan Brooks, from the Quoddy Regional Land Trust, cautions that while sea kayaking does not necessarily present the same problems as other boating, it could if paddlers are not aware of the special environmental and safety con-siderations in these waters. Cobscook Bay may seem rugged, but soil condi-tions make the islands and headlands here quite fragile; people should be very careful not to create paths. Also, the great majority of the land in Cobscook Bay is in private ownership, and this ownership needs to be respected.

Although Cobscook Bay has an inland feel because there is land on every quarter, seabirds and seals are abundant. Common loons, double-crested cor-morants, great blue herons, ospreys, great black-backed gulls, herring gulls, ring-billed gulls, Bonaparte's gulls, common terns, and bald eagles frequent

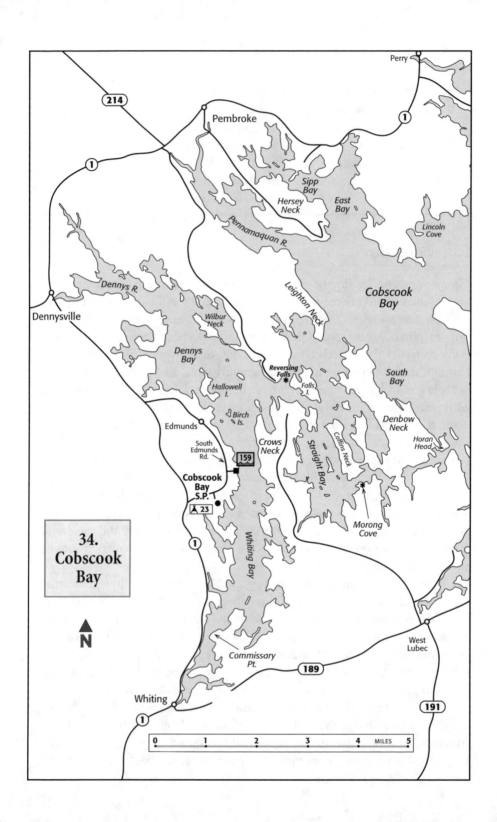

Perry

214

Pembroke

1

Sipp
Bay

Hersey
Neck

East
Bay

Lincoln
Cove

Pennamaquan R.

Dennys R.

Cobscook
Bay

Leighton Neck

Dennysville

Wilbur
Neck

Dennys
Bay

Reversing
Falls
✳

South
Bay

Falls
I.

Hallowell
I.

Denbow
Neck

Birch
Is.

Horan
Head

Edmunds

Coffins Neck

South
Edmunds
Rd.

159

Crows
Neck

Straight Bay

Cobscook
Bay
S.P.

✳

🏕 23

Morong
Cove

Whiting Bay

1

34.
Cobscook
Bay

West
Lubec

Commissary
Pt.

189

N

Whiting

191

1

0   1   2   3   4   MILES   5

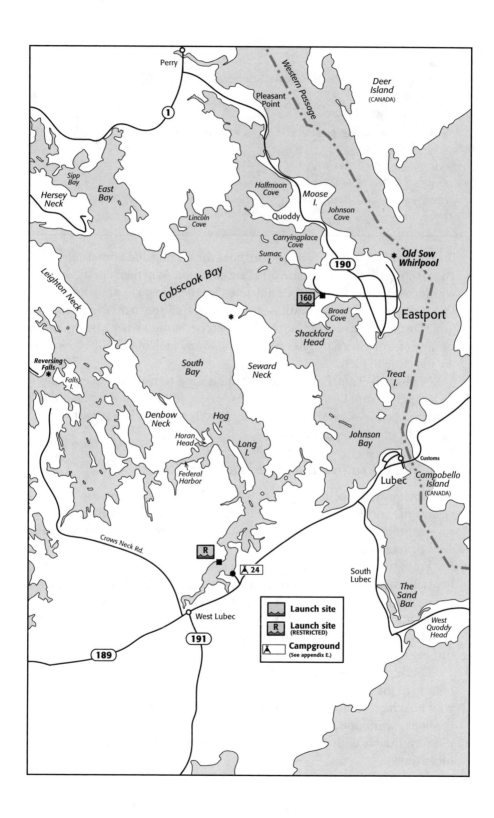

Charts
Chart: 13394, Grand Manan Channel-Northern Part (1:50,000)
Chart Kit: 79
Maine Atlas locator map: 27, 37

Tides (hours:minutes relative to Portland; average rise)
Birch Islands: 0:48 after; 17.6 feet
Coffins Point: 0:16 after; 18.3 feet
East Bay: 0:03 before; 19.1 feet
Horan Head, South Bay: 0:01 after; 19.2 feet
Deep Cove, Eastport: 0:09 before; 18.7 feet

the bay. Cobscook is, in fact, a stronghold for nesting and wintering eagles, and sightings of the impressive birds are common. Whether a nest is located within a sanctuary or not, the guidelines are the same: Do not land near or linger near a nest during nesting season (March 15 through August 15) and give roosting eagles a wide berth. Also exercise caution when you are in the vicinity of seal ledges; if seals raise their head and look in your direction, you are too close to them.

"Cobscook Trails," a booklet detailing nine trails in Cobscook Bay—including information and trail maps for some of the points of interest described below—is available from the Quoddy Regional Land Trust (see appendix D; inquire regarding cost).

Trip Ideas (weather and experience permitting)

Obviously, it is better to paddle with the current than against it. Paddling against the current can range from being a considerable challenge to an engagement in futility. The current is strongest at midtide but continues to be swift throughout its cycle.

From the ramp in Whiting Bay, you can go north or south. To the north lies Hallowell Island, also called Williams Island, which is open to the public (3 to 4 miles round-trip). Catch the bottom of the ebb tide to the island and the beginning of the flood tide back. Although the distance is short, this trip can involve swift currents. If you see eagles or ospreys, paddle by without disturbing them.

Or, catch the ebb tide and carefully paddle to the northern eddy at the bottom of the Reversing Falls. The land along this shore is a town park. Carry your boat high on the shore (it is amazing how fast the basin fills) and watch the boils, whirlpools, eddies, and standing waves build over time. If you are not comfortable with eddies and swiftly moving water, save this trip for another time.

If you head south, catch the flood tide to Commissary Point, managed by the Department of Inland Fisheries and Wildlife (5 to 6 miles round-trip). The same caution regarding eagles and ospreys applies here. Ride the ebb tide back to the launch site.

Two trips—designed for very experienced paddlers—take place in the Cobscook Reversing Falls. The tide information for Coffins Point and the Birch islands (and, for the second trip, Deep Cove) is critical for planning. Approaching the reversing falls from Whiting Bay requires planning around a midday low tide. Either turn around or circumnavigate Falls Island, heading back to the boat ramp on the bottom of the rising tide (about 10 or 11 miles).

To paddle the falls if you are launching from Eastport, it is ideal to have a midday high tide. Plan to be at Leighton Neck, east of the Reversing Falls, as the tide is nearing its height and go through the falls at high-water slack when the falls is completely flooded. It is better to be early and wait than to arrive too late and chance the consequences. Turn around at the west end of the falls or duck south of Falls Island to catch the ebbing tide back to Eastport (13 miles, including circumnavigating the island). Do not linger; slack water does not last long.

A second trip from Eastport has as its destination Horan Head in South Bay (about 10 miles round-trip). This property, managed by the Department of Inland Fisheries and Wildlife, has trails along the shore and looks out onto Hog and Long Islands, both Nature Conservancy preserves. Although this trip does not take in the reversing falls, it does include paddling through the heart of Cobscook Bay—and the heart of the currents—so it requires good skills and better judgment. You can also access Horan Head from South Bay Campground (2.5 miles round-trip).

Safety Considerations, Strong Currents, and Caution Areas

Cobscook Bay. Says the *Coast Pilot*: "In Cobscook Bay and its tributaries, the tidal currents follow the general direction of the channels, but in the coves there are strong reverse eddy currents, and heavy overfalls form over the submerged rocks and ledges. The velocity is estimated at 5 to 8 knots, and some of the buoys are towed under when currents are at strength."

The situation in Cobscook and its outlying bays becomes even more complicated when the wind comes up; if the wind and current are opposed, a very nasty chop can develop. Cobscook is an area where it pays to include the phase of the moon in planning. Tides during the full and new moon are stronger; paddlers can expect that the currents and other dangers will be correspondingly exaggerated as well.

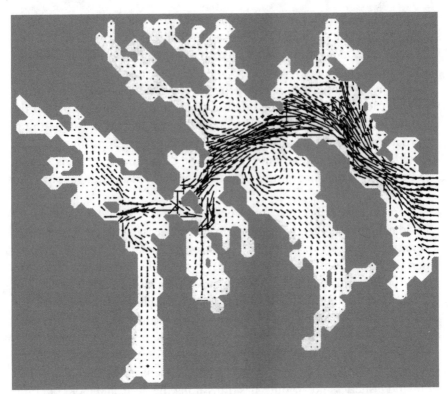

This map shows the tidal current patterns at the fourth hour of flood tide, when two large whirlpools from the middle section of Cobscook Bay (from Brooks, Baca, and Lo 1997, with support from The Nature Conservancy and the Mellon Foundation).

Reversing Falls. Where the bay pinches down, particularly between Leighton Neck and Denbow Neck and west to the reversing falls, the current is extremely strong, even when approaching slack. At strength, the current runs at an estimated 9 to 12 knots through the falls—between Mahar Point and Falls Island—and there is a drop of 12 feet.

Utmost care must be taken when paddling between Leighton Neck and the falls. Just getting into position for a high-water slack transit means dealing with very forceful currents, eddy lines, and eddies. When going through the falls at high-water or low-water slack, start as soon as conditions permit because the slack does not last long. (A *Coast Pilot* chart shows that in an area with a maximum current of 10 knots, there are only 2 minutes when the current speed is not greater than 0.1 knot; only 7 minutes when the current speed is not greater than 0.3 knot; and only 11 minutes when the current speed is not greater than 0.5 knot.)

Passage south of Falls Island. The passage south of Falls Island does not involve negotiating a reversing falls, but the currents are still very strong.

Access

159: Whiting Bay. This launch ramp on Whiting Bay is located on the northern edge of Cobscook Bay State Park, but it is not accessed through the park. The site has an all-tide launch ramp, picnic tables, and pit toilets (no fee). From the intersection of Route 1 and ME 189 in Whiting, proceed north on Route 1 for 4.3 miles and turn right at the sign for Cobscook Bay State Park. Proceed 1.3 miles (bypassing the park entrance) to the launch site.

160: Eastport. The Marine Technology Center (also called the Boat School) has a huge granite all-tide launch ramp that is available for public use. The one requirement is that you must park in the parking lot, not along the ramp, because the school needs access to the entire ramp. Lest you be tempted to cheat, bear this tale in mind. A paddler left his Dodge Caravan on this ramp at 5:30 PM, intending to return by sunset. In his absence, the tide came in relentlessly, engulfing the vehicle until only 8 inches remained in view. At that point a tow truck called earlier by bystanders managed to pull the vehicle from the bay's grasp.

Take Route 1 past Pembroke and turn right onto ME 190 just past the Perry municipal building, proceeding toward Eastport. At a crossroad where ME 190 (Washington Street) goes left, take a sharp right onto Deep Cove Road toward Shackford Head and the Marine Technology Center. Pass the entrance to the Shackford Head hiking trails on the left, and take the next left at the Boat School.

Restricted: South Bay. The Quoddy Regional Land Trust purchased half an acre of land on inner South Bay specifically for clammers and other

Looking north through Cobscook Falls about an hour after low-water slack. Although standing waves have not yet formed here, the water is swift and the marks on the water indicate whirlpools and eddies.

individuals who depend on the bay for their livelihoods. Please do not use this site for paddling trips.

Note. South Bay Campground, South Bay. Campers only can launch from this campground, but as the least-expensive sites are quite reasonable (and you can use the showers and hot tub, even if you don't plan to stay), it's worth the price of admission. The launch area can be used during the top half of the tide. From Route 1 in Whiting, proceed 7.4 miles east on ME 189. The campground is on the left. (See appendix E for contact information.)

Points of Interest

Commissary Point. The Commissary Point parcel, which includes 438 acres, lies at the southern end of Whiting Bay near the mouth of the Orange River. A foot trail follows the shore of Rocky Point; the other points, Wilbur and Commissary, do not have shoreline trails. The Commissary Point tract protects high-quality waterfowl habitat and provides potential nesting sites for bald eagles.

Cobscook Bay State Park. This state park offers day-use opportunities and camping in a truly spectacular setting; the day-use fee is $3 per person (for contact information, see appendix E). The park also provides habitat for some species of particular interest to birders. A pair of merlins has nested in the park since the early 1990s. Merlins, which are about the size of a jay, are members of the falcon family and so have pointed wings and long tails. They are bluish above and have several dark bands on their tail, including one wide band toward the tip. Goshawks, broad-winged hawks, and American kestrels also frequent the park, as do many other species of birds. Seals, beavers, otters, and deer may also be seen.

Hallowell (Williams) Island. This 63-acre island, which is part of nearby Moosehorn National Wildlife Refuge, is open to the public. There are no trails, and visitors must negotiate the sometimes slippery shoreline. Several habitats can be found on Hallowell: salt marsh on the western shore, blueberry barrens on the northern end, and a forest of spruce and fir covering the rest of the island. Dogs are not allowed. Nearby Birch Islands and Dog Island, which are also part of Moosehorn, are not open to the public.

Reversing Falls Town Park. This park, which lies on the north shore of the reversing falls, allows sea kayakers and others to see the falls without paddling them. It's a great opportunity to watch how these rapids change over time—and to watch seals as they surf through the whitewater.

The 32-acre park is owned by the town of Pembroke. Approaching from the west on Route 1, take the right-hand turn between the gas station and the post office. This road would be the extension of ME 214, though it is not marked in this way. At the stop sign, go right, then take an immediate left onto Leighton Point Road. Proceed 3.3 miles and turn right at a sign for the park. When the paved road ends, take a left onto a dirt road and continue for 1.5 miles to the park.

Islands in Schooner Cove. Schooner Cove, located southwest of Leighton Point, contains three public islands: Cat (the largest, not named on the chart) and two other unnamed isles. These islands might make a nice picnic stop were they located elsewhere, but set amid the complex waters that flow into to the reversing falls, they are no place to linger. Those who venture into Schooner Cove should bear in mind that as current rushes through the channel, it creates a strong eddy in the cove.

Falls Island. This 140-acre chock creates the huge reversing falls off its northeast side. The Nature Conservancy acquired the island to protect forever its superb nesting habitat. If you are paddling by Falls Island, cast a

Basalt columns on southwest shore of Falls Island

quick look at the huge black basalt columns on the southwest shore. Most basalt originates in lava that spills from volcanoes and squeezes out through cracks. As the molten flow cools, it commonly forms columns with 3 to 6 sides. The columns on Falls Island run into the water and are easy to spot. Falls Island itself is closed to visitation.

Gooseberry and Parker Archipelago. Maine Coast Heritage Trust owns and manages these two Straight Bay islands and two unnamed isles nearby; they are not open to the public.

Coggins Head, Hog, and Long islands. Coggins Head lies on the south shore of Hersey Neck, on the Pennamaquan River. Hog and Long islands are located in South Bay. The Nature Conservancy has protected these lands for wildlife and they are not open to the public.

Horan Head and Federal Island. The shoreline of Horan Head in South Bay is a mixture of gravel beaches, rocks, and ledge; when the tide goes out, about half of the shoreline opens to mudflats and rocky areas. Trails run along almost all of the 2.3 miles of shore, including frontage on South Bay and Federal Harbor.

Paddling in Whiting Bay

The small island at the mouth of the first cove on the right as you are entering Federal Harbor is Federal Island, unnamed on the chart. This public island is open to visitors.

Horan Head overlooks The Nature Conservancy's Hog and Long islands. Hog is an eagle nesting island and should not be disturbed, and eagles use Long for roosting.

Islands south of Seward Neck. The three small islands in the cove formed by the south shore of Seward Neck are also open to visitors for careful day use. These islands, unnamed on the chart, are called Trio.

Seward Neck. In 2005, the Quoddy Regional Land Trust closed on 128 acres of woods on Seward Neck, with shoreline on both South Bay and Cobscook Bay. The Land for Maine's Future program, foundations, nonprofits, and individuals also contributed toward the purchase, which will be open to the public for traditional recreation such as fishing, clamming, hiking, and hunting.

Sumac Island. This tiny public island, located in the town of Eastport (0.2 mile southeast of Matthews Island near Carryingplace Cove), is open for careful day use.

Shackford Head. The Land for Maine's Future program purchased this headland in 1989. Now a state park, Shackford Head provides incredible views of Cobscook Bay and Canadian islands.

At a Glance: Land in Public or Conservation Ownership

Private organizations and the federal government have protected numerous parcels in Cobscook Bay for wildlife. The lands that are closed to the public are listed in the text and lands that are open to the public are included here.

Cobscook Bay State Park	BPL; campground and picnic area
Reversing Falls Town Park	Town of Pembroke; careful day use
Islands in Schooner Cove	BPL; careful day use
Trio (South Bay)	BPL; careful use
Seward Neck parcel	Quoddy Regional Land Trust; careful day use
Sumac Island	BPL; careful day use
Shackford Head	BPL; careful day use

IF&W Wildlife Lands

These lands are closed as indicated. After the nesting season is over, the lands are limited to careful day use.

Commissary Point (Whiting Bay)	IF&W; careful day use
Wilbur Neck, land to SW (Dennys Bay)	February 15–August 31
Morong Cove (Straight Bay)	February 15–August 31
Red Island (Cobscook Bay)	April 15–July 31
Horan Head (South Bay)	Careful day use

USFWS Wildlife Islands

| Hallowell/Williams Island (Dennys Bay) | Careful day use |

Part III

Maine Coast
Natural History

Glacial Geology

If the wave of a magic wand set Maine back some 13,500 years, sea kayakers would find extreme conditions. Imagine this:

The ocean laps at the base of a sheet of ice thousands of feet high. You can't get too close because the glacier calves mammoth icy blocks that could kill or capsize you in an instant. There is little shelter on islands because they have all been swept bare of soil and vegetation. There is only frigid water, ice, and rock.

Welcome to Maine during the Ice Age.

This chapter of coastal geologic history actually began about 2 million years ago. A variety of complex factors triggered a change in the earth's climate, and more snow fell than melted in the colder regions of the Northern Hemisphere. As snow accumulated, its weight compressed the lower layers into a thick, viscous mass of ice. The ice flowed like a river into valleys and lowlands and grew in size until it finally enveloped mountains and entirely covered the surface of the land.

During the Ice Age, or Pleistocene epoch, at least four separate ice sheets advanced and receded over parts of Canada and the northern United States. The last sheet was centered in the Hudson Bay area and reached out to blanket half of the North American continent. About 40,000 years ago it flowed into Maine and then kept moving south. It reached Georges Bank, Cape Cod, and Long Island about 17,000 to 18,000 years ago. Even though the glacier reached far onto the continental shelf, because so much of the earth's water was bound up in ice (the level of the ocean had dropped as much as 300 feet) there remained a strip of dry land between the ice and the ocean.

In Canada, the glacier was about 10,000 feet thick while in Maine—at the edge of the sheet—the ice was about 5,000 feet thick. The weight of the glacier was so great that it depressed the tectonic plate on which it rested (tectonic plates float on the molten material below them). As the edge of the crust sank, it dropped below the level of the Ice Age sea.

When the climate warmed worldwide, the ice began to recede. By 13,800 to 13,500 years ago, it had retreated to the approximate position of Maine's present coast. Because the land was still weighted down with ice, saltwater came right up to the edge of the ice.

By 13,000 years ago, the glacier had retreated farther and the sea covered the newly ice-free lowland. The ocean reached as far inland as Livermore Falls, Bingham, and Medway. Glacial meltwater carried mud into the shallow sea, and salt water caused the mud to congeal without forming the usual banded layers. This deposit of marine clay, called the Presumpscot formation

Ocean level rise and fall

A. *18,000 to 17,000 years ago: Glacial ice reaches Georges Bank; the sea has retreated about 300 feet below its present level.*

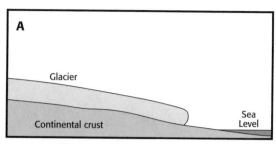

B. *13,800 to 13,500 years ago: The sea at its present level.*

C. *13,500 to 12,500 years ago: The glacier retreats. The earth's crust is still depressed from the weight of the glacier, so the sea floods inland about 150 feet above its present level.*

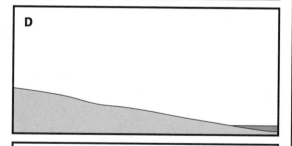

D. *11,000 years ago: The glacier continues to retreat. Because the crust is rebounding, sea level falls to about 150 feet below its present level.*

E. *2,000 years ago: The melting glacier has poured water into the ocean, causing sea level to rise to approximately its present level.*

Note: Height and distance not to scale.
(After Caldwell 1998.)

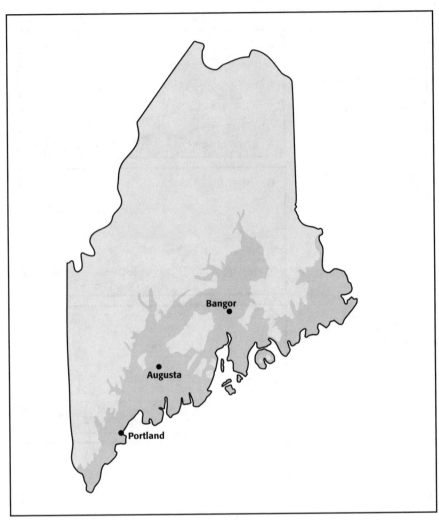

Extent of inland flooding 13,000 years ago (after Caldwell 1998)

after the Presumpscot River where it was identified, contains fossils of clams and snails.

Without the burden of ice, the tectonic plate began to rebound, causing the ocean to retreat. By 12,500 years ago, Maine was dry land. By 11,000 years ago, sea level was about 150 feet lower than it is today. But as glacial ice melted, the water flowed into the oceans and sea level rose worldwide. About 2,000 years ago, the sea reached approximately the position that it occupies today. Maine is described as having a "drowned" coastline because the ocean presently covers areas that were once dry land.

Erratics are boulders that have been transported by the glacier and dropped in a new locality; this erratic is on the western shore of Mount Desert Island.

The balance between ocean and land is ever dynamic. Sea level continues to rise in Maine, about nine (or more) inches every hundred years. If there is a global warming trend, as some scientists believe, then ice at the poles may melt faster and cause even greater flooding along the coast.

Glacial Sculpting

Ice carried rock debris or *glacial till* and spread it haphazardly in a thin layer over the countryside. Occasionally the ice carried large boulders a great distance and deposited them either singly or in boulder fields. These *erratics* are clearly of different rock than the bedrock on which they lie. Erratic, an island in Hockomock Bay (see page 123) features a large boulder that is presumed to have been dropped by the last glacial sheet.

Water-carved valleys have a characteristic **V**-shape, while glacially scoured valleys like those on Mount Desert are rounded to a smooth **U**. Somes Sound is a glacially carved **U**-*shaped valley* that was subsequently drowned by the ocean.

Some Maine islands, such as Burnt Porcupine and Long Porcupine in Frenchman Bay, show an asymmetrical shape that results from glacial grinding and plucking. The north and northwest slopes of the islands are smooth, while their south and southeast slopes are steep and sharp in profile. Ice produced this *stoss and lee topography* as it scoured the stoss (upstream) sides and detached blocks of rock from the *lee* (downstream) sides. These rocky islands are also called *roche moutonnée*, "sheepback rocks."

Eskers are common features in Maine. When meltwater streams flowed on, under, or in tunnels through glacial ice, they carried a load of stone,

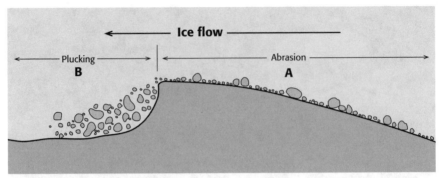

Glacial plucking: A. Glacial ice grinds against the upstream side of a bedrock protrusion, polishing it into a smooth, gradual rise. B. Glacial ice plucks boulders from the downstream side, creating a steep face.

gravel, and sand. After the ice melted, these sediments lay exposed as long, winding ridges that run northwest to southeast, perpendicular to the edge of the glacier. Pond Island in eastern Penobscot Bay is the remnant of an esker.

Moraines were created when ice and meltwater streams brought forward till, sand, and gravel to the outer edge of the glacier, forming ridges parallel to the edge of the glacier. Large moraines like Cape Cod, Martha's Vineyard, Nantucket, and Long Island were created when the glacier was stationary for an extended time. Another large end moraine was deposited on Georges Bank beyond Maine's present shoreline. When the glacier made small pauses in its retreat, it left much smaller "washboard" moraines.

As meltwater streams emerged from the ice, they carried a heavy load of sediments that were eventually deposited as various landforms, including *outwash plains*. In outwash plains, water has sorted the sediments by grain size. Outwash deposits along Maine's southern coast overlay the marine clay laid down when the area was submerged. Postglacial wind and water subsequently transported and reworked the sandy outwash, producing Ogunquit, Laudholm, Crescent Surf, Parsons, Goose Rocks, and other beaches that now grace the southern shore.

Birds and Marine Mammals of the Open Coast

The key to watching marine mammals and birds along the open coast is to notice what's different. Is there a break in the water where, a moment before, there was nothing? Perhaps a seal or harbor porpoise has surfaced. Do you hear a puffing sound that wasn't there? Maybe it's the breath of a harbor porpoise. Are there some terns in a mixed flock that look lighter, more animated? These may be roseate terns. Does a coastal island thick with spruce thin out curiously in one area? Perhaps herons have nested there and killed the trees below with their guano.

Watching wildlife is one of the paybacks for making the effort to get out on the water. There's lots to see, and over time, it's possible to observe some truly spectacular sights.

Marine Mammals

Sea kayakers, harbor seals, and harbor porpoises all frequent inshore waters, and it is a treat when either of the marine mammals swims near your boat. Marine mammals, like land mammals, breathe air, give birth to live young, and feed their young with milk. Although seals have fur and hind legs, cetaceans (whales, dolphins, and porpoises) have only a few hairs and no rear limbs.

Seals. The best time to get a clear look at the head of the harbor seal is when it pops up near your boat to see what is going on. Seals on tidal ledges are very sensitive to disturbance (see pages 28–29), so paddlers should avoid them when they are hauled out.

The harbor seal has a short, doglike snout and large eyes. Its Latin name means "sea calf" or, in a more relaxed translation, "sea dog." The color of the fur is variable, from light gray to dark gray to black, from tan to brown or even reddish. When a seal dives, you may catch a glimpse of its body, which has dark spots on the back and more widely spaced spots on the belly. The average size of an adult male harbor seal is 5 feet and 200 pounds; females are somewhat smaller at 4.6 feet and 154 pounds. Seals eat mackerel, herring, alewives, squid, and other fish as well as crabs, shrimp, and seabirds such as black guillemots and sea ducks. In 1993, the seal population in the Gulf of Maine was estimated at almost 30,000 individuals.

In Maine, seals are most common in Penobscot Bay, around Mount Desert Island, near Jonesport, and in Machias Bay. Pregnant females swim into the safety of upper reaches of bays and give birth, usually to a single pup, sometime between mid-April and mid-June. Pups can swim almost

Harbor seal

EVENDEN '99

immediately. Mothers nurse their young for about a month, after which pups begin eating shrimp and amphipods. After weaning, females mate once again. Both males and females molt their fur in July and August. It is thought that Maine seals move south to Cape Cod and Long Island for the winter, while seals from farther north move south to Maine.

The gray seal also frequents Maine waters, but in far fewer numbers. This species is considerably larger, with males sometimes reaching 8 feet and females 7 feet in length. Young gray seals may be the same size as adult harbor seals, but the heads of the two species are shaped quite differently. The gray seal has a much larger, more prominent nose; it looks more like the nose of a donkey than of a dog. The Maine population as of the early 1990s was estimated at about 400 individuals. Gray seals tend to be seen on very exposed ledges off Mount Desert Island and in outer Penobscot Bay but are occasionally spotted closer inshore.

Harbor porpoises and other cetaceans. The best time to watch for harbor porpoises is on calm days when the water is flat. Be alert to motion: Seals pop up and disappear, but harbor porpoises are traveling. If you catch a glimpse of something moving from one place to another, search along the line of movement and you may see a harbor porpoise skim the surface of the water. Harbor porpoises usually breathe three or four times, then disappear for a couple of minutes.

It's unlikely that you'll confuse a harbor porpoise with another cetacean. Harbor porpoises are quite small, reaching at the most 5 feet in length and

Harbor porpoise

EVENDEN 99

weighing about 140 pounds. They have a blunt head without an external beak; dolphins, which generally prefer more offshore waters, have an elongated snout. Harbor porpoises have a triangular dorsal fin and are dark gray with a lighter gray area that runs along their sides. Each individual swims with strong strokes of its fluke, which is aligned horizontally. When cetaceans come to the surface, they blow out air and moisture. Some species produce an identifiable spout, and while the harbor porpoise exhales loudly enough to be heard it does not have a visible spout. Occasionally, in very calm conditions, a puff of moisture can be seen.

In spring and early summer, harbor porpoises travel singly or in small groups, but in late summer they sometimes gather into groups of 20 or more. The habits of harbor porpoise are not precisely known, but they do migrate south for the winter and then return in the spring.

Harbor porpoises, also called herring hogs, are not part of the family that includes dolphins, pilot whales, and killer whales; they are classified in a taxonomic family by themselves.

Occasionally larger cetaceans come inshore. One famous humpback whale entered Lowell Cove on Orrs Island in Casco Bay (see page 111), and minke whales sometimes venture into Blue Hill and Frenchman Bays by Mount Desert Island. Whales have been reported near Thrumcap Island in Johns Bay next to Pemaquid. Minke whales are solitary swimmers that grow to 28 feet. Although they do not have a distinctive, visible spout, it is possible to hear their exhalations.

Birds

If you can recognize 15 or so species, you can identify the great majority of birds that you are likely to encounter as you paddle along Maine's coast. Some birds, like common and arctic terns, can be difficult to identify without binoculars, but others can easily be recognized by eye.

Cormorants. The double-crested cormorant is a large, dark bird that sits low in the water. It breeds along the coast and heads south for the winter. The adult is black with an orange bill; the immature is similar but is light on the chin and breast. When swimming on the surface of the water, the cormorant holds its bill tipped up slightly. When flying, it holds its head level to the body. Cormorants fly singly, and they also fly in loose lines or **V** formations. Cormorants are often seen perched on rocks, pilings, or trees, stretching out their wings to dry.

Great cormorants are primarily winter visitors to Maine, appearing from November through March or early April. A few birds may linger into May, and a very limited number—about 200 pairs—nest on offshore islands. Great cormorants are larger than their double-crested relatives. The adults are black

Double-crested cormorant; immature (left) and adult (right)

with yellow bills and have a white patch at the throat. Immatures are dark above and white on the cheek, breast, and belly. The flight and posture characteristics are similar to those of the double-crested cormorant.

Loons. The common loon breeds and nests in freshwater lakes of the northern United States and Canada. Loons generally begin appearing along Maine's coast in late summer, but sometimes individuals can be seen during the summer months. The bird's summer plumage is distinctive: dark head, broken collar, white breast, and checkered back. Winter plumage is more drab: dark above and light below. Many loons winter along the coast. In flight, loons hold their head slightly lower than their body.

Common loon

*Common eider;
female (left) and male (right)*

EVENDEN '99

Sea ducks. Sea ducks dive for mollusks and crustaceans rather than eating food from the surface. They also patter along the surface of the water before actually taking flight, in contrast to birds that can spring directly from the water.

The common eider is a regular coastal resident of Maine. As recently as 1907, only 2 pairs nested in the state. Now there are about 25,000 nesting pairs. The striking male is easy to identify: It has a white breast and back and a black belly. Females are brown. In the breeding season, eiders pair up, but during the nesting season only the females sit on the nest. After the young are hatched, several females and their young come together into nursery groups called creches. In winter, males and females sometimes raft together in huge flocks.

Scoters nest in the Arctic and Canadian prairies, so they are uncommon in Maine from the middle of June to the middle of September. After that time they begin showing up to spend the winter. Scoters are slightly smaller than eiders. Three species winter here: the black scoter (all black), the surf scoter (white on the forehead and back of the head), and the white-winged scoter (white wing patch near the body).

Oldsquaws also nest in the Arctic and, like scoters, spend the winter on the open waters of the coast. In winter, both males and females have light bellies (the male has a black breast patch) and are dark underwing. Both are white on the face; females have a dark cheek spot, and males have a dark cheek patch. Males have a long, pointed tail that is not always easy to see.

Gulls. Two large gulls, the herring and great black-backed, are abundant all year long. Of the three smaller gulls that are seen regularly at some time of the year but in smaller numbers, one has a white head (ring-billed) and two have black heads (laughing and Bonaparte's).

Laughing gull

EVENDEN '99

Great black-backed gulls are easy to identify. The mantle (the back and upper surface of the wings) is black; the head, belly, and tail are white. It is the biggest gull on the coast. First- and second-year birds are also large; they are scalloped brown along the wings and back, and there is a dark subterminal band on the tail.

Herring gulls are the ubiquitous "seagulls" of the coast. They are white with a gray instead of a black mantle. The tips of the wings are black with white spots. Young birds are uniformly chocolate through the first winter, then change progressively until they reach adult plumage at three years. If there is a herring gull nearby when you stop to eat your lunch, don't set down your sandwich—they are quick and bold scavengers.

Ring-billed gulls look like small herring gulls: white with gray mantle, black wing tips with white spots. The distinguishing marks are the black ring toward the tip of the bill and yellowish or greenish legs, as opposed to the pink legs of the herring gull. Look for ring-billed gulls throughout the year; they are more common in late spring and fall.

Laughing gulls have a dark gray mantle that turns black at the wing tips; the bill is bright red. They have a shrill call that does sound like laughter. This species is fairly common from the end of May through the beginning of September and uncommon for a month on each end. These birds head south for the winter.

Bonaparte's gulls have a light gray mantle with a prominent white wedge at the wing tips; the bill is black. It is slightly smaller than the laughing gull, and its flight is ternlike. These gulls are fairly common to abundant in May and early June, then again in mid-July through November. A few may be seen during the middle of the summer, and some birds remain through the winter.

Terns. Terns are long-winged, slender-bodied, and much smaller than gulls. They have a graceful, buoyant flight and they frequently hover above their prey, which consists of small fish and invertebrates. The three main species—common, arctic, and roseate—arrive in Maine to breed on treeless offshore islands, then fly far south for the winter. Common terns are by far the most abundant. There are only 250 pairs of roseate turns, which are listed by the federal government as endangered. The three species may nest in mixed colonies. The least tern, which is considerably smaller, is uncommon and nests on only a few sand beaches in the state.

Common, arctic, and roseate terns are about the same size, and in breeding plumage they all have a black cap, a gray mantle, and a forked tail, although the fork is not always obvious at a distance.

It is very difficult to differentiate between common and arctic terns in the field without binoculars, and roseates are only a little easier. Bill color helps if you can catch that feature as the birds whiz by.

- In common terns, the trailing edge of the outer wing (as seen from below) has a short, broad, dark band. The underwing shows a small area of translucence and the bill is red tipped with black.
- In arctic terns, the trailing edge of the outer wing (as seen from below) has a thin, dark band. The underwing shows a large area of translucence, and the bill is entirely red.
- In roseate terns, the underwing lacks a dark line around the primary tips. Roseates are whiter overall and have a black bill.

Common tern

EVENDEN '99

Guillemot

EVENDEN '99

Alcids. Alcids are expert divers that use their wings underwater as well as when they fly. By far the most common alcid in Maine is the black guillemot, sometimes called a sea pigeon. Guillemots nest in rock crevices and on sea cliffs. During the breeding season they are entirely black with white wing patches and surprisingly visible red legs and feet. During the rest of the year, the head and underparts are white and the back is barred; the wings remain dark and the wing patches are still prominent.

Two other alcids—Atlantic puffins and razorbills—nest in small numbers (see pages 178–179 and 301 for more information on these species). Dovekies, pudgy little alcids about the size of a starling, occasionally appear between late October and mid-March.

Ospreys and bald eagles. Although ospreys and bald eagles are not seabirds, they do nest along the coast and on coastal islands as well as inland. They are both large birds, but their distinctive field marks and differing habits make them easy to separate in the field.

Bald eagles are the largest birds you are likely to see when paddling along coastal Maine. They have wide wings designed for soaring. The adult is black with gleaming white head and tail. The immature is dark with some white under the wings and tail. Eagles typically build a large nest about two-thirds of the way up a tree. Maine has over 200 pairs of nesting eagles, most of which are found in Hancock and Washington Counties. Although the federal government may take eagles off the threatened list, the birds are still firmly on the list in Maine. Numbers are up, but the overall reproduction rate is not high enough to safeguard the species.

Birds of the Open Coast

Species	Abundance	Time of year
Loons		
Common loon	Common to abundant	Late summer to spring
Cormorants		
Double-crested cormorant	Common to abundant	May through October
Great cormorant	Uncommon	November through March
Sea ducks		
Common eider	Common to abundant	Throughout the year
Scoters (all 3 species)	Fairly common to abundant	Mid-September through mid-June
Oldsquaw	Fairly common to abundant	October through May
Gulls		
Great black-backed gull	Abundant	Throughout the year
Herring gull	Abundant	Throughout the year
Ring-billed gull	Common to abundant	Mid-April through mid-May and mid-August through mid-December
	Fairly common	Rest of the year
Laughing gull	Fairly common	End of May through early September
Bonaparte's gull	Fairly common to abundant	Most of May and June; mid-July through November (most seen in early fall)
Terns		
Common tern	Fairly common to abundant	Mid-May through early September
Arctic tern	Fairly common to abundant locally	Mid-May through mid-August
Roseate tern	Locally near nests	August through early September
Alcids		
Black guillemot	Common to abundant	Throughout year
Raptors		
Bald eagle	Locally near nests and wintering areas	Throughout year
Osprey	Fairly common to abundant	Mid-April through mid-October

Abundancy ratings (from Pierson, Pierson, and Vickery 1996 and other sources) include:
Common to abundant: Usually seen in moderate to large numbers.
Fairly common: Usually seen in small numbers.
Uncommon: Usually seen in very small numbers, from a few a day to a few a year.

Friends of Maine Seabird Islands (www.maineseabirds.org) and the U.S. Fish and Wildlife Service sell a beautiful 15-inch by 40-inch map of seabird nesting islands along Maine's entire coast. The map also shows topography, towns, and roads. While section maps such as those in this book offer useful details, this map shows how closely connected coastal towns really are.

Bald eagle

Ospreys are smaller than eagles. They are dark above and light below. Their wings are often bent (forming a **W**) and there is a dark patch at the wrist. They have a narrow mask across the eyes, and the tail is banded. Osprey often hover before diving. If they are successful in catching a fish they realign their prey as they fly, turning the fish so that it faces forward and is more aerodynamic. Ospreys build large nests in the top of trees and other likely looking structures. See page 208 for more about ospreys.

Osprey

The Rocky Shore

"This coast is mountainous" with "isles of huge rocks" wrote Captain John Smith in 1614. Captain Smith got it right. Headlands pin southern beaches in place, and the rocky shore dominates the coast from Portland north to Lubec. As the crow flies, Kittery and Lubec are about 230 miles apart. A recent measurement using the latest technology, however, reveals that the coast is 7,039 miles long, including the shore of every cove and all 4,617 islands and islets.

Plants and animals of the rocky shore live in challenging conditions. They are battered by wind and waves, inundated twice daily by saltwater, and exposed to the searing effects of the sun. The tide is the critical factor in influencing the arrangement of life on the shore, for it forces plants and animals into one of five distinct horizontal bands, depending on how much saltwater immersion (and how much exposure to the air) they can tolerate. The zones are labeled subtidal, lower, middle, upper, and splash. Unique conditions in each zone require particular adaptations and allow quite different species to live in proximity.

Subtidal or Kelp Zone

Because the plants and animals that live here are always inundated, this zone most closely resembles the ocean environment. Kelp dominates and crabs, sea urchins, starfish, anemones, sponges, marine worms, and jellyfish also live here. The kelps are brown algae that grow as large, leathery brown plants that may weigh 25 pounds each. Kelps are strong (one species can withstand 600 pounds per square inch before breaking) and flexible (the easiest way to deal with the force of waves is to wash back and forth). They also use a *holdfast*—a mass of rootlike tentacles—to attach very securely to subtidal rocks. In a storm, the attachment rock will often dislodge before the holdfast is broken; many strands of kelp that have washed ashore still cling to their rock base.

Lower or Irish Moss Zone

The lower zone is the area between the level of neap low tide and spring low tide. During neap tides, when tidal swings are muted, this zone is completely submerged. At spring tides it is completely exposed. During the rest of the month, the zone is inundated to varying degrees.

Irish moss dominates here. This algae grows into a shrubby, much-branched plant several inches high. Irish moss has many commercial uses because it contains carrageenan, a colloid used as a stabilizer and thickener in toothpaste, paint, chocolate milk, ice cream, and other products. Irish moss is also the key ingredient in *blancmange*, a traditional pudding made by cooking seaweed, milk, and a flavoring.

Irish moss and associated seaweeds—dulse, laver, and sea lettuce—provide shelter for crabs, sea urchins, starfish, and mussels. Animals that are mobile retreat to the subtidal zone during the lowest tides.

Middle or Rockweed Zones

The middle zone is exposed to the air twice daily. Rockweed is the major form of vegetation. This brown algae has small air sacs that enable the plant to float near the surface when the tide is high. Like kelp, rockweed attaches to rocks by means of a holdfast. This seaweed is often used to pack lobsters for shipment.

Even on a hot day, rockweed is damp beneath its outer layer. Periwinkles, dog whelks, and limpets use rockweed for protection from the drying effects of wind and sun. Periwinkles are small animals with shells. As they move along, they scrape bits of food from seaweed with a sandpapery tongue, called a radula. A large periwinkle population can severely damage or even wipe out a seaweed stand. Periwinkles live in several zones on the rock slope. Darker-shelled animals live lower in the water; lighter-shelled animals live nearer the surface. Each species has adapted to living in its zone and cannot move to another.

Dog whelks resemble periwinkles but are carnivorous. They use their radula to bore through shells of mussels, barnacles, and dead crabs. A clam shell with a tiny circular hole near its apex is an indication of dog whelk predation.

Upper or Barnacle Zone

The upper zone is sometimes but not always immersed during the daily tidal cycle. It is defined by the upper limits of neap and spring tides. During neap tides, when the tidal swings are muted, plants and animals in this zone are fully exposed to the air. During the rest of the month, they are inundated to varying degrees, and at spring tides they are fully immersed. This zone takes the most battering from waves.

Barnacles characterize the upper zone. These free-swimming, shrimp-like animals cement themselves to a rock, boat, or piling and then secrete material to form a six-plated shell. Although a barnacle can be easily crushed by the direct blow of a hammer, the dome-shaped shell can withstand a wave force of up to 40 pounds per square inch. Water does not crash directly against the shell but slides off, dissipating its energy. When exposed to air, barnacles close their shells and wait; when they are submerged, they open up and strain minute food particles from the water with thin, feathery legs.

Laughing gulls rest at the top of a splash zone (home of blue-green algae that looks like black paint); below is the barnacle zone.

Splash Zone

Because the tide does not reach the splash zone, plants and animals are not submerged, but they must be able to withstand being splashed by waves. The dominant plant is blue-green algae, which coats the rock like black paint. This algae is extremely slippery when wet (sea kayakers beware). The rough periwinkle grazes here and seeks the protection of damp, cool crevices in the rock. The rough periwinkle lives almost but not quite on dry land and has adapted in some ways to land living. Females produce eggs that hatch into young periwinkles, for example, instead of eggs that produce larvae that then grow into periwinkles.

Above the Water

A band of bare rock usually separates the highest zone of the rocky shore from the edge of the forest. Plants that grow landward of this band are exposed to salt spray during storms and constantly struggle against wind pruning and dehydration. Black spruce, pine, juniper, bayberry, lowbush blueberry, bunchberry, and a crusty orange lichen called Zanthoria are often found here.

Tide Pools

Rocky basins that lie in the intertidal zone trap salt water, forming tide pools. What lives in a pool depends upon whether the pool is in the lower zone, the middle zone, or the upper zone. It is more challenging to live in middle and upper zone pools because the salinity varies due to evaporation and precipitation, and the amount of water itself may vary. The best way to observe a tide pool is to sit quietly by the side. After the animals have become accustomed to your presence, they will resume their normal activities.

Estuaries

In the broadest sense, estuaries are places where saltwater and freshwater mingle. Specifically, definitions can vary. In one definition, an estuary extends from the head of tide to the mouth of an embayment—the Penobscot River, for example, from Bangor to Fort Point. In another definition, an estuary extends from the place where saltwater measurably infiltrates freshwater to the place at which the freshwater flow is no longer felt—the Penobscot River from above Bucksport to well into Penobscot Bay. In this book, the former definition is used.

Still, estuary is a malleable term. The rivers that flow into Casco Bay contain areas where salt- and freshwater mix, and the bay itself is a mixing bowl for ocean and riverine waters.

Because Maine has a drowned coast, estuaries form in drowned river valleys and bays. Estuaries that form behind sandbars—largely estuaries in rivers of the southern coast, including the Webhannet, Kennebunk, and Saco—are called bar-built estuaries. There are often large marshes behind estuaries with bars.

But not all embayments are estuaries. Embayments that do not have a source of freshwater, like the New Meadows River and the Bagaduce River, are neutral embayments. They may be called rivers, but they are saltwater rivers dependent entirely on the tide.

Within an estuary, there are three subsystems: riverine, estuarine, and marine. Freshwater, which has a salinity of fewer than 0.5 parts per thousand (ppt), makes up the riverine subsystem. Saltwater, which has a salinity of 30 to 35 ppt, makes up the marine subsystem. A mix of the two types of water, anything with a salinity between 0.5 and 30 ppt, is found in the estuarine subsystem.

The salinity at a given point is not static. It changes with the tide and with the season, as snowmelt and freshets determine how much freshwater enters the system. In 1993, for example, the highest level of discharge on the Androscoggin River in January was about 5,000 cubic feet per second (cfs). In February, it was 3,000 cfs. By March, it had jumped to 48,000 cfs, and in April it peaked at 51,000 cfs. By May it had dropped to 11,000 cfs, and in June it had sunk to 6,000 cfs. The Kennebec, Penobscot, and Androscoggin are the largest rivers and discharge the greatest amounts of freshwater, but rivers that have a smaller catchment area also show this pattern.

In some estuaries, like those in the Kennebunk, Harrington, and Pleasant rivers, salt- and freshwater mix freely and the salinity fluctuates widely. When the tide floods the estuary, salt- and freshwaters mix and the salinity goes up. When the tide ebbs—in some cases leaving only river outflow in the channel—the salinity goes down.

But in other estuaries, salt- and freshwater do not mix freely. Saltwater is heavier than freshwater, and if it is trapped, it will submarine up drowned valleys as the tide comes in, forming a wedge of seawater along the bottom of the estuary. The Piscataqua, Kennebec, Penobscot, and other large rivers, which have the greatest freshwater flows, develop these two-tier systems.

Estuaries foster several distinct habitats, including salt marshes and estuary bottom. Lobsters, European oysters, crabs, clams, mussels, scallops, and other species are bottom dwellers. Some, like lobsters, are found in the saltwater-dominated outer reaches of the estuary. Flounder, hake, and other fish also live along the bottom. Eelgrass, which grows along the bottom, provides a sheltered nursery area for many types of marine organisms. It also provides food for geese and ducks.

Many fish frequent estuaries to feed on the phytoplankton and zooplankton that live there. Others, like Atlantic salmon, shortnose sturgeon, alewife, striped bass, sea-run brook trout, American shad, sea lamprey, and sea-run brown trout, live in saltwater and migrate to freshwater to spawn; these are called anadromous fish. Some anadromous species, including alewives, are fished commercially. Others, like the Atlantic salmon and shortnose sturgeon, are threatened and require protection.

Salt Marshes and Mudflats

The creation of mudflats and salt marshes is a slow process. First, waves wash particles of clay and silt into protected inlets or bays. The suspended particles sink when they reach slack water and adhere to the bottom. Layer upon layer accumulates, held in place by natural cohesion and a cover of eelgrass. When the layers have accumulated enough to be exposed at low tide but submerged at high tide, the area is called a mudflat.

Intertidal mudflats are an important component of the salt marsh and of coastal environments where salt marshes have not developed. They support algae, seaweed, several species of clams, periwinkles, amphipods, marine worms, blue mussels, and other species of flora and fauna. They are also the foraging grounds for millions of shorebirds that migrate through Maine each year.

Because the rocky shore dominates Maine's coast, there are proportionally fewer salt marshes than there are in southern states. Still, salt marshes can be found along the shores of many estuaries and backwater bays.

When salt-marsh cordgrass seeds are carried onto the mud, or a mat of grass is washed ashore from an eroding marsh nearby, the salt marsh gains a toehold. This grass is specially adapted to growing in a saltwater environment and quickly sends out underground rhizomes. The grass itself contributes to building the marsh, for as it dies it forms a thick, spongy peat. Silt and clay particles accumulate between stems and in the peat until the mudflats are built up to the average high-tide level, producing a salt marsh. When salt-marsh cordgrass colonizes a mudflat, it provides protection for the other plants and animals that follow.

When the last sheet of glacial ice crept southward across Maine, it scraped away soil and sediments and deposited them on Georges Bank. The relative scarcity of soil and the slow erosion of rock to produce new sediments means that Maine is poor in the tiny particles that form the foundation of mudflats and marshes. Even the fine sediments brought downstream by rivers largely flow out into the Gulf of Maine rather than being trapped in deltas.

Altogether, Maine has about 15,500 acres of salt marsh, which is not much when compared to southern states, like South Carolina, which has half a million acres. There is a string of salt marshes south of Portland, including marshes at Brave Boat Harbor, the Ogunquit River, the Webhannet River, the Mousam River, Goosefare Brook, and the Spurwink River. These are protected as the Rachel Carson National Wildlife Refuge. And there are scattered small salt marshes that line backwater bays and estuary shores along the rest of the coast. The largest salt marsh in Maine—Scarborough Marsh—has developed where the Dunstan, Nonesuch, and Libby rivers flow into the Scarborough River. This 3,100-acre marsh is managed by the state's Department of Inland Fisheries and Wildlife.

Limiting Factors

The salt marsh is not an easy place to live. Plants must withstand regular inundation and a wide variation in temperature—a hot August afternoon bask turns into a cold bath when the tide rises. The roots are continually in contact with salt water, but the salinity varies as streams carry fresh water into the area. Plants and animals are exposed to the searing rays of the sun and the cold fingers of winter ice. Because bacteria and higher organisms living on the mud surface use all the dissolved oxygen brought in by the tide, the subsurface mud has no oxygen, and anaerobic bacteria assume the task of breaking down buried organic matter. Anaerobic decomposition produces hydrogen sulfide as a by-product, which is why salt marshes have the distinctive smell of rotten eggs.

These are killer conditions, but some plants have evolved mechanisms that allow them not only to survive but to thrive. Salt-marsh cordgrass has a

Canada geese

EVENDEN '99

Birds of the Salt Marsh and Mudflat

Note: Not all birds listed here can be found at all of Maine's salt marshes and intertidal mudflats. Larger marshes generally have greater diversity and greater numbers than smaller marshes.

Species	Abundance	Time of Year
Waders		
American bittern	Fairly common; nests in marsh	Summer
Great blue heron	Abundant	Summer
Snowy egret	Abundant	Summer
Glossy ibis	Regular	Summer
Little blue heron	Uncommon to fairly common, southern coast	Summer
Green heron	Uncommon	Summer
Black-crowned night heron	Mostly uncommon	Summer
Cattle egret	Uncommon	Summer
Great egret	Uncommon	Summer
Tricolored heron	Uncommon	Summer
Geese and ducks		
Canada goose	Abundant; the earliest migrant	Spring and fall
Snow goose	Uncommon to fairly common	Spring and fall
American black duck	Abundant; nests in marsh	Year-round
Northern pintail	Fairly common	Spring and fall
Blue-winged teal	Fairly common to common	Spring and fall
Green-winged teal	Fairly common to common	Spring and fall
Common merganser	Fairly common	Spring and fall
Red-breasted merganser	Abundant	Spring and fall
Wood duck	Common	Spring and fall
Ring-necked duck	Common	Spring and fall
American widgeon	Common	Spring and fall
Hooded merganser	Common	Spring and fall
Rails		
Virginia rail	Common to abundant; nests in marsh	Summer

special chemical apparatus to exclude large quantities of harmful salt. The small amounts that are absorbed are collected and excreted by unique glands on the leaves. Thin tubes run from the leaves to the roots to provide oxygen that is not available in the mud. As in any system with severe limiting factors where few species can survive, the species that do well are prolific.

Zonation

Seaweeds and algae that live on mudflats spend half of their lives under water. Salt-marsh cordgrass (*Spartina alterniflora*) dominates the intertidal zone. Milkwort, a tiny plant with rosy flowers, and glasswort, which seems to have

Shorebirds*

Black-bellied plover	Common to abundant	Migration
Semipalmated plover	Common to abundant	Migration
Killdeer	Uncommon to common	Migration
Greater yellowlegs	Common to abundant	Migration
Lesser yellowlegs	Common to abundant	Migration
Willet	Uncommon to common; nests in marsh	Summer
Hudsonian godwit	Uncommon	Fall migration
Least sandpiper	Common to abundant	Migration
Semipalmated sandpiper	Common to abundant	Migration
Pectoral sandpiper	Uncommon to abundant	Migration
White-rumped sandpiper	Uncommon to common	Migration
Stilt sandpiper	Uncommon	Fall migration
Dunlin	Uncommon to common	Migration
Short-billed dowitcher	Uncommon to common	Migration
American golden-plover	Uncommon	Fall migration
Solitary sandpiper	Uncommon to fairly common	Migration
Whimbrel	Uncommon to fairly common	Fall migration
Red knot	Uncommon	Migration
Western sandpiper	Uncommon	Fall migration
Long-billed dowitcher	Uncommon	Fall migration
Wilson's phalarope	Uncommon	Migration

Sparrows

Saltmarsh sharp-tailed sparrow	Fairly common; nests in marsh grass, southern coast	Summer
Nelson's sharp-tailed sparrow	Fairly common; nests in marsh grass	Summer
Savannah sparrow	Common to abundant; nests in uplands around marsh	Summer

*The spring shorebird migration lasts from mid-May through early June, and the fall migration lasts from mid-July through early October.

Abundancy ratings (from Pierson, Pierson, and Vickery 1996 and other sources) include:
Common to abundant: Usually seen in moderate to large numbers.
Fairly common: Usually seen in small numbers.
Uncommon: Usually seen in very small numbers, from a few a day to a few a year.

no leaves but only a succulent, branched stem, grow between grass stems.

The upper marsh, where saltwater reaches only twice a month during spring tides, shows greater diversity. Salt-meadow cordgrass (*Spartina patens*), which is shorter than the salt-marsh grass, dominates the upper marsh. Glasswort also grows here, particularly in small depressions in the marsh that trap water during the highest tides. Subsequent evaporation increases salinity, killing all but the most salt-tolerant plants. Sea lavender and seaside goldenrod add color to the marsh in autumn.

Rushes reach from the intertidal zone into the upper shore. Plants that can tolerate salt spray, but not actual flooding, line the marsh and separate it from the forest beyond. Poison ivy flourishes along the upper shore on both islands and along the mainland.

Animals

Great blue heron

Few animals make their homes in the marsh. Many live on land or in the air and frequent the marsh at their choosing. Others live in the water, entering and leaving with the tide. Immobile organisms have developed adaptations to inundation, exposure, and salinity. The ribbed mussel closes its shell until the tide returns with oxygen and food. Sandworms burrow into the mud. Turtles have a watertight skin. The marsh grasshopper climbs salt-marsh cordgrass to wait out high tide. If rain dilutes the saltwater, softshell clams can close up and live for as long as a week on stored glycogen until salinity returns to a normal level.

Mummichugs and killifish live in tide pools and pans. Visitors from the ocean include many varieties of fish that spawn in the marsh or use it as a nursery for their young. Mammals, including raccoon, mink, Eastern gray squirrel, deer mouse, meadow vole, muskrat, Norway rat, black rat, and white-tailed deer, are usually active at night, but their tracks can be found in and around the marsh.

Birds frequent marshes to feed, nest, or gain protection. During spring and fall migrations, great numbers of ducks, geese, and shorebirds can be seen in the salt marsh and on adjacent mudflats.

Sand Beaches

The last ice sheet that covered Maine deposited large amounts of sand across the state and on what is now the continental shelf. Waves winnowed these sediments, separating them into smaller and larger grains, carrying them from one place to another, and depositing them between rocky fingers. These sediments form the long beaches that stretch across the coast south of Portland, and the more contained beaches that dot the coast north of Portland. All Maine beaches have formed between promontories, although in some cases the headlands are some distance apart.

Because Maine's beaches are trapped between rocky fingers, there is no large-scale drifting or littoral movement of sand that occurs when waves strike an exposed shore at an angle. Drift and currents that run parallel to the shore account for massive sand movement on the large barrier island beaches in the mid-Atlantic states but are less important factors in Maine.

Although the volume of sand in each beach has largely been stabilized, cyclic and small-scale changes still occur. Each summer and early fall waves build up the beach face, and each winter they move that sand offshore. Sand movement is chiefly from onshore to offshore and back rather than from one beach to another. Two exceptions may be the Old Orchard and Popham Beach systems, which are located, respectively, at the mouths of the Saco and Kennebec Rivers. These two rivers transport reworked glacial sediments downstream, steadily resupplying sand.

The rise in sea level is a subtle yet potent element in beach dynamics. Melting of the polar ice cap has added water to the world's oceans at an average of 2 inches per century over the last 7,000 years. As a result, beaches must move inland and upland to keep pace with the ocean. Because beaches draw people, buildings, and businesses, the incremental rise in sea level will, over time, threaten beachside development.

Wave Development and Beach Position

Wind creates friction as it blows across the ocean, transferring energy from air to water. Although energy moves forward in the form of waves, individual water molecules remain in the same place, describing a small, circular path near the surface. Waves that travel for some distance become swells, which have parallel crests. "Seas," the irregular waves that move in a variety of directions, form locally.

As a wave moves into a shallow area, it slows down. Its height increases and length decreases. When a wave can no longer hold its shape, which occurs when it encounters water that is 30 percent deeper than the wave is high, it breaks into a swirl of foam, called the swash. Water molecules no longer

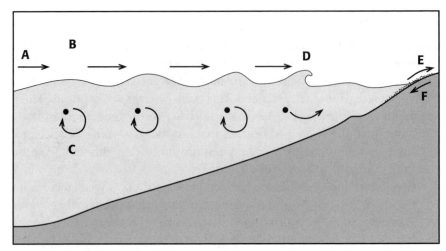

Wave formation. A. Wind strikes water. B. Energy moves forward. C. Water molecules remain in place. D. Wave breaks. E. Swash (water, sand, and shells are carried onto the beach). F. Backwash.

stay in place but are carried up the beach along with sand, seaweed, shells, and other debris. The strength of the wave determines whether the sand remains on the beach face or is carried back offshore. High-energy waves may take away more sand than they bring, causing erosion of the beach face. Typ-

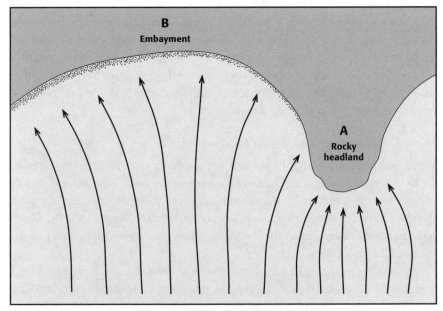

Wave refraction concentrates energy on a headland and disperses it in an embayment. Sediments are deposited perpendicular to the force of the wave.

ically, summer waves have low energy and deposit sand along the intertidal zone, creating a summer berm, or terrace. Sometimes a second terrace or ridge also forms in the lower intertidal zone, paralleled by a shallow channel called a runnel. High-energy winter storm waves (usually caused by

Dusty Miller (Artemisia stelleriana), *also called beach wormwood, has wooly leaves that help the plant survive in an arid environment.*

northeasters) erode these terraces, forming a steep slope next to the frontal dune ridge and transporting sand offshore.

If waves encounter a long, straight, unprotected shoreline and strike it head-on, they shape the sand into a long, straight beach, such as Old Orchard. But north of Portland, incoming waves bump into hundreds of shoals, islands, and peninsulas that influence their direction, velocity, and force. These waves may bend around an island, depositing sediments behind it, or dissipate in a bay, pushing sand landward. Maine's beaches are generally aligned with respect to wave refraction patterns, which means that they have formed parallel to approaching waves. A single bay may have beaches that face south, east, and west, but each beach lies parallel to incoming refraction patterns.

Some beaches in Maine are backed by dunes, where American beachgrass *(Ammophila breviligulata)* is the dominant cover plant. When a shoot of beachgrass is washed ashore after winter erosion, it roots and sends up new grass blades. It also sends out *rhizomes*, horizontal runners that spread like spokes in a wheel. Every 6 to 10 inches along the runner, the plant sets more roots and sprouts. Once established, beachgrass begins to trap windblown sand in the dry area above the tide. Although some plants might be smothered by a covering of sand, beachgrass thrives. New shoots push to the surface and the plant sends out a new latticework of runners, parallel but above the old network. As the plant grows, it traps more sand and continues to grow until a balance between sand, wind, and vegetation is reached. Below the surface, an interconnecting mass of roots, rhizomes, and buried plants stabilizes the sand and creates the basis for dunes. Particular forms and features found in a dune field depend on local wind and sand conditions.

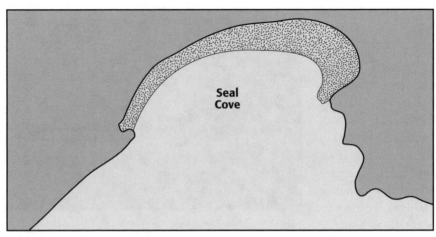

Crescent Beach: A fringing beach (after Nelson and Fink 1980)

Types of Beaches in Maine

Beaches are classified according to their position relative to the shore. *Fringing beaches* usually lie next to bedrock or soil and do not have extensive dune fields or a lagoon behind them. Parts of Old Orchard Beach and Crescent Beach in southern Maine are examples of large fringing beaches. *Pocket fringing beaches* are found at the heads of bays between two nearby headlands and are characteristically small and curved. Crescent Beach in Cape Elizabeth and part of Sandy River Beach in Jonesport are pocket fringing beaches.

Barrier beaches are attached to the mainland at both ends. They may or may not include a tidal inlet behind the beach, but they always protect a lagoon or a lagoon turned salt marsh. Mile Beach at Reid State park is a barrier beach. Smaller pocket barrier beaches are quite common and include Sea Point in Kittery, Pemaquid on Johns Bay, Sand Beach on Mount Desert Island, and Roque Bluffs on Englishman Bay.

Barrier spit beaches extend partway across a bay mouth and are associated with a long, straight dune field, a tidal inlet, and a salt marsh. Ogunquit, Scarborough, and Half Mile Beach at Reid State Park are all baymouth barrier spit beaches. The presence of these spits indicates some movement of sand parallel to the shore, although this movement is small relative to the downdrifting that occurs along mid-Atlantic beaches.

Tombolos are small beaches or bars running between two islands or connecting one island with the mainland. The bars may be exposed only at low tide. Tombolos have formed in the lee of both Fox and Wood Islands at Popham State Park. Popham also features *cuspate forelands*, large seaward projections of beach and dune that often form—as they do at Popham—at one end of a tombolo.

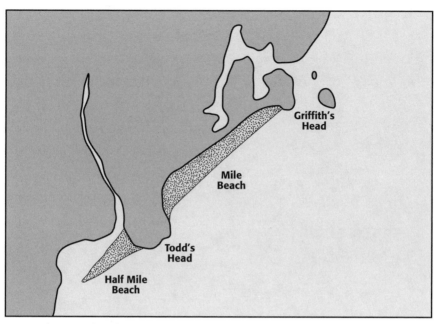

Reid State Park: Mile Beach, a barrier beach, and Half-Mile Beach, a baymouth barrier spit beach (after Nelson and Fink 1980)

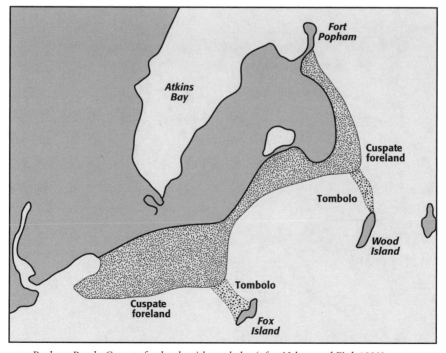

Popham Beach: Cuspate forelands with tombolos (after Nelson and Fink 1980)

PART IV
Appendixes

Appendix A:
Emergency Telephone Numbers

Unless otherwise noted, all telephone numbers are in the 207 area code.

Emergency Search and Rescue, U.S. Coast Guard
(for all stations, cellular is *CG)
Portsmouth 603-436-4414
South Portland 799-1680
Boothbay Harbor 633-2643
Rockland 596-6666
Southwest Harbor..244-5121
Jonesport 497-5700
Eastport 853-2845

Maine State Police
(for all stations, cellular is *77)
Southern Maine 1-800-482-0730
Brunswick-Belfast..1-800-452-4664
Belfast-Eastport...1-800-432-7381

Other Emergency Numbers
Poison Control Center 1-800-442-6305
Fire 1-888-900-FIRE
Red Tide Hotline 1-800-232-4733

Hospitals
York Hospital, York 363-7433
Southern Maine Medical Center, Biddeford 283-7000
Maine Medical Center, Portland 871-0111
Mercy Hospital, Portland 879-3333
Parkview Hospital, Brunswick 729-1641
Mid Coast Hospital, Brunswick 729-0181
Mid Coast Hospital, Bath 443-5524
MaineGeneral Medical Center, Augusta 626-1000
Miles Memorial Hospital, Damariscotta 563-1234
St. Andrews Hospital, Boothbay........................633-7820
Penobscot Bay Medical Center, Rockport 596-8000
Waldo County General Hospital, Belfast........................338-2500

Blue Hill Memorial Hospital, Blue Hill 374-2836
Maine Coast Memorial Hospital, Ellsworth 667-5311
Eastern Maine Medical Center, Bangor 973-7000
St. Joseph's Hospital, Bangor 262-1000
Down East Community Hospital, Machias....................255-3356

Marine Mammal Strandings

For southern Maine:
Northeast Marine Animal Lifeline 851-6625
New England Aquarium...617-973-5200
For Maine north of Rockland:
College of the Atlantic Marine Mammal
Stranding Network 288-5644

Regional Biologists, Department of Inland Fisheries and Wildlife

Gray Office 657-2345
Sidney Office 547-5318
Machias Office..255-4715

Appendix B:
Air and Sea Temperatures

The air and sea temperatures given here for Bar Harbor are representative of those along the rest of the coast. The first graph shows the average low and high temperatures for each month. The second graph contrasts the air temperature (averaging all values during the month) and sea temperature. This second graph illustrates the phase lag between air and water temperatures. Air temperature rises more quickly and cools more quickly than sea temperature. (Information is from the National Oceanographic Data Center and the 1998 *Coast Pilot*.)

Average Low and High Air Temperatures

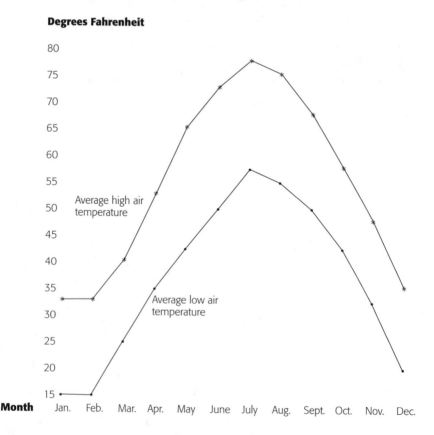

Degrees Fahrenheit

Average Air and Sea Temperatures

Degrees Fahrenheit

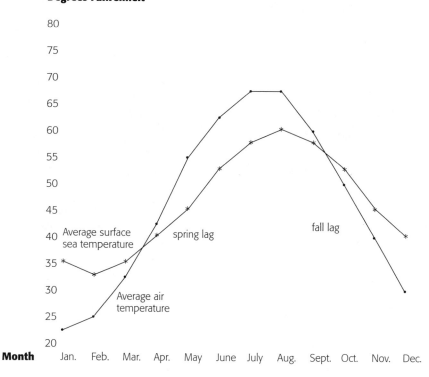

Appendix C:
Wind Speed

The Beaufort scale was developed in the early 1800s to rate wind conditions. For its land report, NOAA weather radio in Maine gives wind in miles per hour; for the maritime report, it gives wind in knots (nautical miles per hour). A knot is equal to 1.15 miles per hour. The Beaufort scale continues past force 7 to force 12 (wind of 73+ mph or 64+ knots).

MPH	Knots	Description	Beaufort Scale	Conditions
≤1	1	Calm	0	Sea smooth and mirrorlike; leaves on trees calm
1–3	1–3	Light air	1	Ripples
4–7	4–6	Light breeze	2	Small wavelets; leaves rustle
8–12	7–10	Gentle breeze	3	Scattered whitecaps; large wavelets; leaves and twigs move
13–18	11–16	Moderate breeze	4	Numerous whitecaps; small waves becoming longer; small branches move
19–24	17–21	Fresh breeze	5	Many whitecaps; some spray; moderate waves becoming longer; small trees begin to sway; flags ripple
25–31	22–27	Strong breeze	6	Whitecaps everywhere; more spray; large waves begin to form; branches of large trees sway
31–38	28–33	Near gale	7	Sea heaps up; foam from breaking waves begins to be blown in streaks; whole trees sway

Appendix D:
Stewardship Organizations & Government Agencies

Nonprofits

Nonprofit stewardship organizations have made major contributions toward protecting vulnerable and valuable land along the Maine coast. The following organizations own land that is open to careful day use (see *At a Glance* entries) or engage in other stewardship activities. For further information— and to support their work—please contact these organizations directly. (All telephone numbers are in the 207 area code.)

Appalachian Mountain Club
(Relating to use of Beal Island)
David Wilson
266 Town Farm Rd.
Augusta, ME 04330
465-9732

Island Institute
410 Main St.
Rockland, ME 04841
549-9209
www.islandinstitute.org

Maine Audubon Society
Gilsland Farm
118 Old Route 1
Falmouth, ME 04105
781-2330
www.maineaudubon.org

Maine Coast Heritage Trust
167 Park Row
Brunswick, ME 04011
729-7366
www.gwi.net/~mcht

Maine Island Trail Association (MITA)
41A Union Wharf
Portland, ME 04101
761-8225
www.mita.org
e-mail: mita@ime.net

MITA's goal is to establish a model of thoughtful use and volunteer stewardship for the Maine islands that will assure their conservation in a natural state while providing an exceptional recreational asset that is maintained and cared for by the people who use it.

National Audubon Society
Audubon Ecology Camp
Keene Neck Rd.
Medomak, ME 04551
529-5148
www.audubon.org

For Audubon-approved puffin tours, contact one of these businesses:
R.N. Fish & Son, Inc., P.O. Box 660, Boothbay Harbor, ME 04538, 633-3244 or 633-2626 or Hardy Boat Cruises, P.O. Box 326, New Harbor, ME 04554, 677-2026 or 1-800-2-PUFFINS

The Nature Conservancy
14 Main St., Suite 401
Brunswick, ME 04011
729-5181
www.tnc.org/maine

Maine Land Trust Network

This network (www.mltn.org) includes land trusts and other stewardship organizations. The following members own and manage land along the coast.

Biddeford Pool Land Trust
P.O. Box 306
Biddeford Pool, ME 04006
www.mltn.org

Blue Hill Heritage Trust
P.O. Box 222
Blue Hill, ME 04614
374- 5118
info@bhht.org
www.bhht.org

Boothbay Regional Land Trust
1 Oak St/P.O. Box 183
Boothbay Harbor, ME 04538
633-4818
brlt@bbrlt.org

Brunswick-Topsham Land Trust
108 Maine Street
Brunswick, ME 04011
729-7694
btlt@gwi.net
www.btlt.org

Cape Elizabeth Land Trust
P.O. Box 265 CCB
Cape Elizabeth, ME 04107
767-6054
celt@gwi.net
www.capelandtrust.org

Chewonki Foundation
485 Chewonki Neck Rd.
Wiscasset, ME 04578
info@chewonki.org
www.chewonki.org

Coastal Mountains Land Trust
101 Mount Battie St.
Camden, ME 04843
236-7091
info@coastalmountains.org
www.coastalmountains.org

Conservation Trust of Brooksville,
   Castine and Penobscot
P.O. Box 421
Castine, ME 04421
ctbcp@prexar.com
www.mltn.org

Cumberland Mainland and Islands
   Trust, Inc.
P.O. Box 25
Chebeague Island, ME 04017
www.mltn.org

Damariscotta River Association
P.O. Box 333/Belvedere Rd.
Damariscotta, ME 04543
563-1393
dra@draclt.org
www.draclt.org

Falmouth Conservation Trust
P.O. Box 6172
Falmouth, ME 04105
www.mltn.org

Freeport Conservation Trust
101 Lower Flying Point Rd.
Freeport, ME 04032
www.freeportconservationtrust.org

Frenchman Bay Conservancy
P.O. Box 150
Hancock, ME 04640
www.frenchmanbay.org

Friends of Merrymeeting Bay
P.O. Box 233
Richmond, ME 04357
fomb@gwi.net
www.mltn.org

Georges River Land Trust
328 Main Street, Studio 305
Rockland, ME 04841
594-5166
info@grlt.org
www.grlt.org

Great Auk Land Trust
P.O. Box 117
Milbridge, ME 04658
546- 7926
info@greatauk.org
www.greatauk.org

Great Works Regional Land Trust
P.O. Box 151
South Berwick, ME 03908
646-3604
info@gwrlt.org
www.gwrlt.org

Harpswell Heritage Land Trust
P.O. Box 359
Harpswell, ME 04097
833-5566
info@harpswelllandtrust.org
www.harpswelllandtrust.org

Island Heritage Trust
P.O. Box 42
Deer Isle, ME 04627
348- 2455
ihttwo@prexar.com
www.mltn.org

Islesboro Islands Trust
P.O. Box 182
Islesboro, ME 04848
www.mltn.org

Kennebunk Land Trust
113 Lafayette Center
Kennebunk, ME 04043
985-8734
www.kennebunklandtrust.org

Kennebunkport Conservation Trust
P.O. Box 7004
Cape Porpoise, ME 04014
967-3465
www.thekennebunkportconservation
trust.org

Kittery Land Trust
P.O. Box 467
Kittery, ME 03904
439-6087
www.kitterylandtrust.org

Laudholm Trust/Wells Reserve
P.O. Box 1007
Wells, ME 04090
646-4521
trust@laudholm.org
www.laudholm.org

Lower Kennebec Regional Land Trust
Att: Jack Witham
P.O. Box 1128
Bath, ME 04530
442-8400
info@lkrlt.org
www.lkrlt.org

Medomak Valley Land Trust
P.O. Box 180
Waldoboro, ME 04572
823-5570
mvlt@midcoast.com
www.medomakvalley.org

Phippsburg Land Trust
P.O. Box 123
Phippsburg, ME 04562
www.mltn.org

Quoddy Regional Land Trust
P.O. Box 49
Whiting, ME 04691
733-5506
qrlt@maineline.net
www.qrlt.org

Sheepscot Valley Conservation
    Association
624 Sheepscot Road
Newcastle, ME 04553
586-5616
svca@sheepscot.org
www.sheepscot.org

State and Federal Government Agencies

Acadia National Park
P.O. Box 177
Bar Harbor, ME 04609
288-5463 (business)
288-3338 (general information about
park)
www.nps.gov/acad/

Maine Bureau of Parks and Lands
(BPL)
State House Station 22
Augusta, ME 04333
287-3821 ext. 3
www.state.me.us/doc/prks/nds.htm

Maine Department of Inland Fisheries
and Wildlife (IF&W)
State House Station 41
Augusta, ME 04333
287-8000
www.state.me.us/ifw

U.S. Fish and Wildlife Service (USFWS)

*The service manages three wildlife refuges
along the Maine coast and is a partner
in the Wells National Estuarine Research
Reserve. The Web site for all refuges in the
Northeast is: www.fws.gov/r5ws*

Moosehorn National Wildlife Refuge
RR 1 Box 202, Suite 1
Baring, ME 04694
454-3521

Maine Coastal Islands National
    Wildlife Refuge
P.O. Box 297
Milbridge, ME 04658
564-2124
P.O. 495, 16 Rockport Park Centre
Drive, Rockport, ME 04856
236-6970

Rachel Carson National Wildlife Refuge
321 Port Rd.
Wells, ME 04090
646-9226

Wells National Estuarine
    Research Reserve
342 Laudholm Farm Rd.
Wells, ME 04090
646-1555
wellsnerr1@cybertours.com

Appendix E:
Saltwater Campgrounds

The following saltwater campgrounds have boat ramps or launch areas for use by patrons. Sites that allow use by nonpatrons as well, denoted here with an asterisk (✳), are also listed under "Access" in each chapter and are not assigned a campground number. (Unless otherwise noted, all telephone numbers are in the 207 area code.) For detailed information on these campgrounds, consult *Hot Showers! Maine Coast Lodgings for Kayakers and Sailors* (see bibliography). Information on camping is also available through:

Maine Campground Owners Association
655 Main St.
Lewiston, ME 04240
782-5874
www.campmaine.com
e-mail: info@campmaine.com

There are many saltwater B&Bs, inns, and other accommodations that have launch areas for use by patrons. Consult *Hot Showers!* as well as:

Maine Innkeepers Association
305 Commercial St.
Portland, ME 04101
773-7670
www.maineinns.com

York to Wells Harbor
✳
Harborview Oceanside Campground
P.O. Box 1
Cape Neddick, ME 03902
363-4366
www.harbourview.com

✳
Recompense Shore Campsites
134 Burnett Rd.
Freeport, ME 04032
865-9307
www.freeportcamping.com

Middle Casco Bay
✳
Winslow Memorial Park
Staples Point Rd., Freeport
Mail: Freeport Town Office
30 Main St.
Freeport, ME 04032
865-4198

1
Orrs Island Campground
Route 24
44 Bond Point Rd
Orrs Island, ME 04066
833-5595
www.orrsisland.com
camping@orrsisland.com

Eastern Casco Bay

2

Hermit Island Campground
Summer: 6 Hermit Island Rd.
Phippsburg
Mail: 42 Front St.
Bath, ME 04530
443-2101
www.hermitisland.com
info@hermitisland.com

✳

Thomas Point Beach Park &
   Campground
29 Meadow Rd.
Brunswick, ME 04011
725-6009 or 877-TPB-4321
www.thomaspointbeach.com
summer@thomaspointbeach.com

Bath

✳

Sagadahoc Bay Campground
P.O. Box 171
Georgetown, ME 04548
371-2014
kosalka@midmaine.com
www.sagbaycamping.com

Wiscasset, Back and Upper Sheepscot rivers

3

Chewonki Campground
Box 261
Wiscasset, ME 04578
882-7426 or 800-465-7747
www.chewonkicampground.com

4

Little Ponderosa Campground
159 Wiscasset Rd.
Boothbay, ME 04537
633-2700
www.littleponderosa.com

✳

Gray Homestead Oceanfront
   Campground
21 Homestead Rd.
Southport, ME 04576
633-4612
www.graysoceancamping.com
grays@gwi.net

5

Shore Hills Campground & RV Park
553 Wiscasset Rd.
Boothbay, ME 04537
633-4782
www.shorehills.com

Muscongus Bay

6

Saltwater Farm Campground
Wadsworth Street, Thomaston
P.O. Box 165
Thomaston, ME 04861
www.midcoast.com/~sfc
sfc@midcoast.com

Tenants Harbor to Owls Head

7

Lobster Buoy Campsite
280 Waterman Beach Rd.
South Thomaston, ME 04858
594-7546

Northern Penobscot Bay

8

Warren Island State Park
P.O. Box 105
Lincolnville, ME 04849
941-4014

9

Moorings Oceanfront RV Campground
191 Searsport Ave.
Belfast, ME 04915
338-6860
www.oceanfrontrvcamping.com
mooringscamp@yahoo.com

*
Searsport Shores Camping Resort
Route 1
216 West Main St.
Searsport, ME 04974
548-6059
www.campocean.com
camping@ime.net

Stonington and Deer Isle

*
Old Quarry Ocean Adventures
130 Settlement Rd.
Stonington, ME 04681
367-8977
www.oldquarry.com
info@oldquarry.com

10
Duck Harbor Campground on
  Isle au Haut
Acadia National Park
P.O. Box 177
Bar Harbor, ME 04609
288-3338
www.acadia.national-park.com/
camping.htm

Eggemoggin Reach and Blue Hill Bay

11
Sunshine Campground
348-2663 or 367-8977
www.sunshinecampground.com
info@oldquarry.com

Northern Mount Desert Island and Frenchman Bay

12
Narrows Too Camping Resort
1150 Bar Harbor Rd.
Trenton, ME 04605
667-4300 or 866-917-4300
www.narrowstoo.com

*
Lamoine State Park
ME 184
23 State Park Rd.
Lamoine, ME 04605
Park season: 667-4778
Off season: 941-4014

13
Bar Harbor KOA Campground
136 Country Rd.
Bar Harbor, ME 04609
288-3520
Reservations: 888-562-5605

14
Mt. Desert Narrows Camping Resort
1219 State Highway 3
Bar Harbor, ME 04609
288-4782 or 866-780-4782
www.barharborcampgrounds.com

15
Hadley's Point Campground
33 Hadley Point Rd.
Bar Harbor, ME 04609
288-4048
www.hadleypoint.com

16
Mount Desert Campground
516 Sound Drive, Somesville
Mount Desert, ME 04660
www.mountdesertcampground.com
info@mountdesertcampground.com

17
Mountainview Campground and
  Flanders Bay Cabins
22 Harbor View Dr.
Sullivan, ME 04664
422-6408
www.acadia.net/flandersbay
flandersbay@acadia.net

Winter Harbor to Petit Manan

18
Ocean Wood Campground
P.O. Box 11
Birch Harbor, ME 04613
963-7194
www.jabinc.org/
oceanwood/ow_campground.htm

19
Mainayr Campground
321 Village Rd.
Steuben, ME 04680
546-2690
www.mainayr.com
info@mainayr.com

Narraguagus and Pleasant Rivers

20
Bayview Campground
39 Rickett Point Rd.
Milbridge, ME 04658
546-2946

Great Wass Archipelago

21
Henry Point Campground
Kelly Point Rd.
P.O. Box 106
Jonesport, ME 04649
497-2804

23
Cobscook Bay State Park
40 South Edmunds Rd.
Edmunds Twp., ME 04628
726-4412
(Launch site nearby)

24
South Bay Campground
ME 189
591 Country Road
Lubec, ME 04652
733-1037
southbay@midmaine.com

Appendix F:
Sea Kayaking Guide Services, Trips Programs, and Rental Businesses

This list of businesses that offer instruction, tours, and rentals is offered as a service to readers but is not an endorsement of any individual business. Tours range from a few hours to a week or more; tours are usually but not necessarily held where the business is located. If you are interested in renting, call ahead to find out what kind of boat is available. Some rental businesses carry recreational kayaks, which are short and wide, rather than touring kayaks, which are long and relatively narrow. Recreational kayaks are more appropriate in protected areas; touring kayaks are more versatile.

Outfitters, guides, and instructors have created a trade group—the Maine Association of Sea Kayaking Guides and Instructors (MASKGI)—whose mission is to foster safe and responsible sea kayaking along the coast of Maine. The group promotes low-impact practices, provides safety education, works closely with agencies and nonprofits, and supports strict standards for guides.

* = MASKGI members
Note: All telephone numbers are in the 207 area code.

York to Wells Harbor

*Harbor Adventures
P.O. Box 345
York Harbor, ME 03911
363-8466
www.harboradventures.com
harboradventures@aol.com
Tours

Excursions: Coastal Maine
   Outfitting Co.
1399 Route 1
York, ME 03909
363-0181
www.excursionsinmaine.com
Instruction, tours, rentals

World Within Sea Kayaking
746 Ocean Ave.
Wells, ME 04090
646-0455
www.worldwithin.com
Instruction, tours

The Saco River

Gone with the Wind
Yates St.
Biddeford Pool, ME 04005
283-8446
www.gwtwonline.com
Tours, rentals

Western Casco Bay

Casco Bay Kayak Rentals
64 New Island Ave.
Peaks Island, ME 04108
766-2650
Rentals

*Maine Island Kayak Company
70 Luther Street
Peaks Island, ME 04108
1-800-796-2373 or 766-2373
www.maineislandkayak.com
info@maineislandkayak.com
Instruction, tours

Middle Casco Bay

*L.L. Bean Outdoor Discovery Schools
15 Casco St.
Freeport, ME 04033
1-888-552-3261
www.llbean.com/ods/
outdoor.discovery@llbean.com
Instruction, tours

*Ring's Marine Service, Inc.
22 Smelt Brook Rd.
South Freeport, ME 04078
1-866-865-6143 or 865-6143
www.ringsmarineservice.com
info@ringsmarineservice.com
Rentals

H2Outfitters
P.O. Box 72
Orr's Island, ME 04066
1-800-20-KAYAK or 833-5257
www.H2Outfitters.com
h20@H2Outfitters.com
Instruction, tours

Eastern Casco Bay

*Sea Spray Kayaking Rental & Tours
412 State Road
Brunswick, ME 04011
1-888-349-7772 or 443-3646
www.seaspraykayaking.com
info@seaspraykayaking.com
Instruction, tours, rentals

Lower Kennebec River: Bath

Up the Creek Kayak & Canoe Rentals
Winnegance Village
Phippsburg, ME 04562
1-866-443-4845 or 443-4845
www.rentkayaks.com
nature@rentkayaks.com
Rentals

The Kennebec River: Merrymeeting Bay

Dragonworks, Inc.
42 Stevens Rd.
Bowdoinham, ME 04008
666-8481
Instruction, tours

Kennebec Tidewater Bike & Boat
7 Front St.
Richmond, ME 04357
1-877-895-2112 or 737-2112
www.kennebectidewater.com
Tours, rentals

Wiscasset and the Back and the Upper Sheepscot rivers

*Chewonki Foundation
485 Chewonki Neck Rd.
Wiscasset, ME 04578
882-7323
Educational programs

Tideway Treks, Inc.
P.O. Box 1333
Damariscotta, ME 04543
1-866-843-3929
www.tideway.ws
Tours in Portland, Wiscasset, Rockland

Lower Sheepscot River and Boothbay Harbor

Gray Homestead Oceanfront
   Campground
21 Homestead Rd.
Southport, ME 04576
633-4612
www.graysoceancamping.com
Rentals

Tidal Transit
18 Granary Way
Boothbay Harbor, ME 04538
633-7140
www.kayakboothbay.com
Tours, rentals

The Damariscotta River

Poseidon Kayak Imports
60 Poseidon Land
Walpole, ME 04573
644-8329
www.nvo.com/poseidonkayaks
lkfjr@aol.com
Instruction, rentals

Muscongus Bay

Maine Kayak, Inc.
P.O. Box 674
Unity, ME 04988
1-866-624-6352
www.mainekayak.com
info@mainekayak.com
Tours in Muscongus Bay

*Sea Spirit Adventures
1440 State Route 32
Round Pond, ME 04564
529-4732
www.seaspiritadventures.com
seaspiritadventures@hotmail.com
Tours out of Bremen and Round Pond

Western Penobscot Bay

*Maine Sport Outfitters
Route 1
P.O. Box 956
Rockport, ME 04856
1-800-722-0826 (tours)
236-7120 (rentals)
www.mainesport.com
adventures@mainesport.com
Instruction, tours, rentals

*Breakwater Kayak, LLC
P.O. Box 627
Rockport, ME 04856
596-6895
www.breakwaterkayak.com
info@breakwaterkayak.com
Tours out of Rockland

Camden Kayak
20 Conway Rd.
Camden, ME 04843
236-7709
www.stormloader.com/camdenkayak
info@camdenkayak.com
Custom multiday trips with instruction

Riverdance Outfitters
Ludwig Rd.
Hope, ME 04857
763-3139
www.riverdanceoutfitters.com
Tours

*Sea Escape Kayak
West Main St.
Vinalhaven, ME 04863
863-9343
www.seaescapekayak.com
seaescapekayak@att.net

Lincolnville to Belfast

Ducktrap Sea Kayak
2175 Atlantic Highway (Route 1)
Lincolnville Beach, ME 04849
236-8608
Instruction, tours, rentals

*Water Walker Custom Kayak Tours
152 Lincolnville Ave.
Belfast, ME 04915
338-6424
www.touringkayaks.com
info@touringkayaks.com
Custom tours

Northern Penobscot Bay: Castine

*Castine Kayak Adventures
Sea St., P.O. Box 703
Castine, ME 04421
326-9045 (summer), 866-3506 (winter)
info@castinekayak.com
Instruction, tours

Eastern Penobscot Bay: Little Deer Isle

Eggemoggin Landing
204 Little Deer Isle Rd.
P.O. Box 126
Little Deer Isle, ME 04650
348-6115
eggland@acadia.net
Rentals

Deer Isle and Stonington

Finest Kind Enterprises
70 Center District Rd.
Deer Isle, ME 04627
348-7714
Rentals

Granite Island Guide Service
66 Dunham Point Rd.
Deer Isle, ME 04627
348-2668
www.graniteislandguides.com
info@graniteislandguides.com
Tours

*Old Quarry Ocean Adventures, Inc.
130 Settlement Rd.
Stonington, ME 04681
367-8977
www.oldquarry.com
info@oldquarry.com
Tours, rentals

Blue Hill

Rocky Coast Outfitters
Grindleville Rd.
P.O. Box 351
Blue Hill, ME 04614
374-8866
Rentals

The Activity Shop
61 Ellsworth Rd.
Blue Hill, ME 04614
347-3600
www.activityshop.com
info@activityshop.com
Rentals

Northern Mount Desert Island and Frenchman Bay

Acadia 1 Watersports
U.S. Highway 3
Bar Harbor, ME 04609
1-888-786-0676
www.kayak1.com
Tours, rentals

*Aquaterra Adventures
One West St., Harbor Place Building
Bar Harbor, ME 04609
1-877-386-4124
www.aquaterra-adventures.com
Tours

*Coastal Kayaking Tours
48 Cottage St
P.O. Box 405
Bar Harbor, ME 04609
1-800-526-8615 or 288-9605
www.acadiafun.com
abckt@acadia.net
Tours

Island Adventures Sea Kayaking
137 Cottage St.
Bar Harbor, ME 04609
288-3886
www.islandadventureskayaking.com
Tours

Loon Bay Kayak Tours
P.O. Box 391
Orland, ME 04472
1-888-786-0676 or 266-8888
Tours of Mount Desert Island, rentals

*National Park Sea Kayak Tours
39 Cottage Street
P.O. Box 6105
Bar Harbor, ME 04609
1-800-347-0940 or 288-0342
www.acadiakayak.com
info@acadiakayak.com
Tours

Hancock Point Kayak Tours
58 Point Rd.
Hancock, ME 04640
422-6854
www.hancockpointkayak.com
info@hancockpointkayak.com
Tours

Mountainview Campground/
  Flanders Bay Cabins
22 Harborview Dr.
Sullivan, ME 04664
422-6408
www.acadia.net/flandersbay/
  campground.htm
Rentals

Southern Mount Desert Island

Acadia Park Canoe & Kayak Rental
388 Main St.
P.O. Box 445
Southwest Harbor, ME 04679
244-5707
Rentals

*Maine State Sea Kayak, Inc.
254 Main St.
P.O. Box 97
Southwest Harbor, ME 04679
1-877-481-9500 or 244-9500
www.mainestateseakayak.com
info@mainestateseakayak.com
Tours

Yak Man Adventures
28 Columbia Ave.
Bernard, ME 04612
244-3333
www.yakmanadventures.com
Rentals

Winter Harbor to Petit Manan

SeaMyst
150 Corea Rd.
P.O. Box 96
Prospect Harbor, ME 04669
963-7223
www.mooselookguideservice.com
Tours, rentals

Great Wass

Jonesport Boats & Bikes
Main Street
P.O. Box 409
Jonesport, ME 04649
497-2463
Rentals

Machias Bay

Sunrise County Canoe and Kayak
Hoyttown Rd.
RR 1 Box 344A
Machias, ME 04654
1-877-980-2300 or 255-3375
www.sunrisecanoeandkayak.com
info@sunrisecanoeandkayak.com
Instruction, tours

Cobscook Bay

Tidal Trails Eco-tours
542 Leighton Point Rd.
Pembroke, ME 04666
726-4799
www.tidaltrails.com
Tours, rentals

Appendix G:
What to Do with Number Two

"Catholes" don't work on coastal shores and islands, which often have a thin mantle of soil. When human waste cannot be properly buried and stays near the surface, microbes found in soil cannot decompose it promptly. If everyone leaves their feces on site—and ever more people are visiting these coastal areas—the areas could become, well, less than attractive.

Federal law prohibits discharging human waste within 3 miles of shore, so depositing human waste in the intertidal zone and hoping it will be carried out to sea is not an option. Besides, human waste can contaminate clam and mussel beds and pose other health problems.

Of all small boats, sea kayaks are the most difficult with respect to handling human waste. Many sailboats have heads and holding tanks. On powerboats, there is room for a 5-gallon pail. But sea kayaks are small, with very limited storage room—and no one wants a spill in a bulkhead.

Solid human waste and toilet paper should be collected and then disposed of at an appropriate onshore facility, like a toilet or an RV or marine pumping station. Several portable toilets have been designed so that they can be carried in the rear hatch of a kayak, used on shore, and cleaned out at a pump-out station. The Boom Box, for example, has a 20-use capacity but is only 13.5 x 9 x 8 inches when folded up for travel.

Sea kayakers on trips have also used other, somewhat less convenient, means, such as an ammunition box lined with several layers of plastic. The drawback is that the plastic-wrapped waste is less likely to be disposed of in a toilet. Another method borrows from the technology of big-wall climbing, as climbers on multiday climbs must also carry out human waste. They use a "poop tube," a section of PVC plastic pipe that has a screw-threaded lid on one end and a permanent cap on the other. Those with good aim can do a direct deposit; others poop and scoop. Because gases can build up in the tube, it is important to vent periodically, especially on longer trips. The contents can be deposited in a toilet.

For sea kayakers on day trips, a smaller system may suffice. Literature from the Leave No Trace Foundation suggests that one way to deal with waste is to invert an appropriately sized plastic bag over your hand, pick up the waste and toilet paper, and turn the bag right side out. Sea kayakers can then store the bag in a watertight container, such as an opaque plastic jar with a screw lid, and dispose of the waste in a toilet. In no case should boaters drop containers with human waste in local garbage bins. This action does not endear sea kayakers to townspeople and, besides, landfills are not designed to handle human waste.

If the process seems odious, think instead about how nice it is to land somewhere that is free of human waste. Once you develop and practice your method for carrying out human waste (and stop complaining about having to do so), it's not such a big deal. Someone dealt with your human waste when you were a baby; surely you can deal with your own human waste now.

Appendix H:
Suggested Equipment for a Day Trip

Sea kayak with waterproof bulkheads or float bags

Paddle

Paddle leash (properly sized—not long enough to go around neck)

Spray skirt

Paddle float

Bilge pump

Sponge

Chart

Compass

* Personal flotation device (PFD)

* Efficient means of making a sound signal (such as a handheld foghorn or whistle)

* Efficient means of making a light (such as a waterproof flashlight or headlamp) any time past sunset

Appropriate clothing (perhaps including a wetsuit or drysuit)

Spare warm clothing in a waterproof bag (wool or synthetic, not cotton)

First aid kit (one per group)

Spare paddle (at least one per every three paddlers)

Tow line (one for every two paddlers)

Boat repair kit (one per group)

Cellular phone or VHF

Flares

Paddlers should also carry food, water, and personal items as needed.

* These items are required by the Coast Guard.

Bibliography

I consulted dozens of articles, reports, and books while researching this book, including (but not limited to) the following publications:

Britton, Nathaniel, and Addison Brown. [1913] 1970. *An Illustrated Flora of the Northern United States and Canada.* New York: Dover Publications.

Bumsted, Lee. 1997. *Hot Showers! Maine Coast Lodgings for Kayakers and Sailors.* Brunswick, Maine: Audenreed Press.

Caldwell, D. W. 1998. *Roadside Geology of Maine.* Missoula, Montana: Mountain Press Publishing Company.

Day, Cherie Hunter. 1987. *Life on Intertidal Rocks: A Guide to Marine Life on the Rocky North Atlantic Coast.* Rochester, New York: Nature Study Guild.

Duncan, Roger F. 1992. *Coastal Maine: A Maritime History.* New York: W.W. Norton & Co.

Eckstorm, Fanny Hardy. 1941. *Indian Place-Names of the Penobscot Valley and the Maine Coast.* Orono, Maine: University Press.

Hill, Ruth Ann. 1989. *Maine Forever: A Guide to Nature Conservancy Preserves in Maine.* 2nd edition. Brunswick, Maine: Maine Chapter, The Nature Conservancy.

Jordan, David Starr, and Barton W. Evermann. 1902. *American Food and Game Fishes.* New York: Doubleday, Page & Co.

Katona, Steven K., Valerie Rough, and David T. Richardson. 1993. *A Field Guide to Whales, Porpoises, and Seals: From Cape Cod to Newfoundland.* 4th edition, revised. Washington D.C.: Smithsonian Institution.

Kummel, Bernhard. 1970. *History of the Earth: An Introduction to Historical Geology.* 2nd edition. San Francisco: W.H. Freeman and Company.

Maine Coastal Program. 1998. *The Estuary Book: A Guide to Promoting Understanding and Regional Management of Maine's Estuaries and Embayments.* 2nd edition. Augusta, Maine: State Planning Office.

Maine Island Trail Association. 1999. *The Maine Island Trail 1999 Stewardship Handbook and Guidebook.* Portland, Maine: Maine Island Trail Association. Membership handbook.

McKenzie, Don, and David Larkin. 2001. *The Kennebec River: A Guide for Paddlers and Friends.* Skowhegan, Maine: Kennebec Valley Trails, Inc.

McLane, Charles G. 1982. *Islands of the Mid-Maine Coast, Blue Hill and Penobscot Bays*. Woolwich, Maine: Kennebec River Press.

―――. 1989. *Islands of the Mid-Maine Coast, Mount Desert to Machias Bay*. Falmouth, Maine: Kennebec River Press.

―――. 1992. *Islands of the Mid-Maine Coast, Muscongus Bay and Monhegan Island*. Gardiner, Maine: Tilbury House, Publishers.

―――. 1994. *Islands of the Mid-Maine Coast, Pemaquid Point to the Kennebec River*. Gardiner, Maine: Tilbury House, Publishers.

―――. 1997. *Islands of the Mid-Maine Coast, Penobscot Bay*. Gardiner, Maine: Tilbury House, Publishers.

Miller, Dorcas S. 1979. *The Maine Coast: A Nature Lover's Guide*. Charlotte, North Carolina: East Woods Press. Out of print.

National Ocean Service. 1998. *United States Coast Pilot (1) Atlantic Coast: Eastport to Cape Cod*. 31st edition. Washington D.C.: United States Department of Commerce.

National Ocean Service. *Tidal Current Tables: Atlantic Coast, North America*. Rockport, Maine: International Marine.

National Ocean Service. *Tide Tables: High and Low Water Predictions East Coast of North and South America*. Washington D.C.: United States Department of Commerce.

Nelson, Bruce W., and L. Kenneth Fink. 1980. *Geological and Botanical Features of Sand Beach Systems in Maine*. Augusta, Maine: State Planning Office.

Newcomb, Lawrence. 1977. *Newcomb's Wildflower Guide*. Boston: Little, Brown and Company.

Paigen, Jennifer Alisa. 1997. *The Sea Kayaker's Guide to Mount Desert Island*. Camden, Maine: Down East Books.

Peterson, Roger Tory. 1980. *A Field Guide to the Birds of Eastern and Central North America*. Boston: Houghton Mifflin Company.

Pierson, Elizabeth C., Jan Erik Pierson, and Peter D. Vickery. 1996. *A Birder's Guide to Maine*. Camden, Maine: Down East Books.

Platt, Dave, ed. 1998. *Rim of the Gulf: Restoring Estuaries in the Gulf of Maine*. Rockland, Maine: Island Institute.

Ruffing, Jennifer. 1991. *Estuary Profile Series*. Augusta, Maine: Maine State Planning Office.

Taft, Hank, Jan Taft, and Curtis Rindlaub. 1996. *A Cruising Guide to the Maine Coast.* 3rd edition. Peaks Island, Maine: Diamond Pass Publishing.

Venn, Tamsin. 1991. *Sea Kayaking along the New England Coast.* Boston: Appalachian Mountain Club Books.

Instructional Books

There are many excellent books about sea kayaking; these volumes are particular favorites:

Burch, David. 1993. *Fundamentals of Kayak Navigation.* Old Saybrook, Connecticut: Globe Pequot Press.
This book is packed with information on charts, navigation aids, dead reckoning, electronic navigation, tides and currents, navigation planning, and other useful topics.

Broze, Matt, and George Gronseth. 1997. *Sea Kayaker's* Deep Trouble: True Stories and Their Lessons from *Sea Kayaker Magazine.* Rockport, Maine: Ragged Mountain Press.
We can learn a lot from other people's mistakes.

Getchell, Annie. 2000. *The Essential Outdoor Gear Manual,* 2nd ed. Rockport, Maine: Ragged Mountain Press.
This excellent book includes chapters on how to maintain and repair kayaks, paddles and PFDs, dry storage and flotation, and wetsuits and drysuits.

Seidman, David. 1992. *The Essential Sea Kayaker: A Complete Course for the Open Water Paddler.* Rockport, Maine: Ragged Mountain Press.
This is a thorough, basic guide.

Dowd, John. 1981, 1997. *Sea Kayaking: A Manual for Long-Distance Touring.* Vancouver: University of Washington Press.
This book shows the outer dimensions of sea kayaking, giving tips about tying into a kelp bed overnight and describing the different kinds of sea ice. It provides engaging reading even if you never want to go where Dowd has gone.

Magazines

Atlantic Coastal Kayaker, Ipswich, MA (508-356-6112)

Canoe and Kayak Magazine, Kirkland, WA (425-827-6363)

Paddler, Eagle, ID (703-455-3419)

Sea Kayaker, Seattle, WA (206-789-9536)

Index

Note: Maps are set in bold.

F

Falls I., **308,** 312, 315
Falmouth, **82,** 86
Falmouth Foreside, 81, **82,** 86
Federal I., **309,** 315–16
Finn Beach, 302
Fires, 30; to report, 352
Flag I., **107,** 112, 114
Flanders B., **247,** 252–53
Flint I., 275–77, **276,** 280–81, 283
Fog, 39–40
Fore R., **82,** 84
Fort Edgecomb, **144,** 149–50
Fort Foster, 47, **48,** 51, 53
Fort Gorges, **82,** 88–89
Fort Halifax, 139
Fort I., **162,** 163–64, 167–68, 172
Fort Knox, 204, **205,** 207, 210–211
Fort McClary, **48,** 54
Fort O'Brien, **299,** 304
Fort Point S.P., and Lt., 204, **205,** 207–208, 210–11
Fort Popham, **116,** 117, 120, 124, 127
Fort Pownall, 210
Fort St. George, **183,** 185–86
Fort Williams, **82,** 84, 88
forts and historic sites: Baldwin, 124;
  Eagle I., **95,** 96, 103, 105; Edgecomb,
  144, 149–50; Fort Halifax, 139; Fort
  Point, 204, **205,** 207, 210–11; Knox,
  204, **205,** 207, 210–11; McClary, **48,**
  54; Pemaquid, **162,** 170–72; Popham,
  116, 125, 127; Pownall, 210; St. George,
  183, 185–86; Whaleback Midden,
  168, 172; William Henry, **162,** 166,
  171–72
Frankfort, **205,** 209
Franklin I. Lt., **174,** 177, 180–81
Frazer Point, 272
Freeport Conservation Trust, 93, 358
Frenchman B., 245–57, **247**
Frenchman B. Conservancy, 251, 358
Friends of Nature, 233, 235
Friendship, **174,** 175–76

G

Gardiner, 135–38, **136**
Geology, bedrock, 100; glacial, 254–255, 320–24
Georges Is., 182, **183,** 185
Georges River Land Trust, 191, 193, 359
Gerrish I., **48,** 50–51, 53
Goat I. (Kennebec), 122, 127
Goat I. Lt. (Cape Porpoise), **62,** 66–67
Goose Pond, **216,** 221
Goose Rock Passage, **144,** 145, 147
Gouldsboro, **270,** 271–74
Gray Homestead Oceanfront Campground, 155, 362, 367

Great Auk Land Trust, 282–83, 291–92, 297, 359
Great Chebeague I., **82,** 84
Great Head, **261**
Great Island Boat Yard, 110
Great Wass Archipelago, 284–293, **286–87,** 291–92
Green I., 67
Green I., Outer, 102, 105
Grindel Point Lt., **201,** 203
Gurnet Strait, **107,** 109
Gut, The, **162,** 164

H

Hadley Point, **246,** 251
Halifax I., 293–95, **294,** 297–98
Hallowell, 135–38, **136,** 140
Hallowell I., **308,** 310, 314, 317
Hamilton House, 55
Hamilton Sanctuary, **107,** 108, 113–14
Hampden, 212–14, **213**
Harbor I. (Muscongus), **174,** 180–81
Harbor I. (Stonington), **228,** 234–35
Harbor porpoise, 326–27
Hardwood I., **260,** 267
Harpswell and Sound, 94, **95,** 99, 106, **107**
Harpswell Heritage Land Trust, 101, 112, 114, 359
Harraseeket R., 94–96, **95,** 98, 102
Harrington B., **276,** 278
Hart I., **183,** 186
Havener Ledge, 173, **174,** 179, 181
Head Beach, 110
Hells Half Acre, 232, 235
Hen I., **239,** 241
Hendricks Head Lt., **152,** 157
Heron I., **270,** 275
Heron Is., **116,** 126, 127
Hockomock B., **116,** 117, 119, 122–23, **144,** 145–47, 150
Hodgsons I., **162,** 169
Hog I. (Cobscook), **309,** 311, 315
Hog I. (Muscongus), 173, **174,** 177
Holbrook I. Sanctuary, 215–19, **216,** 221
Hop, The, **247,** 255, 257
Horan Head, **309,** 311, 315–17
Hospital I., 221
House I., **82,** 90
Howard Mendall Wildlife Mgmt. Area, **205,** 211
Hub, The, 267–68
Hungry I., **174,** 177, 181
Hunting, 19–20, 75
Hypocrites, 160

I

Indian Point I., 113
Indian R. and I., **286,** 291–92
Indiantown I., 151, 156, 160

R

R. Carson Refuge, 56, **62,** 64, 74, 79–80, 360
R. Carson Salt Pond Preserve, **174,** 176–77, 180
R. Waldo Tyler Wildlife Mgmt. Area, 188, 191, 193
Raccoon Cove, **246,** 251
Ram I. (Casco), **107,** 111, 114
Ram I. (Castine), 221
Ram I. Ledge Lt. (Casco), **82,** 90, 94
Ram I. Lt. (Boothbay) **152,** 160
Recompense Shore Campsites, 98, 361
Red Tide Hotline, 352
Reid S.P., **152,** 157, 160
Richmond, **128,** 129, 135–38, **136**
Richmond I., **74,** 74–75, 79–80
Ripley Neck, **276,** 278
Robinhood and Cove, **116,** 117, 143, **144,** 45, 147–48
Rockland, **194,** 195–97
Rockland Breakwater Lt., **194,** 197–98
Rockport, **194,** 196–98
Rolling I., **270,** 274–75
Roque Bluffs S.P., 293–97, **294**
Roque I., **294,** 295–96
Ross I., **174,** 180–81
Round I., **228,** 233–34
Round Pond, 173–75, **174**
Royal R. and Preserve, **82,** 93
Russ I., 232, 235

S

Saco B., **74,** 75
Saco R., 68–71, **69**
Saddleback I., **228,** 232, 235
Safety, 19–20, 22–24
Sagadahoc B., 115, **116,** 117, 120, 362
Sally I., **270,** 274–75
Sally Is., 275
Salmon Falls R., **46,** 52, 55–56
Salt B., 161–63, **162,** 165–67
Salt I., **299,** 304, 306
Sand Beach, **261,** 267–69
Sand I. (Deer I.), 232, 235
Sands, (Kennebec), **136,** 140
Sands, (Great Wass), 284–85, **286,** 289, 292
Sandy Point Beach (Penobscot), 204, **205,** 209–211
Sandy Point Park (Casco), 84, 86–87
Sasanoa R., 115–17, **116,** 119, 126–127, 143–47, **144,** 150
Sawyer Park, 108, 110
Scarborough Beach S.P., **74**
Scarborough Ferry Beach Park, 76
Scarborough Marsh and R., 73–77, **74,** 80
Schoodic, **270,** 271–73, 276
Schoodic I., **270,** 274–75
Schooner Cove, 315, 317

Schooner Head, **261,** 268
Seal Cove, 258–59, **260,** 264,
Seal Harbor, **261,** 266
Seals, 28–29, 325–26
Sears I, 204, **205,** 207, 209, 211
Searsport, **201,** 202, 204
Sebascodegan I., **107,** 109, 112
Seguin I. Lt., 115, **116,** 118–19, 126–27
Sellers I., 237, 241
Seward Neck, **309,** 316–17
Shackford Head, **309,** 316–17
Sheep I. (Dyer B.), 274–75
Sheep I. (Little Deer I.), **222,** 223, 226
Sheep Porcupine I., **247,** 255, 257
Sheepscot R. and Reversing Falls, 143–45, **144,** 147–48, 151, **152,** 153
Sheepscot Valley Conservation Assoc., 148, 360
Ship I., **239,** 240
Shipstern I., 275, **276,** 280–81, 283
Shoppee I., **294,** 297–98
Sidney, **136,** 137–38
Simpson Point, 99
Skillings R., **246,** 249
Small Point, **116**
Snow Marine Park, 196
Somes Sound, 258, **260,** 262–63, 266
Sorrento, **247,** 252
South Addison, **276,** 277–79
South B., **309,** 310–311, 313–314, 317
South Blue Hill, **242,** 243
South Bristol, 161–65, **162**
South Freeport, 81, **82,** 84, 87, 94, 97
South Orrington, 212–14, **213**
South Penobscot, **216,** 219
South Thomaston, **187,** 188–89
Southport I., **152,** 153–55, 157–58
Southwest Harbor, 258–59, **261**
Spring Point Ledge Lt., **82,** 88–89
Spurwink R., **74,** 74, 76, 79–80
Squirrel Point Lt., **116,** 122
St. George R., 182–85, **183**
Stage I. (Kennebec), **116,** 126
Stage I. (Saco), 68, **69,** 71–73
Starboard Cove, **299,** 300–301
state parks and lands: Avery Rock, **299,** 304, 306; Birch Point, **187,** 188–90, 192–93; Bold Coast, 305; Camden Hills, **194,** 199; Cobscook B. **308,** 314, 317; Crescent Beach, **64,** 79–80; Dodge Point, 161–63, **162,** 167, 172; Edgar M. Tennis Preserve, 235; Fort Point, 204, **205,** 207, 210–11; Holbrook I., 215–19, **216,** 221; Kettle Cove, 76, 80; Lamoine, **246,** 251, 257; Owls Head, **187,** 190–91, 193, **194;** Popham, **116,** 125, 127; Reid, **152,** 157, 160; Roque Bluffs, **294,** 295, 297; Scarborough, 74; Shackford Head, **309,** 316–17; Sumac I., **309,** 316–17; Trio, 316–17; Twin Oaks I., 244–45;

Continued on next page